LABOR'S CHALLENGE
TO THE SOCIAL ORDER

KENNIKAT PRESS SCHOLARLY REPRINTS
Dr. Ralph Adams Brown, Senior Editor

Series on
ECONOMIC THOUGHT, HISTORY AND CHALLENGE
Under the General Editorial Supervision of
Dr. Sanford D. Gordon
Professor of Economics, State University of New York

LABOR'S CHALLENGE TO THE SOCIAL ORDER

DEMOCRACY ITS OWN CRITIC AND EDUCATOR

BY
JOHN GRAHAM BROOKS

KENNIKAT PRESS
Port Washington, N. Y./London

LABOR'S CHALLENGE TO THE SOCIAL ORDER

First published in 1920
Reissued in 1971 by Kennikat Press
Library of Congress Catalog Card No: 74-137931
ISBN 0-8046-1437-7

Manufactured by Taylor Publishing Company   Dallas, Texas

KENNIKAT SERIES ON ECONOMIC THOUGHT,
HISTORY AND CHALLENGE

CONTENTS

CHAPTER		PAGE
I	THE QUEST	1
II	"A NEW SOCIETY"	12
III	APOLOGIA	21
IV	WORLD LESSONS	37
V	THE STRUGGLE AT ITS WORST	54
VI	THE INNER REVOLUTION	67
VII	CAPITAL ON ITS GOOD BEHAVIOR	94
VIII	"WHAT DOES LABOR WANT ANYHOW?"	118
IX	LESSONS FROM THE COMMUNISTS	144
X	SOCIALISM	168
XI	GOVERNMENT OWNERSHIP	184
XII	WHO SHALL SPEND MY SAVINGS?	205
XIII	"SOCIALIZING THE MILK SUPPLY"	213
XIV	SOCIALISM AND THE CHILD AT SCHOOL	219
XV	HOW LONG — SHALL WE WORK?	237
XVI	INDUSTRIAL DEMOCRACY AT ITS BEST	252
XVII	LABOR'S TRAINING FOR THE PRESENT CRISIS	299
XVIII	THE EMPLOYERS' CASE AGAINST THE UNION	338
XIX	THE NEW "PROFIT-SHARING"	348
XX	SYNDICALISM	358
XXI	THE NEW GUILD	389
XXII	THE GREATER TASK	408
	INDEX	433

LABOR'S CHALLENGE TO THE SOCIAL ORDER

CHAPTER I

THE QUEST[1]

THE problem here submitted is a study of power rapidly and in part accidentally acquired by labor. More especially it is a study of what labor is to do with its new mastership; what fitness it possesses for the work it would take in hand and how, meantime, other classes are to play their parts.

So far as we have the story, the world seems never to have been without its pangs actual or threatened. The present tumults differ less in intensity than in their international range and motive. The world-touch is now so close; the means of communication so immediate and so universal, that the revolutionary impulse surges about the globe as if no old barrier of mountain, river or sea were left. For proofs, we need go to no labor or socialist agitator. We have only to run through any of the dozen most authori-

[1] In the first writing, I tried to be more exact in the use of words like capitalist, employer, labor, wage-earner, proletariat. The result was either a wordy pedantry or merely tedious by too constant qualifying. The looser nomenclature has the excuse, that it has won a popularity and common acceptance not likely to deceive any reader. Except when distinctions are required, I use "labor" for the whole wage-earning class that comes within the range of my subject. This is not without its awkwardness, because some of the most important of the recent labor programs expressly class all brain workers with other workers. This is doubtless a concession to superior folk who used to speak of two quite distinct classes, one with brains and the other without them. It is in several labor programs that one now reads every one who "renders service" is a laborer.

tative reports on industrial trouble here and in other countries in which government officials, employers and lawyers have the main say. They talk in terms which conservatives before the war would have called reckless and light-headed.

It is from very able business men among these that we hear a new dialect. In all countries they note the flocking additions to trade unions and the still more momentous strengthening of these bodies by strategical alliances which may at any moment concentrate attack where the most vital public interests are at stake. The industrial technique of modern transportation furnishes this opportunity. To find among railways, longshoremen, trolleys, telegraph, telephone, express and truck companies and in mines that labor is pooling its resources; to see why it does this; to see the weakening and even disappearance of the old local isolated craft union and the rise of a more "class conscious" organization, including scores of unions, is to see what is actually taking place.

Not a country has escaped the threats of this new phalanx. An Australian journalist speaks for many countries in thus describing his own.

"The coal miners, for instance, could plunge the continent into darkness and stop all machinery in a couple of weeks, the seamen and railway men could, by united action, starve two-thirds of the people in the same period of time, the rural workers could stagnate the primary industries of the continent in a month."[1]

The contagion reaches wholly new sections,— library employees, bank and postal clerks, policemen, teachers, actors, newspaper men, men of science and college professors.

We see these dropping their old names, "Benefit," "Mutual" or "Equity Associations" and boldly taking the trade union label and demanding charters from the national center of labor authority. We see this very action in dif-

[1] *The Socialist Review*, Dec., 1919, p. 16.

ferent countries and now awkwardly but defiantly in our own.

With a mixture of amazement and curiosity — it is observed from the anxious seat that the terminology of political democracy long in use by labor is actually adopted and put in practice by governments and by many leading employers. New York actors strike; they say they have been "despotically managed" and are now to have their rights. They were carefully coached, and add, "We will have those rights constitutionally expressed." "We will have our own Government and our own politics." "If too much balked, we will have our own theatre and furnish our own management."

The weightiest report of the English Commission says flatly, that industry has been under "an autocratic and absolutist system." There must be an end to this. There is to be a radical re-distribution of power. Two lawyers of high standing who had to do with the "Protocol" in New York garment trades, tell us its purpose was to "constitutionalize the industry." One of them [1] applies the same term to Mr. Rockefeller's scheme in Colorado. From the man responsible for it, I receive an elaborate constitutional program for the largest business firm of its kind in this country. It is unequivocally said that under it so much new power is granted to the various unions as to revolutionize the business. It is admitted that the business must "adjust itself to this new fact."

Here is the struggle of ages against kings and princes to wring from them privileges for the people. Before our eyes, it now passes into factories, mines, railways, shipping and the commonest industries. If labor had won these concessions during peace, far longer time would have been required and competitive tests would have carried their own discipline. In five years, an all-shattering war has

[1] See an admirable study "An American Labor Policy," by Julius Henry Cohen, Macmillan, 1919.

done for labor what a generation could not have brought about.

One who speaks for labor, thinks this "perhaps justifies the war." But that labor should have got its power so suddenly; that it should have come through the unnatural violence of war, may prove as costly to labor as to the public. If labor has won advantages from the war, from the same source it is cumbered by disadvantages. As a whole, it is by no means ready for its job. It asks a share in business management. The claim is just, but fitness for it is not to be extemporized. It has painfully to be learned.

Meantime, labor has acquired a tool to which the rash and impatient will resort — " direct action." It is one of the most specious of syndicalist doctrines. I shall later show that this is not without its uses and its justification, but for all over-hasty, mass-purpose, " direct action " is not only the least democratic thing in the world, it is also the least effective to fit labor for a business director. This is a slow educational process.

All raw and miscellaneous efforts at " direct action " will carry another special harm both to labor and to society; *it provokes authorities to fight its abuses by its own worst weapons.*

The same applied science which tightens us into world unities has in a thousand ways put dangerous tools within easy reach of the many. The wider education has scattered explosive ideas, while popularized chemistry with other sciences has given to the masses the readiest access to material weapons which the more reckless will not leave unused. Here again, war has been a terrible instructor.

In many spots and many times power has gone to the people. It goes now under profoundly altered conditions. It appears on a world stage and with this fateful difference; for the first time the many know they have power and believe they can use it. It is this consciousness which gives to the present and prospective labor chaos its main distinction. It is this which will impose upon us more revolutionary difficulties than the war itself. The strain will be less sudden but its duration longer and not less trying.

Never had those who feel themselves responsible for social order a harder lesson to learn. Where ideas are concerned, we are still grossly superstitious in our appeal to force. As a reserve, force still has and will long have its place.

This must be said with no equivocation. No democracy (especially our own) has yet developed those collective restraints which leave society safe without organs trained in the use of compulsion. But in what is now before us, only in secondary and incidental ways can the responsibility for order be put upon the soldier or the police. Neither of these have the least adequate training for the kind of "order" we must now secure. They can shoot, imprison and club, but not even remotely do these touch the sources of our danger.

Neither can we trust to unreformed legal agencies. So far as the impending strain is met, it must be by other methods and *above all by the assent and coöperation of all that is best in the labor mass.*

The class which Burke called "swinish" and Hamilton "the beast" is now so far in control that it cannot be dislodged. It will retain its power and add to it. Very wastefully and with many rank abuses labor is now to try its hand in managing politics and industry. It has come to believe and upon the whole rightly believe, that the upper classes alone are at the end of their rope; that they are incompetent any longer to direct social forces without disaster to us all.

"Proletariat" is the favored word for those who are to administer economic and political forces "democratically." In at least eight different European programs this has been set down in explicit detail. Including revolting farmers in our Northwest, we have had a still larger output of labor plans less unified, but no whit less determined to make an end of capitalist domination. I say " domination " because many capitalistic functions are not to pass away in any future profitable to discuss. Its *domination* is a proper object of attack and the war against it has but just begun.

In real alarm entrenched and privileged folk in every country are organizing to meet the attack. There are to be prolific " concessions," " betterments," " partnerships " in which labor shall have its share. This is in the open while, with all available secrecy other measures are on foot to keep the insurgents in their proper place.

So far as it is the aim of these attempts to keep labor from *trying out* its own revolutionary program, they will as certainly fail as the futile " Antis " will fail to stop the woman's vote, or as Mr. Gompers will fail to keep the unions long out of politics. We in the United States drift steadily toward the European situation. Labor there at the present moment holds a balance of power which alters every factor in the problem. Before we are prepared for it, it will be true in our own country.

The problem of coming statesmanship is to recognize this fact. It is to learn how the more affluent and those who think themselves superior in qualifications can keep in the game; how they can hold their own and exercise there some restraining influence.

For nearly thirty centuries along the river Nile and in the East, dynasties rose and fell without a thought that " the people " were to have a whispered suggestion in affairs of state.

In the city life of the Greeks, demos had its innings. It made a mess of it, but the idea and hope burned on. It flamed up in Florentine states; it kindled in Swiss Cantons and slowly spread " in spots " as De Maistre thought " like a disease in the blood." Disease or not, its battle is so far won that Kings, Ministers of State, religious bodies, publicists great and small in every land are singing pæans to democratic rule. No one has been louder in this chanting than some of the haughtiest of German junkers and mitered dignitaries in the Roman Church. But labor leadership everywhere knows well that most of this is half-scared phrase-making. It knows that landlord and financier, with the whole more privileged order in the world, will fight as privlege has ever fought to keep its hold in politics and in business.

We in this country, are now caught in the swift current. The task, I repeat is in this one aspect new; power has so far gone to labor that it cannot be turned back. It will here and there go *through*. It will go through to the bottom. In three European states, it has indeed gone through the bottom with leakage and waste enough. All our admonitions to the "ancient and lowly" have dwelt on the value of "initiative" and "self-reliance." Labor now takes the advice. It proposes to initiate and to rely upon itself. It starts schools and lectures of its own — careful to select its own instructors and very shy of all professors in good and regular standing. To be hounded by institutions is the most flattering qualification. Government agents find thirty of these classes in a single coal district. The labor committee tells a visitor, "We'll listen to no college man unless he has shown independence enough to be blacklisted by the trustees." When Debs, Haywood and scores of others are released from prison their influence in the labor class will be multiplied by ten. Not a man of them whose word will not carry weight far beyond its merits. This is the penalty for infantile, primitive attempts to crib or punish ideas. Even those raw recruits of revolution the I. W. W. have had no such backers as those who have shown most violence in their attacks upon them.

Louis Blanqui was the most defiant revolutionist in modern times. He spent more than half of his mature life in prison. The present Prime Minister of France had only contempt for Blanqui's methods, but he gave his best strength to get him free. When the Republic was established, Clemenceau believed society safer with Blanqui free than in prison. August Bebel said his years behind the bars equipped him with influence he never could have approached if he had been let alone.

When will our greater and lesser schools learn what this means? I have just come from an industrial center which has been a hot-house of revolt. No word of the incident had reached me, but I found there a university teacher whose name I had never heard. He had been quietly "dropped." Out of curiosity or perhaps from a vague sympathy, he had visited the hot-house and upon his return had openly spoken of it. Relieved of his job, his entire time is now devoted to a most ingenious way of spreading the ideas which two very influential college trustees said were "to be nipped in the bud." There is a method of "nipping buds" which multiplies them by dozens. These college officials hit upon the method.

For these superstitions and timidities before ideas, we must find substitutes. With an accepted democratic program "for making our rules and making our wealth"; with power so lodged in the hands of labor and its sympathizers, these substitutes are our most immediate necessity as they are our chief security for the future. Together with legal changes to which a growing number of younger men teaching in our schools of law are now giving attention, we shall find these substitutes mainly in the kind of coöperation established with all that is best and most enlightened in labor organizations. These are now to be educated by their own successes and by their own mistakes. The mistakes will be many and grievous, but they must be borne and borne together.

Labor will, for example, shorten its working day until it discovers *for itself* how far it can go. With the entire business responsibility resting upon them, working men have long been struggling with this special problem, as I shall show. In their own factories they have to produce goods. They know that wages must depend upon the quantity and quality of the output. Labor's share (wages) must bear some relation to this product. Though granting eight hours actually or in principle, these workers now argue as any business man argues.

Thus with the whole list of labor standards from minimum wage to social insurance, the workers are to learn mainly by their own exericse of economic and political power. This has to be accepted as something final and determining in the problem before us.

The chief aim of this study is if possible to throw some light on *democracy as its own educator* with the promise this holds out to us. It is also the aim to see what part other classes are to play in those altered relations from which there is no turning back.

After the railroad strike led by Debs in 1894, I was asked by a far-seeing man, " If the war comes between capital and labor, how shall you take sides?" It seemed to me then that no rational answer to that question was possible. Nowhere were the issues clear. Capitalism was top-heavy with abuses. On the one side, it controlled our politics and on the other it fought unionism by methods which forced labor to select leaders in important centers as unscrupulous as some attorneys and henchmen of the capitalists. The entire labor training was one of defiance as against an enemy. The best of unionism now tries to become constructive. This change has gone on with changes in capitalism; through public regulation and a growing admission that labor has every right to organization which all business possesses.

At that time one could only take sides on theories still in literary form. Tentative definitions of all the "isms" aiming at revolutionary change were to be heard on every corner or read in a thousand books and pamphlets, but they had neither bone nor flesh except in utopian experiments. Some of these isms have now passed out of the void. They appear with both bone and flesh. They have sent out their plans of action. They are armed with definite powers to carry the programs into effect. With no evasion, they tell us their purpose toward fundamentals like property, law and the state. We know not only what they think of democracy and representative government, but what substitutes they propose. The one hope of the actual experimental clash of ideals is that (though " taking sides " may be as perplexing as ever) we can see our way as never before to unite the forces in coöperative effort. I hope some evidence of this will be forthcoming in the present volume.

If it is true that labor has won a working influence which gives it a leading part in social direction, the task, I repeat, requires the assent and coöperation of every available section of that influence. There is no contingent however labeled, that can be excluded. For capital, the day of " the lone hand " has closed. A lurking communism, silent and unsuspected in time of peace, now takes the stage. A socialist contingent breaks away from the party " because it has become a corpse." A strong local among the cigarmakers attempts to reshape its constitution. It is " outworn " and " reactionary." It should make " the trade union state the state of the nation as a whole." " Six hours a day and one dollar an hour with the promise of doubling these advantages when all the machinery of production is appropriated." These are the super-demands now everywhere in order and they suggest to us our first lesson and our first opportunity. I set this down at once though proofs must come later. With legal rigors alone, we shall not cope with these intimidations. We must have the help of the relatively cautious groups inside these various radicalisms.

A small minority of cigar-makers announce a soviet policy, " a trade union state " " the state of the nation as a whole."

Who is it that holds these secessionists in check? Not the police or any public authority. It is from within the union that these conscriptors of all land, shops and public utilities receive their most stinging criticism. It is from one of the most powerful state Federations of labor that such as these are called " lawless agitators," " guilty of treason not only to the principles of trade unionism but to the United States of America." The destroyers will run wild until the more steadied labor bodies are brought into acknowledged partnership with capital with all doors open for experiment wherever it may lead.

If without delay the main body of strong American employers would in good faith accept and act upon the conditions of this partnership already sanctioned in a dozen reports by governments and by so many strong employers, more would be done to silence bolshevists of every hue than by all other means. Labor's part in this coping with super-radicalism will be far and away more effective than that of the capitalistic partners alone. As will appear later, the partnership is nevertheless a necessity, and it will impose upon the employing partners a most formidable stunt of proving to labor that it is safer and more hopefully prosperous in the common fellowship than without it. That this can be done is yet to be proved but in the transition it has to be tried and tried through sacrifice and concessions that will also try the souls of the possessing classes.

CHAPTER II

"A NEW SOCIETY"

I

BEFORE the war was half spent, it had become clear that at its close we were to be tangled among forces so intricate as to call for a higher and more flexible intelligence than did the war itself. This is now a certainty. The task is not merely the rearranging of the world map and trade accommodation among the nations; it is quite as much our own domestic re-fitting. No people on the desolated areas will escape. That these trials are first of all economic and concern present property relations indicates plainly the forces of resistance which the new order will encounter.

For what is called "our standard of living" men and women in every class will struggle to desperation. This standard is based largely upon money income, but it gathers about it those sentimental values;— social position and prestige (or the promise of such) which feed the subtlest and most sensitive of human vanities and ambitions. To maintain and to win this "standard" is the tap-root of those hectoring labor demands which so smell to heaven in the nostrils of the employing and capitalist classes.

Yet in this striving to keep and to improve their position, wage folks are only imitating those with higher incomes.

This labor, however, will have one advantage in the coming contest. Its more meager and precarious earnings will shield it from certain leveling forms of taxation which more conspicuous possessions cannot escape. It is certain that labor with its new alliances is to secure immeasurably greater political power. We hear of the whole "white collar brigade" passing into the unions. In England it is the "Professional Workers' Federation, the National Union of Teachers, the Incorporated Association of Assistant Masters, the Association of the Assistant Mistresses, the Custom and Excise Federation, the Second Division Clerks' Association, the Tax Clerks' Association, the Federation of Women Civil Servants, the London County Council Staff Association, and kindred organizations, never before pointly organized to protect their special interests."

In one of our public libraries, employees "unionize." They say "no grievance is corrected by the trustees, they ignore us as the school teachers are ignored. With a strong union we can ignore the trustees." "God help us," says an academic dignitary, "when professors, scavengers and bellboys make common cause." A flustered Boston school teacher comes to me with the question, Shall we form a trade union? With regret she sees that women are soon to have the vote. She says that the witty advocate of woman suffrage, Margaret Foley, is holding large and enthusiastic meetings with the direct encouragement of local Catholic priests. She notes what city employees, backed by votes and active politicians, have got in higher salaries, while teachers with neither organization nor votes still accept a stipend the purchasing power of which is cut almost one-half. I show her a Canadian paper (the Manitoba *Free Press*) reporting the same outcry from half the cities in the Dominion. "We teachers," says one, "are simply forgotten because we have no organized political influence to compel attention." Another says, "There is not an energetic labor organization in Canada that cannot make the Government 'sit up' and listen to its demands. Why are we teachers cowed into silence?" Again, we read "Reporters on the French and English newspapers of Montreal, Canada, have organized a union with a charter from the International," as they have been doing on our side of the line. This entire movement has now a new and most powerful sanction from the State itself. Unions that hold the key to the "life arteries" through which we are nourished from day to day have taught the masses how easy it is to frighten officials into one concession after another. Weaker unions, watching these successes, try to imitate them.

As never before governments have been compelled to take the labor union into partnership; definitely to "recognize" it and deal with it. The representative principle long since in the political field, has now to be accepted in the field of business. War has turned millions of wage-earners from private into government employees. Thus these public servants here and in other countries are being organized and trained for political action.

It was the same intimation of these and other coming changes which early in 1915 led to much speculative suggestion on the social reconstruction to follow the war. In the first year, so much of the old order had been tilted and battered as to force upon us this issue of future readjustment. The lurch toward " state socialism " at once caught the eye because every one could see that the first plunge was only a beginning. To take over railroads, shipping, munition factories, raw materials, insurance: to fix prices on the " great necessities " had an obvious logic. Each step toward collectivism became a cause for further advance. Every new step in state authority produced the necessity (or what seemed to be such) for more authority. Nor is this growth in the power of government (state socialism or collectivism) the most revolutionary fact. The forces of state socialism may be doubled or quadrupled without necessarily undermining the accepted business methods on which capitalism rests. This discovery has produced a little revolution of its own inside the labor world of which we shall take account.

It is because war raised questions which pass out of and wholly beyond state socialism, that our curiosity about the after-days is so alive. Not one of these external regulations is so eventful as are the ideas behind them. Some of these are very old, but their wider, more confident, more democratic international acceptance is new and eventful.

When the President classed those who had been taking market prices on their European shipments among "the enemies of society" as were all those trying to get rich by producing and distributing raw material, the idea has revolution in it. If "profiteering in necessities" is wicked in time of war, *why is it less so in time of peace?* Multitudes who have no knowledge of socialism or sympathy with it will henceforth ask this question. They will get no satisfying answer.

There was revolution in many obscure local events that came and went without a line in the press, of which I give one instance. An authorized official stands before a large body of strikers who refuse arbitration. He tells them coolly that they must accept arbitration or be conscripted. This was a threat and not a bluff by an employer. It was understood to be a direct warning from a Government having at call regiments of armed men to do its bidding. The men broke into groups as they left their work at night. They were trying to understand. At a meeting a few hours later they discussed this threat. "What is its real meaning? If we work for the Government we can't strike or, if we strike and stick to it, we are to be classed with traitors and so treated." One of them tried to justify it "because it is war and therefore exceptional." One better informed said, "No, the French government did just that before the war in a railway strike. The men were whipped in under military control and had to submit."

Close upon this in the local press came comments like this: "Government has power to stop strikes, why does it not use that power?"

Other journals, for years rank in abuse of Mr. Gompers, suddenly began to smile upon him. This high priest of labor was "nobly patriotic" because his great following was to be "loyal." Instead of strikes, we were to have "reasonable adjustments of labor disputes *with compulsion when necessary.*"

Scarcely had our own railways been rounded up by the Government when some hundreds of machinists and shopmen struck in Virginia with the threat of a "general walkout." As reported, the Director General sent a message. "It is the first time in the history of our Government that any employees have attempted a strike against their Government. Such action is incredible. The Government cannot of course be intimidated by any of its employees." These strikers were warned to submit their case at once to the established board of arbitration.

The *Buffalo Evening News* commented thus: "There can be but one answer and that is for the Government to take control and choke the disaffection;— strikes are nothing more nor less than treason. And they should be made a treasonable offense."

This extemporized optimism over force used against labor and strikes would be less strange, if the twenty years since 1900 were not dotted thick with proofs that neither governments nor labor leaders have any such influence as is here ascribed to them. Toward a certain kind of strikes that is steadily growing, the democratic state or any state professing democracy is weak and ineffective. As democracy develops, it will become weaker still through a long transitional period during which labor must be sobered by business obligations.

There is no space here to tell the full story of these new insurgencies of labor which have tested every known resource of public authority on Australian State railways, in Sweden, in Canada, South Africa, Dublin, New Zealand, together with the most haughty challenges of the "labor army" in Europe at bay in the agonies of war. It is a warning record of what awaits us unless some far more fundamental adjustments are found for labor-service under capitalistic management. Increase of organization has so strengthened labor's political affiliations, that the one suggestion to be avoided is over hasty appeal to strong-arm methods. In this industrial strife, these methods alone are as stupidly inadequate as for misunderstandings in a private family. Whatever their use, there must go also very specific constructive adjustments which educate us and at the same time broaden the basis of recognized common interests. International labor troubles are so akin that the history of a strike, lockout, trade union schism in other countries is monotonously like these events in New Jersey or California.

To this foreboding issue of the strike, especially the political strike, I shall later offer other illustrations to prove how inevitable is the reaching out of hope, purpose and imagination toward "a new society." The craving to know a little better how life is to emerge from the wreckage is peculiar to no nation.

It was a German then serene in his confidence of victory, who said "Our children are to live in a wholly new world." A French socialist thought "no trace of the old bourgeois farce is to be left. . . . The infamy we have been calling civilization will be wiped out with all its smut." To him, the allies were already conquerors. The three English periodicals which came to me during the war were never silent two weeks together over this impending social upheaval for which our planning could not begin too soon.

We need not quibble over these guesses. That it will be "a wholly new world" or be "fundamentally reshaped" there is reason enough to doubt.

There will be no lasting change beyond the change in *habits*. Habit in the individual is what custom is in society. Suffering and "mass-emotion" affect us powerfully at the moment, but every revolution records the " sagging back " towards former ways of life. Not to sag wholly back is our task. That we are to have an altered emphasis on many of our traditional ways is a minimum already assured. For any real approach to humanized relations among the nations there is one test; the acquired habit of working openly and generously together as if the prosperity of one was the prosperity of all. That principle has never been fairly and wisely tried within the nation or without that it did not work. If the ghastly and unclean futilities of war are ever overcome, this enlightened coöperation must be achieved.

If so supreme an acquisition is to be ours, a " New Society " is hardly too strong a term to mark the result of tasks which such remaking will impose.

One high service this war has brought; it has forced us to look through and behind the mechanics, the devices, the mere organization of social remedies. It has forced us to re-acquaint ourselves with what has already been done to waken and to harmonize the temper and convictions which are the first conditions of change toward better ways.

In many of these anticipations of future remodeling, we have been told what the employer, the trade union, the State, the rich and the general public should do amidst the ruins which war leaves. I have cut out or copied an interminable list from these proffered remedies — old commonplaces like " free trade," " more authority and power to the State and to the city," " the taking of unearned incomes," " socializing all economic rent," " universal pensions," " minimum wage," " coöperation to replace competition," " multiplied arbitration courts with compulsory powers," " abandonment of secret diplomacy," " complete disarmament," " taking of all private profit out of everything made for war " (which would include most of what is made in times of peace) — these with a score of others like " A new Religion based on Social Ethics," with at least nine varieties of Leagues of Peace — one to exclude all force " desirous only to create an international mind."

In the first months of the war, one counselor was foreseeing. He said "industry must create a new politics." It must begin and be carried on " where the work is done." " In factory, mine and transportation, we must have self-government organized as fundamental law."

If this seer still lives, what a satisfaction must be his to see this " functioning " in hundreds of places. So far has it gone, that a great firm tells the public that democracy once accepted in the plant has already forced them not only to " proportional representation " but to long discussions over the *kind* of representation — finally resulting in the choice of the Hare system.

Midway and later in the war important reports began to appear with remedial proposals in a new tone. They were based on investigations at a time and under conditions which made men serious. We do not look to the New York Chamber of Commerce for language of the pulpit or that of a sociologist with a turn for religion. But the report of that chamber on Industrial Problems makes its final appeal to the moral factor. This, it says, " outweighs all physical factors."

The British Commission on Industrial Unrest finds no way out except in " a new spirit ; a more human spirit ; one in which economic and business considerations will be influenced and corrected and it is hoped eventually controlled by human and ethical considerations."

An accomplished writer at this time saw our only hope in " a revived and democratized science." This should become " the religion of the people." " Un seul idéal peut créer la civilisation meilleure à laquelle nous aspirons, celui de la science. Puisse-t-il être la religion du peuple!"

Behind most of these suggestions is an experience of decades, yes, even of generations. They come, moreover, from different countries and from almost every mode and condition of industrial and political development. Specific forms of industrial arbitration have more than a century behind them. Two forms of coöperation (that of credit and that of producers) are older still. The main organized contention of the trade union, even in our own country, covers nearly four generations. Whether by the State, by labor organization or through voluntary association, the soil has been prepared and the seeds sown for such new harvesting as the future may have in store. The furnace of war consumes a great deal of rubbish, legal and conventional. Its long agonies open the mind to doubts about the past and to questionings about the future. Braver re-beginning may thus be possible. Yet they will neither be possible nor fruitful unless rooted in soil that has nourished generations of our forerunners.

CHAPTER III

APOLOGIA

IN comparing these predictions about the future, I was led to look through a collection of notes by the writer on " Social and Labor Questions " begun in 1881. Except for a part of two years, these observations and guesses represent a record of nearly forty years.

Such bearing as they have is almost exclusively on those industrial and political theories, proposals, agencies which have to do with a conjectural " New Society." There are few or none who do not want " improvements "; that is, some prudent steps in the direction of a new society. From these cautious ones, the demands grow more shrill until we reach the outmost faction of anarchist-communist with his large order already quoted, " not a scrap of the old bourgeois farce with all its smut," to be left. In this scale of desired reforms, we thus deal with a question of degree. But as the old logic books taught us, degree may become so great as to constitute a difference in kind.

In their more general form, my notes touch the increasing friction between capitalism and wage labor; the ways in which politics are molded by the more powerful economic interests, together with the catalogue of " remedies " to set things right. More concretely, they concern socialism, cooperation, the trade union, open or closed shop, forms of arbitration, sliding scales, minimum wage, profit sharing, welfare work, the rise of syndicalism, the I. W. W. and the New Guild.

To write about labor's challenge to the " Social Order " leaves much to be told. Hosts of others attack it too. For thirty-five years a very over-lord of capitalism, Andrew Carnegie, had directly challenged our actual business methods and attempts to equalize conditions. Over his own name he carried this criticism so far that many American trade unionists would protest if the logic of it touched their own interests. In this, Mr. Carnegie is no longer an exception. He is but one among a great many of his class in every country who has subjected capitalism and its reflected politics to revolutionary censure. In the arts, in science, in the church, in letters, among economists and politicians, a very impressive list of critics could be written down in five minutes by any well informed student. Though an individualist to his finger tips and feared by socialists beyond all men in France, Clemenceau has attacked capitalist leadership in *Les Plus Forts* with an acerbity that no socialist has outdone.

At the gathering of business men in Atlantic City after the war, Mr. Rockefeller and Mr. Schwab warned their fellows in language that ten years ago would have classed them before such an audience as *poseurs*. Not only must they and their kind, it was said, cordially accept government supervision to correct the abuses inherent in competing industry, but labor is to have a new deal. It must have " constructive recognition." It must freely choose its representatives to work with capitalistic directors.

After searching personal investigation in Colorado, Mr. Rockefeller, Jr., tells the Commercial Club in Denver that there is to be a new brotherhood in business. He tells of the new purpose in the Colorado Fuel & Iron Co. " to develop a carefully worked out plan of industrial representation, which was adopted by unanimous vote of the board of directors, and a seventy-eight per cent. vote of the employees." Labor representation in the business, he calls " the first outstanding fact." To avoid all intimidations, labor should have the secret ballot with no one to make it afraid.

By secret ballot representatives are chosen annually by

the employees from their fellow-workers in each mining camp and each division of the steel mills, one for every one hundred and fifty employees, but never less than two in any camp or division. Labor is to have its "right of appeal" and also a "Bill of Rights" against unfair discharge with "the right to hold meetings at appropriate places, outside of working hours. The right, without discrimination, to membership or non-membership in any society or organization."

Especially in socialist papers, one saw highly seasoned comments on Mr. Rockefeller's "conversion." One called it "snuffling cant." "It was the same old capitalistic trick of quack plasters for organic disease."

On the other side, I heard in New York from a tory capitalist that Mr. Rockefeller had "sold out to the unions." He had "become an enemy to honestly acquired wealth." We were even exhilarated by his saying that "Mr. Rockefeller is a Bolshevist."

The answer is simple to both socialist and tory critic. Looking long and honestly at the troubles in his own camp, he did what an increasing multitude of employers in every country has been forced to do. They have recognized that business cannot go on without very specific functional and structural changes. They may "lose out" in these concessions, but they are not to be blamed for trying to adjust their affairs to the new pace.

There are now few industrial communities without employers of this stamp. In the chapter on "The New Employer" we shall see in detail what they are aiming at; see also some limitations to the task of "saving capitalism" in anything like its present form.

In my title, I have put quotation marks about "Social Order" as a term much in vogue not merely by the "offensively rich" but by the majority of those who have — or think they have — much to lose from any considerable jolt in the existing business and political organization. "Labor's challenge to capitalism" would convey the same thought. The ordinary method under which business has been done in this country is capitalism. It is buttressed by the wage system. Until it suffered from its own excesses, it glorified competition and swarmed with private profit-makers trying to get the better of one another. Every defender justifies these conditions chiefly on the ground that the intensity of personal self-interest in the profit-making system produces more wealth and distributes it more widely than any other known method.

The enemies of capitalism admit that in its time it was as necessary as it was useful. Especially since the middle of the last century these enemies have been telling us that its days are numbered, because the evils in the wage system and profit-mongering are greater than the benefits. Booker Washington said the enslaving of his people in this country was a step in progress. The feudal system was such a step, but both had to be replaced.

To settle personal differences by resort to sword or pistol, English speaking people have learned to regard with merited contempt, yet the duel was a genuine step towards justice. It replaced the hired bullies who struck in the dark. It introduced the umpire and some sort of equality in the settlement of altercations. For centuries it served its purpose as a link in progress. Capitalism, in spite of past utilities, we are told, must now make way for a new and different industrial order. It is with these critics and with their constructive proposals that my notes are concerned.

In the decade, especially since 1871, the opponents of capitalism have increased in numbers as they have increased in influence. To say that capitalism in its present form is on the defensive is too mild a statement. Its danger from outward attack is less insidious than the loss of confidence from within. For generations capitalism held loyal the large army of lesser salaried officials, as well as the other armies in small business, in the teaching and preaching class, among journalists and farmers.

In country after country, these have been falling away in such numbers as to constitute a crisis even if no other changes were in evidence. They have fallen away solely because they have lost confidence in the " capitalistic order." From the first, primitive societies, customs, structure and functions have always changed when controlling numbers *ceased to believe.* As long as a Dyak medicine man flourishing a bladder to keep off witches had the faith of his people behind him, he was secure. He lost that security by an event so simple as growing disbelief. Voltaire said the strength of the monks in his time was not in *them,* but in the credulity of their followers.

Has capitalism reached this stage? Has it become its own grave-digger? Have so many lost faith that it must henceforth fight against odds? Or is its task one of transformation and readjustment, leaving it still in the field to divide honors with other methods of creating and distributing wealth? Where doubt and suspicion have spread widely enough, we have the friction of an inner *sabotage* in its most disintegrating form.

As the war closes, the proof is substantial that the old order has two enemies where it had one ten years ago.

It is no less clear that capitalism will fight long and it will fight with cunning and with desperate weapons. In the open, it will welcome the more popular " remedies." Whether socialist, syndicalist or communist, few labor agitators have ever learned the defensive power of private property. They have but half learned its skill of adaptation; its ingenuities and its resources to hold its own under new names as well as under legal and other changes. Every month of the present war has been opening the eyes of labor to the need of new tactics. One of the most adroit of capitalistic devices will be in accepting and accommodating itself to reforms, to new taxation and to socialistic encroachments.

For this reason, space must here be given to some of these "betterments" that are of no serious consequence except as educational steps. Most of them have to do directly with industrial and social theories, which range from ultra individualism (anarchism) to an all-powerful State under capitalist control with "law and order" as its ideal. Strangely enough this latter may bear the name "State Socialism." Shifting and uneasily poised between these extremes are individualists, single taxers, at least three varieties of socialists and communists. If we wrote these names about a circle, the anarchist and communist would touch, as if extremes did really meet. Both represent forces that no society can now ignore. They will be so active and annoying in our more immediate future that, what may seem unnecessary space is given to them in this volume. Whether we like it or not, we must recognize that, as the State strengthens and institutions harden, they *breed* anarchisms as our faulty economic organization breeds I. W. W.'s. Nor in writing this do I imply that society in its own defense should not organize strict discipline for those who break the rules.

As regards the wage-earners, my material is mainly with the three great bodies — trade unions, socialists and co-operators, with the sectarian variations in each of them. They are now a world force whose millions are steadily increasing. The war has added immeasurably to their strength. Their direct political influence through closer and more sympathetic organization, will so gain in confidence as to constitute wholly new problems for the present governing class.

The first and largest place in my note-taking is on "Democracy" and on the labored ingenuities to define the word so that it may fit conditions, international and economic, which vast sections of labor are forcing on the world. For some moments, for some areas or groups in history, the word democracy had an intelligible use. There are very ancient, half savage societies in which all the tribal members had a voice in making the rules, i.e., the politics. We in the United States show much bravado over our " democracy," yet no people ever showed more practical contempt for some of its most elemental implications like " the consent of the governed." What meaning can the term have to our negroes? England has some democracy at home in spite of King and House of Lords, but how much in her empire as a whole? Democracy has always begun in spots and among small bodies of homogeneous and like-minded folks. Internationally and racially it is still almost as utopian as pure communism or as the " free autonomous groupings " in the vision of anarchism.

It was from a long and minute study of small " labor democracies " in the three working class sections already indicated, that I was led to ask this question. *" What is labor itself doing with democracy when and where its principles are accepted and tried in its own bailiwick? "*
It has far more economic power, with specific business responsibilities of its own, than is generally believed. What democratic uses does it make of these opportunities which it has itself acquired? If labor hires labor, does it give shorter hours and higher wages? If it takes up the referendum, initiative and recall (as just now at an important labor convention) does it apply them with more logical consistency than is done elsewhere? We know to a surfeit, what democracy is in a platform; in resolutions and in all ceremonial displays.
In all this, there is only an aspiration. It is like saying " the world shall be converted to the practice of the Christian virtues."

In the complicated and interlacing world-industry now reached, really to "democratize" its processes and direct its forces; to pass from wordy proclamations to achieved results is as profound a charge in human nature as to get the sanctities of religion in among the daily practices of men.

Inside its own organizations, labor has been trying for half a century to democratize its own private politics. It has met so many surprises and so many rebuffs from its own members, as to furnish the most valuable of all documents on the subject. One of the older and most successful of our labor leaders says anything like "pure democracy" is "nothing but an attempt to rule by that part of the people who don't know what they want and even less how to get it." He is recording strictly his trade union experience.

Still better for observation is Australasia.

Labor in Australia and in New Zealand has won so much political mastery that we can observe it to great advantage. Labor is there still struggling with political democracy. Only to the slightest extent has it reached the severer test of an economic democracy. One of the most trustworthy correspondents writes from Melbourne to an English radical paper about "Labor's difficulty in governing Australia." He says nothing is to be gained any longer by disguising the truth. The heart of the trouble is in "maintaining cordial and intimate touch between the rank and file of the democracy and the Executive Government." "The more aggressive of the unions and the more independent members of the House of Representatives and the Senate, and practically the whole of the official labor press, are in a state of open warfare with the Ministry," i.e., with its own Ministry. "The organ of the most influential of the unions is in open revolt." Who are these political officials against whom the revolt takes place? The very ones who but a few years since "won fame in the labor movement by the fearlessness of their public criticism of past governments," i.e., before labor came into power.

These new progressives within the labor camp are outraged by the censorship and by the restrictions upon public meetings. That " labor " should disgrace itself by these reactions seems to him disheartening.

But what is it that constitutes the chief complaint of labor against its own political servants? Briefly it is that these men in power refuse to give what labor asks. It will have first more wages and then fewer hours of work.

To indicate the gravity of this protest within the labor party, this reporter tells us of more than 700 serious strikes. He says that " Arbitration Courts are being flouted by a large and growing section which favors direct action," " and within the last six months the central executives of three or four most powerful unions have had their authority gravely imperiled by the flat refusal of the rank and file to await the result of the slow process of Arbitration Court hearing."

The activity of the unions is thus described.

" How is it that with all the powers possessed by the National Labor Government in time of war, the breadwinner can get no relief? Surely with labor enthroned in the National Ministry, and with five-sixths of the States governed by labor men, we should secure the adoption of a policy which will so mobilize national resources that the housewives' purse shall be secure from robbers."

Here we have these extreme democracies shouting protests against their leaders and rent by differences of opinion over the most fundamental principles to which they are pledged.

There are more hopeful interpretations of this Australian evolution, but any one who compares the buoyant expectations of labor in the years following the "political revolution of 1890," with what has actually come about, will see how long and dusty a road it has still to travel before it supplants capitalism by a democratized industry.

An editor of the *Australian Worker* now writes — the workers " are not going to take their orders even from their own political leaders, but that they themselves are going to say what they want, and see to it that their representatives in parliament secure their needs for them."

After long experience with the famous arbitration law he writes of it as a hopeless failure. He says, " its failure to deal with industrial unrest in Australia is largely responsible for the birth of the newer and more militant movement."

Still searching for evidence as to what labor was doing with such political or economic power as it had secured, I turned again to the coöperators. They had become their own employers. I learned with some astonishment that they were having their sore trials with labor. They had at the time perhaps two hundred thousand employees. They were in different countries in businesses as different as banking and insurance are from coöperative push-carts.

Here is an economic democracy wholly inside the labor world that is growing extensively as well as intensively. In organization it now has firm international affiliations. Though it more and more touches politics, its real strength is economic and what is more, its forms of industry determine and shape its politics.

It was from a belated conviction that democracy in this new perspective might throw light upon its outlook and upon its self-imposed limitations, that my notes came finally to take up the struggle for " popular rule " (economic and political) as it appears in the more awakened labor circles — socialist, trade unionist, coöperators and syndicalist. Better even than in small populations like New Zealand and

APOLOGIA

Switzerland, one may see on this more radical frontier what labor does with democracy when it has free hand; what it does when, with caution and sagacity, it adds business burdens to political aspiration. We shall have plenty of instruction in later chapters to show what social stability owes to working men and women carrying on their own business. We shall see, too, I trust, new reasons to encourage labor in taking on further responsibilities of the same kind and to do this with the consenting coöperation of employers.

After "democracy," "socialism, its rise and growth" has the most frequent mention in the memoranda: especially the changes in theory and practice which acquired power and organization bring in every country where the movement gains strength. In the first periods of agitation and propaganda there is a tyranny of dogma. There is the same arrogance, the same hard confidence in fundamental doctrines that are supposed to be peculiar to ecclesiastics in their most reactionary stage.

With no important exception, these theoretic severities soften through the influence of party organization which compels practical fraternization with other political and social activities. Throughout, it was my endeavor to note tendencies and changes of opinion in voluntary association and in legislative purpose, touching social and labor issues. These changes would be startling enough had peace been unbroken. The war has so heightened their significance as to suggest the use of the record in the present study. I set down the title to this chapter, "Apologia," because I know well the imperfections of my material and the risk of too confident inferences drawn from it. It comprises a great deal of conversation with employers and employed, single taxers, coöperators, socialists, anarchists, communists, syndicalists and with our own syndicatist variety, the I. W. W.

Miscellaneous interviewing like this is worthless except

as it throws light on facts and experience which can be verified. I have therefore excluded material, the verification of which is left in too much doubt. For example, the notes (especially those taken in this country) show a change of attitude among large numbers of the employing class which places them among our economic innovators. Some of them are more fundamentally radical than many socialists. In 1908, an Englishman of as large business and political experience as that of Mr. Russell Rea told me of his earlier visits to the United States. His natural affiliation was with our magnates. He said, " I was full of curiosity to know the American opinion on changes in the labor situation which seemed to me very eventful, especially for men of large interests. My net impression was that these strong Americans recognized no issue whatever except the purely practical one of preserving 'law and order.'" He found men with languid curiosity about profit-sharing and other forms of " welfare work " but the United States appeared to them quite safe " from dangers that might possibly be imminent in Europe."

In a following chapter indications enough will be found to show what the years (especially since the eighties) have done to awaken thousands of employers to some lively sense of altered equilibrium. This awakening of the manager is open to the simplest and most definite proofs. It has been amply recorded. For this reason it lends itself safely to my purpose.

Nowhere is the change of attitude toward " pure democracy " greater than among various labor groups. As increased power has brought administrative responsibility, the weaknesses of all " pure democracy " have been discovered. The theory and the practice of socialist executives have also changed. Even if the change is mainly one of tactics, rather than of ultimate goal, it has the utmost importance for the tasks awaiting us in social reparation. As responsibility passes to labor, it learns the complications of its job. It learns that it is not to be done by any sect. It is a job for the collective intelligence, experience and good will appearing in every temperamental difference among men. Neither extreme of radicalism nor of conservatism is at this stage to be shut out.

Democracy has this fundamental character, it has to do with the *uses to which power is put*. Taine's long study of revolutions led him to define a revolution as the shifting of power from one class to another class. This power may be as dangerous as among children playing with sticks of dynamite, or it may be as safe as it has proved among millions of the Swiss.

The forms of democratic power passing to labor are entering upon a new experience. These will strengthen as organization strengthens. It is a *social* discipline because these great labor bodies will be internationally locked together. They cannot work for themselves without more and more working *for and with* others. A national trade union which has seventeen or eighteen millions of money invested in banks, trust funds, real estate and ground rent may have utopian and revolutionary aims, but it will move with cautious reference to institutions and interests outside itself. Unions, socialists and coöperators have hundreds of millions invested in sanitary, unemployment and other " benefits " which leave them no alternative but to work with corresponding agencies under capitalism. " But every one of them," it is said, " is working to overthrow capitalism." Yes, in a sense this is mainly the thing aimed at. But — as I hope to show — that overthrow can only be accomplished through changes that are socially superior to capitalism.

This is the long and inexorable task that labor has before it. To interrupt this task by resort to violence is only to put off the building process to another day. Even if capitalism is doomed, it is the writer's belief that essential features of it (like the retaining of private interest and private profits as incentives to saving and wealth-production) are to remain so many decades that the fact must continue to have wide practical acceptance.

It is as firmly his belief that the wage system on which capitalism rests will be profoundly modified in the direction of far more democratic management. What this means for the future is one object of the present study. The excuse for employing such faulty material as note-book observations is that they confirm and may be tested by other and more substantial records open to us all.

Much is made in my notes of what may be called "labor opinion." I learned that one could easily idealize this opinion. It has all the fallibilities found in any other class, legal, clerical or business. Of the more thoughtful judgments among wage-earners, one may, I think, say this, that in social and economic changes *on which their life-standards depend* their convictions are of more distinctive value than those of their critics.

Of another revolution, the historian Froude long ago wrote —" as a rule, property and influence continued to hold aloof in the usually haughty style. New doctrines ever gain readiest hearing among the common people; not only because the interests of the higher classes are usually in some degree connected with the maintenance of existing institutions, but because ignorance is itself a protection against the many considerations which embarrass the judgment of the educated."[1]

Two authorities on this special question of higher value than Froude's, are Frederic Harrison and John Morley.

In one of the best comments on democracy ever penned, Morley quotes with entire approval this passage from that life-long friend of organized labor, Mr. Harrison: "If any section of the people is to be the paramount arbiter in pub-

[1] "History of England," Vol. I, p. 164.

lic affairs, the only section competent for this duty is the superior order of workmen. . . . (The qualities demanded) are, firstly, social sympathies and sense of justice; then openness and plainness of character; lastly, habits of action, and a practical knowledge of social misery. . . . These qualities the best working men possess in a far higher degree than any other portion of the community."[1] If this is not equally true of corresponding labor in the United States, it must be *made so* by the coöperation of employers and public authorities.

It may humiliate our intellectual pride, but a change so volcanic as that in which we are now caught, leaves us all in a litter of inconsistencies. We can neither "connect things up" nor follow any pet principle to its sequence. When Lloyd George is called "a man with neither tomorrows nor yesterdays" it is meant as stigma. "He has turned opportunism to a fine art." Tossed hither and yon by events, he catches at whatever will sustain him for the hour. He does this in argument and he does it in action.

The accusation is grave but it does not apply alone to this statesman. War first forces this opportunism upon the world and the rough wake of revolution keeps it on our keel. The very desperateness of the industrial struggle is filled with this dissonance among principles. If simplified enough, we all see it. One who says he is an anarchist "because it puts him in great company," insists upon "free speech." He insists upon it as "a constitutional right" and even reads to his audience the words from the constitution to prove his case. He admits, however, that his purpose is to overthrow government and with fine effrontery demands protection of this "fundamental law" while he and his friends engage in its destruction. This lacks sportsmanship, but it has no more inner contradictions than our diplomacies, statesmanship and most of our labor policies.

[1] Essay on Sir Henry Maine.

On one side we clutch at precedents that have lost all meaning and on the other, we grope for new proposals as questionable as they are untried. In the violent thinking and action of the time, this is unavoidable. It is better to acknowledge these inconsistencies than to put up specious pretenses that they are not there.

This volume has its share of them.

CHAPTER IV

WORLD LESSONS

IN the effort to see more clearly what other peoples have to teach us, and we to learn, I made in 1893 a rough chart on which to compare national differences as they appear in the successive steps of departure from capitalistic ways or in attempts at reform. Conservative critics had made much of cultural differences to show that the movement against the social order was incoherent; that, as race contact became closer through improved transportation and trade, these elements of conflict would grow more acute. The great masters of finance and markets could thus play off races with low economic standards against higher races as cleverly as an astute mine operator with a dozen religions and nationalities could in the old days play one trade union against another. Bismarck has told us how he held his own by playing one party against another or one country against another. It is one of the oldest tricks in political chicane [1] and has been just as familiar in the history of strikes.

At a session of the Social Science Association twenty-five years ago, a speaker used this argument to show how little cause there was for anxiety about trade unions on the part of property owners. He knew they could not be exterminated, but they could be "managed." He said anthracite operators easily safeguarded themselves against too

[1] "Abdul Hamid, Sultan since 1876, had become an adept in making promises. Among the people at large, ignorance, race prejudice and religious fanaticism were counted upon to insure the continuance of the sultan's autocratic power and to prevent the spread of incendiary liberal ideas." "European History," Holt & Chilton, p. 441.

belligerent unions by rousing racial and religious sensitiveness. As careful an observer as Paul de Rousier after a long visit expressed the same opinion.[1]

In notes of my own at the bloody riots in Lattimer, 1896, these racial difficulties were set down as likely to form a permanent bar against anything like national federation among miners. Within a half dozen years, Dr. Roberts had shown in his deeper study of this industry how superficial my judgment was. " The United Mine Workers," he says, " have successfully overcome racial differences, national antipathies and industrial prejudices and formed into one body the 15 or 16 nationalities."

Another stage of this ignorance, was the belief that labor organization could never make serious trouble in politics. They were praised for having intelligence enough to see this. They had so often made overbearing claims to wreck this party or that, but only to reveal their impotence at the " show down." There were no shrewder party leaders in the United States than those who believed the unions valuable, " because you could so easily buy up the leaders." In one country after another this complacent fiction has gone as it will go in this country. It will go with another illusion of the same kind. When " trade agreements " between employers and unions were so far won that they had to be accepted in many industries, the employers hit upon the device of so dating them that they expired at different times. This prevented common and " sympathetic " action among the many unions in the same industry. There are industries which have a dozen — twenty, even thirty different craft unions. If these could be dealt with separately, it was far easier work for the employer. If one craft union broke its agreement, public opinion could be turned against it for bad faith, and thus one union be turned against another. One chief source of syndicalism with its " One Big Union " was to break down this obstacle. A great deal

[1] " Les Tentatives de Monopolization de L'Anthracite."

has been done towards its accomplishment. But even if such capitalistic diplomacies fail inside the national boundary, will they also fail on the world area? Having "nothing to lose but its chains," can the proletariat of the world be united as they have been in Pennsylvania and other coal fields? With inconceivably greater difficulties, labor is to try this out. It will try it in the name of some of the noblest instincts, but also with the aid of instincts that would cut every root from which our acquired institutions spring, as I shall try to show.

Meantime I tried to get light on these national divergencies, noting them down as occasion offered to the present year. A miscellaneous few of them are as follows:

(a) Why should the trade union and the socialist welcome "inferior races" in one place and reject them in another? A New Zealand socialist who had made an eloquent plea for "democratic brotherhood against capitalistic exclusiveness" told me "we would go to war before we would permit the 'yellow face' to come into our country." And yet he was telling us in that moment that industry was to be "democratically owned and directed."

This is the tone of the trade union on the Pacific coast and it is the tone wherever increasing blacks come into competition with whites.

It is the tone of the Canadian even against the Hindoo, though they are members of the same "empire." Here are antagonisms, "proletariat against proletariat," fiercer than against capitalism itself. Ideals of democracy are no longer merely local or national; they have an international consecration. Democracy has to be tried out in this larger sphere. With racial misunderstandings and wage standards varying from fifteen cents a day to five or six dollars a day, what equalities are attainable on which democracy may safely rely? What, among diversities so sharp, can the "class struggle." mean?

(b) In the rapid growth of state socialism, why should

the form of government play so slight a part? In a "military camp" like Germany, it kept pace with extreme democracies like Australia and Switzerland.

(c) Why, with socialists so dominant over industrial workers in Germany should the anarchist disappear, while in France and Italy he is rampant in the dress of syndicalism?

(d) Why is a great working class movement like consumers' coöperation so weak among ourselves though we have striven for it and experimented with it for sixty years?

(e) Why has "labor copartnership" left scarcely a finger print in this country?

(f) Why among the Danes should socialism so spread and flourish in a country of small landowners? The small land-owning farmer has been the one hope of conservatives, as it still is in France, against the disporting socialist. It was always the argument of Clemenceau against this party. Even in the United States the socialist vote tends to shift from industrial to farming territory. Within half a century, four very distinct protests of organized farmers have steadily, if incoherently, set their faces toward collectivism. As they appear and disappear, a deeper socialist deposit accumulates. Is it finally to form new terrain on which agricultural populations will control their own political and economic life?[1]

(g) Why in Australia and New Zealand, as labor influence over politics increased, has revolutionary socialism fared so ill, while factional quarrels — labor against labor — seem worse than under capitalism?

(h) Why should state socialism become a sort of snug harbor for capitalism itself, so much so, that many great investors have become the advocates of that ownership?

[1] The Non-Partizan League gives to this tendency a more coherent and socialistic expression with the inevitable result that capitalistic interests fall upon it in a fury of defamation.

(i) Why in the United States should strike-breaking develop into an institution with powerful and expensive agencies organized expressly to furnish spies, " strong-arm-men," employment bureaus and transportation for men " who shall make no trouble "— from " negroes to college students "?

(j) Why in a land " smitten with prosperity " should the I. W. W. appear under circumstances so different from those of France, the land of small industries?

(k) Why in Belgium should the unions, coöperators and labor party work together as if they were a single body? No other country shows any such unity. Are these bodies driven together by the powerful opposition of the Catholic Church?

(l) What does it mean that through all these differences, there is one thing in common; — namely a steady drift against that part of the " Social Order " dominated by commercialism, the financier and the kind of politics with which these forces defend themselves? With every year and in all countries labor in its widest sense closes its ranks against this capitalist dictation.

Stand-patters have always feared these international unities among the workmen as they have feared all advanced, social legislation of foreign origin. In public discussions on proposed changes like the Civil Service Reform, it was (as late as 1893) very risky tactics to lay stress on English or foreign experience. It gave too good an opening to opponents to dwell on supposed success in another country. We would manage American affairs in our own way, if you please. This was thought to be a fine spirit of independence. The approving response of the audience showed how far away we were from the genuine independence open to any and all evidence from whatever source. I have quoted elsewhere an able Massachusetts judge discussing the Australian ballot. He was opposing it because it was "un-American." Whether successful in Australia or not did not concern us. Stung a little by some retort from the other disputant, the judge replied, "We have nothing to learn from Kangaroos." We have moved on since then, but the marsupial argument has still an amazing acceptance in this country. Employers in this State have been opposing a most elementary measure for the "minimum wage." They were only stiffened in their opposition by any reference to wide foreign experience now far more convincing than was the Australian testimony for the secret ballot when the Kangaroo closed the discussion. Yet this thinness of skin among nations and races will long constitute a barrier to those "common international standards," the acceptance of which will definitely mark such progress as we make. Child and woman's labor, some minimum of hours and sanitation are perhaps within sight.

For discussion, however, the war has made it possible to bring in a far wider range of human experience for home use. To cultivate the utmost hospitality is now merely good sense. Our journals are, for example, suddenly filled with articles on industrial councils. When the British Government adopts the Whitely Report with proposed councils of labor and employer, American business men hurry across the seas to learn what this means. They find the councils at work in thirty industries, with "reconstruction committees"; with equal representation from organized labor and organized employers. The visitors look also at the "shop committee." It is very old but now carries a new threat. It is representative government "at the point of production." It brings labor into control with employers on specified questions within the factory. It insists on voting outside the factory, where it may be free, instead of inside where the employer's oversight is feared. One employer yields the point, saying, "It is too frivolous a thing to quarrel about." "Frivolous" does not describe it. This first step "outside" is only a beginning. This joint control will not stop at the shop. It cannot carry out its own program without raising points which concern the entire industry. This at once raises international issues like tariffs, exports and imports. The shop committee is the beginning of a partnership with corresponding responsibilities. Whether in shoes, textiles, oils or foods, the world-market is a part of the job. There is no logical step in this new partnership that does not widen these affiliations. The growing sense and recognition of this make an end of all kangaroo arguments.

Even now we cannot see our way through the simplest problems without immediate reference to that larger world in which labor is definitely organized. Like "the great finance," its international ties will strengthen day by day. This means that we are to *learn together;* together we are to give and to take, as we now draw lessons from England because industry there first developed those labor conditions out of which our own present problems spring. As Italy can instruct us in one of the most hopeful forms of coöperation, France can instruct us by a certain dash and skill in initiating reforms.

After watching on the spot one of the first syndicalist strikes in that country, I wrote down these questions:

Why is France so much more interesting in the staging of her conflict? Is it her "sense of drama," her "passion for logic," her "artistic genius" even among the artisan class? Is it "her greater heroism and disinterestedness in applying ideas"? Is it because small industries develop aptitudes for social initiative? The *idea* of syndicalism no more originated in France than did the trade union, but she first made of this draped anarchism something far more attractive than did other countries stirred by the movement. The same is true of the political uses to which she puts every revolutionary suggestion.

It is partly for this reason that I turn to France where

the revolutionary idea can be traced, to introduce what now comes on apace in our own and other countries. From the first, labor organization there was socialistic in a sense then unfamiliar to us. It passed into politics with dramatic suddenness. There was a paltry 30,000 votes in 1885, for the first socialist candidate for Parliament. Within four years these grew to 200,000.

Nearly a decade of internal wrangling checked this influence but as party strife abated, unified action doubled and redoubled its power. Then followed what we may now observe throughout the trade union world, a closing up in the labor ranks. This unifying in France in 1905, brought 54 members into the Deputies, a number *soon to be quadrupled.*

Let me take a single issue which links up some of our own most revolutionary overtures with what was already clearly outlined in France. Nothing at this moment has more of the earthquake in it than the status of public employees. They have very powerful unions, but how far are they to go? To what extent are they to federate with national labor organization? What classes are we to shut out from this national labor alliance? We are very confident about the army and navy. The police, too, seem to differ from these only in degree. How much do the firemen differ and how much our public school teachers?

A recent investigation [1] discloses the facts in Massachusetts since 1917, at that time " 48 locals of municipal employees with a total membership of 6,691. Seven other national or international organizations have one or more local unions among public employees.

" National Federation of Federal Employees, International Association of Fire Fighters, National Association of Letter Carriers, National Federation of Postal Employees,

[1] *Industrial Information Service,* Oct. 18, 1919 — also *Monthly Labor Review,* Aug., 1919.

American Federation of Teachers, National League of Government Employees, National Federation of State, Town and County Employees."

The five organizations first named are affiliated with the American Federation of Labor. In Boston alone more than twenty different vocations among public employees have been organized: "These organizations send delegates to the Joint Council of Municipal Employees Unions, which is closely associated with the Boston Central Labor Union and hence with the American Federation of Labor." A government organ tells us "the initial membership of 2,800 the teachers' federation has increased in three years to 8,000 members with teachers in some States 100 per cent. organized. Grammar school, high school and normal school teachers are joining the movement." While one university has a "local" of 40 members. Here are issues over which we are to have a contest: the more so because they cannot be excluded from politics and because the labor pressure to include an ever larger number of unions will increase. We shall be told that already we have sanctioned railway, mining and other labor affiliations which possess far more power to disturb the social order than any number of striking police. On what principle, then, does our exclusion of the police depend?

All this is just as evident in other countries, but in France it has a kind of artistic *mise en scène* as enlightening as it is suggestive of the world drift. Though long known, the details are necessary to teach us what that word "international" means.

Before Chicago school teachers shocked our conservatives by forming a trade union, the question had become acute in France. The "Great Act of 1884" gave to labor in that country the right to organize. So instantly did labor respond and in such numbers, as to call for reconsideration, but it was too late. In the discussion, the question was asked, what shall be done with those in the employ of the State and city? " They surely shall not form trade unions," yet steps to this end had already been taken. The great body of aggressive unionism in France is the C. G. T. (General Confederation of Labor). French teachers set out to join this just as Chicago teachers threatened to join the Federation of Labor when convinced that in no other way could they get proper attention. Both wanted more pay and upon justifiable grounds.

French school dignitaries were as righteously indignant at this proposal as were their colleagues in this country. Both pronounced the teachers' step " an outrage." " Every educational value would be endangered if teachers entered a union; nothing thereafter could keep them out of politics."[1] " Only think of a sympathetic strike among school teachers! "

The " Act of Freedom " under Waldeck-Rousseau applied, it was said, only to private individuals and *in no case to State servants.* The teachers still pushed their claim. They pushed it until the highest courts decided against them. They appealed to the foremost radical of influence at that moment and now Prime Minister. M. Clemenceau had to tell his petitioners that the court was right.

Yet the agitation increased. Scarcely two years had passed before a far graver menace rose among post office and state employees of the telegraph and telephone. This is spoken of as a sudden and impetuous rising. It had on the contrary been discussed for years. Its suddenness was a matter of tactics and accidental opportunity.

The gloomiest editorial prophecy as to what society would

[1] In 1917 the " National Union of Teachers " in England met to discuss a refusal by the authorities of a request for a conference. This union had asked for more remuneration. Because they had been ignored, they passed a series of resolutions " Demanding that Government should enforce the payment of the union scale of salaries by all Local Educational Authorities."

suffer if our own railway unions in 1916 *had* struck might have been heard in every part of France. The outcry was at its height when the discovery was made that the police were sympathizing with the strikers and actually giving them money. The police were scolded as our postmaster general scolded the clerks in his own department because of their union activity. This French revolt was the more easily subdued because at that time vigorous sections of organized labor were against the strike. But the spirit and purpose among state employees were unchanged and the agitation did not cease.

In 1910, a privileged body of naval reservists (inscrits maritimes) struck in Marseilles. This too was suppressed, but within two months (May, 1910) the Government had to face an issue which tested every resource it could bring to bear. Ten thousand men struck on the Southern lines. Concessions enough were won by the men to bring temporary quiet. When the unrest appeared on the Northern lines and the companies refused to meet the representatives of the men for discussion, the war was on. Labor on the private railways was joined by the state employees on the " Western."

Not a dozen years had passed since M. Briand had expressed the opinion that not even the army could cope with this kind of problem. He warned against all attempts " to turn strikers into soldiers."

In doing as a statesman what he had earlier thought to be so dangerous, the prime minister for the moment triumphed. The socialist attack upon him was met by heavy majorities. But from that day his power weakened. In the spring of 1911, Briand was replaced and the new ministry faced its task in a different mood. It saw that labor must be conciliated, not by subterfuge or doles, but on some plan commensurate with new conditions, and the coming political influence of labor. This is what the war has at last driven us to recognize in the United States. But large plans, whatever the danger, are not extemporized. The French Government had to temporize. It urged the railways directors to " deal generously with the strikers." This was too vague and did nothing to allay labor's suspicions. There was rank disobedience to orders and what most excited alarm was *that on the government-owned roads, attempts at discipline were hardest of all.*

It is true that " general strikes " from the May Day strike of 1906, the miners' strike of 1908, followed by the electricians' in Paris, including these already noted, " failed." But it is also true that the attitude of state employees and the political sympathy excited for them in their defeat (a sympathy at once reflected in the Chamber as well as in the new Ministry) was to mark a great change in the *relation of politics to the whole labor question.* In half a dozen countries since 1900, public employees have shown all the defiance usually associated with contests in private employment. According to their numerical or organic strength, they have let it be known that government or city is no more an object of deference than are private employers. Nor has any one been quicker or more alert to assist in this defiance than " the glad-hand-politician " in every country. *It is the shifty politician's short cut to political prestige.*

In earlier discussions, it was held that the State had resources — soldiers, constabulary, courts — which strikers would respect, but these agencies can no longer control the discords between capital and labor.

As long as unions are weak, or as long as they were quarreling as in 1910, in France, force is at least a good makeshift. But with every closed dissension in labor ranks; with every addition to their political power, force on the part of governments becomes more helpless to reach a single cause of the trouble. Three years before the war, it was said in France, " We can no longer use force without bringing in interpellations into the Deputies, something harder to cope with than the strike itself."

It was in this year (1910) that the former syndicalist, Briand, became prime minister. Radicals and radical socialists had returned 252 members to Parliament and in October came the shock between Government and its railway employees. In the Deputies socialists fought for the legal right of these and all government servants to strike. A fortnight earlier, Briand had mobilized 30,000 men on the northern line for military training. In the debate that followed the prime minister, stung by the socialist retort, shouted back that if there were no law to preserve order he should act *without law*. He, with his Cabinet, resigned in the following month but not without leaving this lesson of anarchism in high places to those not likely to forget it.

If, in these earlier stages, relatively small numbers of public servants with weak and invertebrate organization could go thus far with the State, what will happen when their numbers treble and quadruple, while their manner of organization gains equally in effectiveness? With state functions growing no faster than they have grown since 1900, this army will more than treble within twenty years.

The general strike on its economic side is a record of failures; but politically, as in Belgium, it has shown remarkable results. Even in France, especially with state employees, the political reactions were such that the prime minister could say: "*It is not a strike, it is a political revolution.*"

Almost in the words of the French prime minister, Canadians have been telling us of their general strike. "It wasn't a strike, it was a social revolution." A waggish scribe calls it "a new and vicious animal in the democratic menagerie. There is nothing for it but ether or cold lead."

My chart proved more serviceable than I knew. In

studying social questions, especially the various forms of workmen's and social insurance in European countries between 1890 and 1893, it became clear to me that our own problems were at the bottom the same problems. The essential unities have ever since grown more evident, while showing only differences in approach and method. Every step in international labor legislation confirms this view. When we are forced, for example, to take up with some seriousness problems as formidable as unemployment and the eight-hour day we shall find the main difficulties essentially the same and the methods of meeting them closely akin in country after country. "How long shall we work?" has its separate chapter, but no issue teaches us more about these "world lessons" and what the war has brought upon us. As if there were no difference in industrial development, traditions or wage standards, the eight-hour-day carries all before it in Finland, Poland, Peru, Spain and Portugal. Holland proposes the 45-hour week by "legal limit." In the Swiss Factory Act, we have a maximum week of 48 hours *in all industries*. The new Provisional Government in Germany sets the same limit with seven and a half hours in mines. Italy is reported as carrying eight hours into agricultural as well as all other work. France will have the same pay for the 48-hour-week as for the former 60-hour week.

What thus becomes of the old arguments against this movement? If we pass to things far deeper than these concrete urgencies, where unities should be welcomed, we find other unities to put us on our guard.

Rumbling beneath a surface separated by no national lines are forces with a common aim. Generally they can be put in one word — communism. They are the passions, hungers, envies, even idealisms aroused and kindled to extreme expression against private property as now held. Here is the "flame-center" of the revolution. It is as international as the atmosphere, raising questions so wholly new to us, as to require a quality of statesmanship nowhere yet in sight. We are now carrying over the war methods to " put down," " crush," " exterminate," *ideas.*

We are to " export our firebrands to countries where they belong." Is this like putting out the fire on one side of the haystack and lighting it on the other, and will exported firebrands have less influence on the world including ourselves where they are finally set down, than in Paterson or Seattle? Will driving them from one spot to another decrease by an atom the total of their contagion? I do not know, but it seems to me grave with doubt. In what does it really differ from turning off teachers, professors and reporters? At what stage are we to face error and questionable opinion where *they are* and *have it out?* If we are unequipped for meeting these insurgencies where they arise, is it not wiser to create the necessary agency? It was for ages the work of sorcerers to transfer disease from one tribal village to another, very much as we have so long dealt with tramps — getting them out of our town into the next town, leaving the national problem where it was or even a little worse.

There is one more phase of these world lessons. A year ago, a popular governor in conference with the President warned us from " bogies." As for him he was an optimist. He gave a reason —" Most of the unrest in this country is of foreign origin." " We must hasten to Americanize them and tranquillity will be restored." This man should be put into some economic kindergarten. The newspapers of any day would show him that England, wholly free from this glut of aliens, is in throes of unrest graver than our own. France, with still fewer aliens, burns with the same fever.

Such control as we have over these distempers will not come through cheerful self-deceit like this. So far as it comes, it will be through very resolute exclusion of all these lazy assumptions that democracy has the least automatic excellence or finality. We have not only to face a new international factor of our problem, we have even more to face changes in our whole tradition of democratic optimism. With the disappearance of profitably available free land, together with a denser population in which the competitive struggle is acute with race feeling, we have yet to discover every real test for democratic fellowship about the world. Not a reality of democracy is to be ours unless we create it anew and under new conditions. A man who gave such proofs of political liberalism, as Lord Macaulay, read Randall's "Life of Jefferson." As the great leader of democracy in this country, Jefferson interested the historian, but excited neither admiration nor faith. In the correspondence between Randall and Macaulay, the latter states his grounds of disbelief in all mass-capacity for stable government. In a letter too familiar to reproduce, he suggested that before the twentieth century closed our worries and our doubts would set in. This letter written sixty years ago has had hard usage among the guardians of "true Americanism."

Macaulay's fear of native despoilers of our own breeding, which too much Jeffersonianism might let loose, is far less important than the reasons for his fear which appear in the completed correspondence with Mr. Randall. Though not the first to see it, no one had then stated so clearly the relation of democracy to circumstances having nothing whatever to do with the *form of government*. With liberal traditions, sparse populations on huge fertile areas — America, Australia, New Zealand — are of course democratic. They cannot be otherwise. To a certainty they will attribute their freedom and prosperity to a democratic régime.

Macaulay saw that when all the land to which smaller folk could turn for security had been appropriated; when populations became dense and we had over-multiplied our "Manchesters and Birminghams" — only then should we begin to know the hard realities of popular rule. We have reached this stage. As if he had read Macaulay's letter, Bismarck made the same point about our democracy to Carl Schurz. " There was some hope of real stability," the Chancellor said, " in princes and dynasties as against government by parliament, press and barricades." Events have made sufficient comment on this, leaving us the hope that whatever profligacies are to infest democracy, we must see it through. No monarch could make a better showing, while most of them now fare ill by comparison. But to see democracy through, we must look upon it as beginning rather than achieved.

Even politically, the democratic ideal is most incompletely attained. But now, industry is to be shorn of every monarchial and autocratic trapping. It is to be made safe for democracy and democracy for industry! Very amazing is the unanimity and unction with which this is said by industrial magnates as well as in the oratory of the labor and socialist conventions.

That we have set out on this long journey seems certain. It is better, therefore, to look first at the sterner difficulties of the task. This involves far more than altered devices or added laws.

CHAPTER V

THE STRUGGLE AT ITS WORST

THIS darker aspect of my subject would be omitted, if its exposure were not an essential part of positive and constructive suggestion. It has required all the haggard evidence of world slaughter to drive us even to serious discussion of a League of Peace. Only as we see the fighting instinct in industry at its worst, shall we feel the need of a commonwealth in which a different spirit and a different method become habitual among men. I have never seen a serious industrial conflict which was not in a very real sense *war*. In the worst instances, there were the tactics of war, there were arms and explosives and they were put to use on both sides. The minds of combatants worked as minds work in war. Before public opinion, both were silent and ashamed of much that was done or permitted. Every variety of secret agent, thugs, prostitutes and professional spies have their uses.

Neither by employers nor labor leaders are these agents well spoken of. This offers a curious study. It was thought to be a patrician virtue of northern and southern slave owners to cast contempt upon men who brought negroes from Africa. These slave hunters were merely furnishing the raw material bought and used for profit by the owners, north and south. It was an odious job to carry rum and gewgaws to those primitive peoples; to hire ruffians to raid a tribe or village and bring away those that were not killed or too badly wounded, pack them beneath deck and sell those who remained alive at some American port.

These negroes could be bought and bred like cattle and

THE STRUGGLE AT ITS WORST

if troublesome, sold for deadly work in southern rice fields, and yet the man who furnished the goods; who made the institution profitable and agreeable to a leisure class was looked down upon as an outcast. If rice-growing paid well, though the death rate among the field hands was three times above the normal and a very cruel overseer was necessary for discipline, the industry went on with little moral uneasiness to those who at safe distance lived upon the gains. The North was as guilty until it discovered that in our climate slave labor did not pay.

In one of our city "vice reports" an investigator of brothels and the sources of supply, told us that a certain "madam" (the keeper of the brothel) took on a very superior tone toward those who supplied her house with girls. "They were a dirty lot and ought to be punished." For herself, "she would have nothing to do with them."

In the whole war zone between employers and employed one constantly meets this complaisant respectability. In denying violence the labor leader apes this respectability as smugly as any mine owner. With mordant irony Ibsen has dealt with it in plays like "Pillars of Society" and Shaw in "Widowers' Houses." If dirty service has to be done, either by labor or by capital, men are found to do it. In several of our industries as despicable deeds have been done on both sides as are done in war, in slavery, or in supplying prostitutes.

The tools used in this work are not held in honor, but they are thought to be necessary when interests are at stake. As I wish to show only the spirit and nature of the industrial contest, I select a single illustration which the present war enables us to see and to appraise. The war produces both the atmosphere and the events through which we may better understand the lesser but more continuous war in industry. There are sickening analogies between the two.

Among the whole more comfortable, investing and propertied class, there is but the slightest realization of the war method as employed by those who manage many capitalistic enterprises in this country and by the unions that oppose them. Employers in great numbers are free from the guilt, even by indirection. So too are many of the unions. But industrial solidarity at highly competitive points is such that innocent parties in the industrial strife can no more be fenced off than could the millions of innocent on European battle grounds. My illustration is that of the hired informer. There is nothing more corrupting in the whole war régime than the education and practice of the spy system. Yet thousands of these have long been doing devil's work in this country among competitive rivals to prevent the growth of a trade union or to furnish information to employers from within unions already formed. The dead-sea fruit which this system bears is a suspicion which spreads like a disease. Whether the spy belongs to the union or to the employer, the excuses are those which any military defender of spies would make. "We have to do it in our own defense." It is a system which deliberately organizes the violation of confidence among men. It organizes the shabbiest of petty treacheries and deceits.

This organized eaves-dropping should be given far greater prominence. It is true that Allan Pinkerton performed in the public interest some most useful services. It was with his help that the most murderous and ruffianly gang of Molly Maguires was hunted down and brought to justice in our anthracite coal districts in the years immediately following the Civil War. But as spying grew into a system its evils developed, attracting the kind of man "who lives and thrives on trouble that he makes." Among them in very large numbers were those skilled in devising trouble if they did not find it.

It is this feature which has eaten like a cancer into our industrial régime. It is this feature which keeps the war

THE STRUGGLE AT ITS WORST

temper alive and makes a mockery of all democratic pretenses. I know so well that this statement about spying and the war spirit will seem lurid and over-wrought to many readers that very specific evidence must be given.

It is not mere chance that, in its really serious aspects, our spy system in industry sprang out of our Civil War. War or the fear of it has been called " the mother of lies," " the mother of high tariffs " and the parent of many ills, but it is a most fertile mother of spies. It has its inside technical literature and instruction, no less important than that of drilling and maneuvering battalions. The term given to Bismarck's allowance for this and kindred purposes was descriptively exact, *" The reptile fund."* It is accurately that in many conflicts between capital and labor.[1]

But a few months after our struggle over slavery, the demand for spies and armed men for use in labor troubles was such that it was commercially developed and extended. Spies and armed men were quietly advertised and put upon the market. In all the fluent ingenuity to account for strikes and especially for the irritations which lead to them, far more attention should be given to what has grown out of the Pinkerton Service.[2] Years ago the gist of this chapter was several times given in lecture form. I was twice very sharply censured for treating this war analogy so seriously. The exaggeration was said to be gross; the evil in no way effected the general soundness of conditions in this country. One political writer whom

[1] When the Persian Darius forced his Kingship upon Egypt and Babylonia, he appointed twenty satraps to govern over as many provinces. An army of spies known as the " King's Ears," or the " King's Eyes " was organized to report all disaffection. With the growth of the great industry in recent times this has had its counterpart.

[2] The Mayor of Jersey City was recently trying to prevent his police force from forming a trade union. He says it is a political game most dangerous to the public. But he also says that before he took office as the city's chief executive, the corporations doing business in the city were continually hiring " thugs " and " guerillas " and " ex-convicts " to " shoot down the laboring men " when

I highly esteem, said the analogy was worthless because in regularly declared war, the rights and interests of all neutrals were carefully safeguarded while in labor wars they were not.

What would some dozen neutrals say about this in the last "regular" war?

But I turn to witnesses as competent as they were disinterested. For most of the time covered by my notes, there have been many important investigations into labor troubles which have exposed the malignancy of this evil. It had grown so that two reports were made by the Senate or by the House in 1892.

Robert Hunter in his "Violence in the Labor Movement" gives with severity and yet with temperance the outlines of this unhappy business. Only a small part of these violences have ever been made a matter of record. But such as we have show us enough. As one illustration, General Pryor, when on the Supreme Court of New York was called upon to study carefully the private detective work in a relatively quiet and orderly strike upon the New York Central in 1890. Congress was appealed to for a bill "to prevent private corporations engaged in interstate commerce traffic from employing unjustifiably large bodies of armed men denominated detectives but clothed with no legal functions." Mr. Hunter quotes Judge Pryor's final opinion thus: "And it is enough to condemn the system that it authorizes unofficial and irresponsible persons to usurp the most delicate and difficult functions of the State and of hireling assassins, stimulated to violence by panic or by the suggestion of employers to strike terror by an appalling exhibition of force. If the railroad company

strikes were called. "They have caused murder and bloodshed," he adds, "in all large cities." I have not verified these statements locally but there is so much general truth in this as to justify its use.

may enlist armed men to defend its property, the employees may enlist armed men to defend their persons, and thus private war be inaugurated, the authority of the State defied, the peace and tranquillity of society destroyed, and the citizens exposed to the hazard of indiscriminate slaughter."

With far wider experience, Commissioner Carroll D. Wright came to the same view.

In the several investigations which have forced a small part of these evils into light we are allowed to see enough of this flagrant mischief to understand the analogies between the greater wars and those in industry.[1]

Just before he went to our embassy in Belgium, Brand Whitlock summed up his experience with employers and employed in the various strikes with which he had had to do as mayor. Toledo has been like a Sunday school model of social order if compared with the main centers of industrial strife, yet the mayor closes one section of this book with these words: "But we had difficulty in maintaining the peace, not only because the strikers, or more likely their sympathizers, broke it now and then, but because when the strikers were not breaking it, the employers seemed bent on doing something to make them. They did not intend it for that purpose of course; they simply thought in old feudal sequences. They hired mercenaries, bullies provided as 'guards' by private detective agencies. It kept the police pretty busy disarming these guards, and greatly added to their labors because the guards were always on the point of hurting some one."[2]

If Judge Pryor and Brand Whitlock could speak thus of these milder troubles, what must they have said of dis-

---

[1] House Committee Report, 1892: the Report of the Senate Committee of the same year, Report on Chicago Strike, 1894, by the U. S. Commission: Report of the Commission of Labor, 1905, on troubles in Colorado, the VIII vol. Industrial Commission, 1901, down to the Senate Document (521), 1913, on the Bethlehem Strike, with a long list of other documents given by Mr. Hunter, pp. 368–373.

[2] "Forty Years of It," pp. 303, 307.

orders in which the brutalities, the detective and spy work were at least ten times more ruthless? When Haywood came East from the Colorado strike in 1903, where I first saw him, he said our eastern strikes seemed to him like " old ladies' tea-parties."

Starting as a common miner, J. E. Williams became one of the most skilled arbitrators in labor troubles this country has produced. As distinct from information or learning, the word wisdom applied to him. In connection with university extension lectures, I came to know him first in his home at Streator, Ill. In the quarter of a century since then, I had many letters from him and occasional interviews. One of the gentlest of spirits, he came to look upon the strike, the spying with the policies that went with it, as the essence of war. He even thought we must *study* war in order to know what competitive industry is and will remain until it is transformed.[1]

The former Canadian Minister of Labor and now the leader of the Liberal party, Mackenzie King, for ten years as mediator, had to do with forty strikes serious enough

[1] After this chapter was written, I have received from Julius Henry Cohen a study, "An American Labor Policy." Mr. Cohen is author of "Law and Order in Industry," a lawyer of distinction who has had long and intimate experience with the interminable quarrels in the New York Garment industries. Though Haywood would also class these strikes as " old ladies' tea parties " they have made up their deficiencies in western mining methods by their incessant occurrence.

It is of this long experience and as Special Counsel for the Public Service Commission that Mr. Cohen speaks of this analogy between the two wars as "perfect." He says both the fighting employees and the fighting unions are now outside industrial law. " Both sides are still in the stage of *military strategy*." " They will not be won over any more quickly than the nations of the world will be won over to a League of Nations unless their assent is obtained to a constructive program in which they are secured."

Of the old "individual bargaining" so dear to our employing class, he speaks as do the half-dozen most important war Reports.

He even says it becomes *a cause of war:* in his own words, " the individual contract between employer and employee protects neither and results in industrial war sooner or later."

to require government intervention. He also had long and intimate experience with labor troubles in the United States. He describes some of our own disturbances "where strikers have been nearly as well provided with rifles and ammunition as the state militia that opposed them. The presence of encampments and the use of machine guns have helped to accord opposing factions an appearance differing little from that of army detachments in time of actual war." He thinks the analogy between wars among nations and industrial strikes is apt and accurate. He warns us to beware of veiling the hard facts under a specious optimism which may conceal the gravest danger. He refers to a speech before the New York Economic Club by a labor leader of one of the largest labor organizations (one of the railroad brotherhoods) in which these words were used: "Industrial war is precisely of the same character as actual war. No battle has been fought in establishing the rights of mankind, either real or fancied, when the hospital has not been filled afterwards and the corpses left upon the field. And it is just so in industrial war."[1]

I have spent days in a northwestern mining district with an employer who had in his pay a body of so-called "private detectives." They had been hired as King George hired Hessians. They were sent in from one of the many detective agencies whose business it is to furnish spies or an armed force to any one who will pay for them. The entire record in these many investigations shows that no more dangerous or lawless men are to be found than some of those who are most active in our extremer disorders. The employer just referred to regretted that he had so "tough a bunch" but excused it on the ground that he could get no others who had the dare-devil-courage to out-face the corresponding element in the labor unions. It was understood on both sides to be war to the knife. The very figures of speech were those of war.

[1] See "Industry and Humanity," Houghton Mifflin Co., 1919.

Many of the best and most peaceable workmen in times of excitement are marked as spies by their fellows solely because they try to check the attempts to form a union or bring about a strike. There is not an evil in the union which is not quickened into activity by the suspicions thus aroused by this paid eavesdropping. If the object were purposely to create violence among the men, no device would better serve the end.

There are many industrial centers where the policing is so meager or so uncertain that employers are forced quietly to organize their own means of securing information or applying to a private agency. "What are we to do," it is said, " if we cannot count on police protection?" There is no answer to this except to admit a political and social responsibility from which few of us escape.

In the building trade strike in Chicago 1900, a man was brought before the Commission who had charge of a detective agency of his own. He testified that he had resigned from another agency because he " had a reputation to keep up in Chicago." "I could not," he said, "very well do the work they wanted me to do."

In his own agency, he employed at the fewest ten and at the most fifty men. After being sworn, he began with the President of the Bricklayers Union. " Gubbins (in testimony just given) made the remark that he had to carry a gun. Well, that is right. It is necessary for him to carry a gun, because there are certain ones of the Contractors' (employers) Association that tried to get me to have my men slug him — that is beat him up — and if possible put him in the hospital six or seven weeks."

Asked by one of the Commission if others had tried to hire him for such work, he replied, " Why, there are at least five, if it were absolutely necessary, it could be proven that they tried to get me to have the men beaten up."

Asked to be more specific as to who it was that made such requests, the detective answered, " As for that, if the time ever comes that it is necessary for me to go before the criminal court it seems to me it would weaken my testimony and I should infinitely prefer not to give those names now." Pressed further, he said, "They are in authority," meaning in the Contractors' Association.

In the mass of testimony upon the character of those picked up about this country, there is entire unanimity upon this one point; that many of the agencies rely largely on men and often women of a shady or criminal record. Even those same "United States deputies" in time of strikes have often caused far more friction than they stopped. When Chairman of the Commission in Chicago, Colonel Wright, asked as trustworthy a witness as journalism has produced in this country, Ray Stannard Baker, what his observations had been, he replied that he had seen more cases of drunkenness among the United States deputy marshals than among the strikers. In the long run, the results are perhaps worse when spies carry on their craft as regular members of the trade union. Any one curious to look further into this underground world should read the testimony March 27, as given in full on pages 219-256 in Vol. VII of the Report of the Industrial Commission 1901.

It is but one blackened page in a stiff volume of our industrial struggles. It is far from being the worst of its kind. Property interests in communities where this goes on, often control both press and police. They are very sensitive about the good name of the town, about real estate and other interests and can therefore easily pervert or hide from the public the real facts.

While the trade unions have again and again played their own ugly game; while they have broken agreements and committed every form of lawlessness, they are under one handicap which puts them at a disadvantage compared with the lawlessness of employers and their interested sympathizers. The employers have means of concealing their own crooks and crookedness which labor cannot command. Labor struggles where its weapons must of necessity be more exposed. Their forms of intimidation and riotous misbehavior may nevertheless be distinctly less injurious to social order than the more hidden wiles of which the property interest may avail itself.

I know the instances here given are extreme, but they have been continuous and in large numbers especially since the Civil War. To omit them or to whitewash them would merely mislead us as to the main facts, and what is worse — mislead us about their possible elimination. It is this strife between the *worst on both sides* which exposes those sources of trouble which are before us for correction. To strip to the skin all that is most vicious in secret national diplomacy as one cause of war is a condition of any possible League of Peace.

To see our industrial spying at its worst and competition at its worst, enables us to see the mischief in every grade and shade of it. Until the excesses are removed, each side will dwell upon and exaggerate every evil report about the opponent as if the relation were solely one of enemy to enemy. In 1887, the manager of a shoe factory running as an " open shop " learned that a union was being formed. From among his employees he selected two men " to keep their ears open and to report to him." Before any one had been turned off, the men learned that they were watched by one or more of their mates. It was the beginning and in this sense a *cause* of the strike that followed. I watched it from its first to its final step. To the employer, there was but one cause — the attempt to form a union. He admitted that the men had a right to a union " if they could get it." He could not use force against them. Spies were safer. He did not like the name. He said they were selected and paid extra " to protect his own interests and the interests of a majority of the workers who did not wish to join the union."

He was trying to defend himself against what appeared to him sharp practices on the other side. I note it here for its consequences. Long before the strike, the spying set one group of men in the shop against another. It was known that spying was on foot, but the renegades could not be discovered. Suspicion centered now on one, then on another, with the result that enmities accumulated which finally turned against the employer. Rancors springing from these suspicions cannot be long confined to the men. They turn against the employer and even show themselves in local politics, always to corrupt it.

In a very commonplace strike of Garment Workers in 1896, in Boston, this secrecy brought results indicated in the following letter given to me at the time. Withholding names, I quote a passage, as spelled, word for word. It is from the labor committee to a suspected member.

Headquarters
District Council
No —

"Will you call and see us before 9.30 A. M. to-morrow morning, it will be for your interest to come. Don't be afraid of the gang, come in the office. Remember if you don't come and you go to court any more against us you will have to leave the City because we will cut the damn heart out of you. We meet you if you don't want to come to the office if you let us know ware. You need not be afraid. we send a committee to see you to-day but you were not in."

From this brutal threat, we descend those easy steps to avenues where stealth and masked procedure are of the essence of war. After its kind and measure, it creates hell, "before hell is due." The deadliest feature is that in this atmosphere *the character of the leadership is determined.* It must be a leader skilled in chicane and war strategy on both sides.

The constant complaint of the employer is against trade union leadership. Even if half friendly to unionism, he often dislikes, fears or despises the actual leaders. We must learn that leadership will never change until the function and character of the union changes. The employers have their own definite responsibility for these changes. The main body of our unions have had no alternative but to fight or to strike. This means a fighter as chief. When Tammany is organized for graft a Tweed is its appropriate boss. If the Manufacturers' Association, the "steel trust," the textile employers are out solely to prevent the organization of labor they will select their most skillful fighting man for leader. This has but one meaning; labor will choose its best fighter in opposition.

I pass now gladly to quite other phases of capitalism, where we may see at least the beginnings of a new order inspired and engineered by capitalist employers who want other tactics. I shall later show these same first steps in adopted labor policies which assume the possibilities of coöperation in the place of war. If this develops, it will strip capitalism of all autocratic authority as it will strip labor organization of its own corresponding vices.

CHAPTER VI

THE INNER REVOLUTION

I TAKE the title of this chapter from a friend who is called a labor agitator. He sees that the war has let loose upon us ideas more dangerous to many of our customary ways of thought and behavior than any of the explosives at the front. He finds the real revolution not so much in the various events as in the new way of looking at things among the masses of men and women in the world. This is as wise as Victor Hugo who said " There is only one thing stronger than armies, and that is: ' an idea whose time has come.' " It is as good as Emerson who thought nothing more shattering and painful than a new idea. To have this intimidating aspect, the idea must carry a real and proximate threat to some privilege in our *mores* which men hold dear.

We long ago saw the new idea at work in religion. The very attempt to put an intelligent meaning into church dogma constituted heresy. We are now trying to get meaning into other dogmas. We have seen the new idea at work in politics; against its parliamentary forms and against control, first by an aristocratic, then by a plutocratic class.

We now observe it as it passes with hardy confidence into the economic and business field. This is our new heresy. The old idea of taxation was to raise money enough to carry on the existing social order. Already before the war, a new idea about taxation appeared — not from negligible cranks, but backed by high and responsible officials. Taxes were to be levied with the express purpose of bringing in " Social equality." This raised a virulent outcry. Among others, a Prime Minister who expressed approval was twitted with being the most reckless demagogue since Jack Cade. Mr. Townley and his friends in the Farmers' Alliance have a new idea. The capitalist press in Minnesota and thereabouts becomes an organized malediction against Dakota and all its works. Everywhere in the shifting power and influence over men and events, no proposal infuriates like the attack on property; especially upon those investment forms to which men look for delicacies of every sort, for social petting and prestige; for prudent and ambitious marriages; for that longing so snugly expressed in the word "independence." I shall trace a few of these new ideas neither to justify nor to condemn them, but to show how they are now acting on labor. It has its own voluminous press — daily, weekly, and monthly organs in which one finds in monotonous profusion new varieties of incendiary ideas. The most inflammable of these are not utterances of labor editors or labor correspondents. They are not even citations from "parlor Bolsheviks." With chapter and verse, they are opinions taken from the most authoritative reports by special commissions, by state legislatures, by statisticians, by government departments, and by employers in large affairs. In syndicalist and socialist press, as well as in the soberer Trade Journals of the unions, upsetting material from high authorities is reproduced in such quantity as to make it clear to the blindest of us why there is "a new way of looking at things."

In communities separated as are Italy, England, Australia and Denmark, the growth of labor's incredulities can be traced. The power to act upon and give effect to its heresy may be marked more closely still. There were decades of suspicion about all the mountainous official statistics as well as of the economic teaching given out by employer and economist. The suspicion passes now from sulky uneasiness to action. Labor refuses for instance to believe that wages are determined by market prices. If asked what does or should determine them, the answer has a truth in it which statesmen, economists and employers have been forced to take into account. "If I have a strong trade union behind me, wages are determined not only by 'supply and demand' but by the kind of trade I am strong enough and shrewd enough to force upon the employer." This heresy has immediate practical consequences. It will be as troublesome as the American disbelief in England's right of taxation before 1775. Labor's attitude toward profit-sharing and much of the welfare work are examples of this hectoring suspicion.

Let me give one other instance. There have been nearly fifty years of experimenting with "Sliding Scales." It was to "realize justice between employer and employed." It was "an automatic adjustment of interests between capital and labor." It was "the most perfect of profit-sharing plans."

In industries like mining where labor cost is high and easily ascertained, what could be fairer than to have wages rise and fall with the market price of coal? After 1870, this partnership in the ups-and-downs of the market was welcomed by English and Welsh unions as it was by our iron and steel workers. Labor was then docile and took its economic instruction from others. Within twenty years troubles arose. It was found very difficult to determine normal prices and the wage relation to those prices. It was found just as difficult to determine the percentage of wages to match the rise and fall of prices. The revision periods proved equally awkward.

It slowly appeared that market prices might fall so low that wages dependent on these prices fell below the "existence level." This was met by establishing a "minimum wage" beyond which wages should not fall, whatever the price of the product. It then appeared that the plan was unworkable except in industries with a measureable simplicity and uniformity in the product. The Fall River Textile Mills met this latter condition so far, that from 1905 the plan had several years' trial.[1] Dissatisfaction steadily increased among employees until it was abandoned. These say —" We never know where we are." " We never can get at the facts about the financing." " We make our schedules from time to time, but they never turn out as we were led to expect."

As in the coal and iron industries, there was suspicion that contracts could be taken — especially contracts far ahead, so as to leave labor with the chances always against it. The more intelligent of the workmen no longer believed in the price index as a test for wage increase. At their meetings they spread this disbelief among others.

It is one of the results of labor organization to make sentiment effective. Suspicion of unfair dealing may be as common among the unorganized, but the trade union turns it into a weapon that can be used.

Anthracite coal owners objected to the sliding scale because as mines grew deeper costs increased and no extra profits were left for such a purpose. The labor objection has no sharp outline like this. It is vague; it talks of " speculation," " occult finance " and " market juggling." Whatever ignorance may lurk in these charges, they disclose a suspicion about these scales and profiteering that is as hard a fact as a bit of steel.

It is a suspicion that no cunning can remove until the hinterland of capitalization with its salaries, insurance, depreciations and other deductions become as open and accessible to wage-earner as to manager.

Labor's education is of course the main cause of these incredulities. It is but few years since economic business and social authorities held that the main difficulty was in " labor's ignorance about the nature of industrial under-

[1] See Stanley E. Howard's Study of this Experiment, *American Economic Review*, September, 1917.

takings." If only the wage receiver could be "educated"; if he could be made to see the "risks run by capital," "the source of wages," "the hazards of management, the severity of competition among employers" and the like, he would know why wages could not be interfered with, hours shortened or much expected of labor legislation.

Here is a passage in a report from the English Commissioners of Education in 1858:

"Next to religion, the knowledge most important to a laboring man is that of the causes which regulate the amount of his wages, the hours of his work, the regularity of his employment, and the prices of what he consumes. The want of such knowledge leads him constantly into errors and violence, destructive to himself, and to his family, oppressive to his fellow workmen, ruinous to his employers, and mischievous to society."

With naïve complacency, these gentlemen assume that they and such as they hold a higher wisdom in their keeping. If the "laboring man" can only be caught and made to listen, then those to impart this instruction will surely be on hand to give it. "Mechanics Institutes" and "lectures on Social Science" were set on foot for this purpose. For many years labor was patient under this instruction. It listened to "the causes which regulate the amount of wages," "regularity of employment," "prices," "sliding scales," with acquiescence and eagerness to learn. We now know that, together with some truth, those workingmen heard a great deal that bore no resemblance whatever to the truth. Most economists of to-day would make merry with those commonplaces quite as much as any labor leader in the land. Millions of workingmen have long carried on their own studies in their own way. With such ardor have they done this, that their betters are often very much afraid of them before impartial audiences.

Professor Clapp in a severe handling of the Adamson law,[1] yet pays this compliment to the leaders of the unions, " The representatives of the men were keen diplomatists, able speakers and quite the masters of the railroad managers who opposed them." Such abilities among labor men are surely not for regret but for rejoicing. Whatever trains them to hold their own in such company adds to " capacity values " at the very points where they become interpreters more and more necessary in social understanding and reconstruction.

At a sitting of the Commission on Industrial Relations, I sat beside the largest employer of labor in his industry in this country and probably in the world.[2] He had listened for several days to the testimony by employers; by their attorneys and by labor men. He turned to me and said: " These labor representatives are really better informed on the subjects here treated and state their case better than we do." Professor Commons was close by, and I repeated the remark to him. " Yes," he said, " employers tell me that all about the country."

It is easy to overstate this, as it is to give it unfair interpretation, but it stands for a substantial fact. Only the exceptional employer has been able, or has thought it worth while, to give sustained attention to the larger aspects of these issues. He hires attorneys to do this for him. Labor has at last produced a leadership without any doubts whatever as to its competence to face all comers. If it admits ignorance, it insists that its opponents have their own shade of ignorance just as dangerous.

The warning is given me that too many pages are here devoted to the trade union. My answer is that these labor groupings in the world;— what they are to do and how they are to behave; what attitude employers and the State

[1] *Yale Review*, Jan., 1917, p. 268.
[2] Mr. Schaffner, of Hart, Schaffner & Marx.

THE INNER REVOLUTION

are to take toward them, is so fundamental that too much emphasis is not likely to be given it. We cannot have even an intelligent glimpse of the military " effectives " that now attack the social order without closest study of unions — not only as they have been, but even more, a study of what they are becoming. We can know neither socialism, syndicalism nor the New Guild if ignorant of unionism and the changes that have come upon it. In a very definite sense, labor organizations in their entirety have us in their grip. They can bring the proudest men in the world into the witness box to answer questions about their rights and behavior. Labor men jolly them as equal to equal. They can frighten politicians into lackeys. So conscious are they of their strength that they can work, not work or half work. It is this sense of power which has devised that most terrible weapon, sabotage — deliberately restricted output, or no output. Like an ill-made bomb, it may be more dangerous to the user than to the one against whom it is directed. We are to have a great deal of this sabotage. It is the threat of this in the entire labor movement; the ease and variety of ways through which it can be carried out that constitute its danger. Strikes, local, sympathetic, general, are forms of it. But the deadliest of all is the spirit of sabotage in action when it becomes contagious. Those who practice it are judge and jury. They feel a grievance. "Let us slow up until we get what we want." When the bills come in, no one will suffer more from it than labor but they will be long in finding this out.

At this point, I am concerned only to show how labor's hopes and convictions are being confirmed and encouraged from the top. A great banker like Mr. Vanderlip, with highest authority in finance and in large affairs, turns serious attention to the new disturbances. He studies it here and he studies it in Europe. On his return, he first warns us that in respect to private property rights, Europe's destiny is our destiny. We are open to every danger that threatens property in other countries. He says in·no sense can we stand apart. "No matter how self-sufficient we may believe ourselves to be, no matter how unlimited are the resources of natural wealth within, we are inevitably part of what is coming to be a very small world, a world in which ideas travel with a freedom and rapidity that must force us to become internationalists in our views and must govern us by international considerations, whatever may be our natural tendencies to Chauvinism, or our disposition toward an insular isolation and security." Of labor's demand to have voice in industrial matters, Mr. Vanderlip says —"I am thoroughly convinced that that aspiration is now world wide and that America will feel the demand as strongly as it is now being felt in Europe. I believe it is a demand that American employers should heed, and that it should be met not merely by forced and grudging concessions, but rather from the point of view which is now held by many English employers."

A group of employers (including such men as W. H. Ingersoll — he whose watch made the dollar famous), E. B. Keith from one of the largest shoe firms in the world, R. J. Caldwell, president and owner of cotton mills, with others of their kind, visited England to report back to the Department of Labor.

The Director General of Information in the Department says: "It may be assumed from industrial history that the United States will follow somewhat later along similar paths as Great Britain; the chairman, a Chicago business man, says, "Our findings are based on overwhelming almost unanimous evidence." They find the country teeming with news of strikes described as the most serious and significant ever seen in England. Of the English employers, the report says: "Nearly all agree that collective bargaining should always be undertaken between associations of employers and the regularly established well-organized trade-unions." "Most employers freely recognize the right of labor to organize; they regard organization as greatly contributing to the stability of industry. Some large manufacturers declare that they wish to see every workman within the unions, so that they must all come under organization control." They are impressed by the interest labor shows in Economics;—that a great amount of study by the workman is devoted to the subject and that a section of the younger workmen is being assiduously educated by certain radical groups along socialistic lines of thought. It develops that in one of the cities visited by us, there are fourteen classes. This is but a fragment of testimony of this kind given by employers. Will our own unions be silent about opinions like these? Will the radical sections of the American Federation receive no encouragement from the admitted drift of our home problems toward conditions in England? This report is cautious and moderate, but it furnishes for that reason the most direct encouragement to labor propagandists.

The visitors had, of course, to deal with a much more thorough-going report than their own—"The Whitely Plan." They found English Employers "almost universally" in favor of it, that they "favor complete union organization of the employed in established labor unions and favor not only collective bargaining, but closer touch with the employed." This plan is now too old a story to be retold, but I select from it a single revolutionary idea upon which labor seizes with avidity, in every country. I specialize on it here because its influence can be so clearly traced and because it fills such space in labor literature and agitation.

We are still very obtuse in measuring the emotional impact on labor from the admitted excesses of profiteering. It is idle to talk of labor's exaggeration of this evil. It has only to take the printed words of hundreds of official and business reports. These have been ransacked with telling effect and spread broadcast through the labor world.

Before the war was at an end, and when Germany was full of confidence, a Berlin business magnate of the first-class as well as an astute student, Walter Rathenau, warned his countrymen against " the ideas that soldiers were certain to bring back from the front."

He said these ideas were " tantamount to a social world-revolution." He wrote in the *Berliner Tageblatt,*

" We shall begin to live again in this harsh world after the war, and it will be tenfold harder than conducting the war to reëstablish order, reason, spirituality, justice, and gentleness. Woe for those who in their business zeal, in order to flatter the masses and the spirit of private profit and to get cheap applause, try to deny this necessity, and who hold out the promise of an easy return to the old prodigal way of living."

He said nothing could prevent " a great shifting of property," " An equalization and leveling down of great fortunes." No minority socialist had used harsher words against the profiteers or more frankly admitted their existence. He was very straightforward in warning the " furred and fine-feathered classes " what they must expect.

Nearly a year and a half later, in a country as different as Canada is from Germany, even staunch capitalistic papers were shocked at the evidence of big profits in war time. The legislative committee in Canada called before it the head of a manufacturing company in Sherbrooke. He was annoyed at the questions put to him and finally retorts, " Our mill wasn't built for the glory of God or anybody else. It was built for the benefit of the shareholders." Before the war, this gayety would have had rounds of applause before any audience of business men. It now draws from capitalistic sources such comments as this: "Following upon an exposure of the profiteering carried on throughout the whole period of the war in the Canadian textile manufacturing industry in open, cynical and criminal disregard of its social and political consequences, the attitude of mind revealed in this statement constitutes a serious menace to the stability of society." The Committee reports the "profits of this concern at the opening of the war as less than seven per cent. In 1915, 72 per cent., and in 1918, 300 per cent. And the comment on this is —"No wonder that Bolshevism makes headway, that discontent is widespread and rampant, that the people are suspicious and angry with their political leaders whose impotence to protect them from these commercial sharks is demonstrated."[1] Of the high profiteering, generally throughout Canada it says it is "endangering the constitution, undermining the safety of the community and bringing democratic institutions into disrepute." Is it strange then that meetings of strikers in the Canadian Northwest should be stirred to white heat by testimony of this kind? The employing class and the press it reads, are ever telling us —" If labor grabs so much, of course prices will go ballooning. Labor, on the other hand, puts the blame on the profiteer. It is denied that the profiteer has any such justification as the working man whose wages as a whole have admittedly not kept pace with rising prices." Neither side here touches the deeper causes, like inflation, but how inevitable that labor should draw the inference that it does. Nothing more than this brings down the avalanche of strikes.

R. B. Stevens of the Shipping Board told the Commerce Committee of the Senate in December 1917 that

"Since the United States went into the war, shipyards alone lost 536,992 working days by strikes and other disputes."

[1] *Manitoba Free Press,* June 19, 1919, editorial.

From that day, there has been an uninterrupted succession of these revolts in which profiteering and its supposed connection with high prices is most conspicuous as "cause" or as excuse. These are ideas long familiar to socialists and for that reason "safe." They are safe no longer because they have now escaped into the open. They have been "democratized"— scattered world-wide among those with new consciousness of power and new determination to make that power felt. Labor's feeling about undue profiteering is very old but such suspicion or belief is harmless so long as it is scattered, vague and without some agency to focus and direct it. That is what organization does when it reaches any such range and influence as it now commands in affiliated unions with hundreds of journals and other agencies to give it expression. In one center, a trade union organization printed and sent out more than 30,000 records of this profiteering. It was a small union of less than 6000 members in the entire country.

II

I here turn back to note events.

In France and England the labor response to the war call was at first immediate and generous. There had been a high level of strikes from 1910 to 1914. For nearly six months, from the latter date they nearly ceased. If some of the severe conflicts of the three previous years had not remained unsettled, there would have been almost complete absence of trouble. In the first six months in Germany, there were less than 3000 men and women out. In the year before the war, there had been above 2000 strikes with a loss of more than eleven million working days. In 1916, came an ominous change in many parts of Europe. Strikes increased ten fold, chiefly in the war industries and in mining. *The friction began with soaring prices, but*

THE INNER REVOLUTION

especially from the suspicion that a multitude of contractors and employers were making " fat money."

In no previous war did such suspicion cause trouble because wage-earners in general were then unconscious of "profiteering" as a manageable issue. The labor press now became filled with it. When the English Government was driven to its investigations of " labor unrest " it found these suspicions as active as they were widespread. The Commission appointed by the Prime Minister in 1917, reports in pages of testimony like this:

" Our attention was called to the contrast between the man who is compelled to serve as a soldier and the man who voluntarily lends to the Government. It was tersely put to us that the soldier is compelled to serve at one shilling a day, while the man with money voluntarily lends to the Government at five per cent. This was pointed out as irritating and unjust.

" Articles, such as milk, and especially milk foods for infants, are already almost beyond the means of the working classes, although they can still be purchased by those with larger incomes, and this in itself causes a feeling of unrest and gives force to the allegation that the better-off people can buy anything they require while the working classes must want."

These ideas had done their work for months before they were discovered and frankly taken into account.

It should not be overlooked that in the United States strikes were not at first silenced by the war. From the first they were a plague. I do not give it as the only cause, but *two years discussion had made " profiteering " perfectly familiar to labor in this country*. English labor leaders were early among us to extend the propaganda and to make their views familiar to labor here as its press everywhere showed.

Every word of President Wilson against the profiteers

has had fresh use to fortify labor's attitude. He admitted the evil and the shame of it. He said "the information with regard to it is available and indisputable." The labor press ransacked corporation reports giving data and page for their authority. They quote a Government Commission which attributes this grosser profiteering "to inordinate greed and barefaced fraud." From this report, they quote nine Steel Corporations with profits running from 78.92 per cent. (the lowest) to 109.05 per cent., the highest. "New Jersey Zinc" earns 95.9 per cent.; a Sulphur Co. 236 per cent.; with lumber, petroleum, copper, packing company in the same running. The Report from the Treasury Department is thus commented on: "it finds large increases," "enormous increases," "sharp upward rise" of profits in 1917 over 1916, with many companies hitting the capitalists' heaven of unstinted incredible loot. And in April 1917, you will remember we went to war, "pledged to economy and sacrifice"!

More than 30,000 corporations were included in the investigation. It shows the worst profiteering in foodstuffs; that the abuses were far higher in 1917 than in 1916 though profits in 1916 were in many instances over 100 per cent. To offset the "egregious wages of riveters and munition workers employers are noted with profits of 1626 per cent. on its invested capital in 1916, and in 1917 made 4337 per cent. Another coal concern increased its 1916 percentage from 1872 per cent. to 5983 per cent. in 1917, an achievement to which it would be difficult to find a parallel, and which *goes far to explain much of the industrial unrest in the coal industry.*"

And now, as this goes to press, both the present Secretary of the Treasury and his predecessor express most awkward opinions about soft coal profits. They have been "fabulous." "The long-suffering public has a right to be heard." Secretary Glass speaks of profits during the war of 100 and 150 per cent. with instances of three or four times that amount.

I shall watch labor papers to see what observations these opinions call out. Nearly three years ago these journals began continuous comments like the following. " Portsmouth, N. H. has its profiteering crew raising prices on rooms and tenements two and three hundred per cent." and it is from some owners of these houses that we hear " most blame for the workers because they ask for higher wages."

" In Bridgeport, Connecticut, many house renters bleed our men without mercy." " They tell us there is very little profiteering. We know better, there is no part of the country in which large numbers of business men are not making profits so big that they do their best to hide them. All the powers of Government center in Washington. It has no big industries, but outrageous profits in rents are made under the very nose of Congress. Think of it. Congress has all power to check this scandal yet what has it done except talk and bring in bills?"[1]

If the administration is so helpless over its own district where the people are denied the suffrage — what can we expect for the country at large? (This was before the tardy law went into effect.) It is of course true that this evil is not confined to employers.

There has been no report worth reading that has not shown profiteering to have its roots in the general habits of our people. No magnate or scheming capitalist has shown more readiness to improve the hour than the small tradesman, the farmer, and the wage-earners like ship workers and miners. Others dropped work on Monday

[1] When our papers began praising Mr. Gompers for suppressing strikes and "keeping labor loyal" notices like the following were appearing in the trade union press to tell us what was quietly going on in Mr. Gomper's own jurisdiction. "Our members are hereby notified that machinists and other trades are on strike in the shipyards of the port of New York. Kindly be governed accordingly."

and sometimes on Tuesday in order to get the double pay on Sunday. Plumbers bringing an apprentice to learn at the employers' expense charged eleven dollars a day for less than seven hours. If these are not "profiteers" the word has no meaning. Labor journals insist, I think with truth, that these instances in their own class are exceptional. They quote high government authorities to the effect that the wage-earning class *as a whole* has not kept pace (in purchasing power of its income) with rising prices.

The belief is an honest one that with such influence as they can exert, other classes have done their utmost to fatten on the war.

Here are other examples cited by labor journals to confirm their belief.

"The great industry at the South is cotton raising. The South is democratic and it is in the saddle at Washington. The cotton representatives come to Washington, but neither President, Hoover, nor any other patriotic bigwig gets one little bit of 'sacrifice' out of these cotton sellers. They stick for the highest prices they can get. From the silver mines we get the same story; they insist on the biggest price the market affords."

Again, "Look at the whole army of farmers. Are they bleeding themselves for the good of their country? As a class they are putting in every stroke to get all the market affords for everything they raise."

The journal of the Coöperators [1] quotes the testimony at length from an inquiry into coal prices. The President of a Missouri and Illinois Co. was asked at the hearing what was his idea of a fair price for coal in this time of war. He answers in the report, "There is no limit, we get what we can. Everybody is doing that, including the farmer."

The Assistant Attorney, General Gose, asked if in such a time as this that was a right attitude.

[1] *Coöperative Consumer*, Oct., 1917.

THE INNER REVOLUTION 83

"I am not qualified to say," was the reply. "I am doing all I can to get what I can."

He said the highest price he had obtained recently for coal was $6.00 a tone for six-inch Carterville lump.

"How can you justify charging $6.00 for something that cost less than $2.00 to produce?"

"Because you can get it. You are a lawyer and you wouldn't do a piece of work for $5.00 if you could get $10.00 for it."

What are the wage-earners to say of such testimony? They see certain big and conspicuous business men or corporations yielding voluntarily or under threat to the country's call. Prices are lowered with guarantees that no advantage shall be taken of the present stress to coin unfair profits. Labor sees too that excess profit taxes reached thousands of employers.

But this is not all that labor sees. It sees that other thousands are so little hampered by threats and taxes that they are making money rapidly and triumphantly. Many of them are so elated that they cannot keep it to themselves. "Give me two or three years of this and anybody may have my business. I shall have all I want." A business man repeats this from one of his friends at a public dinner. He added that it was very common and was exercising an evil influence. Within two days, labor men were quoting this, together with words of President Wilson. He had called this class of profiteers the "enemy." It was such as they who "delayed the war."

But labor is not reduced to eavesdropping or to quoting public confessions by employers. Millions are at work in mills, factories and other industries where they see and know to a certainty that employers in great numbers used the dark hours for their own enrichment.

What is labor's retort to this? Before answering, it must be said that genuine patriotism has been shown in certain unions. Incomparably less has been said of this in the press than of strikes which classed them with traitors. The whole employing and farming class "making hay while the sun shines" can work quietly and without exposure. No irate General can get after these, nor can they be headlined in the entire press.

The striking union is an easy mark. It can be clearly etched. It catches the eye like a blaze at night. But these qualifications do not excuse the unions as a whole. Many of them were as sordid in their self-seeking as cotton vendors, silver men, farmers, house renters and those employers who chuckle over their chance for "big and easy money." It is these which offer labor such excuse as it has.

This is the retort. "As long as this army of profiteers has its way, we shall have our way if we can get it. We refuse to be singled out to illustrate special virtues in patriotism. A multiude of such men have shown great generosity in time and money, but they and their families are not as we are, within a few weeks of want. They can afford it, we cannot."

This retort does not satisfy the public, but it is as natural as it is human. It is above all a *fact*. It has to be taken into account as much as long rains and mud in the trenches. It is this paralyzing suspicion about profiteering that has done its work upon labor from the moment this issue became clear.

For more than a half century, socialism has carried on its world-propaganda against all private profits, as a form of exploitation under the wage system. The converts now number so many millions that they are a power in politics which no statesman can longer ignore.

But one result of this long discussion of profits raises trouble quite apart from socialism. A majority of the American Federation of Labor, says its leader, is not socialist, yet in the "nearly 33,000 trade unions" suspicion about profits has so spread as to give the socialist projectile a higher velocity.

If we add to this, that every new step in the growth of socialism as well as that of trade unionism sharpens this skepticism, we shall see the situation as it is.

III

It is a variant of profiteering, but another idea known as " Equality of Sacrifice " has now created its own popular appeal.

An over affluent American family with a long tradition of copious expenditure began promptly with the rest of us to Hooverize. As the austerities have always had a hard time of it among the rich, so this family did not easily and radically curtail its outlays. The tell-tale evidence of this was a bulging swill barrel behind an outhouse. This would have attracted less notice if the family had Hooverized in its advice to the servants. It gave most audible and repeated instructions to be sparing to the dozen serving people within and outside the house. There was at first some response to this appeal but it did not last. It was soon found that these retainers either did not understand or were not taking kindly to the new régime. One of the family thought them more lavish than ever. The reason for this was at last bluntly divulged by one of them to a serving man in a neighboring household. As I was told, the protest took this form, " They are at us all the time in the big house to economize and save things to help win the war. We want to lick the Kaiser as much as they do — but we are keeping an eye on that swill-tub. It never was fuller of good stuff than since the war broke out. We don't propose to set up in the starvin' line till we see some change in that swill." It was a strike unnoted even in the local press.

English historians have told us of the vast fortunes made and passed down to great families by those favored with army contracts in the four campaigns: that of Marlborough; the Seven Years War; the Napoleonic and Crimean periods.

" To trade upon the necessities even of a starving city," says one, was thought to be " legitimate and honorable transactions."

This incident of the swill-tub shows us how far we have traveled. The Inner-Revolution had reached the waiting folk in and about that house. This " hired help " had talked it over among themselves. Stirring appeals had been made at gatherings in the house. One of the commonest words was " Sacrifice," and what it should mean for everybody high and low. It is my guess that the servants had caught on to this and that their curiosities about the refuse from the table were in some way connected with it.

In these same days, a woman wrote about her troubles to the *Boston Traveler*. She said:

" I have given three sons to the service of our country, and all of them, going to the front, relinquished positions in which they received fairly good wages and did their whole duty to me.

" I was asked last month to buy a Liberty Bond and refused. If the call comes again I shall refuse, and for one reason. My boys volunteered to fight for the flag, and in doing so reduced their monthly incomes by considerably more than 50 per cent. While they are doing this, and I am trying to match their sacrifice in my humble way, I find that alien residents of my city and commonwealth exempt from draft, refusing to enlist, and positively declining to join the colors of their own countries, are nullifying what my boys are doing at the front by stopping construction work for our Government because they demand three, four and five times as large a wage as my boys will receive while fighting for them and for us, and at least twice as much a day as two of my boys obtained in civilian employment." Three sons, besides large loss of income; this was her cross. She pointed out the slackers and asked the Government to do her justice. Like so many in the world, this woman had been made familiar with a new thought, "Equality of Sacrifice." If she had given her sons in 1776, in 1812, or in 1861, this thought would have been as unknown to her as was wireless telegraphy to those then living.

To popularize an idea so revolutionary as *equality of sacrifice*; to talk of it and write of it, so that the man on the street clearly sees what it means, is to introduce an *idée force* as disturbing to the old mechanical order as steam or the dynamo.

There are millions of very ordinary men and women who now insist and will more and more insist that equality of sacrifice be called down from its ethical aloofness, and set to work among men. Its practical application will be as difficult as it is with "justice" or "liberty," but its authoritative acceptance and wide discussion cannot leave things as they were. The "general mind" is already at work upon the idea, trying to define it and give it illustration. We were advised by an Army officer "to boycott those who refuse to sacrifice." What application can we make of this? How much did the man on the fighting front in this war really sacrifice? On the scale of 100 — it is — let us say 80. Is the woman giving three sons and accepting her straitened income at 50 on the scale? Where, by the same test, is Henry Ford? I was told in Washington, "More than a thousand business men have dropped their private affairs and now give their entire strength without cost to the Government." Where on the scale of 100 are they? Are they as high as 10? If the casualty list on the front was as terrible as we know, together with the crippling invalidities to follow after, marks a sacrifice of

90, most of these business men would mark themselves much below even 10. Where in the scale are the buyers of Liberty Bonds? Are they on it at all? Where is the Red Cross nurse in a base hospital? A rich man in New York says, " The Government should take half my fortune." If it did, where should we mark him? Could we compare his sacrifice with that of a college boy driving an ambulance on the front?

It has been a part of the rhetoric to tell an audience, " Every woman who avoids all waste helps win the war." Yes, but the sacrifice is not impressive. She is merely learning good habits. It may be true, as I have heard, that " the man in the mill or mine who sticks to his job may be as patriotic as the boy who takes his chance in France," but they do not take the same cross.

After some change in the French lines, a wasted woman came back to find her home. The husband and her two sons had been killed. News had just reached her of her only daughter's death in a German village to which, a year earlier, she had been deported. And the "home"! So torn and pulverized was the entire region that but for two piles of cinders in one of which some half burnt familiar object was found, she would not have known the site of it. To see this stricken creature as one of a million is to get some hint of what the war has thrust upon the innocent. Where on the scale of sacrifice are such as these?

There is another variant. The war has taught whole peoples to see the reasons why the *property* of those who stay at home should bear a sacrifice, at least as heavy at that borne by men on the fighting line. Nothing more tritely obvious was ever said, yet to think it into practical consistency, so that it may be politically available, suggests social practices far beyond anything yet attained by state socialism.

THE INNER REVOLUTION

The *effort* of the coming democracy to apply this principle of sacrifice to property will be upon no fanciful scale of subjective values like those just given. Roughly and in material ways it will appear in heavier taxation upon every form of property that separates the well-to-do from the less well-to-do. There will be scant justice and little discrimination. The words " unearned income " will be made the target. This will compel a definition of the term or rather many groping attempts at definition. Whose income is earned and whose unearned? The socialists answer this with the same brisk confidence as the single taxer. There is more discord among trade unions and coöperators, but these, too, have a socialistic slant. " Unearned income " will be a larger and a nearer target. The colossal investments in mines, " natural resources," royalties, economic rent of land in cities are already certain to be attacked. The coöperators are as one man against a whole range of distributor's profits now classed as legitimate. To the total of socialist influence against all private investments in railways, trolleys, telegraph, telephones, mines, will be added much of the union and most of the coöperator vote. The millions now cutting coupons from these investments, claim to *earn* their income but this claim will be contested. When the State takes over all such natural monopolies a smaller interest may be paid to the stockholder " during lifetime " or by other concessions that seem politically necessary. This is but a softening of the blow.

Bolder iconoclasts will press for less compensation still or for none at all. With increasing frequency, one sees such analogies as these, " As the time came when serf property had to be wiped out, as property in slaves at the South was destroyed without compensation, so now should the main income from capitalistic investment be taxed off the map." Not one of the old conservative arguments exists for these favored incomes that will not be worse for wear when the wreckage has to be gathered up and all manner of accounts come in for settlement.

The surging unrest will seize every advantage. Phrases like "Equality and Sacrifice" will be carried over from the war, and upon those who have reserves of property will be thrown burdens heavier than they have ever known.

The *logic* of this concept of "Equal Sacrifice" may have this gleam of hope. Really to practice and force it into final equities would do more to stop the savageries of war than all the wordy peace proposals ever made.

Another insurgent idea concerns the uses and justification of extra legal methods to get things done. As labor is trying to put meaning and class consistency into "profiteering," it tries to get meaning and class consistency into "violence." It asks, "Are the political, military, and economic potentates to have their private monopoly in employing violence? Are they alone to define "necessity" and "the law of self-preservation"?

At one of the Hague Peace Conferences, our American Representatives were puzzled to know the real reason why the German delegate held out against specific peace proposals. It finally appeared. German war equipment was believed to be so complete that it was ready for instant use. Who but a sentimental ninny would forego an asset like this? Austria, in the other war, had been conquered in 19 days and France in 45. This was like a man with a gun loaded and finger upon the "hair-trigger" as against one who was still fumbling for cartridges.

Years later our Ambassador to Germany heard this more plainly still. Our Secretary of State urged Mr. Gerard to induce German authorities to sign peace treaties. There was the same hectoring delay before the real motive was blurted out. The Ambassador writes, "After many efforts and long interviews, von Jagow, the Foreign Minister, finally told me that Germany would not sign these treaties because

THE INNER REVOLUTION

the greatest asset of Germany in war was 'her readiness for sudden and overpowering attack.'"[1]

This is I. W. W. reasoning in perfection. Is it either more moral or more intelligent than syndicalist tactics at their worst?

It is not in mere bravado that one writes, " Violence looses the devil among men, but the upper class leaders are no longer to monopolize it in their protection. Violence is no more necessary for them than for us. When they stop it, we will stop it."

What is it that the war discussion has revealed? What in terms of practice have diplomats and political leaders been doing to get these sanctities obeyed and respected among men? We need go no farther back than 1878, when the very greatest of these national dignitaries assembled " to secure the peace of the world." From that most sinister and blundering performance one can count a pretty steady succession of broken treaties accompanied by consequent violence compared to which the entire mass of labor disturbances is too trivial to note. Look at a single example.

It is to the last degree a commonplace of secret diplomacy and in no way worse than a score of others save as the war has made it conspicuous for use *among labor propagandists.*

In 1871, Austria-Hungary signed a treaty in which she made the most definite promises. She was later made administrator and trustee for Bosnia and Herzegovina over which Turkey had sovereignty. In 1908 the treaty was deliberately broken and the provinces annexed. The Powers protested but the Austro-Hungarian Minister would not yield. He said he couldn't because it was *un fait accompli.*

This set to work a swarm of spies. In Servia the out-

[1] " My Four Years in Germany," J. W. Gerard, pp. 60–61.

rage resulted, among other things, in a secret society in which two youths of nineteen and twenty years had their training as assassins of the Austrian Archduke and Duchess. In breaking that treaty Austria was guilty of violence and of a *kind* of violence incomparably more mischievous than any and all lawlessness due to labor outbreaks.

She was scattering explosives where some one was certain to strike a match. This latter was a despicable act, but so too was the nation's broken word. They cannot be separated as causes of the disaster that followed.

My mention of this is only to ask what *labor is to think and how it is likely to act when it thoroughly learns these lessons of violence among the great?* I lay stress upon the fact that labor *is* learning it. For a generation, scholars among socialist and radical groups have noted these scurvy violations of law and order and commented on the devastations which they brought. This war, with the new propaganda *has popularized this knowledge of broken faith and violence at the top.* It has spread it widely and effectively among millions in the labor world. It has produced among these classes resentment and contempt. From an inner diplomatic circle in Frankfort, Bismarck wrote a letter to his wife, "I am making," he said, "great strides in the art of saying nothing — we all play at believing that each of us is crammed full of ideas and plans if he would only speak. . . .

"No one, not even the most malicious democrat, can form a conception of the charlatanism and self-importance of our assembled democracy." This is precisely what the democrat, "malicious" and otherwise, can do and is doing.

Labor has now looked in upon the scene.

It sees among the nations knavish grab-games for the properties of weaker peoples. It sees as a consequence a record of violence in its most devastating form. It sees "*agents provocateurs*" secretly sent among peaceable peoples to *get up* trouble where none existed. The following illustration is not selected because it is German, for that country is in no sense alone in it, but it is recent and the evidence has come from unmistakable sources given out unashamed by the men involved.

"On 1 July Herr Class called at the German foreign office and, failing to find Herr von Kinderlen-Waechter, was received by Herr Zimmerman, the under-secretary. Herr Zimmerman told him: " You come at a historic hour. To-day the *Panther* appears before Agadir and at this very moment (12 o'clock midday) the foreign cabinets are being informed of its mission. The German Government has sent two *agents provocateurs* to Agadir, and *these have done their duty very well. German firms have been induced to make complaints and to call upon the government in Berlin for protection.* It is the government's intention to seize the district."

What, I ask, is labor to think of these diplomatic disclosures which a new literature and discussion are for the first time making perfectly clear to millions of commoner folk in different countries? The Black Hand methods with which Italy seized Tripoli; the partitioning of Persia by Russia and England; the story of France in Morocco are all recent events. They are a part of the same double dealing. The arguments of the diplomats to defend this buccaneering are so specious; their honesty so thinly veiled as to make good sport even in a high school debate. Abraham Lincoln described them in these words: "*They are the arguments that kings have made for the enslaving of the people in all ages of the world.*"

It is the accumulated force of these democratized beliefs with which we have to do. Force alone will deepen every root. The process must in some sense be educational through experimental and coöperative endeavor. To what agency are we to look? I turn first to hopeful changes within the capitalist order.

CHAPTER VII

CAPITAL ON ITS GOOD BEHAVIOR

I

My record contains no change of more significance than the growing attempt to humanize relations among all those concerned in the business process.

During a strike in a mill town near Boston, I was told of a woman prominent in her union who was caught roughly and whirled about by the foreman. She held in her hand a small piece of iron tubing with which she gave a stinging blow on the man's knuckles. "You can order me about," she said, "I will stand for that, but I will not any longer be *handled.*"

This is one of labor's discoveries. It is not a commodity. Or if, in some sense, it is to be bought and sold like nails and lumber, it is something more and something different.

My neighbor, William James, told me of a workman with whom he liked to talk. It had been a question between them, "How much difference is there between one man and another?" Is the best man in a profession, a class of students, among salesmen, or engineers, twenty, ten or five times as valuable as the man of lowest grade? Is there any measure of difference between the best and the poorest carpenter? Professor James' friend was a carpenter. After some days he brought in his verdict, "There ain't so much difference between one man and another, but *what difference there is, is almighty important.*" This is what we are learning about the difference between the commodity view of labor and the human view.

Forty years ago there was discussion about labor as a commodity to be haggled over like cheese or cotton. No book was complete that did not tell us how the great industry with its absentee ownership separated labor from the hirer. From the president of a large Pennsylvania coal mine, I was given a letter to his manager. There had been a serious outbreak on which the manager made this comment: " We can meet the lesser difficulties out here by ourselves, but the worst of them are over misunderstandings which the city owners neither see nor appreciate. They are so removed as to be wholly out of touch with the changes taking place in the miners' point of view." In its own interest these far-off owners have been compelled to recognize this altered point of view, however unreasonable it appears. Thus the remedy gained favor: " Bring owners and workers together."

Welfare schemes were to be " the new interpreters " between the director of business and his work people. Throughout the period, the unions were of course never silent on this theme. In no sense would they admit that labor was a commodity. I can still hear a speaker say, " There's as much difference between you workers and a commodity as there is between a baby and bag of oats. Invested capital increases whether you wake or sleep. Labor's value perishes once for all if work fails."

Meantime, employers were taking part in the change. Some were worried into it by strikes or other friction. Some from awakened forethought like Robert G. Ogden. He had studied the famous Department Store in the " Bon Marché " in Paris. He told me in his store in New York that his business was in many ways superior, but on its *human side* he had found so much to learn that he was introducing agencies to bring the management into more intimate contact with his working force. In more recent years almost every new step is marked by devices to close the gap between the commodity-view of labor and the human view. In books, pamphlets and special journals, we have a new literature to glorify these institutions for the reconciling of interests between labor and capital. We have also a literature of vituperation and contempt. An employer who has put his soul into this work of "harmonizing interests" in his own business confessed that he didn't dare talk of it in public or even to give it a name. "I suppose," he said, "it is welfare stuff. That looks innocent but it is a red rag to labor. Then reporters come round and puff you which makes it worse, so I call it plain business and have done with it." The panegyrics so often dwell on the more ornamental features of welfare plans as to conceal the real excellencies. Although rarely noted in this connection, let me state first one of the best and most promising.

It is the breaking up of routine traditions which have carried along evils so hardened with time as to be thought unavoidable. There is no hardship, danger, or evil in industry that has not been defended as necessary, solely because it was a traditional accompaniment of the business.

Mr. Gladstone's father was much impressed by arguments against freeing West Indian slaves for "what would become of good Christian gentlemen whose income was invested in that profitable business?"

In 1856, a Southerner, whose conscience had become sore over slavery, told H. R. Helper[1] that "abolition was right but he was greatly troubled for the *widows and orphans* that would be left destitute by freeing slaves."

One of our ablest factory inspectors, in 1906, told us of the deaths and accidents resulting from an obtruding "set screw." As later proved, it could be covered and made safer for thirty-five cents, but business men were on hand with objections which seemed unanswerable. There is nothing strange in those Mexican peons who refused to buy American wagons because they did not squeak. There are now volumes of testimony before legislative committees in which about every specific ill known in industry is

[1] "Impending Crisis," p. 329.

excused on the ground that it is unavoidable. Air thick with dust, bad ventilation, too little light or too direct a glare from electric lamps; the long list of dangers in mines, and the millions at work about unguarded machinery, illustrate the tenacity of customs which concern labor. Even where the most revolutionary change and progress had been made in technique and business organization, there was scoffing incredulity that corresponding changes were necessary for labor.

While thirty representative English employers in many industries sign a unanimous report urging the practicability of the eight-hour day —" with necessary variations by joint agreement "— while five American employers return to tell us they are in hearty accord with this view and believe it to be practicable, we still have had in this country recent instances like the following.

In a State requiring employers to grant one day's rest in seven, a Lackawanna Steel Company tries its best to induce the State Board to give it permission to work the men the full seven days. Beginning with the assertion that the plant is "necessarily continuous" six reasons are assigned to show why the enforcement of the six day law would work "great hardship." This mischievous fatalism, whether in politics or in business, has been the main barrier to social growth. In discrediting it, the welfare innovators never have had the recognition they deserve.

It is one of the popular but deceiving half-truths that labor agitation alone has forced employers to put into the human side of their problem the same intelligence to which we owe the marvels of material progress. From the start, organized labor has been so conspicuous in this humanizing of industry; in forcing discussion and legislation which lead to reforms that it can well afford to admit the whole truth. There is no period in the century of betterment in which exceptional employers have not done their part in these ameliorations. Before the twentieth century came in, they had begun in far larger numbers to take their part in wise pioneer work. They have proved in their own business, that some of the most inveterate evils are as unnecessary as small-pox. Yet it has long been the habit in labor circles and among "intellectuals" who attack capitalism to make sport of all philanthropies by employers. Whatever is organized to make labor contented at its job; whatever institutions are built up to amuse, instruct or conciliate the wage-earner are said to be stealthy devices to lower wages, to keep them from rising or to ward off labor organization.

A government department has issued a statistical table to show results of investigation in some twenty industries in which nearly one and a quarter million of employees were given benefits — lectures, moving pictures, health instruction, outings and the like. One hundred and eighty-eight establishments had "dances, banquets and theatricals." Twenty-two had "orchestras." Sixty-three built auditoriums for this special purpose.

A radical labor comment on this is that it is only another sign that capitalism will "die hard." "It has stopped whipping its slaves; it will now nurse them and be good to them." A university instructor of distinction in Oxford, writes a chapter on "Labor's Red Herrings" opening with the words,

"'Social peace' is not the only cry raised by those who desire anything rather than a real awakening of the consciousness of labor. It is felt in many quarters that 'social peace' by itself is not a sufficiently tempting repast and consequently dealers in 'red herrings' are beginning to do a thriving trade."

He advises the unions to resist "Scientific Management" as well as the "premium bonus system." This is only "a method of getting ninepence for fourpence extra." Profit-Sharing and Labor Copartnership come in for the

CAPITAL ON ITS GOOD BEHAVIOR 99

same gibbeting. Among these critics are able economic students and investigators like the Secretary of the National Guilds, Mr. Mellor. Asked by an English editor what he thought of the outlook, Mr. Mellor answers, " Chaos combined with deceitful kindness." He thinks this threatened kindness on the part of employers very ominous. " During the war," he says, " the capitalists are busily at work securing the foundations of a new type of wage-slavery. They have discovered that it is to the interest of all employers to make *their* workpeople happy. Their methods are obvious. They intend to buy off the leaders. Through Industrial Parliaments, through bogus workshop control, through extensions of the Trades Boards Act, through joint committees of every conceivable kind, and, above all, through fairly high wages and comparative security the employers are trying to keep down the hostility between labor and capital."

There is a deluge of abuse still more caustic than that of these highly trained men. Much of it is richly deserved. Employers have a shabby record of extemporized pieties and philanthropies expressly to keep down wages.

I was in a Virginia tobacco factory where the proprietor told me he had a " singing class." By some sign, he started a long row of colored girls crooning a folksong as they picked the leaves apart. " It keeps 'em good natured," he said, and " they do more work."

It is a motive like this which our critics still see in the whole movement. The criticism is as indiscriminate as it is unfair. Governments have already got their best help from some of these experiments and will get a great deal more. If socialism were to arrive within a twelfth month, nothing would better test its administrative good sense than the uses it made of many hundreds of these welfare institutions. In the latest government report, this definition is given: " Anything for the comfort and improvement, intellectual or social, of the employees, over and above wages paid, which is not a necessity of the industry *nor required by law.*" [1] What seems to me unfair in labor's harsh treatment of Welfare Work as a whole, is the ignoring of a new temper among an increasing number of employers and even more, the ignoring of educational results upon which I shall dwell. I begin with what one critic calls the " poor fripperies of the movement."

II

There is practically no sort of experiment which may not be found on our own territory. Under " Education " we have the wage-earners invited into classes as literary as in a fashionable boarding school; " universal history," Bible history, oftener United States history; sometimes in the rise and growth of general industry and again in the history of the special occupation. At one end, instruction is given in the drama, in tango and war on alcohol; at the other in wireless telegraphy. Under " Health " (largely educational also) nothing that goes on in an ordinary gymnasium from dancing and breathing exercises to fencing and boxing is left out. Indeed practical hygiene training at the very heart of the business world has reached proportions which rank it among the real national assets.

Physicians as well as a large army of trained nurses are now a part of this new industrial régime. Hundreds of classes in " First Aid to the Injured," are regularly carried on. Rest rooms and even instruction in their use with reasons why and when one should rest are frequent. In prevention of accidents and guarding against the use of dangerous products, educational agencies are widespread.

There are already above thirty varieties of workingmen's pensions.

[1] " Welfare Work for Employees," Bureau of Labor Statistics, 1919.

Occasionally we find an exercise in idealism with inspiring hints of what may some time become habitual among our business habits, as in the last agreement of Hart, Schaffner and Marx, in which an added ten per cent. to wages includes (by consent of the trade union and the firm) the lowest paid labor, or, where we find inventors of safety appliances against disease and accident refusing to take out patents, because these advantages should be free to all.

In the so-called profit-sharing, there are so many kinds of "bonus," including Mr. Ford's "bonus on brains" as to defy classification. There are "product-sharing," "progressive wages," "collective wages," "industrial partnership," "copartnership," "gain sharing," "common benefit sharing," "collective sharing," "prosperity sharing," "management sharing," with several kinds of "sliding scales." The varieties of stock-holding by the workers is again as bewildering as the variety of bonuses, especially if the conditions under which shares are obtainable are taken into account.

Further, we have payment "deferred," and payment in cash or half cash, and half something else; we have payment by shares and by rights to a pension; payment according to wages; according to length of services and by a combination of the two.

These plans for raising working standards among employees run the whole gamut from the most primitive and patriarchal dispensations up to the boldest democratic adventures. Every gap can be filled by practical object lessons now found in three-fourths of our states. They are in our public utilities and in about every kind of private business. Many of the most interesting have no public recording and are beyond narrow local boundaries.

As truthful a picture as I have seen is in Ida Tarbell's "New Ideals in Business." No one who knows her work will suspect her of undue capitalistic bias. She closes her volume with the hope that "we may finally really democratize our industrial life." This hope is grounded largely on the new kind of employer whose spirit and activities she reports in much detail. "He is seeing, she says, a significance and a possibility in humanizing his relations that he formerly did not dream. He is developing the inspiring consciousness that it is possible for him to be not a mere manufacturer of things for personal profit, but as well a maker of men and women for society's profit."

The University of Berlin, in 1912, sent a representative to the celebration at Princeton (Prof. Alois Riehl). He wanted to see "anything that was new and significant in the way of education." Without telling him where he was going, I took him for three hours through the department store of the Filene Brothers in Boston. When we left he said, "But this isn't a store, it's a university."

In most parts of the country in the last thirty-five years, I have seen a large number of these attempts in stores, factories and other industries that had the character of a well-ordered school. Often in a single business, we may see at a glance a compact natural history of this Welfare process. Miss Tarbell finds instances to fill a volume. There are more than enough to fill another. I select one not mentioned by her to indicate the origin, growth and tendency of this service,— the Solvay Process Company. It began in 1887, with the children of the employees, because that seemed easiest and safest. For local reasons, sewing was first introduced, other activites being added, up to the "Guild House" under the auspices of the "King's Daughters," and a welfare secretary. Here are "mothers' clubs, with instruction in cooking, dressmaking, housekeeping, dancing and embroidery." There is a day nursery, clubs for play, for the drama and (until Carnegie came to make it superfluous) a library. There is a gymnasium with physical instruction for adults and children; dining rooms and lunch counters are provided, and an emergency hospital with a physician in attendance and classes in "First Aid to the Injured." There is a general accident committee under which are sub-committees for the different departments in the plant. These meet weekly to discuss accidents and their prevention. There are trained nurses not only for the men at work but for their families. These nurses are charged to report any conditions requiring change in the workmen's homes. The company contributes one-half to a "mutual benefit society," with the unusual showing that more than four-fifths of the employees are members. It has a "mechanics' school" for boys. In 1888, profit-sharing was adopted so far as to include officers and foremen and a picked élite of the workmen. In 1910, the bonus system was added, based on wages, with plans for its further extension.

There is in this instance, nothing startling or distinguished. It has no peculiarity that cannot be found in many other enterprises. It is, however, a good instance of welfare work which has grown slowly under careful plans. There is no thought of "playing with the democracies or with other fads." It brings us squarely to the frontier which separates an accepted capitalism from all those insurgent ventures which imply timidly or aggressively — that capitalism is on trial, both for its sins and for its incompetence.

The illustration is also useful in showing us what so many of the friskier critics of the present order unite in despising. To them it is all the worse because under it, capitalism still gets on so thriftily. It acts as if all attainable equities are to be had under the wage system if it is wisely and generously administered. There are no shrewder men in industry than those who cherish the latter opinion. They are in great numbers and are acting together either in defined organizations or with tacit understanding. Together with possible improvements, they believe capitalism to be from every point of view a mode of industry more certain to insure freedom, opportunity, ample production and fairer distribution than socialism can ever promise. They do not listen meekly to radical attacks. They are even rude in describing the various socialist sects and their proposals about whom these employers tell some home truths as they do about many professional reformers. Not infrequently these latter left business because they failed in it. In great numbers reformers live on contributed money while they instruct the world in the exacting art of inaugurating a new and more perfect behavior among men.

Now the business man who organizes production and knows how hard it is to create surplus goods does not like the easy ways of these social critics and exhorters.

Aristide Boucicaut long ago became supreme in welfare work and in one of the world-famous department stores, he refused to " do good " on borrowed money. He thought any improvements he could make would be far more permanent *if they were paid for out of wealth that he was himself creating.* To pay his own reform bills gave him rights and responsibilities which became a basis for educational influence. It was a principle as sagacious as it was sound. When people breathless for reform came to him, he wanted to know what they did toward earning their own living. Not to earn it at all, he thought was a poor recommendation for one who would instruct others how to earn theirs. To earn one's living by the pen, by teaching, by public speech was also a most doubtful qualification for an industrial director.[1]

This precursor among welfare masters was indeed as suspicious and critical of all would-be-instructors of literary or clerical turn, as are many of the new labor organizations —" trade union colleges "— now creating their own educa-

[1] A dispatch now tells us what has happened to this most famous of department stores: "The Federation of Unions of Catholic Employees has decided to join the strike at the Bon Marché department store, where 6000 employees walked out last week to secure the 44-hour week, old age pensions and increased wages."

tional agencies. Nor was he cynical about it like an advisor I once heard quote this sentence, " Don't try to reform the world until you are well convinced that the world can't reform you."

Yet labor was never more distrustful of these schemes than now. It is not only the less worthy traditions in these philanthropies, it is the open and express purpose of welfare plans on every hand that still rouses suspicion. The new pension plans of the American Woolen Company " free to all without cost " excite the widest comment in labor ranks. In the titanic struggle among steel workers to unionize labor in this great industry, the elaborate pension service is spoken of as the old game " to break up their organizations and make them merely a part of the running machinery of the various industries."

The very attempt through these benefits to keep labor in its place calls out most sarcastic comment.

With the Cadillac (Mich.) Lumber Co., the object is frankly to induce the men to remain with the business. After one year's service three per cent. of their earnings are given; after two years five per cent.; after three years six per cent. The great railroad systems were most elaborately equipped as one or two illustrations show. Of the Atchison, Topeka & Santa Fé R. R., we read: " Since 1907 all who have been in service fifteen years secure pension at 65." A motto displayed in club reading rooms runs: " Give a man a bath, a book, and an entertainment that appeals to his mind and hopes by music and knowledge, and you have enlarged, extended, and adorned his life; and as he becomes more faithful to himself he is more valuable to the company." The Union Pacific set 20 years for the pension, while granting the 65-year limit for certain classes, but setting 70 for all others. Yet there is no end to the attacks on these features. " They just want to keep the hook in our nose. It is all a trick to tie us up so we can't move about freely to get a better job or to prevent us from striking."

In the past there has been every ground for this criticism, but in the actual conditions of labor replacement: — in the restless come-and-go rising to several hundred per cent. in a year is there nothing to be said for plans to counteract a waste so excessive?

Lake carriers tell us the turnover among their men is above 600 per cent., i.e., six hundred of a thousand men will leave within a year. An employer submits an analysis showing that the come-and-go among his mechanics costs him $100 for every man who leaves. Another reports that in his case this sum is too low.[1]

My men, says another, are as if they all owned motorcycles and wanted to use them to see the whole country, — stopping a few days here and there to earn money enough for the next stage in the trip. There are three lumber camps now near me. From two of them, more than half the men leave every month, and from the other, oftener still. The manager says " Most of my time is spent in replacing to-morrow the bunch that leaves me to-day." At a Florida sawmill, the foreman says, " We used to keep niggers till we buried 'em, and now we are lucky if they stay a month." In some degree this is the situation everywhere in the United States. It is an inconceivable loss for labor, for employer and for society. The question therefore has pertinence. Are wage earners likely to suffer by checking these fluctuations? What habits useful for any form of industrial organization are being formed by these wandering hordes?

This pulling and hauling between employers striving for stability and the more restless unions striving to keep labor

[1] Quoted pages 60, 61. " Profit Sharing " by three active business men and two professors of Economics. Harpers, N. Y.

"free" is not a bad illustration by which to judge the value of welfare appliances.

It must be conceded that if the economic order — not merely in its abuses but root and branch — is so rotten that it cannot be destroyed too soon or too thoroughly, then everything tending to its downfall should be welcome. If the present system is as far gone as was our slave labor in 1861, the present labor turnover is a matter of rejoicing.

The facts have no such simplicity as this. However thoroughgoing industrial changes are to be, they have to come in some order of growth, and above all with decades of education for every party involved. In consumers coöperation, in socialism, in labor unions, this education is an awakened and advancing movement. But the awakening is also among increasing numbers of employers who are readjusting their minds and their methods. The best of these methods is giving to labor the one educational opportunity they need to prove their own case. If employers were flabbily to concede what the many radical labor contingents demand, we should have change indeed, but change under which labor would be the first and longest sufferer. The unions insist that they offer superior advantages to workers through their organization. Even if true, the claim should not go uncontested. If by his pension plan working through the coöperative association in the factory, Walter Lowney can hold his thousand employees faithful and satisfied, he is within his rights. Let the unions prove that they can do better.

Private welfare work may in time yield to other devices, but what meantime are employees to do? Are they to be stampeded for making the best of the present system and for trying to keep labor satisfied?

The wholly legitimate desire of the employers is to identify the conscious interests of their work-folk with the business. No employer, if he can help it, wants a divided allegiance. He does not want his men to look for guidance first to some trade union leader or committee. His ideal is for the simple and direct loyalty of all his employees. Business leaders realize the steady drift of labor organization toward the socialist position. They are more and more alive to the fact that this means a resolute and progressive demand to oust the capitalist and make way for trade union control of industry. Every convinced opponent of socialism will act accordingly. He will do his best to prove that the public and labor alike are better served by an improved and progressive capitalism. He may not win out, but he would be a poltroon to yield without a contest. Knowing as well as another, that to save capitalism it must undergo constant readjustment and bettering, he will seek out and apply such ameliorations as appear to him practicable. This is justified and for this reason. No one — except youthful iconoclasts, know with any precision how society is to develop; what form it will take or what names will fit it best. From temperamental preference, we may feel and express strong opinions on the society that is to be as we swing between conservative and radical extremes. But the future is so far hidden from us; the conceivable alternatives are so many, that allowance must be made for industrial and political unfoldings, very different from those on which we happen severally to have set our hearts. Are we to cast out the wage system? Is the system of property not merely to be amended but in its private forms to be destroyed? Is the democratic principle to be carried through to its limit by immediate control by the masses? Will the name "socialism" most accurately describe the society of the year 2000 in any given country and perhaps in all countries in the year 3000? It is because we have no certainty about these issues that ways must be kept open for well nigh infinite experiment. We can only wildly guess if the wage system is to pass away or how long it will be with us. As long as it is here, it should be made as efficient as any other tool in use.

This is what all decent welfare work does. Even the rough and common average of it springing up everywhere in the United States, has enormous benefits. Even if the wage-getter finally goes the way of the slave and the serf, he will not go in our time. So long will the majority of men have to take wages, that most employers meantime can serve in no way better than by increasing the comforts and the security of the men and women working with them, and what may have an even higher importance, to work seriously within their own business at the fundamental but unsolved problems like unemployment, housing, pensions and minimum wage as a secure base on which and from which bonuses, sliding scales and the like may have more promising trial. A private business with the good will of the working force has every advantage for such experimenting. It has close personal touch, freedom from politics, direct personal interest and responsibility. The State with all its power can never possess some of these advantages which the best of private business offers. Even if there is more fundamental work to be done than what is inspired or directed by employers, much of this latter is an open way toward more democratic control. Every step in the practical logic of it brings labor closer to management and begins the business education which in any event must guide us in the future.

There are hundreds of employers in the United States who have done so much for the instruction, fun, economic well-being of labor and what is more, they have so cleared the field of routine and runt-minded ways of doing business, that their achievements will be found invaluable for all further experiments toward a more democratic administration of industry.

Here, too, is the employer's opportunity to prove the excellencies of capitalism and at the same time prove his case against the "agitators." In overwhelming majorities in this country labor is still unorganized. It is, moreover, little realized what large numbers have tried the unions and left them in disgust. A carpenter several times in my employ stands for thousands of these. Four times here, and in California, he joined the union. He says he has done with it. He is a rapid, skillful, high-priced man. He settled the eight-hour question himself. He will work longer for no man. He says he objects to the goose-step; to being told when and how he shall work. He says "they lie when they tell you there is no restriction of output." He objects to the petty politics of the union. There is no statistical approach to the number of these men but it is very large. The most thoughtful of them admit both the necessity of the union and its utility. They admit that it must have still larger growth and influence. That unionism, however, is to cover all industry with closed-shop monopoly, they believe to be neither possible nor desirable. They see in it a tyranny more to be feared than that of private employers.

This man points to the automobile industry to ask what the unions have done for labor better than Ford, Cadillac, Packard and a host of others. The unions have done as little to raise wages here as they have among the household domestics. These freemen do not loudly express it nor have they any press propaganda, but in enormous numbers unorganized labor is also watching and thinking. It sees how socialist tendencies are gaining. It is weighing these two in the balance. If the most powerful labor body in the world (the English " Triple Alliance ") succeeds in forcing the mines and railways under state management, this freer labor will have plenty of time to judge whether it proves advantageous or not.

That greatest of all tests has not yet come, namely, Will *production* so thrive under socialist direction as to give labor generally and permanently the promised high returns? It is possible, but the proof is not at hand.

Socialists who admit this usually reply, " Oh, but things go badly under state management now because the State is capitalistic. Give us a people's government and all will go well." This, too, is possible, but it is a claim still to be justified. The attempt will go far, but it will be watched. At every stage it will be critically observed, not only by a conventional opposition but by much unconvinced labor.

Australia has gone very far towards a " people's State " but the internal friction was never more troublesome. When they get more people's government will the friction lessen? We do not know. That, too, is under scrutiny.

What is now settled is that for much of the greatest industry, employers and employees are to face each other in more compact and more democratic organizations. Employers agree to this, while States advise it and encourage it by their example. In the next decades we are to observe this alliance, to see (a) what portions of industry it will leave uncovered and (b) how far capitalism holds its own in the partnership.

In the intervening time, as we seek light and training to guide us, the welfare pioneers have no apologies to make. In doing their best to save the existing order through reform and adaptation, they are as squarely and as soundly on the side of progress as the most confident of their critics.

III

I should not give a line to this welfare beneficence except for its experimental values. These are among the real forces because they educate in two directions. They educate the employer and they educate labor. Especially upon younger employers, the best of this work opens the mind to the very questions on which change depends. As these experiments develop, they force him to reconsider and to restate every problem. With whatever bias or economic preconceptions he starts, these are certain at some stage to get a jolt. Many employers who begin with the most rigid views about the minimum wage, piece-work, new machinery, profit-sharing, bonuses, rights of stockholders as against those of wage-earner have been led to change their views solely through these experiments.

The change comes where it is safest and socially the most serviceable. It has no taint of the "parlor socialist" or mere theorist. The changes of which I speak are in the minds of practical men tugging at their own business and at the same time tugging quite as hard with experimental methods like shortened work day, labor insurance, seasonal variations, unemployment and higher health standards.

These innovations must pass through every rigor which business success imposes and are all the better for the friction. Though the experiment may finally fail, the educational result is often greater than if a nominal success were reached.

We are deluged with advice about the workman's need of education. It is excellent counsel for labor needs it, but for the unavoidable changes before us, the employer and the rest of us need it quite as much. With the new forces now at work, that employer is hopeless who is not prepared for these changes by struggling with welfare plans. With whatever variety he begins, he will be driven to one modification of it after another. If he does not flinch, he will be led to look at the whole industrial relation in a different spirit. This is not a theory or a conjecture, it is a fact, open to observation in most cities and industrial centers.

In my immediate neighborhood are first-rate illustrations, one of which I offer because it raises the deeper questions that are to aid our economic transformation.

As successful an employer in his line of business as is known to me in Massachusettts confesses that he had long believed invested capital "earned every cent it could get and had a right to every melon it could cut." Solely from a close study of his own business in relation to welfare plans this employer made the discovery that in his own words he "had been carrying a fool's head on his shoulders." "Capital didn't earn any such return as it got year after year." He admits that much of it was "at the expense of labor."

He knew of Massachusetts mills which had rewarded the stockholders three or four times beyond the current interest on capital, while the public was being told that the business could not afford any higher wages without financial risk. He quoted a well-known treasurer of a famous mill as saying, "If our dividends stopped altogether, great numbers of the older stockholders would have got back their original investment five times over."

Long discussions in one phase of welfare plans had made my informant face this question. *Why should the mere investor get all this rich cream while so much less goes to labor?* "Those who 'earn' it should have it." Nobody, he thought, would dispute that. Who, then, in my own business are the *real earners?* Wages had been raised, but he thought not a penny more than costs of living had risen, which plainly meant no rise at all. "If it was true that capital was getting unfair and unearned income, then labor is defrauded." In this spirit he spoke out his thought.

In trying to improve a profit-sharing scheme he was forced again to answer "who earns the profits?" In a quite socialistic sense, he said "those who do the real work make the profits and ought to have them. Capital is sure of its 6 per cent. in my business and as the risks are normal, they should have no more." "We make a great deal more than that, and I want to get it clear who it is that earns this extra profit."

Asked what he meant by "the real workers," he named certain inside men, different heads of departments, foremen, salesmen and advertisers. At this point he said he was "stuck." He was sure that men who organized departments and kept them up to date; a few men who improved machinery and designs; a number of buyers and those who extended the sales —" the planners and the drivers "— were the real earners of all the surplus which could go to profit-sharing. "If I were to drop out those men, my business would slump in a month, with common labor only. I could not hold my own against any one of my competitors."

Why, then, should he give more than the market price to the others? There were highly skilled workmen that ought to have more if any one did, but how could one pick these out for favors without making the less skillful dissatisfied? If he began with the wage class, he must give it to everybody and these, he was sure, did not create the extras out of which a profit-sharing fund was made up. He could not see that more than "one in forty" contributed anything to the extra product on which profit-sharing must be based. Yet he wanted to extend the plan just as far as he could enlist interest in the men. He thought if it were extended to the rank and file, it would be a straightout gift. He did not object to the gift if it would "work," but this he doubted. This doubt is at least intelligent. If his labor force had consisted of 80 or 100 men with whom some personal touch was possible and especially if he had their confidence, the plan might reasonably have included all. Or if the plan had been long established far larger numbers might have been added. But to begin anew with more than 3000 men (if profit-sharing history teaches us anything) he would fail.

Easiest and safest of all is profit-sharing with what he called "the real drivers at the top." Nowhere has this device wider or more secure scope. But with an advancing

CAPITAL ON ITS GOOD BEHAVIOR 115

state socialism or in syndicalist reactions organized over against the State (as well as in labor copartnership) we shall later see what perplexities even this "management sharing" has before it. To "democratize business" is to bring in the rank and file. They are in some manner, to have voice in choosing directors and in deciding policies. They will have their own opinions about the distribution of plums and about the payment of services.

Now it was the shadow of this difficulty which caused the hesitation of this business man. He had thought far enough to admit that since the business had become solidly established, a lot of investors had been getting a great deal of wholly unearned income. In spite of legal sanctions, this seemed to him a plain injustice and he was furthermore convinced that it was storing up trouble for the future. "It gives labor a good case against capitalism." By talking much with those who had experimented and by thinking out the problem in his own business he had come so far on the road. Neither advice from outsiders; threats of a trade union nor any book study would have convinced him that he was "carrying a fool's head on his shoulders" in thinking that stockholders had a sort of natural right to those successive additions to dividends which had been accepted as a matter of course.

Here is one of many intelligent and hopeful proposals followed at every stage by an education calculated to open and broaden the mind for whatever lies in waiting. It is an education which makes it easy to understand the advancing claims of labor. "Mere ownership apart from labor service has been getting too much." This has long been labor's claim. Here at last are employers frankly admitting it. Here, too, is a plan to *begin* at least the correction of abuses. So far as labor is socialistic it will accept the plan only as a first step. The importance of the step is that it makes further understanding possible between the two parties. We know this because labor *as employer* has already met among its own employees precisely the same difficulty, namely, how far will the mass of ordinary labor respond and intelligently take part in *any* industrial organization?

The one desire for big dividends may conflict with the prosperity of the corporation as directly as too importunate demands for more wages on the part of labor. Neither all stockholders nor all laborers can be trusted with immediate power over the business.

How many can be trusted? On the labor side, how many can be brought over the line of mere wages really to interest themselves in improving and enlarging the business? This is not merely the crux of the matter in democratizing business, it is the crux in democratizing politics.

The advantage of turning to the ablest of the welfare directors is that their experiments are under the most favorable conditions. They begin in their own business and with a labor force of their own selection.

There is not a man of them who has not run foul of this difficulty of interesting enough of his employees to make more democracy work. Some of them had to sift and re-sift their workers before they could gain an inch in extending power to labor. Until safe majorities of wage-earners are in some way educated to something more than the day's income, " democratizing business " will remain an aspiration only. I shall show the desperate struggle in the labor camp with this same difficulty. What political as well as economic democracy must prove is the willingness and ability of the *mass* to take on such measure of responsibility as to insure orderly and progressive administration of the thing at hand. Courageous and intelligent attempts to do this on both sides have now begun.

It is said that Rousseau's books were bound in the skins of the aristocrats. Are the records of our later drama to be bound in the skins of the capitalists? There are threats of this kind, but the danger of such distinction is not imminent. There are business bourbons who have neither learned nor forgotten, but hosts of younger leaders and many old ones are so alive to what is before them, that time and leeway enough are theirs to insure, let us hope, a long and fairly safe transition to newer and better ways.

Before these are taken up, intervening obstacles must be considered; " the unreasonable claims of labor "; the attitude of many and resourceful employers and also certain features of the revolution now upon us.

CHAPTER VIII

"WHAT DOES LABOR WANT ANYHOW?"

I

AT least twice a week we have heard this impatient or angered inquiry. Labor is asking and receiving what most employers and hosts of the consuming public think outrageous. While this is not true of labor as a whole, it is true of a luckily placed minority. Even of these, it is not confined to factories or mines, to carpenters or railway men. Yet it is these and the ways of many household domestics that just now set so many " real nice people " a-worrying. We are credibly informed that a cook in a prosperous suburb sent orders upstairs from the kitchen that the mistress and her guests make less noise and the order was obeyed. Another tells the mother that the daughters returning late from evening gayeties cannot laugh and talk " as if nobody else wanted to go to sleep. This must stop or I will leave." These are the new ways. They are many and will increase. The irritations of the superior are especially nettled against the " aliens " who it is said lived hungrily and very meanly until they reached this country. Here we have been heaping upon them all sorts of benefactions: quadrupled their wages, given them twice the leisure they ever enjoyed, only to receive this black ingratitude!

A Sicilian in Boston confesses never to have earned above 30 cents a day in his own home, and usually less. He began here with a dollar and a quarter and within eighteen months had two and a half dollars a day, and now a good deal more. He has more and better food and as for clothes, " it is as a new kind of man I now dress." His religion is that of the I. W. W. He says that capitalism is "the new slavery." He read it in his first English book. He says that of five dollars the laborer earns, capitalism takes four. It is therefore for the working classes to "see this," "to think it together," and then to "become free by taking the place of the robbers." There is nothing unusual in this except the rapidity with which this man's views had developed in his American environment. With his income and opportunities improved five hundred per cent., his wants, his claims and expectations had increased a thousand per cent. When I asked him if there was not more capitalism in this country than in Sicily, he said, "Mountains more." I suggested that this excess of capitalism had somehow improved his lot materially and educationally at least five hundred per cent. He agreed to the per cent., but would not admit that capitalism had anything to do with it. He was even trying to persuade his mother and two younger brothers to sell their scanty belongings and cast in their lot with him among these "mountains of capitalism." He could give his mother luxuries that "only the rich man" in his native village could have, and as for his brothers, "they should be educated better than the sons of those rich men" and "all for nothing." And this is accurately the fact about some millions of other immigrants who have brought the gifts of adaptation and the will to use them.

As these world migrations turn their backs upon the old home to seek and to find a freedom, an economic and educational opportunity they have not known, they merely hold the mirror up to human nature. Who of us that finds a new satisfaction — added income, freedom from drudgery, new power of any sort, does not want forthwith to multiply these acquisitions? One of our humorists says, "*the trouble with satisfying a new want is that it begets triplets.*" The quick claim of our immigrants to new advantages is one of the most hopeful, as it is one of the most practically embarrassing elements in our social problem. The pressure toward higher standards is so brusque and determined that economic adjustments are full of rasping friction. Foreign domestics come to us who never got above fifty dollars a year. I have known two such to reach wages five times that amount with more leisure, less work, and no penny added to their expenses except of their own choosing, and to do this before the third year. One of them said that within two months she "was dressed so proud she didn't know herself." At a social settlement in San Francisco in 1911, I saw a group of Finns just leaving for their home lands. One of them told me they were going home "until the strike was over." They were six and seven-dollar-a-day men in the building trades. It was their chance for a vacation.

These cheerful illustrations are of course from the upper, luckier side of our immigration, but they are everywhere and in great numbers.

It is the lower, unluckier and less skilled portion of our immigrants which presents the uglier features. But among these less fortunate ones, the new wants are as quickly learned and as keenly felt and because of stubborn checks upon their gratification their importunities become all the more troublesome. There was general jocosity last year at the expense of the Osage Indians.

A discussion of the House Committee on Indian Affairs is quoted to show that "these aborigines are the richest people in the world." "The 2,200 of the tribe have about 1,500,000 acres of Oklahoma land, about one-tenth of which has been leased for oil purposes. There is now paid to them annually between $4,000 and $5,000 per capita from the oil production." With economic opportunity and a taste of luxury, we see them rise cheerfully to the ways of civilized men. They even learn to employ "higher costs of living" to justify the request for enlarged income. They petition for more of their lands to be leased in order that the new necessities may be eased.

"WHAT DOES LABOR WANT ANYHOW?"

One commentator says it is a national disgrace that these half civilized creatures should be allowed to have luxuries " which they cannot appreciate and which they certainly do not *need*." " They are not satisfied," he says, " six months with a Ford, but must change it for a more expensive machine "— as if this were in the least peculiar to these dusky inhabitants.

Very early in my note-taking, a strike of shoe workers in Brockton (1885) led to a discussion on the question " What is it that labor wants anyhow? " It was put to me in a letter by an employer. He said he was anxious to find out. He had been in business twenty-five years and the men were always trying for more, always for more. It would quiet his mind if he knew what to expect. " I never give them an inch that they don't ask a foot."

This was an exercise in irony, but inquiry showed that in his own mind the question was already answered. He said that for women, " a dollar to a dollar and a half a day " was enough. More variation had to be allowed for men, but the best of them ought not to get more than three dollars, and most of them not more than two dollars.

He had no theory such as older economists devised to justify these or other limits, but a vague idea of " what the women needed and what the men needed " best expressed his convictions.

I confess that never before had it quite come home to me that labor had as much right to ask and try to get whatever it *could* as investors do and people generally. I had friendly relations with this employer and when I asked him how much income he himself wanted, he answered, " whatever I can get out of my business." He *wanted* still more, but had a " right to whatever profits came to him from his business." For his men and women, he had a different standard. Labor in his factory was " unreasonable " because it was asking more than it " needed." It had not occurred to him to apply this standard to himself. He was to have whatever he could " make." The question of his needs he thought had nothing to do with the discussion.

A few years later at a club in Cambridge, a trade union speaker was asked, " What would labor take if it could get it?" In terms that to-day seem ascetic, he answered, " five dollars a day and eight hours' work." " But would you be satisfied with that," put in an employer, " when you got it?" " Of course not," was the reply. " We should then try for six dollars and for seven hours." I walked away with this employer who grew merry over what he thought the discomfiture of the speaker. " Let them get seven hours and soon they will clamor for six, then for five, and so on until we have to feed them with pap from a spoon." " The audience saw that the speaker was crying for the moon." When I asked this business man what he and other employers were crying for, he said, " Oh, well, I suppose we're crying for the moon too." Why, then, should crying for the moon be less natural to labor than to capital; to one class than to another?

If it is true that individuals and "group interests" in business and politics are all striving for an unlimited *more*, controversy and strife must follow unless our world home is so stored with supplies and satisfaction that no one need be denied. Buoyant optimists have maintained that nature is thus amply provided. They have made many questionable phrases like this: " If God makes mouths, He makes food enough to fill them." " That the soul has cravings only means that satisfactions are there to meet them." It is true that metaphysical refinements or utopian schemes are usually brought in as a condition of securing these blessings. We are usually warned that we must first acquire a new behavior or some thorough-going remaking of society. Meantime, we seem bent on a great deal more than nature sees fit to grant. Everywhere the nations have been asking more territory than could be had without making trouble among their neighbors. Everywhere political parties and business associations seek acquisitions that must be checked or others will suffer. If the multitude of us are engaged in this over-reaching, the result is conflict and competitive struggle. The strife of interests, as each group conceives its interest, is somewhat softened by various methods of "accommodation"; by forms of arbitration and legal regulation, but accepted business methods under capitalism leave this passion of over-reaching in the entire field as aggressive and probably as unintelligent as ever.

It summarizes the most frequent charges against the trade union that business would be ruined if it granted the power, the wages, etc., which the union demands. Yet how old and how universal is this out-reaching.

We want more money than we get. We want a great deal more happiness than we get. We want more distinction among our fellows — more influence and power than ever comes to us. This last craving for distinction and influence over our kind (to dwell on a single example) is indeed so deep and so importunate that its omission leaves us blind to the most open of all human records.

In any race study like that of Professor Frazer in "The Golden Bough," one sees through many centuries to what portentous lengths this hunger for attention, repute and celebrity goes.

To become the center of popular attention which carries prestige with it, men eagerly take an office for a year, a month, a week — yes, for a single day, knowing to a certainty, that they are to be killed (often most cruelly) at the close of so fleeting an adventure.

From the primitive horde which precedes the tribe up to the present day, there is apparently no jot of abatement in this thirst for some form of distinction and difference from their fellows.

The infinitude of personal decorations from kings covered by "orders" as a savage is by paint, down to servant girls and their mistresses seeking a hat that shall attract attention by differing from all other hats has its explanation in this desire to be set apart a little from others; not to be lost and overlooked in the colorless mass of everybody and nobody in particular.

Nothing can so handily and so variously gratify this passion as money. A labor class dependent on wages satisfies its wants like other people chiefly through money income. It is absurd to suppose it will be "contented" with a fixed wage any more than a contractor, portrait painter, manufacturer or actor cheerfully accepts limits to income far within the circle of things desired.

The most intelligent and energetic class of labor no longer believes a word of the old economic warnings about those inflexible barriers as to hours and wages. They know there are limits, but they prefer to find them out by their own effort and experiment. The union organizes its strength for such experiments, determined like others to get — what it can get. Labor is merely falling into line with the rest of us.

What would be left if the gentlemen in the stock exchange got all they wanted? Where would physicians, lawyers, dentists, farmers, stop if there were no limit set to the incomes that would satisfy them? Or how low would the whole body of consumers crowd down prices if they could?

In the demands of labor, the employer meets that in human nature which he is himself practicing every moment. Does he ever set the limit to desired income? Yes, in the first glow of business success, men now and then say something like this: "If I get enough to give me seven or eight thousand dollars a year, I'll quit and take it easy. That will satisfy all the wants I have or that my family ought to have." I have known well three men who told me when they were going to stop working. Their limits differed,— differed as their ambitions and traditions differed. They all reached and passed their goal. Only one of the three ever had a serious thought of stopping. He told me when past seventy, that he should die when he dropped work. "I go away," he said, "every year, but after two weeks the only happy thought I have is that of getting back to business." Exceptional men here and there do deliberately say to themselves, "I have enough and will quit." But so exceptional is this that it does not seriously modify the larger fact. Business and professional men strive to swell their earnings just as labor has learned to reach out for more. The labor method is unpopular because no one has yet learned how to do a really disagreeable thing agreeably.

It mistakes about everything in human nature to think that labor will set limits to its climbing any more than the rest of us.

Because of mounting costs of living and the terrible exigencies to get things done whatever the costs, governments for five years have been feeding labor with one concession after another. It could not be helped, but labor's appetite was merely whetted for more. It is a new and formidable difficulty that this appetite now turns to politics as the chief agency of securing and enlarging labor's hold on ultimate power. We see this in organizations which have nothing whatever to do with making and distributing goods. A good example is in the rise of unionism among our city firemen. Organizing these city employees was discussed and I think attempted in a Pennsylvania coal district as early as 1904. Pittsburgh soon followed with affiliation of its union with that of Allegheny City. In several States, the attempts failed until the war. They were at first very wary about public opinion. They were too uncertain as to what would happen if they defied the city. Even their own journals warned against rousing the public against them. The insurance companies threatened to cancel all insurance in Tampa[1] if a union was allowed to form.

When the war came, these firemen's unions took their chances. They struck boldly for " recognition." They flocked to the American Federation of Labor, and in 1917, we hear of the representatives at Washington forming " The International Association of Fire Fighters." In Massachusetts a " State organization " is now asked for. So rapidly did the firemen now act that thirty-five cities had " organized " in the first year of the war. These had doubled in 1917, while at present nearly 120 are reported, "the movement growing as lustily in Canada as in the United States."

This is labor's discovery the world over. In democratic States as now organized, we have no adequate means of holding it in check. It must make its own experiments, meantime turning to politics in quest for favors. Because it so accurately foretells what is before us, of a growing alliance between labor and politics, I note an occurrence in my own neighborhood.

In spite of an act of 1909 forbidding the city council to interfere in the administration of the fire department or in fixing hours of labor, the politician had seen his opportunity. Organization had given the fireman voting power with the exceptional chances to influence local politics. A commission was set to work. It reviewed the history down to 1905, when they had *one day off in eight,* but organization and political coaching meantime were doing their work. In 1905, says the commission, " each of two candidates for the nomination for mayor promised the firemen a decrease in the hours of labor." Here the pestilence of the demagogue begins, as we see it in Athenian democracy in its decadence and among outbidding candidates in Rome with

[1] I learn that the firemen's strike at the "cigar city," Tampa, Florida, was a year earlier than the above date.

their circuses and free bread to the populace. It now appears in lavish promises to home-coming soldiers, all to be paid — not by the candidate, but at public expense.

Thus the hours of the firemen were reduced in 1905 to one day off in five, "although Fire Commissioner Wells made repeated objections." In 1909 the three-meal periods of one hour each were extended to an hour and a quarter each.

The firemen also got two hours' "church leave" every other Sunday; also from 5 P. M. to 10 P. M. after working a full day on detail; also 8 A. M. to 10 P. M. on Sunday, when the member has worked full time on detail for three preceding days; three days of 24 hours each in case of death in the immediate family; an extra dinner hour on Thanksgiving and Christmas, and 16 days' annual vacation.[1]

Let no reader think there is anything exceptional in this, so far as motive and intention are concerned. Without the asking, these organizations can now secure adroit and fluent spokesmen who compete in proffering favors. Before an inquiring committee from the Chamber of Commerce, one of them took high ethical ground. Here are some of his answers:

Q.—"You say that the reduction from one day off in eight to one in five has not impaired the efficiency of the fire department?"

A.—"I do."

Q.—"You are aware that the underwriters hold a different opinion?"

A.—"They, as theorists, may have one opinion, and I, as a fireman of experience, may have another."

Q.—"And you maintain that a further reduction from one in five to one in three days will further increase the efficiency?"

[1] A little later the Boston Waiters' Union was threatening a strike to secure *one day off in fourteen,* but these were not city employees and they have so far slight political influence.

A.—" I do."

Q.—" And one day off in two would still further increase efficiency? "

A.—" Yes."

Q.—" And one day off in one and a half still further? "

A.—" Yes."

" I would say," continued the witness, after much sparring, " that the firemen would be perfectly satisfied with one day off in three, and would not ask for any further reduction, unless the workingmen generally asked for a six-hour workday; then we should ask for the two-platoon system."

The picture is incomplete without the following:

" Firemen and their friends packed the old aldermanic chamber in City Hall last evening, in support of the firemen's demand for one day off in three instead of one in five, and Councilman Walter L. Collins, who, as chairman of the committee on ordinances, presided, found it impossible to restrain the tumultuous applause, cheers, and even whistles, which rewarded those who spoke for the proposed ordinance, or the jeering laughter at the expense of Francis N. Balch, who, for the chamber of commerce, in opposition, undertook by questioning to refute the arguments of those who favored the ordinance."

To keep the issue clear, it should be said that more leisure for these men was as advantageous to them as to the public. But it is the excess and abuse of favors to which attention is called.

Here is a most favored body of men well pensioned and retired early enough so that many of them still earn good pay for years in addition to pensions. Within and without the body, efforts increase to secure the " double platoon " under which still more leisure comes to them.[1] Though

---

[1] Then came the press announcement: " Following the example of fire fighters in many other cities, the 3,600 members of the Uniformed Firemen's Association of New York — almost the entire

"WHAT DOES LABOR WANT ANYHOW?" 129

it adds a half million to our bill for taxes, candidates now urge it in the name of "justice" while in four cities we have the "*three platoon*" system claimed by the men and oratorically defended by political sympathizers. Ten months after the above was written the report circulates that these firemen who required one day off in three "to see something of their families and keep physically fit for dangerous work" are found here and there "working on the sly for good pay." This forces the commissioner to issue orders "prohibiting the use of the one-day-off-in-three privilege for purposes of private employment on any official matter."

While this discussion over the firemen was in progress, we were told that twenty thousand dollars a year has been set apart for the maintenance of a four-year-old child in New York City. The mother finds this sum stingily illiberal. In her distress she turns to the court for relief. Last year she says the outlay for the little one was $27,593. The harassed parent begs for an additional seven and a half thousand to make good the deficit. It was impossible, she said, with $20,000 to supply all the child's yearly wants. Close upon the heels of this comes another; this time a lad of seventeen years, from Pittsburgh. In law, he is still an "infant." With the sympathetic assistance of his governess, the child's minimum necessities are thus itemized:

Rent and electricity	$ 5,000
Household expenses	12,000
Education	1,500
Clothing	1,500
Automobile	3,500

membership of the force here — have joined a branch of the American Federation of Labor. They expect through this unionization to be able to bring stronger pressure to bear on the city administration for higher pay and the adoption of the two-platoon system or, if possible, a three-platoon system.

> Spending money 1,500
> Incidentals, traveling expenses, and
>   medical expenses 3,000
>
> Total $27,000

The surrogate had to appoint a referee who admits that ordinary boys could not live quite so lavishly without "grave risks." Upon examination, however, the referee finds this special lad of a quality so "firm and austere" that $25,000 a year is free from perils. We are not told why he is deprived of the extra two thousand. No details are given of the forced economies which this restricted living represents. The account continues: "He lives almost a military life, rising at 6 in the morning, taking regular exercise, being personally responsible for the neatness and tidiness of his room and clothing, and in other ways disciplining himself most vigorously. Moreover, he is very careful about how he spends his money. He even practices great economy in the purchase of gasoline for his motor car."

One is reminded of the elder Lorillard, who was asked how much money a man really needed to live like a gentleman. "He should have," was the reply, "a thousand dollars a day and *his expenses*."

If these illustrations excite gayety, in which of them is the humorous element the more lively? The gilded infants are at one disadvantage — they cannot use political pull as directly as the firemen. These latter make it plain that with time they may show the superior "efficiency" of two days' work or even of one. A labor tribune says our troubles would end if we paid the wage-earners "what they ask."

Hearing of defects in our Civil War, because of jealous bickering among the generals, Artemus Ward did better still; he said the remedy was simple. Make every man in the army a general and there could be no jealousy.

This contagion quickly reaches the unorganized, skill-less labor on the street as it comes within the circle of city politics.

In a suburb of Boston, it is just announced that the, " Mayor gladdened the hearts of the city employees yesterday when he announced that the minimum wage for those in the service of the city would again be raised. It should be at least five dollars a day."

This mayor will, of course, be the idol of the beneficed labor until some other political aspirant outbids him. Not even the most unskilled and leisurely labor on our streets will long *stay* gladdened. Without the least trouble, they will find as many pressing reasons why they should have five dollars as that they should have four. It will not occur to these employees, nor indeed to any one in town, that more work is to be done for the higher pay. They will make no more extra effort than will our Massachusetts legislators after voting their own higher pay. The comment on these grasping importunities is almost too obvious. They have nothing to do with poor or rich as a class. They are as universally human as hunger and ambition are human. If this overdraft is sin or miscalculation it holds us in a common frailty.

Is the time at hand when we may learn a common lesson in social restraint? The earth-home has no store to satisfy all cravings stimulated by artificial wants.

Is there any solving of a dilemma like this? With perfect certainty it may be written that neither laws, systems nor " isms " in any kind will either now or ever bring us a snail's pace nearer such a goal, except in creating atmosphere and conditions in which, all together, we learn a spirit of accommodation, of yielding, of give-and-take in a world either too poor or too wise to gratify the total of desire.

I have somewhere read that with none of us does the devil have so easy a time as with those who can satisfy all desires. Though this impatient urgency of labor has in it the very soul of progress, it is at present an obstacle.

II

There is another, no less formidable,— the feudal and warlike temper of too many employers.

If it could be decided by secret ballot with no fear of public reprobation, a majority of employers would quickly make an end to trade unions in this country.

It is a common belief among them that men and women workers would be better off without unions, that they would be more steadily employed and suffer no diminution in wages. This is the other obstacle which the very preliminaries of industrial reconstruction must encounter in the United States. It would of course be said, " We do not object to labor organization." " They may join or not as they please, *but* "— we then have the familiar qualifications about " interference " especially of outsiders, together with the flag-raising and a fine defense of American freedom. The one meaning in these solemnities is that — unless forced to it — they will not accept the logic and the reality of collective bargaining. Yet if the labor union has come to stay, if its organic strength steadily gains from multiplied locals up to national and international bodies, it is ill-considered to have no plan or thought about it except to abuse, oppose or circumvent it. If the world over, industrial development creates trade unions as naturally as it brings new and closer organization on the side of capital, it should convince men still under the influence of reason that some constructive adjustment is necessary between the two forces. In an age of high industrial organization, labor must also have the help of that most dreaded nuisance "*outside*" representatives. It must have it if for no other reason than to bring upon the scene those who run no risk of discharge. But this one is of minor consideration. From local organizations labor like big business has passed into district, state, national and international associations. Accepted representation is as essential here as it is in politics. It is as essential as are those walking delegates for big business called attorneys. In many industries, mere local representation in no sense stands for the full strength of unionism in that industry. Many of these outside labor agents display an arrogance which fully explains the employer's hostility and too often justifies it. But these defects are incidents to every growing democratic movement, political or economic.

Forgetting the parental eye, Bacon says that all reforms at birth are like new babies, ugly and misshapen. Both collective bargaining and full industrial representation (as distinct from individual, local and craft and representation) must be recognized and embodied in the nation's workshop in spite of its ugly features.

Meantime the employer's antipathy has its own explanation. His day's job has little to do with "long run views," or with large social views of any kind. It has even less to do with imposing forecasts of industrial reconstruction. The employer is concerned and rightly concerned with a mechanism for turning out the best possible profit on his investment in a future over which he has some practical influence. It is from the exigencies of this more immediate task that he thinks and speaks. It is for this reason that for years the public will have to listen to tales of trade union abuses. They have been many and often gross. As with democracy itself, these abuses are rank enough everywhere, but in the United States we have been so belittered by an overhasty immigration as to add four-fold perplexities. Nowhere will this friction and misunderstanding baffle us more than in adjusting industry, law and public opinion to the growth and federation of the wage-earner's power.

Labor's fight for the "closed shop," for example, will result in friction so dangerous as to call for all the intelligence and fair-mindedness available. The American people are by no means prepared to admit the "closed shop" for universal application. They now oppose it because they believe it to involve a vicious discrimination against millions of wage-earners who want some freedom of their own. Hardly one worker in a dozen belongs to labor organization in this country. The Government cannot dragoon this great majority and force it into unions, though governments are going far in this direction.

While discussion need not be wasted on this issue, it would be folly to ignore labor's dread of the open shop. It would be another and greater folly not to recognize that what is practically the closed shop has got to be recognized under certain conditions and in certain industries. There are conditions in which collective bargaining is impossible without it, and what is more, situations under which state action in relation to labor assumes the necessity of what is in reality completely unionized shops, organized with employers' associations.

None of our industrial centers are without employers who combine expressly to use the open shop to destroy unionism itself. Their legal spokesmen are very astute in appealing to "liberty" and other sacred names dear to the public. Collective bargaining, when it was as legitimate as any employer's association in the land, has been crushed out so often and by means that many employers do not dare disclose, that labor has felt itself driven to this closed shop propaganda. In collecting material on this subject ten years ago, I was repeatedly told by trade union men, "We know of course that the closed shop can't cover the whole labor class, but we have to fight for it in many industries as the only weapon against employers who stop at nothing to root out unions."

The war, moreover, has brought its crisis in the attitude of governments and in the reasoning of a great many employers. Bewildered or outraged because the Government makes friends and partners of organized labor; bewildered by their own sense of helpfulness before the autocratic ignoring of the old business ways, these men of affairs have had to think things out anew. "What can it mean that about every competitive principle on which we were brought up is overruled?" A great many of these have set their teeth to "get even" after the war. The result of their thinking is to clean the slate of all the nonsense involved in "democratizing" the administration of business. They believe it to be as impossible as it would be injurious. In spite of price fixing, collective bargaining, living-wage and other sentimentalities, these practical men propose to take their chances. They believe that things will come their way again. Labor has been on the run during the war, but the running was by the employer eager to offer a higher wage. In the days ahead the running is to be reversed. It will be toward the employer. This gives him what he has lost. Under "supply and demand" with labor competing against itself, we are to have once more the good old days.

It would be a gloomy outlook if views like these were to control the main business leadership of this or of any other country. It would be for the nation what it would be for the world to drop back into the secret, autocratic ways of the old diplomacy,— each nation administratively organized to trick other peoples out of any and every advantage open to superior cunning or force. Too much business in this country has had this character and still has it. It has been attended with inconceivable waste of every natural resource. It has left a curse of periodic unemployment and of glutted town life with forms of poverty and artificial inequality which made the growing unrest each year a greater peril.

To go back to these costly crudities would discredit every claim even to ordinary prudence. When the smoke has well cleared, we shall be left in an atmosphere far more highly charged with democratic expectation and democratic purpose.

In all our loquacity about the coming democracy, the fact has to be taken into account that an army of strong men no longer believe in its desirability. As a matter of course, they accept a nebulous political liturgy to which the name democracy has been given. But as the demand arose that the implied equalities were to pass into economic and business activities, disbelief and cynicism are outspoken. One acute expression of this skepticism is in their attitude towards most of the popular peace methods to prevent industrial strife. To them, strife is what competitive industry means. Like those who hold it to be an amiable sentimentalism to think that wars can be stopped, these realists in business ask us to face the facts. Their real belief is that it is all a "struggle for existence." Such as cannot or will not hold their own, naturally go to the wall or euphemistically "fall into their proper places." Group interests, it is held, are too touchy, too numerous, too diverse; above all too shifting for permanent peaceful settlement. "Let us then so arrange our business that we can fight with the best weapons in our hands."

Before the war closed, on an occasion which brought together business leaders in the big industries from different parts of the country, I could find but one man who did not say plainly that he should use every means which he considered safe to beat unionism. Most of them had had plenty of experience with labor organizations. Almost to a man, they were in the fight because the union, in proportion to its strength, prevented or hindered *discipline and control*. " I had collective bargaining several years," said one. " I couldn't discharge a man without fooling away days with a committee. My output dropped and I was simply losing my hold on the thing I had built up." This fairly summarized the objections of others. Every one of these men belonged to a capitalistic organization — some of them against their will. Most of them admitted " in theory " that labor had every right to organize which was claimed by the employer. But only one of them would admit that labor could be trusted with the power and leadership implied by strong organization. These vigorous men thought power in their own hands was perfectly safe but " if employees organize, that means the appearance in my office of a union official from another State or half way across the continent to direct the men in my plant. No business can stand that, nor do we propose to submit to it."

It was this offensive practical nuisance of what was felt to be ignorant interference, which closed the door to all general reasoning on the question. Again, these employers had learned through their own associations that they could as a fact circumvent the union. They had collectively given their minds to the subject. They had learned to stand by each other and to deal summarily with their own scabs, that is, the weaker employers who wanted their own " liberty " even against their own business associates. Some of the employers' associations have agencies through which the blacklist is as effective as it is safe from any law.

In a word these and thousands of others of their kind have come to believe quite honestly that the abuses of unionism are so extreme as morally to justify their opposition. Yes, even justify the systematic use of spies, detectives and thugs if the occasion calls for them. It is tit-for-tat between both organizations. There is not a trick in this industrial war that is not known and practiced by some of our trade unions, and it is so little realized how much of this rough work goes on in both camps and *why* it goes on, that I give a single illustration. It is not a fancied, but an actual, strike — one of scores from the fighting lines of industry. In terminology, in tactics, in ruthless disregard of neutrals, it has every characteristic of war. In a great industry with but a tiny fraction of violence which blackens the tradition of mining and building industries, we take up the strike at that moment when it quivers on the edge of failure or success.

In this inflamed hour, it matters not a fig whether we are considering employers or employed. Both are extremely likely to resort to force and lawlessness. It has been done by both sides hundreds of times since 1890. If you ask either party why lawlessness was resorted to, you get, in essence, Germany's excuse for entering Belgium; "It's too bad, but we just had to do it." They think this because, when on that tremulous edge of winning or losing, everything depends (with the employer) on keeping just enough men at work to make the strikers (and perhaps the public) believe that business can continue without the help of those on strike. The employer may be wholly honest in trumpeting before the pubiic all the great terms about "liberty" and "human rights." Many of his men and women want to stay on the job, many have debts, many have families, sickness, and every possible reason not to strike. It is the best moral and tactical defense of the employer to focus attention on these and on their protection. He may thus strengthen a good cause for himself or he may conceal a bad cause.

In the actual strike here considered, in the most strained and doubtful moment, those remaining at work — scabs from the labor point of view — go to the employer asking protection in reaching their houses or leaving them. If intimidation or slugging has begun, the police will protect the workers *for a certain distance* about the factory, but obviously cannot personally conduct every man and woman to and from the dwelling-place. *This is the danger zone for thugs of both parties.* The police cannot cover it, therefore private agencies or their own men are appealed to by employers to frighten or beat up troublesome picketers.

On the other side, labor in this decisive hour knows that it must scare or win over scabs enough to prove to the employer — to themselves and to the public — that they have the game in their own hands and that the employer is at the end of his rope.

To secure a balance of numbers at this parting of the ways the union often falls back on lawlessness. It must persuade or terrify enough of those at work to get this favorable balance. Its intimidators or hired thugs go straight for that area where police protection ends and there get in their work. It is part of the hilarity to jockey with the employers' thugs or bribe them — to add a few dollars daily to what the employers already pay them to see that the protection for the employer doesn't jeopardize the strikers' cause. Here, of course, the spying and the bribing run indiscriminately across the line between employer and employed. To add scores of strikes far blacker in detail, is to look upon the actual picture of a great deal of industry in the United States. Nor should it be omitted that in this sombre story the hired attorney is often a more subtly mischievous influence than are those for whom he works.

As between pot and kettle in the industrial clash, no one will nicely balance the guilt or make it easy for us to take sides. No one, however, gets a hearing (or deserves to get it) before the employing class and its beneficiaries if he ignores the glaring evils in labor organization.

I therefore hasten to say that I am fully aware of trade union treacheries and improprieties. I have a most ample record of them, corrupt leaders, hired thugs, despicable forms of violence, restricted output culminating in sabotage so stupidly destructive as to suggest dementia. All these brutalities are a part of trade unionism in the United States, but in the large total of the movement it is exceptional. In judging it, we are dealing with labor at its worst.

But what is the employer at his worst? What has been the worst in much of our great financiering, in railways, insurance, sugar, capitalistic exploitation of our natural resources; in our mining and contract building in cities? Which party in these deviltries has touched the lower level?

To raise the sins on the side of capital does not free labor from its guilt, but we shall avoid hypocrisy if we tell the whole truth, namely, that the record of misbehavior is just as ample on the other side. There has been in the United States nothing dirtier or more lawless than that done directly under the dictates of capital. Instigated corruption of legislation and the spy system have more rotting effect on social tissue than most of the misdeeds of labor. This common sinning is here mentioned solely that we may have a fairer start in our discussion.

No scheme of industrial peace can avoid reckoning with this class. It will have no such tether as it had during our civil war because the public has been roused to some sense of the iniquity and because thousands of employers are honorably awake to the danger and are themselves setting an example of disinterested public service.

It is an illusion however to suppose that other thousands are not in this primitive fighting mood as a permanent possibility. Least of all do they believe in such peace "democratically determined." They are good humored about the "pretty fooleries" of welfare work but as something to tolerate and nurse along as one would deal with an extravagant whim of wife or child. Even if a minority, we are blind to the real influence they exert in combative industry.

In proportion to their strength and success, they compel other employers to imitate their methods.

As war literature has its great authorities who defend war as a permanent physical and moral necessity, so business has its able cynics who tell us the struggle for existence will go on in trade and commerce, as it has in the whole animal creation.

They hold it to be only a question of selecting "fitness" or what they call such. To be "unfit" is to fail as you deserve. Now that transportation and the mechanics of communication have thrown every race and continent into this competitive conflict, the sources of strife and the necessity for it are multiplied. To discover and to train the instincts and the faculties required for leadership, every spur must be sharpened for this larger cockpit. This is their tone. It is also the tone of a great deal of trade union leadership.

For the individual money maker they draw one comforting conclusion. As in the older and bloodier warfare, there are industrial "peace periods" in which productive work goes on and savings accumulate, so our industrial militarists believe it to be just as true in the commercial world, but they hold out this hope. The individual may always have his gamblers' chance of "making good money" in these quiet spaces.

Their reasoning is simple, strikes are always to be expected; destructive theories of taxation, socialism, communism are in the air and they are not to be stopped. "Let us then get to business!"

A great landowner told the Governor General of Canada, Earl Grey, that the single taxers were probably right, but added "the present system will last as long as I have any use for it." In every busy center are men to whom that is a first principle of action. Many of them have flirted with arbitration or even welcomed it so far as they could use it to protect their interests. They have tried welfare work only to turn away because it was troublesome and still more because it was likely to stir up expectations that could not be satisfied. " I will deal squarely with my men, pay good wages and take my chances " is the attitude. The best of these are often respected by their labor force quite as highly as those who have elaborate " benefits " or even a closed shop. Why then should they bother? " Let 'em strike — I can make money enough between drinks."

From the point of view of their direct material " self-interest, I have never heard a good answer to these employers. With intelligence and tact, they may save themselves from much nagging annoyance. Yet something is now in the air upon which these industrial belligerents count as little as did the German General Staff upon the easily awakened moral and democratic forces of the world. Even on the plane of a dwarfish self-interest the good old days are passing. On a plane even a little higher, where we see capitalism in process of change and readjustment, this " between drinks " policy is every day of more doubtful value. The pith of it is a surviving fatalism, the overcoming of which is as good a definition of progress as one can give.

The world has never been without it. For centuries wise men thought slavery a necessity from which no society could ever free itself. Only as the slow evidence came in (as in our own South) that industry was safer and more productive without slaves did these obstinacies die out. When Denmark freed her serfs, disaster was predicted. The serf, it was said, was indispensable to agriculture. There were of course great evils, but they must be borne. Only when it appeared that free paid labor was more productive and better for the employer did the illusions about serfdom give way. Close upon the eighteenth century an English queen died of small-pox. Men great in the state, in the church and even in the medical profession, took this scourge as a "visitation" and as such unavoidable. I have heard a kindly and very distinguished German professor argue that no nation could give up the duel without loss of the most precious social possession, "personal honor." We have made gains enough over some of these superstitions to give us hope. It is a hope based on changes in the employing and in the labor class. We have the new spirit growing among employers. We look now to such indications as there are, that an answering spirit is at hand in specific labor groups which may make possible, enough coöperation to guide us through the unknown vicissitudes ahead. This involves critical study of the isms unfriendly to the present order as we know it.

I begin with the most ancient and close with the most recent.

CHAPTER IX

LESSONS FROM THE COMMUNISTS

I

ESPECIALLY at this time, no adequate statement of socialism and its probable destinies seems to me possible without reference to communism. Five years ago, this would not have been true. It is not an accident that communism follows upon the heels of war. War devastates not only property but it devastates ideas about property. It is not an accident that the war-impact turns the communistic impulse from its peaceful tradition to one of threat and violence. Between the "communism of persuasion and good will" and that of an armed minority, the difference is like that between the Quaker and the fighting Moslem. The peaceful communisms furnish the best documentary evidence of the value and necessity of private property as distinct from its abuses. In our own country, practical attempts to realize communist ideals have converted some thousands of men and women — not in the least to the "capitalist system" but to the cultural uses of private possessions.

Socialists are wholly right in their vehement protest against confusing their ideal with that of communism.

I deal with the latter first, not only because it had the field many centuries before its more scientific variation, but because war has inflamed every communistic passion. In the past this most daring economic ideal had been put in practice by millions of people, as it had been repeatedly given literary form by men of genius in different lands.

Yet if socialism gets control, its enemy the communist will be instantly at the gates:— indeed it will be already inside the gates. The communist has always chaffed the socialist as the socialist chaffs the capitalist and the bourgeois. He ridicules the socialist prudences, opportunism and truckling to the property instinct. From its first day, any socialist society would have its main problem with these more sweeping perfectionists.

Utopian colonies, especially in our own country, throw so much light upon this world-issue, that I turn back to them.

The recent war has created a communistic revolution. If democratic sentiment gains headway, we shall have no future war without these ever more radical uprisings. If private property is to be preserved, wars should be stopped. In three countries, we have been watching this extremest of all theories about property. We should have kept cooler heads if we had seen in Bolshevism something as old as the stone age. Property in common has had about every trial that man can imagine. It has been backed by brute force, by legal sanctions, by religious appeal and by secular persuasion.

Recently we have observed it in Russia, Hungary, and German cities with the use of all the old weapons. In every progressive stage man has eventually got the better of it, as he will in the present instance, if labor be given a fair chance. With such opportunity and with business burdens of its own, no class will oppose communism more than the working class.

It is more than twenty-three centuries since one of the wisest men in any age wrote in his utopia that no mother should know her own child. Women in the world now have the vote. What would they decide on this feature of Plato's Republic? Would a half of one per cent. stand for it?

At Guise in northern France, I visited the Familistère where certain very timid approaches were made in " socializing babyhood." But there was also motherhood which soon set at naught every extravagance in carrying it out, leaving some cautious experiments which have promise of much larger usefulness. Since the ninth century before Christ, men have looked for regeneration to communistic utopias. They were to be the great solution. Bands of men and women have set themselves apart at great sacrifice to realize some embodiment of the perfected life as prefigured from Plato to Lenine.

Rationalistic disapproval, raillery and the common sense objectors have had no effect in discouraging these millennial braveries. The check upon them came mainly through accumulated experience *from the inside.* This explains my present use of the topic. There are few records richer in suggestive guidance for our present needs. Only actual trial could teach a lesson so elemental as that isolated colonies implied asceticisms; an intimacy of contact and incessant fraternizing intolerable to all except the dullest or most exceptional in the membership.

These defects could not be guarded against by warnings or by instructions. They had to be learned by trying. Though rarely of working class origin, American utopias have had the most effective criticism from socialist writers, and especially from those who have lived in them.

Their age and world diffusion alone give value to these ventures.

For five thousand years, there has probably been no century in which individuals, larger or smaller groups have not tried outright to create a New Society. Both in despairing and in hopeful periods, men of idealistic inclination have revolted against the harsh facts and limitations of existence. In their effort to escape, they have turned to utopia. No resource of metaphysics or of religion; no degree of self-abnegation has been left unexhausted to realize these "visions of perfection."

Every kind of government has been tried, theocracies,

oligarchies, republics and extreme democracies. Some in their vicissitudes have tried each in turn. Some have passed from purest democracies to practical despotisms; some have reversed the process.[1]

In preparing a course of lectures on the history of utopias, besides gathering literature, I visited in Europe and in this country several of these societies. Six of them were still struggling on; a few others had passed out so recently as to have left stranded members from whom one could learn even more of the facts than in the hey-day of success. In selecting them, I tried to cover as far as possible different types;— religious and secular, socialist, communist and anarchist. It has been frequently recorded that these attempts have had their quietus. The utopian spirit has been subdued, but in no sense has it passed away. Much present day socialism; some of our single taxers, coöperators, syndicalists and " New Guilders " are as distinctively utopian as was Sir Thomas Moore or Edward Bellamy. A wise conservatism would set the highest value on the excursions of these knight-errants. They are the adventurers in an unknown that needs explorers even more than the physical world in older times.

The war has again roused the utopian impulse in the world. It is internationalized. Over fearful spaces it now returns to the savageries of force to get the will of the minority obeyed, even to the destruction of everything we know as democracy, these minorities copy too well the very vices they would overthrow. We shall try force as a remedy, but with that alone we shall fail. Until we supplement force by something more powerful and more dur-

[1] The Therapeuts among the Jews before the Christian era were strictly communistic in property distribution. In the midst of an accepted slave system, they refused its allurements and even went so far as to have nothing made for exchange or trade. This meant a life of ascetic severity. It also meant dissolution or dependence on charity; that is, allowing other people to pay their bills.

able, the welter will remain. It is from the voluntary utopias — those with " the holy scorn of force "— that we get our best instruction. It is these which tell us so much about ourselves in relation to property and self-government. It is in these that we see democracy its own critic and educator.

The millennial flight is easy and exhilarating in a book, but to trace the vision among men and women trying to get it into daily practice is to learn a great deal about all democratic aspiration and its possibilities. Some months ago, I saw a letter from an I. W. W. jailed in Aberdeen City. This is the utopia which he sees:

" There are no capitalists, only workers receiving the full value of the product of their toil. Central employment offices furnish jobs for all.

" There is no poverty, there are no jails, police, judges, armies or navies.

" The cities are clean and beautiful. Everywhere there are parks, wide streets, flowers, rows upon rows of fine, cozy and comfortable homes.

" The workers are no longer stoop-shouldered and consumptive-looking; the parks are filled with lovers; clean, healthy, beautiful women and handsome men are everywhere. They have plenty of pure food, shelter, good warm clothing, pleasure and education. All hearts and minds are turned towards solving the mysteries of the Universe."

This is the " good time coming " when all shall be better than well. Every school girl could put it on paper with variations dictated by temperament.

In More, Bellamy and in bits of Wells one sees this transition from dreaming to doing; from " the clean vision to the grimy fact " in quite amazing ways. No one who read Bellamy's " Looking Backward " on its first appearance, will re-read it to-day without new appreciation of the author's insight and genius. Much that excited laughter thirty years ago, is now read with the feeling that Bellamy is out-of-date; that science and organization have out-run his dream.

In the Utopia of Sir Thomas Moore a good deal of what his contemporaries thought harmless poetic fancies is now a political and social commonplace;— so much so as to put this dreamer among the most practical of men.[1]

More than this, some of the most successful businesses in the world are at this moment on the borderland between the utopians and our prevailing capitalism.

In Italy, France, England, Germany, the industrial field is dotted with working business models, in origin and intent, consciously connected with some one or other of the old dreamers. I saw an old workman at Guise whose faith in Fourier and the Familistère was still firm as was the faith of Albert Brisbane when in 1842, just before Brook Farm, he won Greeley and *The Tribune* to his cause.

Between the best of the utopias and much of our most enlightened business there is an unbroken trail. In following this trail with its beckoning by-paths, one falls in with all the economic and political ideals.

It is the road along which the thing called democracy is trying to find its way. Always a small minority breaks from the beaten social path to try experiments. Every would-be democratic movement (socialist, trade union and

[1] There are of course other than communistic utopias like Dr. Bode's "Indivi." ("Indivi, Ein absonderlicher Reisebericht," Leipzig, 1892.) I saw much of the writer in Germany in 1893. He was in correspondence with Herbert Spencer to whom he looked as the world's Savior from the curse and servilities of Socialism. Dr. Bode's religion was to interpret Spencer's individualism and that of lesser men like Auberon Herbert to his fellow Germans. It was either "Staatszwang oder Freiheit." There was no alternative between this brow beating State and the free activities of individual men and women.

coöperative, wherever these appear at their best) there we see specialized ability (political or economic) carefully selected and trusted with power. Wherever there is weakness, corruption, factional discord, leadership degenerates and loses stability.

Boucicaut's Store, Maison Leclaire, Godin's Iron Works are instances. I note these three because they sprang straight from utopian speculators. With scores of others, they are in that transition which separates us from still greater changes. What has happened to those that remain alive? All of them, like that one perhaps completest of all, the Seiss Optical Works, have found that no utopian departure from the property instinct was possible. The instinct could be modified and modified toward greater equality. But the social utiltiy of the instinct, gets powerful recognition in the whole field-practice of these idealisms.

Because of abuses, we are querulous now about minorities. On vital issues involving the necessity of change, a minority may be oftener right than the majority. It is the minority which breaks up the habitual herd-like ways of men. It is the minority which has among its members those with courage enough to face obloquy. This is what Frederic Douglas meant when he said, " One with God is a majority." The minority feels itself hampered in religion, in politics, in the property relation. Direct revolt against the inequalities of private property has led especially in the nineteenth century to hundreds of utopian endeavors. Even those laying conscious stress upon other features like religion or freer sex-relations were profoundly influenced by new ideals of property holdings.

The question is always there, " Must we forever go on with the table overloaded, its extreme upper tip possessing all the costly titbits, while poverty scrambles for scraps at the other end?"

" Is there anything of sacredness or finality in a distribution of wealth which surfeits the few while it pinches the many?" In most utopian programs is the expressed belief that these extremes are largely due to laws and customs made by the strong and the lucky. It is believed that law, custom and conditions may be so changed by the infused democracy that at least all "undeserved poverty" may be removed. Only in a negligible few of the programs is there a claim for anything like absolute and literal equality. But an equality in which "every faculty shall have its chance"; in which artificial privilege in its grosser and subtler shapes shall be cut out — this is everywhere in evidence in these schemes of regeneration. Oftenest too the concept of property is the rock which causes the first schism. So clearly is this seen in the religious period by the more spiritual leaders that all means are used toward utmost simplicity of life. Twenty-eight centuries ago, Jewish "Rechabites" refused property for the same reason. In Conrad Beissels' Community in Pennsylvania, founded in 1732, a gift from the Governor of 5000 good acres close at hand was refused because, as they replied to him, "it would be injurious to our spiritual life to accumulate much property."

What then is it which slowly undermines this abnegation? Why do those who start, careless of private possessions end by quarreling over them? It is chiefly because men gradually discover that property, personality and power go hand in hand. As long as the religious motive is supreme, this connection is obscured, but every step toward the secular standard shows the relation between private possession and personal realization and control over men and over events.

This personal influence (or power) is what all leaders in these communities seem most to crave. In no social groupings are the guides more jealous of their control over their following than in the most religious settlements. Nowhere do we find the autocrat more sharply etched. With Brigham Young in the saddle, the Mormon motto "Holiness to the Lord" had a sanctity and authority that the most absolute king might envy.

Once settled in Utah, the hardest and the dirtiest work was seen to be a necessity for all. The lack of water forced them to drudge at an irrigation system and to work out a plan of land distribution of the most difficult character. If one would have land, he must promise that he could make it fruitful. If he would have water, he must show that he could use it productively. There was no flirting with a communistic formula like "to each according to needs." Favors went according to *results* approved by the authorities. "If you will have two acres you must first show that you can improve one acre."

Long after it was known that rich mines were beneath their feet or in adjacent hills, they stuck to their spade-work because they were so ordered. If told to arbitrate a quarrel, they arbitrated. If told to buy only at their own coöperative stores and boycott the gentiles, they did not hesitate. Though Lehi brought the idea of coöperation from England, "democratic management" so vital in the English store, was not even discussed. "Holiness to the Lord" sufficed. This despotism was of course concealed as adroitly as the third Napoleon managed "the vote of all the people" to put him in power. The Head of the Church could not have a plebiscite; he could "refer to the popular vote" but the result was as certain as to any ward boss under Croker who had already counted the votes and knew the result. This veiled and unveiled autocrat, as we shall see, does not disappear from the trade union. Socialists and syndicalists alike know him. He has indeed a persistence which raises the question whether democracy can altogether dispense with him. The more enduring utopias (like the Rappites just faded out) have been religious bodies usually with the leadership of some impressive personality that could command discipline. A faith or a person of unusual influence serves the one highest test in these experiments, namely, that of selecting the type of adherent that will work, obey and submit to the conditions of social order.

Many of the colonies that die in the teething are made up of miscellaneous, unselected persons. Of one of the more recent failures we read: "From first to last, about five hundred others joined them, some from almost every State in the Union, and many from countries in Europe. This list of membership itself is a curious study. It is the United States in microcosm; among the members are old and young, rich and poor, wise and foolish, educated and ignorant, worker and professional man. There were temperance men and their opposites, churchmen and agnostics, freethinkers, Darwinists, and spiritualists, bad poets and good, musicians, artists, prophets, and priests. There were dress-reform cranks and phonetic-spelling fanatics, word purists and vegetarians." They try "pure democracy," but at the end we are told, "Every member was an equal partner, and while theoretically he was bound to obey his selected chief, practically he only did so when he pleased. His officer had no power to compel obedience, and no remedy against insubordination except his own resignation." To the last item, this is like the more extreme "Self-Governing Workshops" in which the workers choose one of their own for manager. If he happens to be a man of real quality, he may command discipline enough to keep the business on foot. The chances however are at least four to one that he will not be such a person and for this reason the "pure democracies" break up, or like some small profit-sharing copartnership, they continue with just enough business success to hold them together for longer or shorter periods. This educational process must be traced.

II

Whatever else democracy is to signify, it stands for an associated life in which the members generally have something to do in shaping the rules under which they are to live. Under capitalism, plutocracy has employed all the genial rhetoric of democracy to cozen the populace into the belief that it was the real law maker. The political awakening in the United States with the clamor for initiative, referendum and its congeners has come in part because people have learned how destitute of all real control they have been. They have learned that authority and legislative power were ingeniously concealed from them. But this happens even in some of the most religious of the utopias and much in the secular ones. The tablets of the law are brought down from some mountain height with precepts which leave a most democratic impression on the awed listeners. Very tardily in the religious group, the members discover that authority is not in their hands.

So long as there is extreme simplicity in the common life all goes well. Among the "Separatists" they so stand out against the world, even in the nineteenth century, as to make in most primitive ways almost everything they use. With every increase in material prosperity and closer contact with the outside world trouble is at hand. The sharper-witted see that those in control somehow acquire new power and new authority. This finally excites criticism and discontent. From this stage, the struggle is against what is essentially autocracy whether religious or secular. It only develops more rapidly in non-religious societies.

This uneasiness at the sight of power passing to the few suggests something about the future of democracy which deserves more study than can here be given.

When John Stuart Mill had conceived his main plan of economic and political reform; after it had been repeatedly discussed with Austin, Roebuck, his father and other men of distinction, he was profoundly disturbed by asking himself the simplest question: "What if all these reforms are carried through?" It came to him that not very much after all could be accomplished; that other and harder problems would instantly arise.

Thinking men in the utopias have this experience. It is first believed that if only property can be distributed in some spirit of justice all will be well. As some approach to this is made; as the idea of it and the logic of it become familiar to the mind, doubts arise. Men ask, "Well, what of it!" What if the earth becomes common property and all the members get at least "all the product," what difficulties, questions, tasks will still be there for solution? It is like asking the ardent single taxer, when you get every penny of economic rent and every foot of land is accessible to all, what then? The struggle will be on more equal terms and this is ample to justify the agitation. But with single tax in full swing, the deeper *human* problems remain over for settlement.

This at any rate is what comes to the surface at some stage in utopian experience. It arises among the meditative type as distinct from the man of action. It appears, I think, because the spirit of equality among men is not reached through any manner of wealth distribution.

In some of the most unworldly and fraternal of these utopias there is little trace of "consent of the governed" much less of "crowd direction."

The leader may be a saint with all the outward marks of humility, he is yet almost certain to remind us of the dictator. Let me take one of the best, E. L. Gruber, one of the founders of what is now "The Amana Community" in Iowa. He was a model of piety 200 years ago in Hesse where this society began. But he seems never to have doubted that he was to be a Boss not of man's selection but of God's. Amana boasts of large community life, three generations without a lawyer or a beggar, some claiming they have no beggars *because* they have no lawyers.

The twenty-one "Rules for Daily Life" left by this founder are an exhortation to piety and extreme puritan simplicity. The first Rule reads, "To obey God without reasoning and through God our superiors."

If a colony of 2000 souls like Amana implicitly believes this rule and willingly acts upon it, what a power is possessed by the leader! He too like God is to be obeyed "without reasoning." Whatever their saintliness, few men can so represent the Almighty without overplaying the part. This is what happens in autocracies, religious and profane. People were very saucy with the German Kaiser because the Deity was so exclusively and noisily appropriated for imperial uses. There was nothing in the least peculiar about this. No monarch who accepts or to whom his people concede an authority divinely bestowed will be silent about it. If a people once acquiesce in the claim that their ruler holds his power directly from Heaven rather than from common folk, that people will hear about it so often that they cannot forget it. No solemn occasion will pass without mentioning it.

To bring God upon every scene where your own private or family interests are at stake; to bring Him in clothed in your own colors, with sword drawn in your own cause, is a sanction and an asset which no practical politician will overlook. A Deity so accommodating can even be made the scapegoat for blunders and for sins.

When he was outside Germany, the "philosopher-chemist," Professor Otswald said, "in our country God the Father is reserved for the personal use of the Emepror."

When Bluntschli led in the teaching of political science, he received a letter (1880) from the first of German soldiers, Moltke: "War," he said, "is a part of the eternal order instituted by God."

The divine favorites in utopia are an improvement on

the military uses of the Deity. There is no blood lust in our American utopias. There is however a most dangerous appeal to divine sanctions to cover personal and private policies.

Without those imposing approvals from the spirit world, mormonism never could have collected its tithes or withstood its enemies for a decade.

Some of the wildest communistic supervisors have been the sturdiest autocrats, hiding the fact by their gift of religious interpretation. They have brought in God or God's word whenever these were needed. The fling at the capitalists that they will do anything for the people except get off their backs is true of many of these religious preceptors.

Though no better for illustration than a score of others, I select one known well by many who are still in the flesh.

Because they were against all war the forerunners of Amana were welcomed by Philadelphia Quakers in 1817.

We know their history for a century. It is full of gentleness, simplicity and good faith. The very minimum of sacrifices necessary to the communistic life never could be secured without devout faith that God was pleased by the offering. When the head of a society loses this ghostly support, the skeptical, the energetic and especially the young, with eyes already upon the outer world, begin to leave. The docile ones remain to carry on the tradition even when they know the end is not far off.

An old " Separatist " still alive in 1900, told me his old faith had not changed.[1] All of them, he admitted, had

[1] To Dr. Howard N. Brown, Emerson gave a conversation he had with Mr. Alcott. He thought Alcott should go out of the world first. Asked why this compliment was paid to him, Emerson replied:

"Because I can give a better account of you to the world than ever you could give of yourself."

expected the millennium too soon. He was as sure as ever, however, that Heaven was "the perfect communism" and "all of us," he said, "are worthy to go there only so far as we practice communism in this life." He would no longer take orders from "mere man." He had transferred his autocracy directly to the other world. He wanted no man to stand in God's place, but he also saw that his society could not survive this change.

He knew that the dry, secular motive was not enough. He had studied other colonies and saw how rapidly they fell by the way, if no kind of religion bound them together and furnished human directors who could command obedience because God was at their side. He had come to hope men might finally be educated to "the great unselfishness" of communism by purely earthly experience of its benefits. He thought "some generations" at least would be necessary for this training. A faithful utopian of such intimate experience as that passed through by W. D. Hinds, wrote late in life: "While the author's experiences and observations have given him an abiding faith in Communism as the ultimate basis of human society, they have also given him a lively appreciation of the losses and miseries resulting from ill-considered and ill-conducted social experiments; and he would cry 'Halt!' to every one proposing to found or join a communistic, semi-communistic or co-operative colony without the fullest consideration." [1]

This is the inner history, not of one or two, but of scores.

Nor is there any greater change in human relationship than in this slow passing of the leader "obeyed without

The most enlightening and judicious testimony I have ever heard of utopian ventures came from those who thus followed after; sometimes with fond and regretful criticism, sometimes, as with Charles A. Dana of Brook Farm memories, with a reminiscence half raillery, half cynicism.

[1] "American Communities," close of Introduction.

reasoning"; obeyed because, as interpreter, he speaks as God speaks. Leadership with God in the background is the full equivalent of autocracy. When the gods fade the colony fades.[1] The elected guides must now appeal to purely human motives. These bring in the prizes and the glitter of the outer world to compete with the meager satisfactions which communism affords. Most profound of all the changes is this slow substitution of secular motives for religious sanction, but the autocrat does not disappear.

At the dazzling height of Ferdinand Lassalle's power over his followers, he was not only a ruthless dictator, but he openly defended it. All the fine words about equality were true, he said, but they could not bear their proper fruit, he added, except under long cultivation. Meantime ordinary folk were to be led, they were to obey, and none but Lassalle should be the chosen one. He could privately jeer at this, but he delighted in the super-human attributes with which his followers clothed him and in this does not differ from religious dictators.

III

I have dwelt long on this feature because it is inseparable from the property relation under these communisms. Time brings its reflection and doubts to many members. They bear the taunt from the outside, " Ah! they are growing prosperous in their business. That will bring them off their high horse." If this has its grain of truth, another feature was more important. Thousands of colonists had to be taught by the very severe trials that all equality forced

[1] Without the devoutness of a real religion, we should not have had in this country fifteen distinct settlements of Shakers who " for more than a hundred years lived prosperous, contented and happy lives, making their land bloom like the fairest garden; and during all these years never spent a penny for police, for lawyers, for judges, for poor houses, for penal institutions or any like improvement of the outside world."

from without or narrowly interpreted in their constitution, stifles liberty.

A Communist, faithful but of singularly open mind — a leader at the Putney, Vt. Colony, tells us very frankly that many become restless under the communistic division because of its " hampering effect on individuality."

If those possessing this gift get into leadership, they may find satisfaction in exercising their strength. But all cannot be leaders. The steady exodus of these more vigorous spirits may everywhere be noted. Their testimony would form the best of all commentaries on communistic limitations.

A man like Josiah Warren of idealistic temper but of intellectual force joined the Owenite Colony at New Harmony. He did his best to " submit " and to live its life. In his " Sovereignty of the Individual " we see the crisis in his thought from experience in the colony. John Stuart Mill borrows a phrase from Warren whom he calls in his Autobiography a " remarkable American." Warren was interested in what we to-day like to call psychology. He found men and women acting from most unexpected motives after they had solemnly committed themselves to " a great and unselfish cause."

It was " the weakness (or strength) of the individual " that broke up the Colony. Here was the disease. There was no cure save in more vigorous personality. If communism failed in this, it was not a discipline but " an asylum for weaklings."

When the crisis of 1881 came to the communists of Oneida, this desire for " more individual liberty " was an articulate ground for bringing in again individual ownership of property. Two socialists wrote to the " Altruist " (Apr. 1909) : " We could never think of placing ourselves where we could not decide for ourselves what to do with the proceeds of our own labor."

An explanation like that of Warren is too simple. Much of the revolt leading to utopian ventures results from competitive intensities in capitalism which are intolerable to many men and women. They would welcome a simpler life and we should all be the richer for faculties they might there develop.

Well on in the nineteenth century, as machinery quickens its pace and town life becomes more congested, communities appear in which "release from slavery," "more leisure" are set out among the attractions. Men and women leave a mill town because they "will not submit to become mere cogs in a wheel."

"Let us go out where we can live in quietness and in dignity"; "Let us escape from the slave lash of competition where every faculty is warped by struggles that have neither meaning nor profit," are sentences which get instant attention from many types of men and women in our high-pressure society. These are not all the lazy or the devitalized. There are among them those whose faculty and capacity for enjoyment seem to be stunted in a company of business hustlers.

I found that admirable editor and citizen, Henry Wallace of Iowa, much impressed by this feature in a visit to Amana. In one of the "communist villages" is a mill of which I have a picture. Set down in Lowell or Manchester it would look like a whale oil lamp beside an electric light. One asks how it can hold its own against those huge modern structures which "scrap their machinery every ten or eleven years." The answer is that the people in Amana have been satisfied with relatively meager returns.

Talking with a farmer, Mr. Wallace notes the spirit of the place in a discussion on silos. The man said he was interested in silos. "I am a subscriber to your paper. I mean to have one, but I haven't got round to it." Yet he was not in the least unhappy in this belatedness. Going to the mill, Mr. Wallace finds the same atmosphere. He says, "The mill hands were not 'hurting themselves' by too much work, but looked placid and contented. There was a coffee pot in the center of the room, and one man took time off to pour himself a cup. Every one was working, but there was not the vigorous bustle noticeable in most American factories."

What would happen if a half hundred of these "placid and contented" people were shipped to Lawrence or Woonsocket? A few of them would take the quickened step and rejoice in the added income. A larger number might adjust themselves, but the placidity and contentment would vanish. Others would fail and become a charge upon the community.

It is one of the most damning counts against the present competitive wage system that its selective process — so stimulating on one side, is so destructive on the other. With automatic ingenuity, it picks out every gift useful *for immediate business ends,* while it ignores or discourages other capacities that may have equal or even higher worth. One may safely admit that these picnickers will always be with us. It may even be that they are the forerunners of a far-off way of living together in which "the right to be lazy" (I have a pamphlet with this title) will be acknowledged, in which the property relation will be as communistic as now in many private families.[1] One wishes that our present society were strong enough — not only to allow but to encourage voluntary experiments in this kind. They would jeopardize no social value because they cure or expose their own limitations. To see how this is done is to learn our best lesson about the tenacity and the utility of the property instinct. The changes now required are those which preserve and democratize this utility by ridding capitalism of all domineering privilege.

[1] A recent Community in Missouri explains that "it is only an enlargement of the family."

The tribute from the utopias is in the increasing recognition of these property values as they appear in changes in their constitution and by-laws. With a mass of other utopian evidence, we see in these concessions how long the instinct of private property is to survive.

In their first printing, these constitutions have high and confident appeals to the most disinterested virtues. It is taken for granted that men are naturally and miscellaneously so fond of each other that all sorts of obstacles may be overcome. There seems no doubt, for example, that they will hasten to overlook the nervous irritabilities which close and continuous personal contact — as in habitual eating at the same table — often induces.

In setting out for the millennium, their covenanters assume a collective sobriety, forbearance and self-mastery which require only new conditions and perhaps " a generation of proper child training " and the promised land will be theirs.

There is also another assumption; that liberty and equality are natural partners, whereas nothing has hitherto been found more difficult to harmonize. The documents tell us what equality is to mean. It has at first a hard literalness that would more surely stifle liberty than would the most ruthless of autocracies. There is scarcely an experiment of any duration in which this is not made bitterly clear.

In practically all the communistic and in some socialistic ones it is assumed that the property instinct is something accidental — about as easily removed as the appendix, or, at least that it will readily yield to an ideal of common possession.

If there is no religious bond, or if the bond has weakened, protests gather head until truculent majorities insist upon an overhauling of constitution and by-laws — as I once heard it put —" to give relief to what seems pent up in everybody."

"What is pent up in everybody?" Here is the crisis with its trail of experience centuries old. Even Rousseau said civilization began when men first put fences about their land. To the common good, they have taken down many of these barriers but only to erect and preserve them about other kinds of property. Whenever it is believed that the chief individual and social values depend on clearly definable ownership, "what is pent up in everybody" asserts itself. Nowhere is this better seen than in the agitations to revise their first utopian laws, so that these personal vigors may be expressed.

If differences in education and ordinary refinements among members were too marked, the result was a bluntness of personal criticism very trying to most men and women. In that most faithful account of frontier life, "The New Purchase," Mr. Hall who became the first Professor of what is now the University of Indiana, tells us what happened to them because of a "worked screen." "Powerful proud doing of stuck-up folks" was the comment on those who wanted some privacy or in any way to be screened. The author says (p. 81): "And I am sorry to say that in the 'Purchase' as in some other places, such opinion is found similarly expressed about extra cleanliness, decency, modesty, learning and the like, if these things exceed your neighbor's they subject you to suspicion, often to dislike and not infrequently to rancorous persecution,— scorn, envy, hatred, are felt for your real or supposed excellencies and acted out at the first opportunities." This long Icarian history is full of changes to escape these troubles but most significant of all are the changes which recognize the necessity of control over one's earnings.

Thus new rules were finally made against members "absenting themselves from labor" and then the majority decide "that those who would not work should not eat."

Toward the end, the battered constitution admits the right of private property.

In one of many, a Colorado colony founded in 1894, in a southwestern county to "maintain harmonious relations on the basis of coöperation" soon discovered that it could not "dig the necessary ditches for irrigation under its fundamental law." It practically discarded the first constitution and changed the articles of incorporation. Under the first by-laws, we read what kind of equality was aimed at. "All workers and officers should receive the same wages." The members stand this until the results are seen. Then the revolt begins. In this case it appeared that the surplus out of which all capital is made was so slow in coming, that they could not even continue their journal. After some six years' discussion we see the transformation in these words, "*to engage in no business except on the profit plan.*" They "could not get the necessary work done" and consequently had to "compromise." This shift from communism to all business "on the profit plan" is not a compromisae but a somersault.

The Icarians led by a man of genius broke (within some forty years) into seven differing colonies. In our own history, no utopian following had more persisting, ideal enthusiasm or displayed more practical efficiency than at Nanvoo. Yet, midway in its career, the members began to tire of each other at the common table. One member thought the disruption came, not because of the plan but because of "personal criticism that became intolerable."

The Australians who set out for Paraguay after the great strike in 1890 to create a "New Australia" were energetic, like-minded and singularly free from cranks or degenerates. If their leader fell short of what he asked "the brain of Jay Gould and the heart of Christ" he was clean, honest and far above average ability. A local Secretary of Legation who visited them was impressed by the appearance of the men and women as he was by the fertility of the great area to be made their home.

At first in the Constitution, "All the means of production in exchange and distribution" was to be held by the community. There was to be "community saving" to supply the needed capital, then "Division of the remaining wealth production among all adult members equally *without regard to sex, age, office or physical or mental capacity.*" A first payment of $300 before migration shut out the "undesirable." A Foreign Office Report of 1895 said these were "as fine a set of men and women as it was possible to collect anywhere and of a stamp much superior to any emigrants yet seen in South America."

As with Cabet's colonists, journeying from New Orleans to their Texas purchase, the first grumbling was over "what was omitted in the glowing prospectus." "Why were the swarms of mosquitoes never mentioned?" "Why were they not told that bachelors and those with small families must support the lazy and those who had large families?" When they found this out, several bachelors left the colony for good.

At the start these were not to work for each other for wages, or lend to each other for interest, or take rent from each other for land or houses, but to care for and work for and share with each other in fellowship.

Every one of these prohibitions slowly disappears.

Native labor is brought in and paid wages with the published excuse that this labor was from "the outside and they couldn't apply their principles except within the colony."

At the end, what one of them called "the day of freedom" arrived; "By a vote of the majority, it was decided that the Constitution should be altered; henceforth every man would be entitled to dispose as he pleased of the fruit of his own labor, and a new incentive was given to industry."

LESSONS FROM THE COMMUNISTS

I have often heard the communistic features of our first Colonies at Plymouth and Jamestown scoffed at as " proving nothing for our own time." It will instruct any such doubter to go back to those records and compare the psychological reasons for restoring some form of private ownership with the same experience as in most of the modern communisms.

CHAPTER X

SOCIALISM

Less noisy at the present moment than Communism (with its more panicky name), socialism is a world-fact to be seriously reckoned with. With varied and instructed guidance, it leads in the attack on capitalism and on those who are trying to make the best of it. Every syndicalist sect, all anarchists and communists are of course among the enemies, but socialism has the leadership. It offers the most definitely reasoned case against the present economic order. We are told with precision what forms of private property are to be destroyed and what the destroying means. It is often indignantly denied that socialism would "destroy" any property. As in Bacon's figure, wealth too much heaped up is like a manure pile which rots and is a nuisance until spread widely over the ground. "We would diffuse wealth, not destroy it," "In socializing property, we strengthen it," are modes of exposition. When the metaphysical display is over, it is admitted that quite stupendous individual possessions are destroyed in the sense that all control over them is taken from the individual and handed over to the community. Then, with marked differences of opinion, we are told what forms are to be left in strict private control or "ownership." We shall gain much if we put aside all the refinements of literary, poetic, metaphysical and ethical definitions of socialism. In all these, there is too little that is in any way distinctive. Socialism asks a very radical overturning in our notions of property. It attacks other objects, but most property as now privately held is its enemy. To call it a struggle between capital and labor is not exact. It is not a strife between capital and labor, but between human beings,— a minority of whom own and control certain forms of property. By a lusty and ever more clamorous majority, this restricted ownership is disputed.

The possessing minority appeals to a sacrosanct legal system under which their holdings should be secure. " We have earned our property or inherited it under laws made by the people. Except through taxes, it cannot be taken from us unless by breaking faith with rules which all of us have made." " Yes," is the reply, " but you made those laws because you were on the inside with influence enough to control politics. Every one of your laws was made to protect your own individual or class interests. By the same methods we, the people, can unmake or modify every act. To that we are consecrated. For that socialism exists."

To save the reader from a tiresome rehearsal of these discussions already threadbare, I submit both for statement and for argument a series of very simple cases. The whole wage-earning class has now come into the discussion. It is my belief that it will have far more to do with all final decisions than any other part of society.

My choice of illustrations is therefore determined largely by their fitness to call out this final judgment of labor about property and the forms under which it is held and disposed of, as well as the extreme to which labor is likely to carry out the more radical projects.

Before passing to these illustrations, one concrete instance of the larger theoretic aim may be given. At an election a few years since, it was said in the socialist appeal for votes, that $6,000,000,000 go as " a free-gift to mere owners of land and capital. This of course is taken from the nation's yearly income. These owners of land, machines and money are *as owners* not workers in any sense. They are paid the stupendous six billions solely for owning things."

Socialists ask why these fortunate possessors should get such rewards added to their ownership. Is not ownership its own sufficient reward? Should one *own* and be paid for it besides?

They say further that the six thousand million is taken from the wage-earners. It is "a free gift of an amount that would put hundreds of thousands of families above the poverty line." Our present business system is thus convicted of robbing labor to an extent which becomes the chief source of national weakness, creating meantime all the grotesque extremes of material inequality which have brought ruin upon so many peoples.

Now these statements are not from some penny-a-liner in an obscure socialist sheet. They are signed by a long list of persons many of whom have national reputations for various and deserving public service. These names are upon the faculties of leading universities from Columbia to Wisconsin.

While the six billions of our national wealth goes yearly from earners to owners, these signers of a " new Declaration of Independence," say further:

" The Federal Public Health Service states (Federal Public Health Bulletin No. 76) that an $800 income a year is required to enable a family to avoid actual physical deterioration through lack of decent living conditions; that more than half the families of working men receive less than that amount, that nearly one-third receive less than $500 a year, and that one in every ten or twelve receives less than $300 a year.

" Furthermore, in most cases these figures represent the labor, not only of the father, but of the mother and children of the family. While poverty stalks through the land like a spectre, the property-owning class amasses, by virtue of ownership alone, fortunes of fabulous size."

Thus are our capitalistic parasites put upon the grill. Is it true or partly true that labor is so shorn of its earnings? It is beyond measure more important to answer that question or to get light upon it than to waste good hours on issues which in no sense distinguish socialists from other faiths.

All the anxiety over poverty, unemployment, prostitution, crime, drunkenness, child labor, etc., is not a monopoly held by socialists. This party brings its own remedial proposal for these ills, but it is only one of many. Destitution and all the unmerited ills have long excited the growing sympathy of those who bring quite other solutions.

So important is the message of socialism; so obtuse and witless is a great deal of the opposition, so great a rôle is it to play in our immediate future that the first need is to know what differentiates it from those who admit the necessity of great changes, but seek to bring these about by different methods.

This six billion theft from labor is an assertion which really tells us something. We shall never intelligently take sides for or against socialism until we come to some decision on this claim.

With many others, I should have long ago joined that party if statements like the above (the six billion theft) had carried conviction. The statement does not call attention to the sentimental drapery which hangs about the subject, but touches the economic heart of it.

About no subject is there more verbose irrelevancy than that which fills the literature condemning socialism, as well as that which defends it.

It is now without excuse to mistake what socialists ask in the strictly business and political relation. To them the whole surplus in wealth production which passes into private hands from rent, interest and profits is a thievish deduction from what labor produces. As the rent of land should not be taken by the individual, but by the town or the State, because "the community creates it," so interest and profits should go to the whole of us and never privately to any of us. To believe only that the rent of land should go to the community, makes one a follower of Henry George but not a socialist. Socialism will have all that George would have, with interest and profits added. Practically every claim that socialists now make throughout the world has for its aim to get some slice of rent, interest and profits away from private persons into public possession. If in cities they ask to take our gas, trolleys, lighting, or to take railroads, mines, insurance, and other great business, it is because the public may itself secure this surplus. The socialist note in the "Plumb Plan" is that it takes away private profits and gives them over (if any are left) to all of us who are served by the roads.

In its age of innocence and freedom from responsibility socialism was thorough-going. It was a sin to hedge or qualify. Its first definitions are therefore important because they show what experience teaches in securing a response to great principles requiring sacrifice. If made by mature and disciplined men, socialist definitions have come to have so many qualifications as to be embarrassing. I listened to a recent discussion in which an able defender of the movement said his party did not want to take over "all industry," much less to destroy all private property. He wanted everybody to have a great deal more property "for individual disposal." He thought socialism would bring this about. If it reduced the dropsical incomes at the top, it would immensely lift up and broaden the level at the bottom. He said the nervous old women among the financiers were always talking about "leveling down" but never a word about the leveling up that was sure to follow. When asked why socialists did not want to take over all industries, he said it was impracticable and besides it was unnecessary. "All we need is the *basic* industries."

Then followed long quibbling as to what "basic" meant.

It appeared that the socialists in the audience differed among themselves quite as much as they did from those opposing their cause.

When asked what kind of property under socialism was to be so amply held and disposed of by individuals, he gave the classic answer "consumable property"; that is, property not derived from profits, interest, rent or inheritance. Here again the socialists present showed wide and even violent difference of opinion as to the amount and kind of individual possession this would leave.

Though somewhat too simple, this is what has come to pass in the history of socialist opinion and definition. It is not in the least to their discredit. It only shows the flexibility and intelligence which every growing movement must possess.

At first, we heard, "Socialism will do away with all poverty." Attention was called to this until criticism by socialists themselves made it appear absurd. The definition then changed to "Socialism will cure all *involuntary* poverty"— much closer to the fact — but still leaving us to flounder over the word "involuntary."

In its dogmatic beginnings, "Land, capital, and *all* the means of production" were to be taken from private possession. These were to be socially (or democratically) managed. In slip-shod discussion one may still hear or see in recent articles that *all* means of production are to be socialized"; "*all* private inheritance of property (except for consumption) stopped," "*all* the school children fed and medically cared for by the state" and of course "all private interest, profits and rents turned over to the public."

Politically, everybody is to rule and have voice in management. Socialist and labor representatives have long since learned a wholesome skepticism about all these first formulas. Even those have learned it who are in the purely political stage, as in the United States, long before the actual business control has been reached.

I have gathered hundreds of these definitions from which I select one to indicate fairly this turning from dogma to facts and practical possibilities. It is what happens in science, in religion, in education, everywhere indeed where there is progress. Socialists were first to point out these changes and to approve them.

No one in this country is more careful in his definition than Mr. Hillquit. To him, socialism is "the collective ownership of the social tools of production and the collective arrangement of industries based upon the use of social tools." Here we pass from "*all* tools" to "*social* tools." This little word "social," like "basic," so transforms the earlier characterization as to present the problem in a radically different aspect.

First it is "all the means of production," now it is only the "social means of production." The older definition was finally seen to be impossible when it was carefully thought out and even more when it was subjected to such tests as any socialist or coöperative community could supply. Socialists themselves came to see the absurdity of "taking over" or socializing thousands of the lesser "tools of production," from the woman's sewing machine (even when used to prepare goods for the market) to the machines on the farm though worked by wage labor. The aim of the new definition is to assure us that only the larger, more complicated and important machinery is to be socially owned and collectively managed. We know what is meant by "all machinery of production." Accurate inference from the term is possible. But we do not in the least know what any individual means when he says "only the *social* tools." "Social" is not only vague, but it is a term so subjective that it swells or shrinks according to the standards and experience of the speaker. One has but to ask socialists as I have often done, what the word means, to see how safely elusive it is. Mr. Hillquit (pg. 113 "Socialism in Theory and Practice") fairly takes the logic of his own definition. He says, "There are certain industries dependent on purely personal skill, such as the various arts and crafts, that from their very nature are not susceptible of socialization and other industries such as small farming that will, at least for many years to come, not be proper objects for socialization. These may continue to exist in a socialist society as individual enterprises side by side with the larger coöperative works." He concludes that "by far the greater and most important part of wealth production will be conducted by coöperative (socialistic) establishments."

In every country men of Mr. Hillquit's rank have come to this larger and looser description of their aims.

We are thus left where we may at least surmise what socialism will do to us if it proves victorious. We should have the combined arteries of transportation, the mines, shipping, factories, milling, meat packers, bakeries — indeed everything in the way of greater industry all run as we carry on the Post Office in which no one of us can invest a penny. For no individual is there any chance for profit or for interest. Now if all this comes about, we shall then be living under a system to which the word socialism would properly apply. It would so apply even if a good deal of small farming and small industry still went on with individual appropriation of profits and interest. To have industry so overwhelmingly socialized, that it could do as it liked with these little private dependencies — merely tolerate them because they could exert no influence — would leave us no name so properly descriptive as socialism.

Any one convinced that we are passing into such a régime may fairly take the name. If on the other hand one believes that however much is run by the State or "community-unit," there will be enormous developments of strictly private industry and land culture still with interest and profits;— believes moreover, that this free competition outside the socialistic and political control will be as necessary for industrial growth, as it will be to keep a bureaucratic state efficient and on its good behavior, he may legitimately decline to class himself as socialist. On the little " curve of evidence " presented in this volume, I have never seen good ground to doubt that though the socialistic function is certain to extend, the individualistic and voluntary forms will also extend. This is to be the great contest of the future. I thus lay stress upon the gulf which separates the original orthodox ultimate of socialist theory from the whole actual and practical problem presented.

I have heard a physician speak of " The New Science of Health and its Promise to eliminate all Sickness." We had only to take his health principles to heart, make them a part of our habits, and disease would disappear. This may be conceivable, but it has to do with a future and with a race of which we know nothing.

All the older and the present extremer claims of socialism are of this character. They ask of the race what it has neither the capacity nor the disposition to give. During the war it was natural for the strict pacifists to demand a tax of 100 per cent. on *all* profits. Over the whole field of production for everything necessary for war, from foods, clothing, medicines to munitions no one was to have a penny of profits.

But millions of socialists wanted the war fought through to a finish. Many of these were as uncompromising " for the complete elimination of profits," " Do not tax a scandalous twenty-two per cent. like the French or an eighty per cent. like the English," but " leave no blood money at all " was the tone of those who wanted " the victorious conclusion of the war." What conception of human motives have we here? What would have happened in every country if the millions of those making profits, normal as well as abnormal, had been deprived of this motive? Supplies would as certainly have failed as if every producer had been struck by paralysis. No class shows this with more absolute proof than the wage-earners or if we like the term better, " the proletariat."

Nowhere would these be put off with mere patriotic appeal. Like striking ship workers, they would " deliver the goods " but not a further stroke unless their wages went up and were kept up. Mr. Hoover showed his genius for good sense in insisting that normal profits to the producers were as essential in getting the war through as was the patriotic motive itself.

It is to these motives, as every man and woman may observe them, that I now turn rather than to the conventional objections against socialism. It is to have a great and increasing influence, but only as a partner in the coming reformation. From within, it is creating its own limitations and getting its own larger social education. It is learning that to the sense and value of private property, the race will cling with tenacities which communist and near-communist as little realize, as advocates of " free love " realize the forces — especially in women — that will oppose it.[1]

Even communistic history furnishes all the proofs we need, to show the steadily increasing belief that personal as well as social growths require an even higher value on individual control over what is fairly earned or honestly believed to be earned. Far more is this true of socialism as seen in its last three decades. This, I say, may be best seen *inside the labor world*. We shall there find quite amazing conservatisms in property ownership and in political management. Like others, socialists have found that their claims must be submitted step by step to economic possibilities and *even more to human acquiescences*. They have been at work trying to find out what forms and what measure of private property the people will demand. They have many surprising discoveries still to make.

[1] I am not classing socialists among these advocates.

The entire first claim for the "*all*" of interest, profits or inheritances has undergone changes that show how we may finally work together in cutting out "unearned increments."

For more than twenty-five years, I was speaking to audiences in different parts of the country in which socialists were often leaders in the discussion. Except in a small minority of those who thought themselves orthodox, or "the real thing" in the faith, there was never a sign of agreement over that word "unearned." If the lecturer was either tired or hard-pressed, it was almost too easy to set the socialists quarreling among themselves over its definition. The most conservative economists admit the fact of huge unearned increment, but between them and the real communist to whom all private ownership is "unearned," are the differences to be accounted for. It is between these extremes that we find the most influential socialist leadership of to-day. This leadership represents opinions as far removed from the communists as from the capitalists. There is thus far not a hint that the main strength of the labor class will take sides with communists. Conditions of abnormal and violent character will have communist outbursts. We may even have this on a national scale in some European states. If it comes, we shall have slowly and at immense costs to recover from it as from any other disease. Nor in saying this would I close the door upon the communist hope, that in some very distant future a race and a society may emerge, spiritually strong enough to subject the instincts of private property to common uses. But with men and women as they are or as they are likely to become — let us say, if we will, in the year 2000, no general, sanctioned communism is in the least more probable than that all men will be of equal height or of equal capacity. I believe this will prove true of every extremer aspect of socialism.

Not separable from its economic features is another which has undergone transformation.

It is from the inner circles of socialism that we now get the most intelligent verdict upon the political weaknesses of the movement. The family jars referred to have never for a moment been absent, but their critical value had little significance until socialists got power enough to elect officials. We had plenty of socialist mayors long before the war. Once in office, they had to deal with their own party followers, with the public and with a critical body of intellectuals or independents not members of the party, though voting the socialist ticket. Stitt Wilson, socialist mayor of Berkeley, California, was speedily attacked by his regular following, some of whom told me there, " He is behaving just like any bourgeois." " He's cleaning streets and trimming trees all right, but no socialism." The mayor replied that he represented all the public interests and not alone socialist interests, and from this he would not budge.

No party officials in our history ever had more rasping difficulties with their backers than these men. It is among the first discoveries that the socialist electorate not only fails to represent the main interests of the community, it does not in any sense represent *the full labor interest*. Here the quarrels begin. Scores of these experiences can be given in a single instance.

Congressman Geo. R. Lunn was a socialist mayor of Schenectady. No one had severer training in the political methods of his party. He writes without bitterness in the *Metropolitan* —" An enrolled socialist party member who does not join the local organization has no voice in party affairs. That is, he has no voice except at the primaries, where he is expected to endorse the various candidates selected by the local organization or machine."

" If a group of enrolled socialists opposed to the candidates suggested by the organization should bring forth a different set of candidates at the primaries and should succeed in having them nominated, the socialist machine would at once repudiate these nominees as traitors to socialism." "The moment socialists enter the political field they are guilty of grossest tyranny at every point where they seek to disfranchise from active and effective participation in nominations for office — all socialist voters who are not members of their small coterie." A socialist to the manor born, John Spargo, says the socialist local "becomes a little sectarian gathering giving its time and energy to the party machine."

Mr. A. L. Benson was socialist candidate for president in 1916, receiving nearly 600,000 votes. Finding that the party "doesn't work" he waits some months to see if it will "right itself." He says, "It has not righted itself. I therefore resign as a protest against the foreign-born leadership that blindly believes a non-American policy can be made to appeal to many Americans." Several of these former leaders are now welcomed contributors to some of the most conservative periodicals in the country.

American socialism has few names that stand for more inflexible loyalty to its principles than A. M. Simons. In the *New Republic* (Dec. 2, 1916) he speaks out in such paragraphs as these: "With the sorrow that comes with the destruction of one's dearest ideal, I say that in many a city the socialist organization is to-day *little more than an organized appetite for office* — a socialist Tammany, exploiting the devotion of its members instead of the funds of corporations, for the benefit of a little circle of perfectly honest, but perfectly incompetent and selfish politicians, who still persist in thinking themselves idealists." As if he were describing the history of socialism in every foreign country, he says, "I have collected the names of nearly fifty people who have filled the highest unpaid positions in our party, who have been candidates for office when election was hopeless — writers, speakers, organizers — the type of men and women who gave up what the world called careers to devote their lives to what they believed to be the one fight worth fighting — and all these are to-day leaving the movement in the principles of which they still believe."

He charges the officials in control during the 1916 election with " a complete lack of comprehension of American democracy." " Every effort to secure a national convention was thwarted. The attempt to maintain an open forum for discussion of party affairs was choked off by relegating such discussion to an unread supplement of the party organ. Not a single socialist paper of influence permits that freedom of discussion which was once our greatest pride. There is also that contempt for the membership which always accompanies distrust of democracy." If the note in these confessions is a little too acid, it is in the main true, as it is true in most other countries. There was never more contempt shown for popular rule than by the executive socialist management in Italy, France and Germany.

As in Europe it has also in this country had its record of petty chicane and of cheap factional opportunism; its frequent exercise of cliquish autocracies which put it side by side with the commonest tasks of party politics. Between the higher and more disinterested aims of socialism and the lower, narrower and more self-seeking elements, there is the same perpetual contest for power which one sees in the trade union, in older political parties, in competitive business, or in international rivalries. Socialists are painfully like other folk.

As long as they are out of power and are smartly abused, there will be the appearance of harmony. But with power partially attained their troubles begin.

They begin because the *administration* of official responsibility brings out every cliquish, separate interest and nowhere do these differences assert themselves more than in the labor field. Conservatism is a relative term and labor has it in abundance. Now that labor programs broaden their definitions to include a wide "intellectual" following, these interests multiply. They will constitute new checks within the entire movement. In this country, organized labor courts and is courted by "non-partisan" farmers, but a great body of grangers tell us in the present week that their interests do not coincide with those of the unions. One strong state body of farmers scores the miners for standing by the Plumb plan. Because of our geographical bigness, racial varieties and industrial complexity, nowhere will these divergencies more certainly defeat any and all narrow "class-conscious" proposals.

It is this which gives the defenders of the "social order" every chance they deserve. They cannot take that chance without a great deal more organized coöperation with that relative conservatism both in the unions and in socialism. These strictures on socialism are not quoted to cast aspersions on this movement. For half a century it has shown heroisms and self-sacrifice which put it securely among the idealisms to which the future will point with pride.

It has, moreover, won its place in the world's practical politics. We must work with it as we must work with labor organizations; as we must work with other parties and with the State. It is as shallow to condemn the cause as a whole as to condemn the unions as a whole. In Italy at the present moment there is a swing of the socialist vote toward the "revolutionary reds" but another strong body still struggles to keep its hold on ordinary political methods and in affiliation with other parties. It is with these in every country that society must learn to work.[1]

[1] To see how the sense of differing interests has grown, we may turn to a good example in the English House of Lords representing land. A great pet among them (their Prime Minister) listened to one of the early attacks on this interest in favor of tenants. Lord Palmerston came to the defense of his mates in these words "tenants' right is landlords' wrong." Based on Prins' plea at the next stage, a Danish scholar (A. Christensen) in his "Politics and

Though socialist sentiment about it has undergone great changes in recent years, I turn first to one aspect most easily open to ordinary critical opinion, the socialism of the State where we see new opinions and new resistances from labor's rank and file. We also see one change in *motive* with significance of its own.

Crowd Morality" has given a brief statement of these trade and professional interests as a more appropriate basis of politics. A translation has been published by E. P. Dutton, N. Y., see especially the two closing Chapters X and XI. This author thinks the three-fold division so marked before the war in Germany,— Landlords' League, League of Trade and Commerce and Socialism representing Labor, indicates "the most distinct finger-post of the course of future politics which any country has thus far produced." But labor already shows within its own ranks at least three " interests " very differently interpretated.

CHAPTER XI

GOVERNMENT OWNERSHIP

WHETHER from socialist, syndicalist, or New Guild point of view, some settlement must be had with government and city management of business. To increase this public control to the utmost has been the ideal and the practical endeavor of a most important section of socialists as it is now of some of the greater labor organizations.

In the study of "Municipal Ownership" in the United States, published by the *Intercollegiate Socialist* (Nov., 1916)[1] it is said "if government ownership under the present political control is a failure, then the keystone of the arch of socialist argument would be shot through with a fatal flaw. This first and most crucial test of the essential practicality of socialism has been successfully met by cities in every part of the United States." There is the usual qualification that socialism cannot arrive without the control of the Government by the working people and democratic management of all industry. Mr. Clark rightly insists that they have to fight their way through and out of the present "class government" and boldly submits the case to actual comparative tests as between public and private ownership.

If capitalist writers are half as confident as they would have us believe, they should rejoice to meet the issue thus presented. It puts the discussion on a scientific basis in the sense of submitting it to proof or disproof by methods that command respect. It is the war, however, that compels a

[1] The best and most impartial study is "State Socialism Pro and Con," by Walling and Laidler, Henry Holt, N. Y., 1917.

restatement of the whole case. Throughout the world the instances available for this treatment steadily increase. It is, for example, now possible to compare the individual and social benefits under public and under private *insurance* so as to form some opinion on the merits and defects of each. For five years we saw the play of new motives at work in this extension of state functions. We were given a new estimate of private profit as the main driving force in industry as compared with motives of another kind.

In war, governments multiply their economic activities because they cannot wait. Though the costs be four times normal rates, the demand must be met. But another reason is more to our purpose. States have taken upon themselves much of this great business in order to satisfy labor. " State Ownership as a means of quieting Labor Unrest " heads a discussion and a defense of such ownership. It is the poorest of arguments, but it points to a fact no longer to be ignored. War again has made terrible exposure of wastes and bungling in much private business that had been held up to us as a very model of efficiency.

The abler students had long before warned us that no comparison between public and private direction was possible unless these defects of private control were discounted. We had by heart the story of political chicane and corruption due directly to big business secretly manipulating our legislatures and Congress. It is a most obvious peril that government ownership will " take the railroad into politics." But they were already in politics with a record so sinister that the evils have to be set off against evils incident to public management. Which will prove worse? We do not yet know. Many of these utilities had come under a financial control that used them *first* for its own enrichment. Is this driving force less dangerous to public interest than the motive behind government ownership? As great a railroad man as Collis P. Huntington said twenty years ago, " We can't continue private management of railroads. A sentiment is developing among the people so critical that government will have to take them." Mr. Huntington did not believe in public ownership, but he said it was inevitable for the reason given. It is to forces of this kind that we look to account for the whole movement away from private ownership.

By the help of my chart the collectivist drift in seventeen countries proved the more interesting because its motive and tendency could be studied in communities as different as New South Wales from Russian Czardom, or as Switzerland differs from Japan.

Seen in graphic form, the increase in state and city functions has been as steady as it is universal. It has grown faster than population or than national wealth. The form of government is of slightest consequence. State and city functions multiplied as rapidly in autocratic Prussia as in ultra democratic New Zealand. This steady and continuous growth raises one awkward question for the opponents. They are now uniting in a chorus of denunciation! Organizations are springing up which have the express object of informing the public how disastrous this tendency is proving. " Initiation, enterprise, personal responsibility, all alike suffer as state business increases." " Nothing that the State touches is done as well or as cheaply as in private business."

That shrewd and eloquent man of affairs Mr. Otto Kahn returns from a tour of investigation in Europe to warn us against " the paternalistic system and the spirit of Germany." It is a grave slip for so ingenious a man to identify state socialism so especially with Germany. One could now make most telling points against increase of state powers if Germany were in any sense alone in this drift. It is but one of at least forty governments under every form of political control. Moreover, in the very years when German prosperity was astonishing the world, her " state socialism " was increasing fastest. Was it in spite of her collectivism?

But the question I raise is this: If one after another, throughout the world, the nations deliberately choose this ever wider extension of state powers, is it to be inferred that they are all dupes? Are they collectively so incompetent as to blunder on from bad to worse as they add one state and city function to another? Through innumerable commissions they have all been studying this question at home and abroad. They have reported upon it in every imaginable aspect with the result that state powers have everywhere been increased. They have done this for many reasons but one reason stands out, namely, the practical failure of much private control *to hold the confidence of voting majorities.* This is what Mr. Huntington had in mind. A former editor of the Boston *Transcript* still active in his profession, tells me that the greatest railroad man New England has produced, John M. Forbes, also held this view.

But what a fact is this loss of public confidence! So it has come about that more and more the people about the world are asked for confidence in state management. They have given it to an amazing extent.

Are we then to believe that the whole world has been fooled? That is not an encouraging outlook. In the address quoted, Mr. Kahn professes to be extremely optimistic about the future. What are the grounds of this cheerfulness if the nations so deliberately unite in adopting policies which he tells us are so destructive; destructive, moreover, of those most primary human energies on which progress must depend? This could have no other meaning than that the world's senility is already upon us — not a good ground for hopefulness.

Yet Mr. Kahn's charges are not to be ignored.

Especially the last quarter of a century has shown so many flagrant economic and political defects in public management as to raise grave questions as to its further extension. With equal fanaticism we are told " public ownership has failed," and that "public ownership is a success." A great deal of it has met with disaster, but much of it (as compared with the preceding private management) has been successful. Switzerland, Scandinavia, English and German cities show a record on which, if submitted by referendum to the people concerned, the vote would be twenty to one in favor of public as against private control, and this strictly on a basis of experience.

It sounded queer to me to hear Mr. Bellamy, manager of the street railways in a big English city, refer to the objectors to city ownership as cranks and a wholly negligible body. He came to this country to examine our street car system, its administrative and financial management. He returned to Liverpool with the conviction that in both respects English city control was a distinct improvement and safer than our own. But a few months since, Sir Eric Geddes, former manager of the Eastern Railway, said, "*Except in the one bright instance of the municipal tramways,* the transportation systems of this country to-day are not prosperous."

Never was there so favorable a moment to make a new valuation of this issue. As we look back to the earlier discussions, the advocates of "collectivism" or "state socialism" thought it sufficient proof of their cause to show what rare economies could be made by "eliminating competition and unifying control." The State and city could borrow money at lower rates than private persons. Better wages and shorter hours were also easily within the gift of public authorities. There is proof that here and there these advantages have been considerable, but as measured by the expectation of the advocates, the results are depressing. It is proved that much public ownership, imperfect as it is, was the only possible alternative because capitalistic control had become economically incapable or was believed to be so by the people. Moreover, some of the strongest influences at work for public ownership were long unknown.

Even before the war these were in evidence, but the war has put them on the screen with startling vividness. We knew neither the political leverage of redoubled armies of state employees compactly organized, nor the adroit uses which political leaders could and would make of this fact. I saw much of Dr. Theodore Barth in Berlin thirty years ago when this special phase had become acute. Both as editor of a liberal paper (*Die Nation*) and member of the Reichstag, he attacked the whole Bismarck policy chiefly from this point of view. With other powerful liberals he believed this rapid extension of state control was building up a servile bureaucratic State that would destroy every free initiative in church, university and in civil life.

It was here that the motive in much of this state aggression was first made clear. Everywhere the expense account of State and city was rising. The traditional forms of taxation were proving inadequate and as direct taxes are a terror to politicians, the shrewder ones everywhere were searching for new and indirect ways of getting money. No one knew better than they how easily the ultimate costs could be hidden from the public. Yet even this demand for funds tells but part of the story — the part that may prove most dangerous to the public, and the part which we now face in this whole issue of greater or less collectivism.

In all political rivalry, strong men seek power and security in exercising it. Bismarck wanted the revenues from state-owned railways, but far more than this, he wanted the enhanced prestige which the control of transportation would give him. Not a private road would be brought within the State, without adding its horde of officials and employees whose loyalty and political influence could be more surely counted on. How easily the important posts could be given to the faithful! Far too little has been made of this in the discussion.

Macaulay thought Lord Halifax the rare political sage of his time. He is quoted as saying, " Every party is a kind of conspiracy against the rest of society." When Bismarck got his state railways, he wanted to monopolize tobacco, just as Japan takes a coal mine to feed the furnaces of its navy. Whether the public in the end pays more is a question not even raised. Or it is the brand new Czecho-Slovac State that at once seizes tobacco " because it must have the revenues."

Bismarck knew the French Government had this tobacco monopoly from which it received fat returns. Earlier, as diplomat in Paris and then as conqueror, he had burned quantities of tobacco there and knew it was poor in quality and very expensive. This did not interest him. He wanted the money to strengthen his hold on government. He had political ends in view which required funds and influence. The German ambassador in London has told us that Bismarck was like Napoleon in his passion for power "— gleich Napoleon liebte(er) den Kampf als Selbstzweck." For the same reason he wanted the " brandy monopoly " to strengthen him politically. Its revenues would add just so much to his control over his enemies.

This statesman professed to be above all parties — to be the " honest broker " working for the interests of the Fatherland as a whole. Every hour the struggle goes on by the party in office to hold its own against the " outs." In this sense it confirms Halifax, " Every party is a conspiracy against the rest of society." " Government " is not an abstraction. Practically day by day it is the party in saddle. Especially when its hold is threatened, the temptation is to seize any profitable industry that promises fiscal or political support. That it can do this better for the consumer does not even occur to it. If the ruling party in Japan can get revenues by " socializing " camphor, it will do it solely for the support which a profitable monopoly gives. France now asks for a state monopoly of such an enormous busi-

GOVERNMENT OWNERSHIP

ness as the control of petrol. The last question asked will be that of cheapness and excellence of the product in which the public is most concerned. Perhaps the most brilliant of living literary men long ago became a socialist very much in the manner of the "Dean of American letters," Mr. Howells. But Anatole France has been singularly free from all utopian illusions. In "Sur la Pierre Blanche" he speaks of the logic in the collectivist drift as "inevitable." But he says "*justice* has nothing to do with it." "Le collectivisme se réalisera un jour, non parce qu'il est juste, mais parce qu'il est la suite necessaire de l'état présent et la conséquence fatale de l'évolution capitaliste." Just as little do those business efficiencies in which the great body of consumers are most concerned enter into the motives which inspire a large part of added state functions.

At least ten governments (including Swiss Cantons) make salt a monopoly. In Venezuela it is absolute over the manufacture, sale and importation. France does not hesitate to make the product of her tobacco and match monopoly costly to the consumer for fiscal reasons. The state monopoly of powder has again and again been attacked for wasteful and expensive management, while no one more than socialists have criticized and exposed the abuses of the government printing office.

At that safe distance which lends enchantment to the view, an English writer on finance and a prolific author on government ownership, Emile Davies, writes thus of our own government printing office at Washington: "The greatest publisher in the world is the United States Government, which issues over a thousand different publications and sends out over a million publications a week. It is the proprietor of two daily publications, the *Congressional Record,* and the *Daily Consular Report,* five weeklies and seven monthlies — one of them illustrated. The Department of Agriculture sends out no less than thirty-five million publications every year; practically every publication issued by the Government is distributed, most of it gratuitously and for the asking. The United States Government has its own printing plant, which is said to be the largest and most modern in the world." Not a word of caution about the traditional abuses of the trade union in this department or of the notorious extravagance and expense of operation. This author in his "Collectivist State In The Making" has a passage too good to miss (p. 125).

When public control has reached its climax a man is to be "brought into the world by a state doctor or midwife, reared in a state nursery, educated, clothed and doctored at a state school, and, if needs be, fed at the cost of the community during his school days (except, in London, on holidays and days of public rejoicing). He can earn his living in government employment in any country. In most big towns he can live in a municipally owned house. In New Zealand the Government will lend him money with which to buy a house, and it will also lend him, free of charge, the plans on which to construct it. If sick, he may be treated by a state doctor or in a state hospital. He may read at the state or municipal library until he goes blind, when the State will take him into a state blind asylum, or until he goes off his head, when he will be cared for in a state lunatic asylum. If unemployed, the State endeavors to find him work. In most of the towns in Italy or in Buda-Pesth, he can buy his bread from the municipal bakery, and in other countries he can get municipally killed meat from a municipal butchery, and flavor it with government salt, after having cooked it over a fire made with state-mined coal. Or he can partake of this meal in a municipal restaurant, drinking municipally brewed beer, wine from the state vineyards, or state spirits. He then lights his state-made cigar with state-made matches, and can read a municipally produced daily newspaper. By this time, feeling more cheerful, he can draw some more money from his account at the state or municipal savings bank, and can visit the municipally owned racecourse, where he gambles with the State or city, and can end up the evening at a state or municipally owned theatre. If he likes he can even take a municipal ballet girl out to supper, after which he may, if he feel so inclined, confess to a state-supported priest. Then, if he can afford it, he may go to recuperate at a state or municipal water-spa or bath in France, Germany or New Zealand, after having insured his life with a state insurance office and his house and furniture with the state fire insurance department.

" He can buy state gunpowder at a state shop and blow his brains out; or if he likes, blow out some one else's. The State, having brought him into the world and made him what he is, will finish the job and kill him, this being a monopoly jealously guarded by the State except in war time. In Switzerland, Paris, or many another city, the municipality will bury him."

I should like to submit this passage to Mr. Dooley and hear his comments on this all-mothering State which takes us both to blind and to lunatic asylums; which so easily deprives us of our own brains and enables us to deprive other people of theirs. Yet this is the situation we now meet. In spite of all that can be said against many features, we are to hear much more of it. As a whole, it cannot yet be stopped. The evidence is but partly in, nor have we yet " suffered enough to be wise." Democracy is cowardly before open and direct taxation. The politician knows this and how to take advantage of it. Organized labor now enters the movement. It brings an influence so great and so immediate that collectivism also must *go through*.

Like other theoretic extravagances of socialism, these " inevitabilities " must go their lengths until all of us and especially labor discover the costs. " La conséquence fatale " has now to work itself out until its limitations are disclosed. If the railways in this country were to " go back " to the old ownership and anything like the old ways, the aggressive discontent of the employees would alone destroy efficiency. By impartial authorities one task is possible and cannot begin too soon.

State owned business in different countries has gone so far and into so many kinds of industry that a comparison of relative desirability of public and private ownership is more and more open to tests. The comparative merits of city lighting by public or by private methods in the United States will very soon be known; in some instances may now be known.

A prolific capitalistic literature is in circulation showing us in great detail how inefficient (in its opinion) and how wasteful public ownership is. One of them writes, " It is high time to call the bluff of these socialists. In transportation, electrical plants, insurance, gas works and others, it can be *proved* that private ownership is more economical and offers better service to the public than work done by the city or State." He calls my attention to a long series of publications by the " Municipal Ownership Company " in New York to show why state telephones failed in Glasgow and in England; why the whole Australian " state socialism " is breaking down; why and how France is suffering from the same cause.

He could " furnish a list of more than two hundred municipal lighting plants already defunct "—" sold, leased or abandoned." He notes especially a series against " this public muddling of business " by that well-informed English publicist Sydney Brooks.

There is more hope in this challenge because it includes the world movement. It dares the collectivists to compare notes on the two methods in Switzerland and Scandinavia where there is much state control with great efficiency and little political corruption, as well as in countries like Italy, France, and in the United States where politics has been

GOVERNMENT OWNERSHIP

at times so depraved that no experiment in city ownership has a fig's value. When Philadelphia some years since "municipalized" her gas and "it failed," there was proof of nothing except that Philadelphia at that time was very corruptly governed, and the same is true of many other "failures" over which my informant gloats. With the more doubtful cases, we should watch what seems a wise and fore-handed purpose reported from Sweden, "the electrification of railways is in active progress, the Swedish Government has its own state waterfalls board, which has acquired something like 70 per cent. of the water power available in the country, and is constructing vast hydro-electrical works, so that it may supply its railways with power from this source." Or, Victoria, which began in 1909 "to develop a coal-bearing area, and constructed a railway 27 miles in length to the field. It laid down a township on modern lines, and at the same time established state brick works and quarries. For the year ended June 30, 1910, it produced 201,000 tons of coal, and in the following year 376,070 tons," selling meantime 115,000 tons to the public. We may have here an admirable instrument if used with prudence, to curb private monopoly. To feed their railway systems New Zealand, Hungary, Victoria, Sweden, Prussia and Austria have taken over mines and if they have a surplus it may be sold directly to the people.

To take the world movement has this promise: any one who can show that state and city ownership has proved generally inferior to private management in Switzerland, Sweden, large parts of Australasia and England makes a strong case. The challenge is fair, and everywhere groups of able socialists eagerly accept it. They are doing in this a distinct public service. We should meet the challenge not with epithets but as sportsmen. Both the strength and the strategy in this country are now on the side of private property. It has upon its side the real powers — the courts, the press and vast institutional organizations.

A city manager of a trolley system who had been in control twenty-four years said at a Boston meeting, " It is up to us. We have got to *prove* to the people that we can serve them better and more economically than those cities which own and run their own cars." That is as gallant as it is true. I asked this gentleman, if he thought it easy to do this against the example of so many cities in the world that get on pretty well under city ownership. He maintained that our situation both for steam railways, telegraphs, etc., as well as street cars, was so far different from Europe and Australia as to give the advantage to capitalistic control. " In the first place," he said, " we know this fight has to be made. We have been preparing for years on a basis of comparative costs. We *know* we can beat city ownership. To my skepticism about "*proving* this to the people " he answered, " we are willing to trust the people with the evidence." Nothing fairer than this can be put in words. It is all the fairer, because the city ownership believers are just as ready to argue it out on the same basis of relative economy and efficiency. The public has now to watch this rivalry, seeing to it, if possible, that the dice are not loaded on either side.

What will try our patience in this contest is that labor organizations are everywhere adopting the Bismarck policy. They, too, demand government ownership, not first to serve the public by cheaper product, but to enhance their own power. They will show quite as little concern about the final expense account as the French Government with its monopoly of matches, tobacco and petrol.

Labor asks for increased state activity because it has learned the possible uses for its own ambitions. It sees what good fighting ground opens before it. It has discovered that it can strike with even more favorable chances than private strikes offer. As governments take over one great business after another, labor notes that wages are raised as in Japan in 1906–08; in Switzerland, 1908–10, nearly thirty per cent.; in Italy twice between 1903 and 1908. When France took over the "Western" wages at once went up. They see, too, that France and Switzerland cut off one working hour in the day. State and city are of course to be "model employers." To whom it is said should we look for an example in raising the standard of living if not to our great governing bodies. The State has power to grant eight hours, to fix wages at a good level, to grant pensions and other benefits. "Raising the standard of living" also has a generous ring from the lips of the politician. He will not miss his opportunity. He knows how unpopular it is to stand out against any alluring phrase like "model employer" and "living wage." State powers will be enlarged for another reason.

If facts are concealed or omitted in public employment, the employee does not worry, because he knows as well as Postmaster Burleson that the taxpayers must foot the bill. In Massachusetts, Mr. Endicott is called "the most successful arbitrator of strikes in our history." Hardly a hold-up bothered him more than a few hours. But what arbitrator picked haphazard from the street could not win honors as peacemaker if offhand he could give the strikers what they asked? Organized labor has had its eye on these "successes." The war excuse for "keeping the men at work at all costs" has gone, but political influence on public officials may become a good substitute. *Collective bargaining thus passes into politics.*

These are the later reasons to show what forces are at work to extend state socialism. They would justify real pessimism if they were not at the same time slowly exposing the weakness of this collectivist fatalism, and especially exposing their dangers to vast sections of the consuming public including a majority of wage-earners.

Unorganized labor as well as syndicalists already express

their dread of the "over-padded State." It has come largely, I think, from a closer scrutinizing of government activities.

This testimony pours in upon us from the very countries where conditions are as nearly like our own as Canada, Australia and New Zealand. In these two latter countries, there is no longer a question as to a great deal of political fumbling with public enterprises like state and city managed transportation. These are inefficiencies which certainly play their part in the higher cost of living. However its deficits are concealed, every public utility, post office, railway, telegraph, has to be paid for by the people, and the movement will go on until the people find it out. As trained an observer as Professor Mavor of Toronto now gives us an account of "public ownership and operation of telephones in the province of Manitoba." The Government purchase was in 1908. The purchase was made as a political issue and politics in its eviler sense has shadowed it from the start. Politics extended the service far into rural districts. "Something must be done for the lonely farmer." It proved to be a bad buyer of raw materials and fittings. There was over-stocking of supplies. The announced profits were found to be fictitious because no adequate depreciation had been allowed for though separately urged by the Telephone Commission. In 1909 charges were reduced when the business was not "carrying itself." When, in 1911, higher rates were proposed, a storm of disapproval swept over the Province. Then, of course, came a Royal Commission to make inquiries. Of this report Professor Mavor says: "An inconclusive and unsatisfactory document at every point, the inquiry led to the threshold of the Government, but there it stopped. Instead of honestly taking their share of the blame, the Government chose the dishonorable course of virtually prosecuting the commissioners, whose faults arose solely from the fact that they were loyal to a government which was disloyal to them." I give this because even in details it is so exactly like reports for Australia (as well as for countries like Italy and France). The criticism will not yet stop the movement, perhaps not even check it until the people suffer enough and widely enough to bring these evils under some form of control. This educational process will be hastened by every new and further attempt at businesses politically managed. But state socialism has gone so far that criticism is more and more directed against the State acting as "producer."

It is here that doubts accumulate on every side and socialists and labor critics join in the warning.

With all our devices to extend power to the people, offering to every climber as they do, a way to throw expenses upon the public, we see clearly where this slope leads, unless checked by political capacities and devotions extremely rare in the world's bureaucracies.

There are businesses of first utility like insurance that offer instances of success which may be quoted, like the following:

"In Wellington the other day the New Zealand State Fire Insurance Department laid the foundation stone of its new home and the speakers for the occasion had an instructive story to tell. To begin business (in 1905) the department issued debentures to the amount of £2,000 ($10,000). It immediately cut the rates of the private companies 33 1-3 per cent. on dwellings, offices, and similar risks, and 10 per cent. on trade risks. Prophets assured the people that the taxpayer would have to make good the losses which were inevitable, but the department proceeded to organize to compete with the thirty-three fire insurance companies doing business in the Dominion. After fourteen years of open competition, it has paid off its original debentures and has built up reserve funds to the amount of £214,000 ($1,070,000)."[1]

[1] *The Public*, Dec. 6, 1919.

But insurance has a relative simplicity that puts it in a different class from the big mining, milling, and those "basic" industries where the great issues will have their decision.

If the State is to own and operate these, it must add to economic values — to "goods," foods, materials in such quantities and of such quality as to insure an expanding prosperity. This must be done with enough improvement over present capitalistic methods as to justify the change.

This superior production must give year by year immense additions for repairs, business extensions, education and every kind of public betterment. The rising standard for these requirements demands higher and higher expenditure just as our schools, hospitals, "clean milk" social insurance make constantly growing demands on surplus wealth.

Up to date, one sees that a generation of wide international experience in "political business management" has thus far given us too scant evidence. We have been flooded by a literature in which slip-shod assertion made it appear that *"distribution"* is the central fact — that production would somehow take care of itself if we could get "fair" or "equal" distribution.

Production must first do its work before the question of distribution arises. Everywhere it awaits the creative energies from which wealth first springs. That "distribution" is itself a great part of production should not conceal the issue. That the first emphasis on distribution is puerile is seen, I repeat, by a growing number of socialists and labor men. Mr. Spargo in his recent book on Bolshevism is one of many when he says, " Every serious student of the problem has realized that the first great task of any socialist society must be to *increase the productivity of labor.* It is all very well for a popular propaganda among the masses to promise a great reduction in the hours of labor and, at the same time, a great improvement in the standards of living. The translation of such promises into actual achievements must prove an enormous task." He says it will require such an organization of industry upon a basis of efficiency as no nation has yet developed. If the working class of this or any other country should take possession of the existing organization of production, there would not be enough in the fund now going to the capitalist class to satisfy the requirements of the workers, even if no compensation were paid to present owners. From the most conservative economist or business man, we could have no stronger or more sensible statement.

It is such as these who are also watching the world movement. Among the nations over the globe they are observing the State and city acting as "wealth-makers." Railways and every sort of transportation, mining in several metals, manufacturing, repairing, cattle raising and butchering, have reached dimensions in a score of countries which enable us to do more than guess at results so far attained.

One may pick out favored instances, but of the mass of this state and city functioning as "producer" the showing is meager and doubtful. Much of it (as in our own country) is like putting dollars into one end of the machine and getting out (if lucky) seventy-five cents.

Only in rare instances is there even a pretense of strict business accounting. All sorts of deficits are thrown back on the tax-paying public. I tried hard in Germany to get at these concealed deficits (like enormous sums for rentals and many indirect costs) in the sum total of expenses for national workingmen's insurance. It could not be done. Bismarck wanted the working classes to help him defeat a dangerous liberalism. He tried to buy these classes as he went to Canossa to buy the catholic vote that had beaten him in the Kulturkampf. If this insurance system had not been profoundly modified by those (in this case) wiser than he, it would have failed as this giant always failed when he ignored moral forces. It is often and for many reasons worth while to be taxed for these deficits. But how far shall the multiplication of minus signs go on? If state socialism is to justify itself as producer, then at some point it must honestly pay its way or the social product falls. During the war state socialism showed a few instances of high and efficient production. But it showed still more blundering and bureaucratic inadequacy.

The war-motive, however, cannot safely be copied for peace industry. We are thus left — not as denying that political management may some time learn its lesson, but with results that warrant the utmost caution in adopting collectivism as a headlong principle. From several countries there are practical illustrations (state coal mining in the Saar and fish supply in New South Wales) of what governments may do to hold greedy private monopoly in check. Most of this has been done — not to " socialize all business " but solely to regulate abuses of private ownership.

If Sidney sets up its own flour mill and bakery with the result of keeping prices on a lower level, the step may be welcomed. But all this is as far as possible from what every extreme of socialist doctrine asks of us.

No bounds are set to this desire to get things for nothing or to get them at other people's expense. Before the street railway commission of this State, advocates appear urging that we all ride free upon our trolley system. Mr. Bauer of Lynn, puts it in familiar form: " The trolley rider is a money asset to the community into which he travels." " When he goes out of it daily, he leaves behind something of permanent value in the form of work done with his hands or with his brain or else actual money. Instead of making him pay for this service he is rendering, he should be allowed to give it free. A couple of generations ago it was the custom of the people to tax those who used the toll roads. Later it was found that this was a poor public policy because it discouraged business. Business expansion is now being discouraged through the tax imposed upon the trolley rider."

If this " free rides for all " had become an issue in practical politics, this gentleman would have been rebuked by some competitor for public favor because he asked so little. " The analogy of the toll road applies not only to trolley systems but most especially to the railroads." This has been seriously put in print and publicly argued. Railroads are one of the " basic industries " but so are a dozen others from steel and iron to milk, food, and clothing. This side of an absolute communism, there is always an opening for the more radical man to further his personal influence by pretentious solicitude for the people. One of our consuls tells us what these out-bidding politicians are now doing in Uruguay. They advance a project for the expropriation of all cigar, cigarette and tobacco factories and for the monopolization of the business by the Government for the purpose of " improving the situation of the military class and the organization of national defense and furthering the merchant marine and the navy, without the addition of new taxes."

The last word comes from the Chicago convention of the new labor party late in November, 1919. " Abolition of the United States Senate," " Government to own and operate the banking of the country," " Incomes of individuals to be limited by law." Not only are all public utilities to be nationalized, but " all basic industries." All government work is to be done " by day labor." A university man, as fraternal delegate from England, tells them that in his country " it no longer was a question of whether the coal mines would be nationalized. The only question now is whether we will confiscate the mines or pay for them."

With an approved " national referendum, initiative and recall " a close guess is possible as to what is before us with such a program: the more so, as all federal judges are to be elected by popular vote to hold office "not exceeding four years."

Whatever may be said of the previous resolutions, this last one would leave us, within half a decade, with a judiciary of as little independence as in the very worst of the Latin republics.

As the case now stands, we are to get our instruction about the extension of the socialistic principle in fields where there is the widest possible experience.

No academic or theoretic discussion will have any such value educationally, as an application of principles to such questions as the rights of inheritance, school feeding and "state burying of the dead," state doctors and "socializing the milk supply."

CHAPTER XII

WHO SHALL SPEND MY SAVINGS?

No point in socialist orthodoxy tells us more about essential ownership and what all those possessing even small sums are likely to say, than the "rights of inheritance." For stimulating and maintaining certain inequalities, nothing has done more than our inheritance laws. If artificial inequality is bad, here is one great source of the evil. For more than a century, these abuses have furnished rare sport for the enemies of capitalism.

It was easy to show that no "natural right" inhered in this form of distributing property. It was plainly a custom,— a custom in constant change like fashions and methods of taxation. Socialists have made the most of this; putting inheritance laws on a par with the evils of private profit, rent and interest.

If, in their hunt for traitorous persons, our senatorial committee had heard socialists and even a college-bred I. W. W. use the words of a president of the American Economic Association, they would have had a perfect case for prosecution. Though he shocked no one in his audience of economists, this is what Professor Irving Fisher said. Being a mathematician he used Pareto's logarythmic law: "The number of wealthy men at the top is two and a quarter times as great, in proportion to population, in England as in the United States, presumably because the number of generations through which fortunes have been inherited are much greater there than here."

He quotes another Italian economist (Rignano) who urges "the State co-heir of all bequests so that it will receive one third of the estate on the first descent, two thirds of the remainder on the second, and the residue on the third descent.

Dr. Fisher speaks of the inheritance system as "the first great factor responsible for the undemocratic distribution of wealth." If our medievalists set out to penalize authoritative opinions like the above, they would have to close the economic departments in at least a hundred colleges, or leave them so enfeebled in the hands of timid conformists as to make them objects of general contempt. Nothing can now prevent an overhauling of our inheritance customs. As with profits, interest and rent, it is a question of degree. Socialists began with their "all-or-nothing" demand.

"The State shall take entire charge of your property at death. You shall not give away a penny of it." Note carefully that the earlier agitation against the rights of private inheritance ignored altogether the wage-earning class. The proletariat was long thought and spoken of as having nothing to leave at death and therefore was omitted in the discussion. Richer folk were the target. Among these were abuses so many and so gross as to be the easiest mark. Little as it is, there has been change enough to put a new face upon this question of inheritance.

Especially in the last half century, it has appeared that some millions of the workers have invested savings in banks, in business, in building and loan associations, in insurance so that attacks upon "all inheritance" had to be reconsidered just as the saner socialists have reconsidered the "all" of machinery and private profits.

Within a much shorter period another source of doubt has arisen,— one that is to play a star rôle in the whole socialist discussion. State socialists long glorified and idealized the State — not the actual bourgeois State but the coming "People's State." When the many conquered and possessed the governing function, it could be trusted because "it would express the general will": "the new State is nothing but all of us acting for the general good." "Each for all and all for each."

If "the people" have nowhere yet become possessors of the State, they have had quite enough to do with it in Australia, New Zealand, Canada and the United States, Denmark and Switzerland to raise no end of suspicions about ultra democratic control and its supposed logic. Nowhere more than among the masses is this doubt spreading. More and more is the practical wisdom of this centralized political power (whoever controls it) put in question.

One sharp aspect of this incredulity takes this form: "Is the politician in power likely to spend my money more wisely than private persons spend it?" With every extension of this political power and the exhibitions given of wasteful and irresponsible expenditures, the doubts multiply and they multiply in the labor world.

If the State is to take my savings at death, will it use them more wisely than I can use them? If it cannot, then, in this respect, the State has a poor case. Even for its minimum existence, it must and does take a portion of those savings, but is it to feed and strengthen those functions by taking to itself *all* inheritances?

Before the answer, let us look at a second phase of the discussion which seems to play into socialistic hands. "What I inherit has been earned by others. Shall I accept 'unearned increment' and therefore class myself among the parasites?" This is one ground for socialist opposition to all inheritance. In the most recent book I have seen,[1] nearly 300 pages are given to a passionate attempt at argument for the entire "destruction of the inheritance principle." This is the tone of the older socialists. It is that of the most famous of all manifestoes which calls for "the abolition of all inheritance." Though he makes interesting qualifications, John Spargo speaks of "society being

[1] "The Abolition of Inheritance," H. E. Read, Macmillan, 1919.

the only possible inheritor of property."[1] For many years before the war, August Bebel was the intellectual leader of German socialists. In his book "Die Frau," read by millions, he has a passage beginning (p. 346): "In the new society nothing more is to be inherited — nichts mehr zu ererben ist."

For a final criticism of this "logical asceticism," we need not turn to capitalists or to economists in their pay. From within the socialist ranks it has its own correction, as I believe many another excess will find its cure from the inside rather than from without.

As so many real authorities among socialists now drop out the "all" before "the means of productions" and even before "interest," so discussion and experience have led them to drop the *all* before inheritances. They have made it a practical question, as more and more the whole progressive sections of labor will do.

Some years ago, I visited in their homes two of the most distinguished of European socialists. They lived as amply as the best paid college professors. They were well served by wage-paid laborers in their families. In this issue of inheritance, they held opinions in no way different from that of Mr. Wells in a later phase. It had come to be solely a matter of what they thought common sense. To leave the children merely "consumable goods" (always permitted in socialist theory), they thought to be not only a "pedantry" but a danger to one of the most powerful of human motives — saving for the offspring.

I have no fling against those socialists because they did not at once "divide up." This charge of not "dividing up" is perhaps the most childish of objections.

The craftsman-poet Morris was fairly rich. After one of his lectures, I heard the silly question put to him by a simpering lady doing her best to be polite, "But Mr.

---

[1] "Socialism," 236.

Morris, as socialist why do you not divide with the poor: how can you live as you do?" She got the answer, "Because, Madam, I am not a damned fool."

If we are to believe those now most in authority among socialists, there is not the least fear that "*all* inherited property" will be taken from the individual or the family.

We are now told right and left that it is not proposed to stop all inheritance but only "dangerous accumulations" and "those which become the nest-egg of privilege." "Consumable goods"—the home with its furnishings, garden plot, etc., are of course to pass to survivors as at present. As "the old and helpless are to be cared for by pensions," we are assured, "there will be no need to invest savings with the object of securing independence."

These investments aiming at an income from interest and profits are indeed the super-vice to all good socialists. Every guilty investor of this sort "becomes a parasite in proportion to his success." He "merely encourages a system under which he can make the real laborers support him." In an attack upon one of our richest men, I heard it said, "This Crœsus with three palatial houses besides a yacht-palace on the water pays every bill out of the wealth earned by nearly ten thousand workers."

Strictly as investor of capital, it was denied that he has the least claim to any income. "When he dies, his children and those who marry them for their money, will be called 'independent' when as a fact they will be ordinary dead beats living off the labor of others." The abuses of great wealth and the gaudy scandals so often associated with it lend themselves to most effective propaganda against inherited wealth. If it did not easily lie within the practical possibilities of taxation to deal with these excesses, multitudes of voters in little sympathy with socialists would flock to their standard.

It is when we come to the smaller and commoner incomes that the inheritance problem becomes interesting. As this side of it has received critical attention, no one has raised more rational objections to doing away with all private inheritance rights than those who now direct socialist discussion. As the issue has been brought home to those with small possessions, the property instinct speaks up. It is discovered that parents are often very fond of their children; that as parents, they enjoy foregoing many present gratifications for the sake of the children and the children's future. Among these weaknesses is a most obstinate inclination to leave one's possessions — savings bank book as well as other belongings — to these intimate survivors or indeed to make the gift after their own choice whatever it be. In quoting Mr. Gronlund's riper conclusion, I am giving the recorded opinion of a great many other socialists when they deal with what are called "legitimate possessions." Illegitimate possessions are usually much larger sums than those held by the critic. I heard John Burns say in 1886, that twelve hundred dollars a year was all that anybody should receive. Prosperity so changed his standard of estimates that he publicly justified himself in the receipt of several times that income. That is what happens to the general body of the workers whose wage standards have risen. Their property sense quickens and becomes sensitive to its rights. One New York bank has 4000 distinctly working class depositors. Socialist logicians asking to do away with " all inheritances " would get instant enlightenment if these investors should record their vote on the issue.

Without being at all prosperous, Mr. Gronlund became interested in this question and so far faced it as to realize, even thirty years ago, what a large part of the wage-earners were likely to say about parting with their property. He says socialists have learned something — in his own words —" Socialists used to insist upon the abolition of the right of inheritance and bequest. But if what I gain by my own labor is rightfully my property — and the Co-operative Commonwealth will, as we have seen, declare it to be so — it will be inexpedient in that Commonwealth to destroy any of the essential qualities of propertyship; and I can hardly call that my property which I may not give to whom I please at my death."

If we can intercept him at the right moment on "his great curve in changing opinion," no one surpasses H. G. Wells as a reporter. In his most socialistic mood he takes up this issue of inheritance. In his "New Worlds for Old" (page 145-6) he insists that "posthumous property will also persist in a mitigated state under socialism. There is no reason whatever why it should not do so." He even appeals to "a strong natural sentiment" in favor of this form of possessions.

"Widows and widowers again have clearly a kind of natural property in the goods they have shared with the dead; in the home, in the garden close, in the musical instruments and books and pleasant home-like things." Nor does he stop at "consumable goods." "*Even perhaps a proportion of accumulated money may reasonably go to a friend or kin.*" "It is," he says, "a question of public utility; socialism has done with absolute propositions in all such things, and views these problems now as questions of detail, matters for fine discriminations. We want to be quit of pedantry. All that property which is an enlargement of personality, the modern socialist seeks to preserve."

Pages like these could be quoted bringing us out on to the familiar highway of practical social utility where every one of these doctrinal niceties will be fought out within the labor world very much as they have been of old in other classes. But this is conditional.

If our economic system so adjusts itself to the new order that it offers an increasing portion of labor a chance to add to its income with available opportunities for investment, no one within the social order will stand more stubbornly than labor for its right to dispose of its possessions as it will. Many socialists insist that this " available opportunity " exists for a negligible minority only and that these facilities are slowly diminishing. If they are right in this, their judgment is as sound as their cause is good. A social order in which the conditions of economic security for the many are steadily lessening is obviously bankrupt. It is thus " up " to the powers to make good their case. To make it good they must learn and learn soon to work understandingly with all that part of labor that has learned enough to take a common ground on which social and constructive coöperation is possible.

CHAPTER XIII

"SOCIALIZING THE MILK SUPPLY"

I

FOR many years this has been claimed as one of the first and most necessary to be socialized. From four larger cities there has come a serious threat "to take the milk supply from all private vendors."

A New Hampshire senator is reported as saying, "Government should take over the distribution of milk. Then the farmer would get a decent price for his milk." Yes, if "Government" secured better organization, directed by more intelligent and faithful service, but that is what we want to know.

One milk center draws supplies from more than 22,000 farms. Many very inaccessible; many doing the work with no hired help. Under such conditions, will Government take over all these properties and keep account of costs, so that we know even approximately what they are?

The best sanitary reasons exist for greatly enlarging the community control of this product. Several countries offer successful experiments along these lines. But are we to believe that the entire milk business — production and distribution — will be so controlled? Milk flows into many of our cities from farm areas four and five hundred miles in diameter. Boston gets milk from New York State, from Vermont, New Hampshire and Maine. In this area are thousands of farms employing many thousands of laborers. Shall the City, the State or Government take up this work in its entirety? Shall these public bodies hire and direct this vast body of workers?

There are plenty of advocates even for this, but there is not the least danger that our people will submit to it.

They will submit to and even demand more inspection, regulation and experimenting with "municipally owned cows and farms." There is much room here for further public action. But for years too many people have been watching government and city operations. Too many farmers have the new experience with hired labor to make it in the least likely that we shall entrust the whole milk business to Government.

From my own farm, I have seen a neighbor's hired men take to the shade of a tree when he was safely out of sight. If absent long enough, they have a game of cards and even when working, they so "slow down" that I get from the farmer this account: "If I'm with 'em every minute, they work fairly well. When I'm away I'm lucky if they earn their board."

Another neighbor with like experience, allows a considerable part of his hay to go uncut in the present year telling me, "It's no use! the kind of help you can get won't earn their money unless you are at their heels all the time, I'll now raise what I can myself and let it go at that."

From a large "fancy" farm having a very large labor body, I hear the same story of costly supervision to prevent this "soldiering." The proprietor says, "I don't know what it is, but something in the last few years has got into the men I hire. They seem to me a different breed from what I had even a dozen years ago."

Work of this kind on one of the largest estates in New England was abandoned after long trial for the same reason.

"With the kind of help you can get" (for there is no other) to what expense would city or state be driven, in keeping these scattered thousands reasonably at such tasks in raising, feeding, milking and caring for publicly owned cattle? Here is something to the point; *the change that has come in the spirit of hired labor!*

It is this change which makes the call for further state

socialism so ridiculous even to a large part of labor. The trade unions now demanding it, do it solely to strengthen their power. They do not even propose to be more efficient until that power is secure.

It is this which leaves us our one out-standing problem; namely to get such share of business risks and burdens on to labor that it stiffens under it as well as the employer. Even if the state is finally to take up the total of milk-producing and delivery, something must intervene to train and interest so vast and so scattered an army. There are already other movements and other hopes in this direction, but I touch upon one in this field of milk supply which has special promise. It is that of consumers' coöperation. It already has its educated groups furnishing a stable market. In many places, it has tried farming at least enough to learn its difficulties. It has educated its labor for many kinds of industrial service and sees clearly that agricultural labor must have its scientific schooling and *be given a stake* in the business. If this can be done on farms accessible to the coöperator's market there is no reason why sound beginnings should not be made.

One of the most successful of our American groups is now seeking such a farm with the clearest understanding that its labor has to be " made "; that scientific instruction has so far to be given as to make these men and women feel the attractive power of a service which has every charm which science gives. The Manager tells me they have members eager to leave town life for this work. " We can then furnish our own milk, vegetables and fruit with no middleman's profit." But this too is a long road. Its merit is in the education and experimental proofs it affords for further advance. However far it extends, we shall find practical limitations which will leave a large part of this business in private possession, ownership and control. There is as little danger that the people of our generation will elect to carry the socialistic logic to a finality, as that all farming tools, sewing machines and motor vehicles " run for profit " will be appropriated and run by the community at community cost.

II

I read a collectivist generalization " The Dead should be buried at Public Expense." Because of evils we all observe, we are told " the state should take entire charge."

It is true that if some graphic representation in moving pictures could be made to the American people of the costs, profits, competitive wastes of over-stimulated extravagance in our whole private burial system, there would be shock enough to make some change possible. If there followed immediately another display of burial customs in many European cities, we should perhaps be led to take some steps toward rational control. But this would not involve a complete socialistic disposal of our dead. It would involve a very definite extension of public agencies to meet abuses. The loose orgie of private profit-making in this field which we have all sanctioned is as unworthy of our intelligence as of our morals. We have allowed the mystery of death to be played upon by competing undertakers, armies of insurance agents and other money-seekers as if this solemn event is in no way different from a public auction.

It is disheartening enough that we have so long allowed the loan sharks free leave to bleed the needy. It is even more humiliating that we permit indiscriminate competitors to combine and bid against each other in this funereal traffic.

An investigator tells me " The undertakers are quite as good as the rest of us. Many of them make only a living but none of them can help taking advantage of a situation with the bargaining power all on one side." He was told by one reporting to him: " I have only to show the poorest woman a photograph representing the fine funeral of a neighbor and she wants one like it, even if she has not a cent except her insurance money. Folks don't ask you the price of things in a time like that."

Older communities, from which we should learn, have taken proper measures. Several Swiss cantons restrict private profit-making almost completely. A public hearse and carriage for the family is furnished free. The poorest may take the last journey with no shame. By paying for them, any who chooses may have more expensive trappings. In other sections of Europe only recognized associations are allowed to own crematories and these shall not be money making companies. Thirty or more cities own them.

Other cities fix regulating tariffs expressly to check the old private abuses. Cases brought against the city by private undertakers have been decided by the courts solely on the ground that death offered too dangerous temptations to private trade. This is like Sir Edward Grey's conviction that powder and armament production puts too great a strain on human motives and should be taken out of private hands.

Yet even in these illustrations, for which so much may be said in favor of extreme public control, there is no indication that any influential part of the community would for a moment tolerate the logic of any economic or other doctrine. There is to be no hard uniformity of burials, no attempt to prevent added tributes to the dead. It is to check abuses and to assure to all a "minimum of decency" in these last rites.

That ancient terror that socialism "will level us living and level us dead" is as groundless as that "every one in the next century will have no doctor except a state doctor and pay no fee except as prescribed by the State." There will be great checks put upon scrambling competition among physicians, but there will be private ones. Among patients who choose a doctor after their own liking those of superior skill will doubtless get an extra fee privately paid.

Labor's hold upon us is now so secure that it must be convinced with the rest of us. It must learn the great lesson of limits in applying any doctrine or any principle. Every radical proposal must be "put up" to all the labor groups. I have chosen therefore these homelier problems that are less easily kept in cloudland than are those socialist fundamentals "the three rents." Though it may seem prosily overdone in detail, I give one further experience from which I got more instruction about those practical limits in extending socialist theory than from any other. In a French commune under socialist control, I heard these plans for "socializing school-feeding." The conviction had been reached that *all* children must be fed or vicious class distinctions would arise. The conviction was also expressed that this socializing would stop with food, but at that time, this presented no perplexities.

CHAPTER XIV

SOCIALISM AND THE CHILD AT SCHOOL

I

ONLY the most determined reader will endure the details of this chapter. My excuse is that a great deal of time was given to it and that no investigation proved more enlightening on changes of opinion which come to those who try to crowd a supposed " principle " so far as to lose all relation to other realities equally important. As a principle, individualism is as persisting a reality as socialism. As the former tends to anarchy, the latter tends to communism and we shall stand out against the excesses of both. Radical labor groups are making this discovery and what is more, they are acting upon it. This means the acceptance of that broader social experience which makes " progress of the whole and by the whole " possible. In this illustration, we see collectivism and individualism at grips with each other in a field where the human reactions appear in their most elementary form.

Like many a proposal having the sound of novelty, this proves (like " shop committees," or " social insurance ") to have roots of most unexpected age and depth, so " schoolfeeding " has a half century behind it. It sprang up among very different peoples and was inspired and directed by all sorts of motives, religious, charitable, political and scientific. The story shows the struggle among voluntary, official and compulsory methods. With the help of two devastating wars, the nourishment of the school child has now become a question of survival and social security.

Simple as it seems, nowhere can we study with more profit the immemorial conflict between collectivist and individualist ideals. Collectivism has made immense gains but it has also revealed weaknesses full of warning.

As no theoretic view upon this question has half the value of actual experiment, the appeal should be made to fields where there has been trial enough to show how the " great human average " acts under the more-or-less of bureaucractic management. The clear record of these reactions is very enlightening. As the democratic impulse widens, the passion for freedom and self-direction declares itself as unmistakably as does the fear and hatred of all red-tape lethargies. I select therefore instances in which we may see the socialistic logic at work; where men's decisions and preferences on compulsory collectivism may be observed and passed upon by ordinary folk; where there has been experiment enough to draw some conclusions about what " the people " will do when the full meaning of the problem comes home to them. I dwell upon the actual history and variations of opinion, because the subject is everywhere so alive that a wide basis for inference is possible. With the proposal to do away with " all profits " " all interest," " all rent," we have not yet any avenue for instructed " mass opinion." [1]

At the Paris Exposition in 1889, I first heard of socialist proposals to " feed, clothe and hygienically care for school children." Five years earlier, this work had begun, though the idea of the *" cantines scolaires "* had been long familiar. As the world destruction of young manhood has now again set new values on the child, so the Franco-German war of

---

[1] The following are recent books which I have found instructive, especially that of Miss Bulkley.
Forsyth —" Children in Health and Disease "— 1909, Page 102.
Rapeer —" Educational Hygiene "— 1915, Chapter 16.
Brown —" Health Aspects of School Lunches "— 1916.
Bulkley —" The Feeding of School Children "— 1914.
Bryant —" School Feeding "— 1913.

1871, made it almost immediately an issue in France. The caisse des écoles (school fund) was founded in Paris in 1874. The real work was at first voluntary, but as the logic of compulsory education was thought out, one question was more and more asked, " If all children are forced to attend school and many of them are found to be so ill-nourished and ill-clothed that the teaching process is wasted, what is to be done? This was before socialists had captured a single commune. When a few years later, I visited communes where socialists had control, I heard the same large purpose expressed about the public care of school children that Bernard Shaw gives us in the preface to " The Doctors' Dilemma."

" Be careful to go to a school where there is what they call a school clinic, where your nutrition and teeth and eyesight and other matters of importance to you will be attended to. Be particularly careful to have *all this done at the expense of the nation* (my italics) as otherwise it would not be done at all, the chances being forty to one against your being able to pay for it directly yourself even if you know how to set about it. Otherwise you will be what most people are at present: an unsound citizen in an unsound nation, without sense enough to be ashamed or unhappy about it." This was the note of the French socialists. To socialize public utilities, eliminate middlemen, private contractors; to take over drug stores (as they had begun to do) would of course furnish ample funds.

In the earlier period, however, collectivist theory had no part in it. Individualism was in full vigor and very fluent with arguments about " weakening parental responsibility."

Wherever the first investigators reported the facts of malnutrition — France, England, Holland, Belgium, the United States — the public was long stolid in its incredulity. Very slowly it had to be educated into curiosity enough to look seriously at the evidence. After London was feeding 60,000 school children, a more searching investigation showed that the number must at once be doubled. A few months after his testimony, I saw and spoke with a physician of such eminence as Sir Lauder Brunton. In 1907 he expressed this opinion after careful study. "In spite of all the charitable organizations and benevolent institutions in the country, they found that children were starved by thousands, they became weak, they were growing burdens to themselves and useless to others, and instead of being a strength to the country they weakened it." We should be more than suspicious of this extreme emphasis if it were not supported in one country after another by men of this competence. Dr. Collie said, "Apart from infectious diseases, malnutrition is accountable for nine-tenths of child sickness." Dr. Eicholz: "Food is at the base of all the evils of child degeneracy." The Health Officer of Manchester, Dr. Niven, Dr. Leslie Mackensie, Sir George Newman, reported results of their investigations in the same strong terms.

The Secretary of Ratan Tata Foundation (University of London) in 1914 called the opposition to this freer feeding "a mean and short-sighted parsimony." In 1913, the estimate of those actually suffering from malnutrition was 600,000. The evidence so accumulated that the national standards of vigor seemed threatened. Causes like war and a sinking birth rate have given new and startling impetus to child saving and thus to adequate care.

When agitation had done its work, "the health of the child as a national asset" became a shibboleth. Parliamentary committees and city councils yielded to argument. In 1913, it was a Chief Medical Officer of a Board of Education who said, "From a purely scientific point of view, if there was one thing he was allowed to do for six million children *if he wanted to rear an imperial race,* it would be to feed them. The great, urgent and pressing need was nutrition. With that they could get better brains and a better race."

As we now re-estimate the human losses, especially in Europe, every objection to adequate feeding will fail and should fail. The real issue will be over the *extent and method of it and over the raising of funds.* Shall the State bear the whole expense or shall the bills be divided between the public and the parents? What division of the cost shall be made between government, municipality and smaller towns?

For a generation socialists have been very withering in their attacks on the " stinginess " of all bourgeois and charity treatment of this question. It has been written into scores of platforms that children should be fed and clothed without any puttering hesitations as to costs. " All children, destitute or not, should be fed and fed without charge at the expense of the State or municipality " appears again and again. Every new investigation is rich in material for those who urge this generous program. Neither child nor parent was to be " humiliated." All should be treated alike, and feeding " should be made free and universal," or " Medical officers shall determine the whole question of physical needs and local authorities be definitely obliged to feed all children thus determined to be necessitous." We are told " It is intolerable that legal technicalities, the dead weight of administrative indifference and the mean individualism of a small section of reactionaries should stand in the way of recognition of a principle which the vast majority of a community accept." This epitomizes the *drift* in every country.

We are assured by those who urge " large and generous policies," that in " principle and idea " this supplementing of home feeding is widely accepted in private schools as it has been adopted by thousands of business establishments. Many employers say that it pays them if they furnish the meal at considerably below cost. A few testify that lunches entirely free are found to be " good business." These witnesses are used by those who would adopt the same policy for our schools. "If it pays the private employer, it would as certainly pay the public."

Loose reasoning like this will be as popular as it is misleading. The private employer is personally responsible for his business and for every direct and indirect cost. For every miscalculation he has to pay. He cannot, like the politician or official, pass his blunders on to the public. Those who urge free feeding tell us that in the end, "it would so enrich the community as to cover the preliminary costs many times over." Month by month, the private employer could test this. Public officials have neither the motive nor the qualifications for such tasks. It is this aspect that I wish especially to note.

In the year following the agitation in England, I received from the correspondent of the London medical journal, the *Lancet,* an account of his visits to ten Continental cities for the purpose of reporting results of "Free Feeding of School Children." He told me he had been profoundly impressed by the need of systematic feeding. In his pamphlet on this subject (printed in the office of the *Lancet,* 1907) we see the movement at every stage as we see the conflict and changes in discussion.

A city physician examines the clothing on a large number of very poor children. In her "Child and The State," Miss McMillan, who gave years to this subject, thus comments on the doctor's findings: "Some little victims are sewed up in their clothes when the cold weather comes and are not taken out again till spring. Some have one garment piled on another and are often in a state of steady perspiration. Some have nothing in the way of linen and are dreadfully underclothed, and many — very many alas! are devoured by parasites! This last can be tolerable perhaps to the child living a free life in the street. It is unbearable in the restrained life of the class-room, and is doubtless one reason why a great many can hardly fix their attention on any subject taught in school." A Boston teacher of twenty-seven years' experience in schools of the poorer quarter tells me of cases differing little from the above.

It is among these classes too that the consequences of our child labor restrictions and compulsory school attendance are acutely felt. There is no more accepted tradition among our aliens than that the children should begin early to help out the family budget. Compulsion *plus* labor-laws stop these aids. A widowed mother who had daily to leave her home for ten hours, tells a visiting teacher, "Oh, the rich folks make a law that our children *must* go to school. They are not even allowed to work and earn anything for us until they are nearly grown up. How can I and those like me feed and clothe them so they are fit to be seen in school?" Meantime we, in the United States, have accepted the necessity of this added care of the child. We read that in Chicago 123,897 children were examined in 1909. Out of 63,000 found physically defective, *44,000 were defective in oral conditions* — that is, their teeth and mouths were in a bad state. In the schools of Princeton, Ind., *805 cases* were studied in 1909 — to take a town — and of these *193 boys and girls* had good teeth, and *612 bad teeth*. Five hundred and seventy-nine had never been to a dentist, and only twenty per cent. of the 805 used toothbrushes!

The United States Commissioner of Education, after stating the reasons for school feeding, says the idea is now "well-rooted" and "will spread very rapidly." The practice is already reported in over fifty of our cities. Individualistic opponents, it is said, can have no argument because the parent is to pay the bill. There is to be no "charity element."

If we include the European movement it is already evident that parents are not going to pay the full costs of this institutional feeding. The "deficits" to be paid by the public are growing in this country and will continue to grow. As with a large part of city and government ownership, all of us have to foot the final bills and the question, I repeat, is *how far* are we to follow the "large gesture" of the socialist?

I do not myself believe this to be an objection to systematic school feeding. I wish only to bring out the issue and its consequences. With the inevitable growth of socialistic sentiment we must accept the fact together with its implication. "If we compel children to be educated, they should go to school in such condition as to make their education possible. If the child is under-nourished at home, he should be supplied at school." When the opponents saw the experiment to be inevitable, they insisted that voluntary and local agencies should alone be trusted with the work. "Let us first appeal to the parents in their homes." A French Commune experimented for two years, only to find that "not one parent in ten could be moved to the least practical response." Another reported that seventy per cent. did not take the trouble to read the notices sent to them. Even where a small majority did respond, the interest was found to wane after a few weeks. The "defenders of the home" kept up the fight in spite of discouragement. One irate objector said he would "give them just one generation of this pampering to break up family life and put children into public institutions as Rousseau put away his bastards."

Investigations in the poorer homes meantime brought out most ominous evidence. " Mere children drinking strong coffee often with no nourishment." Boston found " hundreds that come without any breakfast at all." Others " lived so far away that their stomachs were unfit for study by ten o'clock." "Sometimes it was coffee or tea and one or two cents to buy something on the way — usually cheap candy." It is thus admitted everywhere that some

SOCIALISM AND THE CHILD AT SCHOOL 227

children must have free food. Are the rest of the children to know this? Often it is kept a "profound secret" or they are allowed to "sweep and wash up, so that no charity stigma shall lie against them."

Again it was found, as in Boston where 22,000 homes had been visited, that "large numbers of children from 'perfectly good homes' go to school with no breakfast." These well-to-do mothers answer the inquiries, "The breakfast is always there, but they run off without touching it." One ruffled mother says her children "go to bed so late that they have no time for breakfast if they are to get to school on time."

Pages of these half tragic, half comic experiences could be given to show how practically difficult it is to reach the homes by mere voluntary or persuasive appeals. Item for item, it is like voluntary attempts in any country to insure the "working classes" against accident, sickness and old age. Voluntary approach easily reaches the strong and more successful; that is, those who least need insurance. The weaker, the unlucky, the shiftless; in a word, the large numbers for whom insurance is socially and individually most necessary have to be dealt with by the rigor and uniformities of state compulsion. This, for good or ill, is the price we pay for the "Strong State."

The longest and the completest experience of school feeding is that of Paris. In the very midst of the social revolution of 1848, a body of scientific men in France studied and reported on "the causes of diseases"—to which the children of the poor were exposed. They found the chief evil to be lack of animal food: that fresh meat should be given them "*once a month.*" Political convulsions soon stopped all efforts to meet these suggestions, but Victor Hugo was so moved that some years later he furnished the suggested meal to forty ill-fed children. The results reported in England led to the "Destitute Children's Dinner Society."

In 1870, fifty-eight dining rooms had been opened to carry on and extend the work. From once a fortnight, we pass to "once a week," then to "twice a week" until we have daily feeding with the demand that "holidays be included." From 1867 we can follow a movement that seems to be irresistible. Less and less do we hear the argument about "weakening parental responsibility."

In 1884, in her elementary schools, Paris was furnishing food on a large scale at public cost. In 1905 she was giving more than six million free lunches.

In the report above indicated is a passage which sums up at that date so much world experience that I give it at length. "The municipal councilors and others, whom I have recently seen at the Hôtel de Ville, entertain very little doubt as to the upshot. It is evident that only a third of the parents pay and then they do not pay the full cost of the meals their children eat. So that all the children and all the parents derive some advantage at the cost of the general rate-payers. When attempts are made to get more voluntary subscriptions for the school funds, the persons solicited very often answer that they pay such heavy taxes that there should be no need to add to these any further sum. Not a few of the parents also, when it is pointed out to them that they should endeavor to pay for meals given to their own children at school, object that they are already paying through taxation, and this is perfectly true. Thus the number of those who individually pay for the meals have steadily decreased from year to year and it is already an open question whether the money thus obtained is worth the trouble of collecting. Its collection causes friction, creates invidious distinctions between individuals, gives rise to accusations or the suspicions of favoritism, necessitates somewhat inquisitional investigations into the private concerns of numerous families to ascertain who should and who should not pay, and occupies a large staff of persons on an unpleasant and unproductive investigation. Then why should a workman who is just a little better off than his neighbor, because, for instance, though earning the same wage he has two children instead of three, be made to pay twice over for his children's meal, once to the *caisse scolaire* of his district and once to the tax collector? The section of the population that can and does pay for their children's meals are beginning to realize that it would be very much to their advantage if *the entire cost was defrayed out of public funds."*

In the following year, 1908, I again visited several smaller communes in control of socialist officials. There was but one opinion about school feeding, namely, that it should be done far more generally and with still more ample funds, at public expense. This is the socialist urgency in every country to do away with distinctions and qualifications. Their organ in New York, *The Call,* shows the spirit in these words.

" There have been numerous pigmy attempts to supply penny lunches to school children, but the efforts in this direction have been so feeble, so niggardly, so half-hearted and so tainted with charity that they are hardly worth mention.

" There is only one way in which this problem can be solved satisfactorily, and that is by a generous, comprehensive system of free midday meals for school children without any stigma of poverty being attached thereto.

" All school children would benefit by a noon-hour school-meal system, the well fed ones as well as the underfed ones."

II

This feeding, however, is but a first step. If " sufficient food, properly cooked and properly eaten " is a necessity under our system of compulsory education, then clothing, medical care of the lungs, throat, skin, eyes, teeth, and indeed of every other hindering imperfection may be just as essential and certainly as logical.

One after another these actually appear. From two poor quarters of Paris "clothing was found so scant that in cold weather the children brought infectious colds dangerous to the whole school." Paris began moderately with a budget of 8500 francs for boots and another budget for clothes. Later a single district of the city (Batignolles) was paying 12,877 francs for boots alone with public agitation for "less red-tape and more substantial benefits."

As successive socialistic additions were made (books, stationery, food, clothes, care of teeth, throat and nose) came reasons why many pupils could not pay the bills. We have had, for example, many examinations of the teeth and of the relation of "bad teeth to the mind." Four Cleveland schools report "above ninety per cent. of the pupils' teeth require immediate attention."

Another larger group of schools shows "eighty per cent. with nearly half as many defective throats and noses." From Buffalo we hear at the Congress on School Hygiene of "an appalling number with faulty eyesight and hearing." A special commission in Boston reports that "5000 is a conservative estimate of the total number of tuberculous children in the public schools" besides a large number "poorly nourished and thus favorable candidates for infection." A special place "in the open, with extra food and clothing," is recommended.

We are warned in the report from Illinois where "it was recently shown that the State each year expends $1,187,000 in educating children who die of tuberculosis before reaching the twentieth year. Massachusetts probably runs a close second. And hundreds of millions are thrown away on pupils who do not actually die, but whose faculties, dulled by improper feeding, cannot grasp and retain their instruction. School lunches are therefore as much a part of education as schoolhouses, textbooks, or teachers."

As in a mass of older European experience, we have at this point the frank admission that voluntary associations cannot be depended on to do this work; cannot " long feed upon the willingness of wealthy contributors to a society of philanthropists." Belgium and Holland, it is said, " give free meals to the under-fed," while Paris with the longest experience " includes the subsidy in the city budget." This tendency to put the expense upon the public is as universal as are the other features of a growing state socialism.

As thrifty politicians are this moment loud in their demand that civil service rules for returning soldiers should be dropped; as they first asked in New Bedford that all needy soldiers be given fifty dollars; elsewhere that they should be given $100; a candidate for Governor demanding " as many dollars for each brave man as there are days in the year," and finally that they should all get five dollars a day from the time of enlistment (this from a Congressman), so we find the politician in the story of school feeding. Each wishes to outdo the other in public beneficence and to have the credit for it.

At Toulon, in southern France, the first committee was very firm at the start. " Each pupil should pay." As it became noised abroad that many poor children could not pay, the question at once became political. Selected ones who could not pay were first fed free, but required to wash the dishes and help clean up. This soon became an issue. " Why," asked a socialist official, " should they be compelled to advertise their poverty before all the other pupils?"

The political stage of this movement is always the same. Any local politician acquires an enviable reputation by appealing to the electors for " large and generous treatment of this question."

This is the history in scores of French communes, as it

is in Italy. In the latter country, I think with no exception, the first steps were in the name of charity and private initiative. Then the municipality begins part payment. This invariably grows to more and more until the timid objector is silenced. He is silenced when rival political parties take up the issue. It was a socialist pleading for free public feeding who says, " In time, however, the contending political parties accepted the principle, the Government gave its approval, and now the rival factions compete with each other as to *who shall feed the children in the best and most complete manner."*

In San Remo this issue had a dramatic history. As long as the Conservatives were in power, free feeding was held to the old lines, but socialists in 1903 got control. They more than doubled the 6000 lire and turned the " charity subvention " into a direct municipal appropriation.

An interesting variation in Italy may be seen in the little town of Vercelli. Here it was not primarily a question of feeding, but of " educating a sense of equality." One party thought this could be done " without any collectivistic attack on the social order." The socialists, it was said, are teaching class hatred. Their talk is always of enemies and class war. This must be met in the schools not merely by the book and oral instruction, but even more in the daily practices of eating alike and dressing alike. Masters and mistresses were advised " for example's sake " to eat as the children ate. A leader in this was the local member for Parliament, Signor Lucca. He thought the socialists' theory of " class war " so dangerous that it should be met by a " realized equality " in the schools. Let all alike be compelled to take the same meal. This was carried into effect. But gross inequality in *dress* was next observed. This too should be met by a subvention for clothes,— the town supplying raw materials for the sewing classes. A list of 500 articles of clothing is given as the year's work. We then read, " Several hundred little children are gathered together here; they belong to all classes of the community, there is not the slightest difference in their appearance, and all are treated exactly alike."

Socialist agitation has nevertheless played an honorable and most serviceable part in overcoming the scandalous apathy of the public on this question. Far more has to be done at public expense to insure the healthy vigor of the child at school, but the central issue remains — *how far and how much* shall the collectivist principle be encouraged?

Between those who would center all power in the State and those who would progressively leave her less and less, the pendulum has always swung — and always will. Unless an unqualified communism is before us, the people will somewhere draw lines; they will find practical limits as with school-feeding, inheritances, state doctors and milk supply beyond which they will not pass.

All attempts to be "scientific" or sham-accurate about the exact tracing of this line is the idlest casuistry. From place to place and from time to time it will be differently drawn in the endeavor to preserve some balance between the forces of organized compulsion in State and City and the free competitive activities that are sources of our strength.

I have known three socialists with long and definite experience on this phase of school work who would lead in the fight against any and every proposal to do anything like what was called for by the socialist Mayor of St. Ouin: "Wherever it leads, the State must pay the costs of food, clothing and medical care with no discrimination of class, rich or poor."

Collectivism will never wholly dominate any vigorous and growing social organism. We are not all of us going to work for the city or state either in the letter or the spirit of state socialism. A hardy proportion of the race will go on with its own tasks. It will insist upon doing these freely in its own way and after its own humor. The evidence of this comes from the most socialistic authorities. More and more they rebel against all "blanket-universals" of their own or of any other theory. We expect these practical adaptations from Fabian opportunists and from "reformists" generally, but they come from the ablest Marxians like Kautsky. He believes that socialism will free whole reservoirs of energy out of which new activities and new undertakings will spring into existence and that these "*shall freely compete with the state.*"

It is in this spirit that another lifelong leader and defender of Marx, W. H. Hyndman, ridicules those of his own following who constantly tell us "all wars are capitalist wars." In his "Future of Democracy" he sets down a list of wars — South Africa, Tripoli, China, Burmah, Morocco — which were capitalist —" whose primary object was to obtain an extension of trade and commerce." But another list, he thinks it nonsense to call "capitalist":— "Wars of emancipation like those of Cavour in Italy and the great struggle in Hungary." He thinks it as absurd to call the war just closed a capitalist war. Mazzini and Garibaldi wanted war and started war but what capitalist motive ever cast its shadow on their thought?

The whole batch of "logical consistencies" expressed in the "all" of socialist, syndicalist or communist claims finally gets so little welcome among the very ones who apply them that the rejection or limitation comes most convincingly from within.

"Beware of the Orchestra." This too I have heard from one who said he spoke from experience as a musician. He was a "philosophical" anarchist. "If you play in an orchestra," he said, "you must take orders from without. Not by a hair can you show your own individuality. Over you with his stick is the leader who becomes 'great' only

SOCIALISM AND THE CHILD AT SCHOOL 235

as he compels submission. You have a sheep-flock of fifty to one hundred men watching his stick. They submit like slaves with the result that slave *habits* are formed which will show themselves socially and politically. They can't be musical slaves and free men in other relations of life." For this very free lance, only the soloist should be trusted with this art and the artistic values it conserves. The first man to attack him was another anarchist. In the chaffing that followed, he was asked if the duet wasn't the first entrance of the devil upon the scene. Another asked why a higher self-expression or at least a different kind of self-expression wasn't possible through the group-work of the orchestra. But none of these levities impressed him. He would have no dallying. Freedom was his god and compromise was mammon. This bravo in logic has his counterpart among extremer vegetarians who will not eat an egg because it contains a potential fowl. I had a schoolmate of rare purity of mind who would not kill a mosquito or a fly. He thought it lacking in hospitality, but if too many, he rather gently shoo'd them out of the window. Neither religion, politics nor reforms are without these types. If not too much in their company, they are a great relief from conventional monotonies, but no complicated society will entrust them with powers to dictate conduct to unconvinced majorities.

If history has a single hint for our guidance, one of them is this: that in the sections least supervised and regulated from without, a great part of those qualities most indispensable for social growth first come to life. This is but part of the impending problem of the lesser, self-determined community as against the greater.

At no time are we without first-rate witnesses to the excellence and necessity of the small free unit as against the ponderous and highly organized unit. When the glory of " The Great State " began to fascinate the German mind after the victories over Austria and France, a cosmopolitan publicist of such rank as Karl Hillebrand admitted that nothing could withstand this tide until it had spent itself. He treated it, however, as a danger to every "spiritual spontaneity which had made the greatness of the Fatherland." "We must," he said, "at length free ourselves from this weight of super-organization and restore again the free conditions that made Kant and his peers possible." If Treitschke teaches that the supreme achievements are inspired within and by the State, Lord Acton (at least the equal of Treitschke as historian) sees the richest growths free from and outside the State.

So, too, Lord Morley: "History derives its best virtue from regions beyond the sphere of the State." It seems a far cry from these august inquiries into the desired size of states and empires to the pros and cons of nourishing and caring for the child at school. Yet it is in experiments like those in government ownership: — supplying milk, disposing of our savings at death and school feeding — the degree of it, the ways and means through which it is done, that will instruct us because we can observe them among the more intimate and human motives that must determine public policy as democracy extends.

CHAPTER XV

HOW LONG SHALL WE WORK?

EVERY conflict of opinion raised in the chapter on socialism and in the illustrations which followed has become a part of working-class psychology. With long political accountability it acquires its own restraints. With continuous business responsibility, it learns so much in common with employers of the better class, that a tentative fellowship is as immediately possible as it is essential.

Where labor has taken up and carried the burden of production with its risks and obligations it adopts a new tone. Definitely responsible for business results, these workmen grow circumspect. For twenty-five years labor, as employer, has discussed and experimented with this question of hours and production. The managers hired by labor have become fluent in the use of the old arguments against too much cutting of hours.

In actual practice private employers have outrun anything the labor-employer has yet brought about. It sounds droll to hear a workingman coöperator say of the great employer at Port Sunlight, "He can cut his hours to six because he has a stupendous and successful business. He can afford to try any experiment, we cannot."

At a meeting of the Cambridge Club at which some features of Mr. Rockefeller's welfare work had been presented, an employer made this intelligent objection: "Mr. Rockefeller has business resources so vast that he can safely try anything he likes while in small businesses we should run too much risk."

This was the defense of the coöperator, "We are put to

it by competitors. Our business is not large enough or secure enough to cut the working time. We got it down to nine and then, in some departments, to eight. We can't at present go further and maintain our output."

This is what labor has to learn with all other problems raised in this study. Once actually under the burden, its gait grows steady. With something like 400,000 of its own employees, labor is hard at work on the time it will devote to industry.

The *principle* of eight hours has been won. It has been conceded by governments and municipalities. An army of employers has tried it, and justify it, but the working time remains one of the really great problems of a democratized industry.

As we can no longer discuss the strike on a mere wage basis, or government ownership on a basis of profit and loss, so we waste our time over the eight hour issue if the deeper purpose under it is not seen.

Since the war, we have seen trade union men opposing eight hours unless they could make it a basis of highly paid overtime. They were after this higher pay and not the shorter day. With real power in its hands, how will labor decide this question? When it sees clearly the relation between the quantity and quality produced, and wages, what will be the decision on hours? Millions of workers know as well as any one that scant production means in the long run scant wages. Other millions have this still to learn.

In a large shoe factory, I tried thirty years ago to find out how many of the men and women *wanted* eight hours. The question had been discussed at a series of meetings in which conflicting opinions about the desirability of the eight hour issue got vigorous expression from workmen. As most of them were paid by the piece, I found that only a minority even pretended to desire the shorter day except through some scheme that would give them as much money for the shorter as they got for the longer. No such plan had been devised. I could find but few who had any wish to substitute day wages for work by the piece because they believed their wages would fall off. These few, moreover, were older — less vitalized or in some way below standard as compared to the average worker. With the help of a foreman, I selected both men and women who were conspicuous for skill and capacity. Not one of them could have been induced to accept eight hours if this involved less income. They wanted the extra money for other gratifications more than they wanted the extra hour.

If the question had been put to vote, the ambitious would have been overwhelmingly against any cut in hours if it meant less pay. I do not present this as a final reason against eight hours, but we shall see what an issue it will make when labor takes the helm. I had seen in England a " Profit Sharing Partnership," in which a body of men and women were running their own business. They had " democratized " it. They had very complete independence and they liked it. If they wanted a day off, they took it. If they didn't like their manager, they changed him. If they disliked the successor, they changed him. They were very proud of this independence and enjoyed displaying it. " We've no boss or master here," was the tone. They knew their business was not very successful. They were keeping on some older men and women at a loss rather than turn them off. They had to do this " because there was no pension system." Especially in marketing their goods, these industrial partners had learned their weakness. They were behind their competitors in shrewd and timely purchase of raw materials.

They were making just enough out of it to keep going, subject, of course, to industrial and market changes that might sooner or later close them up.

And yet this group of " co-partners " had to all appearances deliberately chosen this easier and freer way of life quite content to take the consequences. They knew that many private employers in their trade were making better goods and higher profits; were quicker to put in new and better machinery and in most ways had a higher efficiency. They knew, too, that many men and women, in some capitalistic establishments got higher wages than their own industrial democracy could pay. These independents, however, claimed not to care a button about such superiorities of capitalist enterprise. They had got over the illusion that they could beat anybody in the field. They had set up another ideal.

To have control of their working lives; to call no man master was their chosen luxury and they were apparently happy in paying the price for it. They insisted that a more leisurely life was better than the slavish drive all about them. Life should be more than meat even in their day's job.

There was something very admirable in this. One shrank from putting it to the test of " general availability." The world may some time grow wise enough to arrange its toil in the same spirit, but there is a difficulty because at present, nothing is more certain than that the younger and more energetic will refuse submission to second or third rate achievements in wealth production. They will work at higher pressure partly because they want the higher income and partly because they want the satisfaction of using all their faculties. For both reasons, these more ambitious ones would soon quit a picnic shop like the one described.

A referendum vote in the Brockton factory would have instantly made this division between those who cared more for the extra satisfactions which higher wages gave and those who were willing to forego those satisfactions for the sake of the lighter tasks and a freer life.

The division is not simply between the lazy and the unlazy. It is not solely between the strong and the weak. It is between one type and a different type both among employers and employed. Much is made in the psychologies of the distinction between the active and the meditative types. Labor has as many of this latter as any other class. These are more keenly interested in other "goods" or values than any cash return can represent. They rightly want a society elastic enough to allow them to work three, five or any other measure of time after their tastes. We may be astonished at their numbers and at the variety of gifts they bring. It is my belief that these will prove of inestimable value in future reconstruction.

It is these who will help frustrate all attempts to shut the race too rigidly into any form of bureaucratic state socialism. This is why the developed syndicalist and New Guild impulse against every industrial autocracy is one of the soundest instincts. It is as inseparable from the "right of small nations" as it is from the "rights of individual liberty and growth." It is only a part of the great quest to subject all mechanism to a higher and worthier purpose than quantity of output can express. The employing class has its fair share of those making the same quest. They have the sense of freedom and the mood of the artist.

In very different businesses, enough clear-headed managers have already proved the feasibility of fewer hours to show that far wider use may be made of the shorter day. The slow reduction from twelve to nine hours has already carried its own irrefutable proofs that keeping labor too long at its tasks is bad business and even worse social policy. And now from nine to eight or less, the list of successful experiments is so long and in so many different industries as to appeal powerfully to a disinterested public opinion.

For what is further involved, I turn to a little of the history as set down in my first notes. It is a history rich in suggestion. We see how men argue on a basis of self-interest; how and why they oppose change. We see what uses labor makes of this opposition in its own propaganda for the shorter day.

In 1872, I went from Cambridge into Boston to hear evening talks upon the eight hour day by that clear-headed apostle of labor, George E. McNeil. There was no oratorical fustian, but only quiet conversational appeal. He carried this quality into the discussion following the talk.

I can now see that some of his reasoning was fanciful, especially his stress upon eight hours as a cure-all for unemployment. But the ever-recurring emphasis upon broader social reasons for the change left an impression never effaced. Strongest of all, and wholly new to me then was his insistence that the first question to ask and answer must be in terms of the man's whole working life. Not how much could he do in a day, a month, a year or in his most vitalized decade, but under what conditions should he work to secure the best results in the thirty to forty years before him? How should he work so as not to be scrapped ten or fifteen years too soon? This gives the questions its social importance.

As a shoemaker (with the coming and going) McNeil had worked eleven and a half hours a day. He made it clear how hard it was to save energy or even the wish to use the mind after so long a day. In the nearly fifty intervening years, all sorts of employers in all sorts of industries have frankly come to these views. This business confirmation of his view, McNeil could not know in 1872. As we now see it, he could not then know the full force of another of his favorite arguments. It was this, "What did our democracy imply, but that every citizen should cast an intelligent vote?"

Intelligence in this relation means substantial and varied information that does not come by accident. If labor is ever to reach an equipment fitting it to take part in democratic, self-governing societies, it must have at least as much leisure as an eight hour day makes possible. The long day then offered no such chance to any but very exceptional men like McNeil and another shoemaker, Henry Wilson. McNeil did not believe that one man in fifty among Lynn shoe workers could meet — or at any rate would meet — any of these educational requirements under working conditions then prevailing.

Even at that time, few students could help being influenced in favor of eight hours by the opposing arguments. The stock reasons, then current, showed but too clearly an interested bias. What would labor do with the extra time? They would, of course, go to the saloon or in other ways form bad habits. Production too must so fall off that wages would sink and the workers be worse off than ever. How often I heard another objection in this form: "I wouldn't mind lowering the time a little, but it is an entering wedge. If they get nine, they'll be sure to ask for eight, and then seven." This is the familiar warning of the illiterate father to his boy: "You better not learn the first letters. If you do, you'll have to go through the whole dern alferbet."

As a matter of course, we are still told how the docking of another hour will mean only that the men will abuse the leisure. But every student knows the uses of this argument when the working day was 13, 12 or 11 hours. Never was a time when a little more leisure was thought safe in the hands of labor. Did not employers tell us of those English wives who flocked to them begging that the working day be put back from nine to ten in order to save their *husbands from the pothouse?* What a part these wives played in the shabby farce to point a moral against a rational day's task! Never was one more skilled than McNeil in naming the kind of argument with which employers defended their case. Even in 1844, complaints were so resounding in Massachusetts that the legislature was forced to appoint a committee to look into the hours and conditions of labor, especially in the mill towns. The Report was so conservative as to bring the taunt of being entirely controlled by the employers. The Report concluded that "twelve hours and over" was not too long for the day's work, besides it was not in the province of the legislature to remedy such evils; the men should "trust to their own strength." This rebuff was but one of many in this and other states. In the two following years the discomfiture was the same, the employers fighting hard, as they do to-day, in fear of competition from other states and in fear of legislative interference. Machinery, too, "must be run twelve hours or no profit would result."

Yet through it all a growing part of the more influential labor world had set its heart on eight hours — *or their equivalent*. In spite of ignorant or malicious misrepresentation, the more intelligent advocates did not ask for any hard and fast application of eight hours; no one knew better than these petitioners that, in many industries, the literal eight hour day will not everywhere work. No one states more clearly that a great deal of elasticity will be necessary in its application. What was asked was that an eight hour minimum might be worked out wherever practicable; that "overtime" receive extra pay as an automatic check upon abuses of the principle. Thus the *idea* had come and it had come to stay. It got itself well phrased: "Eight hours' work, Eight hours' sleep and Eight hours' play." Capitalism generally has kept men, women and children at the task as long as they would stand it.

Labor itself has made the chief protest against the abuses of overwork. But from the first, a small minority of employers steadily growing in number and influence has been no less useful in proving to the world *how and why* the shorter day was as good business as it was good statesmanship.

These men are no more to be omitted in the long story than are great advocates of the reform like Shaftsbury and Macaulay. In this country the experiments were at first timid and hesitating. In Massachusetts in 1881, a textile manufacturer told his experience in the Bureau of Statistics of that year. He began, he said, with the thirteen hour day. He began also to watch his men and women at their work. He soon saw that "something was wrong with the hours and more so with the arguments popular among employers.

"Soon after I took charge, I persuaded the rest of the directors to allow me to reduce the hours to eleven. Before this, the weekly product of the mills had been 90,000 yards of print cloths. After it, with the same machinery, the weekly product rose to 120,000 yards.

"Now granting that a part of that increase was due to improved management, yet it is clear that this improvement could not have been made nearly so effective without the improved physical conditions which so great a reduction of hours afforded."

A few years later Frederick Hazzard went to Europe to study the effect of the prevailing eleven hour day. He became convinced that even eleven hours was a business blunder. At the end of long and varied tests, he concluded that in spite of high wages per unit of time, "the result in cost is less than it was before the eight hour change was made." Since then experiments in great numbers have shown at least this: that *with high class management,* the case for the shorter day is among the practical possibilities for almost every kind of business. The United States Bureau of Labor shows the lopping off of hours from 1907 to 1914, in eighty-nine trades, with results that show this to be a reform as practicable as that of properly guarded machinery. We now have ample and trustworthy industrial history reporting the facts. It does not contain an authentic page to prove that labor has made worse use of its leisure than has any other class that ever won leisure. It is true that the practical difficulties of a shorter task in certain industries are far greater than labor is likely to concede. It is for this very reason that forward looking employers are furnishing us with better arguments for eight hours than economists or agitators ever gave.

The debate on this question is more and more between two kinds of employers rather than between labor and employer. Those who resist eight hours usually tell us they would welcome it if their competitors could be forced into line, but in what business is there fiercer competition than in the clothing industry? Yet in a late agreement of Hart, Schaffner & Marx, the largest firm of all, we read: " It reduces hours from fifty-two to forty-nine a week with an increase of ten per cent. in wages." Here too we find the minimum wage.

With a party of delegates to the Paris Exposition of 1889, I visited glass works in the north of France where experiments with shorter hours were under discussion. Eight hours was then a mere dream. But twenty years have done their work.

A recent article in "Science" by Dr. F. G. Lee, reports that the proprietor of this same business is now convinced that the eight hour day and even a seven and a half hour day may be made more productive in that industry.

The best evidence is from old and well organized firms where welfare work has reached high water mark. The Seiss Optical Factory at Jena is one of the most carefully planned in the world. I was two months in that town when its organization was undergoing changes thought by timid people to be as dangerous for the men as for the business. It had long tested the nine hours with results so favorable as to make the eight hour day " only another step in better business."

These experiments are in many countries. In the Engis Chemical Work of Belgium it is instructive because *labor opposed the change from fear of lower wages.* The manager, M. Fromont, after twelve years' trial, pronounces eight hours "a success that convinces every man open to evidence." He points to improved health of labor and a larger output of the plant. The range and variety of these successes is far too great to be explained away on grounds of some peculiarity in the location or in the business. The English President of the Iron and Steel Institute says: "We commenced the forty-eight hours week system twenty-two years ago. We began with a thousand men. In May, 1914, we had six thousand and now (1917) we have fifteen thousand." He adds, "We are now unanimous that we would not resort to the old system."

Since Robert Owen voluntarily lowered hours in his mills from fourteen to ten more than a century ago, the evidence has accumulated. Yet a few months ago a Massachusetts employer thus scoffed at President Wilson's approval of the eight hour day: "Of course, as politician he has got to do that. If he ran a big business, he would know better." Fortunately, it is from the hardest heads in business that we now get a reasoned judgment on eight hours, which no person fully alive can ignore.

From one of the largest businesses (Endicott-Johnson Shoe Co.) we have a report which concludes: "We think the eight hour day has arrived." This industry is notoriously competitive and therefore open to all the classic objections to any initial shortening of the day by single firms.

Another shoe company, W. H. McElwain, with nearly 7000 men, subjected this issue to every searching test, with the result that lowering the time from a nine hour day (55 hours per week) to almost eight, the "production per man" has increased.

The war is producing the kind of evidence upon the effects of long and short hours that should settle a few of the most disputed points once for all. At a time when England was fighting for existence; when every motive was for utmost, immediate output, many competent boards were watching results of hours ranging from eight per day to thirteen. Over a wide field, concentrated observation was directed upon small groups occupied on many varieties of tasks.

The result is a crushing refutation of all pleas for long hours. In one of many reports under the "Ministry of Munitions," written by the physician in charge, we read such items as these:

"Observations extending over a period of 13½ months upon the output of workers showed that a reduction of working hours was associated with an increase of production both relative and absolute."

In the illustrations given we have tests of the twelve hour day, the ten and nine hour day down to eight, with the final conclusion that a considerable addition to the leisure time of the operatives would have substantially improved the total output of the factory. This is like the Victor plant in New Jersey, with its 7500 employees. From the management we read: "The company believes that the shortening of the hours will greatly reduce the nervous strain which is so evident in modern industrial organization."

The head of an old and prosperous business with ten thousand employees, Lord Leverulme, has experimented enough to express the opinion that six hours may prove still better for business. Watching the effects of long hours during the war and speculating on the future of English industry, he suggests that efficiency alone will require at least the eight hour day. He joins the revolutionists. A large well-to-do idle class is no longer to play the deadbeat. "We cannot consent as a nation to there being any idle (rich or poor). Nor can the British Empire become a loafer's paradise if it is to continue to exist."

This employer of so many thousands has a most fertile suggestion about the unnecessary idleness of *capital* (mainly machinery) which he thinks should work longer and more efficiently through shorter shifts. Here he finds a source of so much more production as to make fewer hours for labor easily possible.

This is not a twentieth part of the evidence easily available for the eight hour cause, but it is enough to show the part wise employers have played in convincing public opinion and other business men that the labor claim has upon the whole been justified. That a trade union like the Cigar Makers could win eight hours after a long struggle and finally convince employers in that industry that it was an improvement would not have satisfied employers in other industries, but as scores of practical managers fall into line and add their own testimony to the superior efficiency of the shorter day, the main battle is won.

No "eight hours by legislation" shows anything in the least comparable to this proof in private business that it is possible and at the same time a wiser way in conducting industry. It is in no way necessary to the argument to show that it is at once desirable under all conditions. What employers are showing is that the case is clearly made out for larger extension of principle.

As it is my hope in this study to avoid all pleasant lying, even if on my side, an admission must be made. In a good many industries and among many sections of labor the shorter day will result in lowered product. No reform ever brought its "easement" without furnishing attendant troubles. The eight-hour day will be abused, as it has been already in well-known industries in this country, and especially in much public employment. Government — whether federal or municipal — will have long and serious difficulties with this feature. They are difficulties, however, inherent in all political management of labor and not only in the eight-hour aspect of that labor. In conceding this reform, governments have shown good sense because the *principle* is itself sound. It has slowly to be worked out like social insurance in spite of incidental waste and blunders. It is better that we should not be spared the record of abuses.

Inquiries like those of the New Jersey Bureau of Statistics show a " reduction of output in a majority of establishments when hours were reduced." In more recent investigations like those of the National Industrial Conference Board we read that more than sixty establishments report lower product with the shorter hours. Thirty-two claim that the reduction is proportionate to the lessened working time; a few that it was more than proportional. These conclusions are to be taken with great caution because of their origin. Yet they tell a good deal of truth which all cocksure persons who insist that product has not fallen off should take into account.

In most concerns where product has been maintained and even increased under eight hours, there was long and careful planning with strict supervision over the labor force or where that force had passed a long selective process. There was also in the main good will and confidence between management and men. Where these conditions are lacking, it is not to be expected that the general body of workers will invariably respond.

We now know well that great numbers of wage-earners do not mean to work as hard. They are very frank in posting their program. It is this: " We do not accept the ideal of competitive industry with its interested prattle about quantity, always quantity. The old ideal put machinery and output first. We are going to make it second. That life is more than bread and meat has a practical meaning to us. These are words to the preacher but to us they shall be deeds." The attempts to reach this ideal will go hand in hand with much waste and idleness. The evils will probably increase until the whole wage system is brought under greater democratic control. Labor must then face this question of pace and of quantity of output precisely as it faces it in the self-governing workshop and in the coöperative movement where labor has long been its own employer.

As I recall again the little hall, in 1871, what strikes me is the utter simplicity of the issue as those working men and their leader conceived it and indeed as many scholars conceived it. Labor wanted eight hours, the employers opposed. It was one against the other. Scarcely a shadow of this simplicity now exists. Employers are in two camps, thousands of them accepting the principle and many of them long since practicing it.

As for labor, with every new accession to strength, it begins to question and dispute as to what it will have and how it will get it. These differences are not about mere trifles but as often about essentials.

Some will have it by law. Others insist that trade unions are a safer agency. But more and more eight hours are asked as a *kind of minimum* on top of which a higher and more favorable wage income can be secured. As governments and many employers have granted the principle, labor uses the occasion and the favoring settlement to drive the best bargain within its power.

As labor gains still more control, the struggle in its own camp over wages and means and even over " principles," will increase. If labor, as it hopes, should get the mastery, all that is really vital in this eight-hour issue has still to be fought out. We shall then learn that we can *democratize nothing in politics or in industry without carrying the dispute further in among the masses concerned, where the " ache of responsibility" is felt by all alike.*

CHAPTER XVI

INDUSTRIAL DEMOCRACY AT ITS BEST

I

IF we looked solely at the history of socialism, we should get from it very little encouragement of mass-capacity for democracy. Its ablest leadership has been from bourgeois intellectuals who after long trials have bitterly commented on the capacity of the masses. Even in the entire record of trade unionism, we see how acquired power leads to gradual imitation of the old checks on mass-interference and the adoption of old machine methods against which the young radicals of labor protest like mugwumps against our own standpatters.

Wrinkled with forty years' service among the unions, one of our A. F. of L. gives his experience in a quotation. He said he thought at the start that he knew what democracy was and could define it any hour of the day. " I have lived," he added, " to see that I knew nothing whatever of the tribe I belonged to. Most of them haven't a grain of interest in the duties which make real self-government possible. If we trusted the whole crowd to have a hand in everything, we should only be shifting tyranny from one shoulder to another. It would be harder to fight than the old tyrannies because it would continually slip from one bunch to another."

Consumers' coöperation does not solve this problem of " pure " or indeed of any other democracy, but it takes a brave step and holds it. It does a great deal more; it carries the responsibilities so far into the labor membership that it can see *where the fault lies,* namely in apathies and frailties of their own class. Thus capitalism is seen to be only one of the sinners.

One does not even get a glimpse of the movement in its larger aspects unless coöperation is seen as a sort of economic interpretation and embodiment of democracy itself. Among those who are caught and held by its spirit, it carries the democratic purpose into industry. It assumes approaches to equality in the only rational conception the word can ever have among those of differing gifts. It becomes selective. It sifts out a new order of capacities on which democracy must build if it build at all.

To hard-headed men bred in the stress and strain of industrial conflict, these new capabilities appear freakish. Yet no one, even a little familiar with the history, can sit through the sessions of a single coöperative congress without a profound and sobering experience. He is in an atmosphere of rigid business procedure, but there is no hour in which he does not recognize the presence of something more than business. It is this something over and above which holds his attention. He cannot define it but it is very real. It is most conspicuous in the higher leadership.

It is now nearly a quarter of a century since I first met at a trade union congress, Horace Plunkett, then on the threshold of the great work to which his life has been given with rare and enduring consecration. He expressed an opinion, the meaning of which, I did not then half guess. "Ireland," he said, "will never have a worthy politics until she changes her economic life." There is not one of the great coöperators who did not have at heart this something over and above business and its material, individual gains.

Here it was a new hope of religion, there of politics, again of social regeneration. Owen, Dr. William King, Raiffeisen, Huber, the heroic group of "Christian socialists," deBoyve, Pictet, Robert, Luzzatti, Plunkett — not one of them is to be thought of apart from his overthought of a cleaner and richer social life. Not one of them who did not see coöperation in its relation to more essential equality and justice among men.

One other name must be here recalled, with a message from his death-bed. I saw Albert Grey first when, upon an estate of some four thousand acres, he was trying to organize the coöperative endeavor among his work-folk on the land. Though interested chiefly at that time in the copartnership phase of the movement, the thought strengthened and enlarged until it became what he called "the nearest guess at the way out." Years later, as president of the Coöperative Congress, he spoke with deeper confidence of coöperation as a world movement carrying with it the surest hope of industrial fellowship which man had yet achieved.

Just before his death it was in this spirit that he sent out his final message.

"You know the idea of those words — he being dead yet speaketh? A voice from the dead often gets a hearing. That's what I'm after. I want you to make my voice sound from the grave. I want to say to the people, there is a real way out of this mess materialism has got us into. I've been trying to tell them for thirty years. It's Christ's way. Mazzini saw it. We've got to give up quarreling. We've got to come together. We've got to realize we're all members of one family. There's nothing can help humanity — I'm perfectly sure there isn't — *perfectly sure* — except love. Love's the way out and the way up. That's my farewell to the world."

If democracy has any hope, it is in the discovery of such men and in the acceptance of their leadership. That coöperation tends to educate and to select this type is the truest word that one can speak about it. Its economic and business training so lightens the strain on the more selfish, competitive motive as to make it easier for such men to gain and to retain real influence. If this is the greatness of the movement it is also its most chastening difficulty, especially in this country.

Nowhere do the uncertainties, risks, doubts so swarm about the subject as on our own domain. The very violence of our material prosperity, the extent and variety of unexhausted, natural opportunity, with the habits thus engendered, have until very recently, made the economic modesties of this movement rather ridiculous to us. The savings were so meager and the troubles so many. It is now certain that in this country coöperation is to have its first real chance. It has gone to the working class where it belongs in all its first stages. It is upon this broader basis that it must be built up and for one reason upon which too much stress cannot be placed; like other labor groups, these coöperators will go into politics. They have taken this step in Belgium and in England — " three millions of coöperative households " because government officials threatened to tax them as if they were making profits like private business.

The coöperators struck back with the threat to put candidates for Parliament in the field. Once there, these members will have at their bidding an enormous vote. In alliance with the Labor Party, they could at once block legislation as easily as allied socialists and radicals do in France. But here is a difference. These coöperators do not take into politics the untried theories or utopian aspirations of so many socialist members. Coöperators can send representatives far better trained than average middle class or upper class representatives. This is the safety of the selective and long economic and financial training which coöperation has given. From farms and oversea trade, to great manufacturing, banking and finance, there is not a business activity in which they are unschooled. If they take to politics, it will be with constructive policies based on business experience as severely practical as that of any representative in Parliament.

It may seem a too sudden transition from utopias to the most solid business achievements yet won by the working-class. It is justified because the coöperative movement not only had a utopian origin, but a spiritual idealism has never been absent from the élite of its leadership. A late book (and a most useful one) by L. D. Woolf ends with vision and prophetic suggestion as distinctly utopian as if the "Great Father" of the movement were still speaking to us.

Robert Owen was "The New Employer" of his day. He was a very prince in welfare devising as well as a forerunner of the syndicalists. He was a "road-breaker" between the old ways and the new. He was a textile manufacturer who could hold his own against any man in England. We know business men believed in him because they would lend him money.

In spite of so much writing about him, he cannot go quite unmentioned in my account. In perfect outline, the syndicalist idea first appeared in the circle influenced by this man. Even the "One Big Union" was there. It is, however, as father of the coöperators and as one whose religion was in education and its possibilities that he here has place. Never was it so clear as now that the supreme service of coöperation is in its educational reactions. Though it prove — as I have heard it called —" The Great Bluff," we are committed to democracy. Though no baker's dozen of us may mean the same thing in using the word, we look to "education" for its realization. We have learned that the book part of this training is secondary to the daily discipline "at the point of production"— where men and women earn their bread and most continuously exercise their faculties. It is this education that we may see in those solidifying labor groups with supplementary "shop committees," "councils" and "partnerships" of every kind. Owen's is the great name in the transition between utopia and the large business achievements of working class democracy.

INDUSTRIAL DEMOCRACY AT ITS BEST

Owen appears to us first as a master in the ways of capitalism. Very minutely he knew the processes of textile production. He was adroit as a buyer and as a seller. Year after year he could much more than double his money. In one year he turned above 400 per cent. on the output of his mills. But over and above these gifts was another; something in him difficult to name. He saw the competing mills sweeping children like dust into a furnace. He consulted doctors to know why they died so fast. He consulted economists and his business peers only to be snubbed. All about him among good people of the upper sort, he heard this devastation of human weakness ethically and economically excused. It was done in the name of liberty. Very great people in 1830, had ideas about competition and freedom just as fantastic. One of the very foremost economists tried to make people believe that profits were made in the last hour of the working day. If this were true, what a smiting argument against cutting off that hour! If thirteen hours were the day's task and the profits were made in the thirteenth, what ruin to the laborer if his time were lowered to twelve hours!

To his honor, Owen showed his practical contempt of these pedantries in the service of high profits.

In a western mining camp, I saw an advertisement of a salve to heal the sores upon overworked mules. Such charmed efficacy had it, that the mule with skinned back need not be taken an hour from his load. "The salve worked best while the mule worked." From the earliest slavery down, no institutional evil known to us was so lacking in resources that its defenders could not hand out a salve under which the old ways should continue undisturbed. Yet this innovator became a crank and to many people an intolerable bore. Owen put his own work in jeopardy by his utopian extravagance. The fault was in part his, but not less the fault of a troop of snubbers about him, those who hated the new idea. He began sanely pleading for his new hope of education and elementary justice to the child. But the snubbing process set in. He had to fight for it and to fight so hard and so long, that the strain drove him to reactions and extravagance in defending his views of which his enemies took every advantage. This is the history of many another herald of new ways, forced by contemptuous opposition into dangerous and excessive overstatement of his cause. It is very rare among men to make allowance for this.

II

As educational restraints have already come from inside labor and socialist organizations, so they have come, as nowhere else, from two generations of coöperative tugging at business undertakings.

If democracy is to finish its job; if it is to go into and through the economic process as well as that of politics, this coöperation has more immediate instruction for us than any of those political science departments in which Bryce found such distinction in American universities.

I say this, not as one of the utopians about the future of this movement, for its limits will prove much narrower than ardent apostles believe. But on the ground it is to cover, its educational influence is certain to rank among the very foremost aids to that self-direction on which democracy depends.

As against all headlong radicalisms, these coöperators are at the present moment a steadying and educating force in the world which would stir enthusiastic approval from the rich, if these but knew what schooling in political and industrial realities millions of coöperators receive. This is true, in its measure, of other sections of labor, but of the coöperators it has a distinction and a difference first to be considered.

Thirty-five years ago, I called at the Children's Mission in New York to ask that noble-hearted man, Charles Loring Brace, what he thought most instructive for study on a trip to England. Without hesitation, he said, "Oh, the coöperative movement. It has more promise for the future than anything known to me." I took the advice and met there one of the veterans who told me of its first trials. After his own long day's work, he lugged two miles across country his share of store commodities. He remembered the jeers of the bobbin boys and the fearsome doubts of certain members before the shutters were first taken down. Ten years later, I saw much more of these activities in England and on the Continent.

In 1908, I was asked by Mr. Glenn of the "Sage Foundation" to look over again the European ground. Six months were spent in this research. As the purpose lay wholly in the possible uses of such report as applied to the United States,[1] I was led to look more carefully at the history and actual present condition of coöperation in this country. The difficulties at that time proved so serious that no report was published. The situation has now changed.

For the first time in the United States the tide of a working-class Rochdale coöperation is rising on a scale that has real promise. In the world turmoil, it is probably the most *conservative* movement now observable — conservative because it throws upon labor groups sharp and specific business responsibility. Except to take profits in the capitalistic sense, labor has to do about everything done in ordinary business. To succeed, it must match capitalistic management in its own field. Much smug advice is being given to labor about its behavior. It will take very little of it. Labor is now to try its own hand in business and in politics.

[1] I wish here to acknowledge the help which enabled me to make the journey of 1908. Such return to the Sage Foundation as I can make will be found in the present volume and in a later more complete study of the world movement with which the writer hopes to follow the present volume.

If it has more special need of "education" than any other class, this form of coöperation will furnish it more directly and more wholesomely than all other agencies combined.

There have been many coöperative experiments in farming with many failures. They have so far won modest success that now comes a bold venture. We read that they have bought 10,000 acres in Canada for growing their own wheat. What will they not learn of the farmer's problem in hiring help, supervising it and so mastering this "mother-industry of the world" as to get their wheat cheaper than it can be bought from the profit-makers!

They may accomplish this, but not without facing and overcoming every prickly obstacle with which other farmers have to deal.

To see how labor is using its acquired economic power; to see further what guidance we may get from it, bits of its history must be reproduced. The Russian story is in many ways more arresting than that of England, but for my purpose something of the latter experience must be given especially for readers unfamiliar with the record. The war has added great hope to the movement. We will look back for a moment to the English Congress in the year before the war.

In the report we read, " This business now administers £55,000,000 of capital, has an annual trade of £123,000,000, employs 135,000 wage-earners, and carries on its enterprises in no fewer than ten different countries. Nor is its work confined, as is commonly supposed, to the retailing of groceries. These fifteen hundred popularly elected committees of working men do their own printing, their own banking, and their own insurance. They have their own tea plantations in Ceylon; their own butter and bacon factories in Denmark and Holland; their own buying depots in America and on the Continent; their own ships on the sea to bring imports to their own warehouses."

A London paper in commenting on this congress expresses astonishment that " our governing classes seem so little to realize what this huge commercial enterprise means, with its three million (now nearer four millions) wage-earning families, combined in fifteen hundred societies, united in a hierarchy of federations, *officered and directed entirely by men of the wage-earning class,* governed by committees of manual laborers who are elected, quarter by quarter, at mass meetings of all the membership, male and female." To this observer the puzzle is why so little is heard of business of this magnitude in the ordinary accounts of trade. " Lombard Street," it says, " knows them not, because there is no floating of loans, and their bills never appear in the banker's portfolio. Though they are buying continuously at the rate of something like a thousand pounds in every *minute* of the working year, they always pay cash. They have at all times more capital from accumulated savings than they know what to do with."

The founder of one of Boston's older and most successful department stores, Mr. Hovey, delighted to tell of one of his largest buyers who complained that nobody seemed to know him in the store. " The trouble with you," said Mr. Hovey, " is that you pay cash. We have no evidence of debt circulating about, so there is nothing to make you talked about." I have heard an alert business man going regularly to England on business maintain that coöperation couldn't be much, because " one hears so little about it."

Is this lack of noisy assertion in the coöperative tradition to be explained by the tranquil and uneventful character of its growth? If news is " what ought not to happen " coöperation has little of it, yet in no half-dozen of its seventy-five years has it failed to show steady and wholesome growth. Our competitive industry, like war, furnishes the startling and provoking detail. It satisfies the adventurous instinct on which gambling feeds. The price variations of joint-stock companies and other commercial enterprises are a never-ending object of fascination to the gaming impulse. Coöperation has few of these primitive enticements. It is as uninteresting as health or a happy marriage. It is even short on scandals. It is not, I am glad to say, wholly free from strikes. They have been great educators, but the wreckage due to them is so much smaller as to leave us in a world almost tiresome for lack of melodrama. You cannot even go slumming among coöperators. As an individual you cannot buy for a rise, or in any way satisfy the gamester's passion. Though you have many shares, you shall have but a single vote. You cannot get other people's proxies in the hope of securing that power so dear to the capitalist heart — "*control over the business.*"

There is nothing to "corner," nothing out of which to make monopoly. Coöperation does not have to exhaust itself in great phrases like "putting the man before the dollar." This is done by the very structure of the enterprise. It is really the man and the woman who vote rather than the amount of their property. So, too, does it economize in the most dazzling ingenuities of the advertiser. So stripped is it of flambuoyant appeals that nothing is easier to overlook.

One may revel among the Swiss peaks the summer through; may become absorbed in the daring and in the restraints of social legislation among those excellent democrats, and yet get no hint of the 11,000 coöperative societies, or that one Swiss in nine is a member of one or more of these associations. In the decade just passed the membership has more than doubled while the turnover has more than trebled.

Just as little did the passenger on the Rhine boat realize that as he touched at small towns like Neuwied, he was in a vast coöperative network. In the Empire were 35,000 societies with a membership of some five millions. If other continental countries had been as careful of their statistics, we should have a still better story to tell. In the opening decade of the century the coöperative credit societies in Germany grew from twelve to eighteen thousand; the distributive societies from sixteen hundred to twenty-two hundred. The credit societies alone had a membership of nearly two and a half millions.

And thus one passes from country to country among peoples, conditions, stages of industrial development so widely differing as to meet once for all the old objection that coöperation may fare prosperously " in a small country " with a " static labor class like the English workers," or among " fanatical Belgian socialists," but " not in a country like our own." In every variety, credit (rural and urban), agriculture, insurance, production and distribution, coöperation thrives increasingly in communities as distinct as Finland (with two thousand societies), Japan (with six thousand), and Italy (with eight thousand). Everywhere it is helping to carry democracy into the main business of life.

A college professor told me he had traveled about Denmark and " couldn't see that there was any coöperative movement there." He didn't see it once referred to in the papers and found it hard to get any native literature about it. That is as easy as to spend a summer among French peasants and not notice their thrift or that the women are as good business men as their husbands. My own first blundering impression in Denmark was that the socialist party must be of no account, because I could nowhere find an adequate literature of its activities. It happens that these did not yet express themselves mainly in print, but in practical action. It is partly because the Danes are *living* coöperatively that they write so little about it. There is an immense activity through special and general unions, but the statistical display of this energy does not blatantly stare at you from bill-boards. It was yet perfectly easy to note the presence of more than five thousand coöperative societies. This, in a population of but little more than two and a half millions, gives us *one inhabitant in every four* as a member of a coöperative society. From 1901 to 1910, the number of affiliated societies increased from 684 to 1,259. The paid up capital more than doubled, the reserve fund grew sevenfold. This means an essentially coöperative community, even if there is " nothing to see." It means that this plucky folk, living on a niggardly soil, have added immeasurably to their strength and resources by developing the coöperative habit among the people. It is these " working-together-habits " that have helped this admirable Dane to become what a popular American minister there, Dr. Egan, called " so truly civilized that he can teach us (in the United States) many a lesson which we need to learn."

One European traveler who did not wear blinders must have mention because he makes a luminous comment.

The *aim* of coöperation is to wipe out all parisitic waste in making and distributing products. It tells us we have too many middlemen, especially that we have some ruinously expensive kinds of middlemen like " advertisers of everything it would be better for us not to have." It does not deny a proper function to advertising, so far as it excites interest in and calls attention to what we really need. A business man engaged in advertising assures us that directly and indirectly advertising costs us more than two thousand millions a year and sets great armies of men and women at work upon utterly useless or positively harmful goods.

By common consent, a large part of it is waste and much of it worse than waste.

The traveling advertising manager, to whom reference is

INDUSTRIAL DEMOCRACY AT ITS BEST 265

here made, studied the European coöperators. He was much astonished at the magnitude of their business and the kind and negligible amount of advertising. What I shall quote from him sent me back to turn over again the pages of "Looking Backward," where one sees how painful an operation it is to get a new idea safely into the mind. That business can be done with the sole motive of serving the user of the product is such an idea, yet the word "service" has won great popularity in recent years. At least with the lips, it is pretty well democratized. The politicians now are glib with it. Two of our richest men have said their wealth had no meaning to them except service. But when Glenn Plumb says the railways should be used for service and not for profits and *means* it, I hear him called a demagogue and otherwise very profanely spoken of as if he were a public enemy. Recently I heard Mr. Plumb state his case under fire before a small audience but with lawyers, business men, professors and engineers to question him.

It was perfectly evident that the *implications* of running our railways "for service and not for profit" presented the greatest difficulty in adjusting the mind to his idea. Yet here is the essence of consumers' coöperation as seen in the Bellamy store.

As the awakened visitor from the nineteenth century he saw "no display of goods in the great windows, or any device to advertise wares, or attract customs. Nor was there any sort of sign or legend on the front of the building to indicate the character of the business carried on there. . . . ,"'Where is the clerk?' I asked, for there was no one behind the counter, and no one seemed coming to attend to the customer.

"'I have no need of a clerk yet,' said Edith; 'I have not made my selection.'

"'It was the principal business of clerks to help people to make their selections in my day,' I replied.

"'What! To tell people what they wanted?'

"'Yes; and oftener to induce them to buy what they didn't want.'

"'But did not ladies find that very impertinent?' Edith asked, wonderingly. 'What concern could it possibly be to the clerks whether people bought or not?'

"'It was their sole concern,' I answered. 'They were hired for the purpose of getting rid of the goods, and were expected to do their utmost, short of the use of force, to compass that end.'

"'Ah, yes! How stupid I am to forget!' said Edith. 'The storekeeper and his clerks depended for their livelihood on selling the goods in your day.' . . . She smiled as she added, 'How exceedingly odd it must have seemed to have clerks trying to induce one to take what one did not want, or was doubtful about!'

"'But even a twentieth-century clerk might make himself useful in giving you information about the goods, though he did not tease you to buy them,' I suggested.

"'No,' said Edith, 'that is not the business of the clerk. These printed cards, for which the Government authorities are responsible, give us all the information we can possibly need.'

"I saw, then, that there was fastened to each sample a card containing in succinct form a complete statement of the make and materials of the goods and all its qualities, as well as price, leaving absolutely no point to hang a question on.

"'The clerk has, then, nothing to say about the goods he sells?' I said.

"'Nothing at all. It is not necessary that he should know or profess to know anything about them. Courtesy and accuracy in taking orders are all that are required of him.'

"'What a prodigious amount of lying that simple arrangement saves!' I ejaculated."

Now this is what our American advertiser saw. He says:

"We live in a competitive system. If we lived under a coöperative system, there is no doubt that hundreds of millions spent in advertising yearly might be saved to the consumer."

In far greater detail as to the grounds of his opinion, another spokesman helps us out still further. The chief literary organ of our national advertisers had an able article by one of the staff (April, 1912) under the title, "Does Consumers' Coöperation Threaten?" It is partly an alarm cry. The coöperative movement, which he had studied in different countries, appears serious because he could reckon a membership which totals 10,000,000 of families or 50,000,000 of people. "In England one family in every four is represented in the coöperatives," and in Scotland the percentage is higher still. He, too, was astonished at the magnitude of producers' coöperation. "The largest bakeries in the world," he says, "under one management are those of the Glasgow coöperation, and Vienna comes next." He is told of a coöperative textile mill, now building in England, "that will be the largest in the world." More astonishing still are the salaries of men who manage these great undertakings,— less than that of the average college professor. He then adds:

"So it is evident that the movement holds something more for the American manufacturer than merely academic interest, even at this time when such consequences as those described must be remote in respect to our own land, because the continuous and complete extension of the system in this country would soon begin to handicap many manufacturers, *impair the value of their trade-marks and good will,* and progressively destroy it.

"It would *restrict* and finally *destroy advertising* as we know it, inasmuch as the advertising of the coöperative is for the most part confined to simple announcements, and there is no competition within the societies to stimulate its development."

The article, as printed in Professor Cherington's volume, closes with these words: "This outlines the sort of competition the manufacturers of the United States may have to face before many years."[1]

As one who hopes that democracy may go to the utmost length consistent with social well-being, I should not dare to paint the danger as quite so imminent. But the core of truth in this adventurous observation is sound. I faithfully reproduce his own italics, adding, as they do, their own emphasis to a quite up-to-date practical business opinion. If to-day this gentleman were to walk into the store of Bellamy's fancy, he would have no need of Edith Leete to guide him or to answer his gasping inquiries. The ravages threatened by European coöperation upon private advertising have so prepared this man of 1913, that Bellamy's daring "phantasy" seems to him a platitude, and so we leave him in pleasant comprehending fellowship with that gentle dreamer.

Of Russian Coöperation I first heard from Kropotkin. It began twenty years later than in England. Kropotkin saw in it the prophecy of a future in which man's exploitation of man would end. Returning from frequent visits to Russia, Charles R. Crane told me of its progress. The educational director with several high officials are now in this country. There is the Peoples Coöperative Bank in Moscow which its representative here calls, "the heart of the Russian coöperative movement. The bank has a capital of 10,000,000 rubles, divided into 40,000 shares of 250 rubles each. Of these shares, only 647 are in the hands of private individuals, most of whom are coöperators. The present shares can be acquired only by coöperative societies, so that the bank is owned and controlled by the coöperators them-

[1] Pages 90, 110–113, "Advertising as a Business Force."

selves. A new issue of shares voted by the shareholders in December, 1917, will at the close of the present year bring the capital to 35,000,000 rubles. The amount of deposits in the bank increased from 2,000,000 rubles in 1913 to over 150,000,000 rubles in January, 1918. During 1917 the bank loaned to various coöperative societies over 25,000,000 rubles, and did a total business of 3,000,000,000 rubles.[1]

" In addition to consumption, the coöperative consumers are also energetically devoting themselves to production, thereby contributing powerfully to the industrial development of the country. Soap, candy, tobacco, matches, preserved fish, boots; paper and starch factories, factories for the treatment of leather, wood and sunflower oil, flour and sawmills, printing presses, mineral water establishments, salt works, iron works, and coal mines are a partial list of industrial undertakings which have been launched by the consumers' societies. In the field of agriculture the coöperative societies of producers now control, in whole or in part, the production of flax, hemp, butter, eggs, grain, hops, and bristles, besides naval stores, timber, fisheries, and the fur trade. The Central Association of Flax Growers comprises 46 coöperative unions and 142 local societies in 22 flax-producing provinces and has a membership of 1,500,000 peasant households.

" The coöperative societies in Russia hold themselves strictly aloof from politics, and have carried on their activities with remarkably little interruption, all things considered, from the war. In 1918, in spite of the hindrances connected with the blockade and the disturbed state of the country generally, their total turnover was 8,000,000,000 rubles, or about $1,600,000,000. In that year they operated over 500 industrial plants, and had a total of over 50,000 employees."

[1] " It should of course be stated that one reason for this rapid growth is the absence of an aggressive middle class distributive system. These coöperators had the field to themselves, thus avoiding many difficulties which labor must face in this country."

It will at once be evident that business of this scope and variety makes its own labor problem for the working class conducting it. Here is its kindergarten, its high school and its college. I was glad to be told by a coöperative Russian director here, Mr. Zelenko, that they had occasional strikes. Labor managers must in some way learn to deal with strikes, for there will be plenty of them as business control passes to the workers. Strikes — labor against labor — are to play a great part in the new education. Labor will learn in these contests, how many troubles are not in the least peculiar to capitalism. The coöperators are already showing us what democracy has before it. Already these Russian democrats are hiring men of their own class by many thousands.

We shall soon see what this means for discipline and for the common safety if other classes bring practical good sense to the problem.

III

In this hasty glimpse at the world movement, one gets some estimate of what democracy may yet work out for itself as it molds its economic life toward freedom steadied by its own business burdens. That within the memory of those still living, the humbler masses of men could reach these results would have excited among the educated and practically minded in the upper classes only scouting incredulity.

This cynicism has indeed been the history of all democratic changes. In his "Democracy and Liberty" (Vol. II, 1) Lecky tells us that Queen Victoria's prime minister, Lord Melbourne, looking back upon some mistakes in judgment made by wise men whom he had known, said: "All the d——d fools in England predicted one set of things, and all the sensible men in England another set, and the d——d fools proved perfectly right and the sensible men perfectly wrong." We do well to recall this as it applies to the countless supercilious predictions of those thriving and worldly-wise doubters who made merry over the first awkward attempts to apply democracy to trade and industry. With no less advantage shall we recall another fact — that many of those early coöperative pioneers were too strident and too cocksure. Especially did those who wrote the literature and voiced the movement claim too much. English forerunners looked for the swift oncoming of results which only generations can bring. It is also true that coöperation has developed along lines that were heart-breaking to some of the noblest men on its early roll of honor. They wanted to preserve capitalistic features that had to pass away. Yet if those brave men could have sat in the last congress and listened to the story of working-class triumphs; if they could have looked over together the ordered record of the International Coöperative Alliance and note the tables of its growth and its varieties with its ever wider acceptance among the thoughts and practices of our time; if they could see that many an old feud (as between limited and unlimited liability, self-governing workship and consumers' associations) was not, after all, so weighty a matter — would any one of them count an hour or an effort in the cause misspent? Its unfolding has been different, but in most important ways far better than they dreamed. It is to-day the rock on which the whole democratic structure is seen for what it is — not the sole and exclusive temple in which the world's work goes on, but one of its stateliest and most spacious wings.

Until struck by war, its growth was as astonishing as anything in the history of modern industry. In its various forms it was already doing a yearly business of more than three thousand millions of dollars. And it was doing it at the same time that it was schooling its millions of members in the highest of all arts — self-government. Apart from formulas and mere agitation, "industrial coöperation" has become the most democratic thing in the world. As a great movement, like the new social legislation, it has won its place in the last generation. I say the "most democratic" because it has once for all proved that democracy is possible on the economic field; or, more accurately, on large portions of that field. "Democracy" is as easy as lying in a document or on the platform, but in the production and exchange of wealth it is so supremely difficult that many wise men have pronounced and still pronounce it impossible. Yet in more than one hundred thousand successful associations — in insurance, purchasing and selling groups, credit and banking, production and distribution — coöperation has begun its highest task of training for applied democracy by carrying its equalities into the very structure and function of business dealings among men.

Like parrots men keep on repeating, "Oh, coöperation does good work in distribution, but in production it fails." This is an error. In its own self-created market "coöperative production" has won the most brilliant successes. It is this feature, indeed, which showed in later years some of the most astonishing growths. One of the ablest of London weeklies reports the Coöperative Congress in these words:

"The International Coöperative Alliance has silently grown into the most gigantic of all our non-official world federations. Its 24 national units now include something like 130,000 separate coöperative societies, having no fewer than twenty millions of (family) members, representing three or four times that number of persons. . . . The essential feature of the world-wide coöperative movement has become the control of 'industry,' the 'elimination of the middleman'— that is to say, of the capitalist entrepreneur — and the democratic organization of all branches of production and distribution directly by collectivities of citizen-consumers."

As distinct from distribution, it adds:

"As a matter of fact, the coöperator's success has been even more remarkable in production than in distribution. The coöperative movement runs five of the largest of our flour mills; it has, amongst others, the very largest of our boot factories; it makes cotton cloth and woolens, and all sorts of clothing; it has even a corset factory of its own; it turns out huge quantities of soap; it makes every article of household furniture; it produces cocoa and confectionery; it grows its own fruit and makes its own jams; it has one of the largest tobacco factories, and so on."

For sixty years, objectors have set every sort of theoretic frontier that was to call a halt upon the movement. At first "only the English working-man had the genius for it." "It must be confined to small local trading." It could never hope to do banking or manufacturing or take the risks of insurance. In no case could it reach any considerable part of a nation's business.

These solemn incredulities now appear humorous. Within less than thirty years Denmark became a coöperative nation. Germany was sown thick with societies. In at least twenty nationalities coöperation has struck such root that it can no more be stopped than popular education. The first failures in Italy were said to prove that "coöperation did not suit the Italian character." Its growth there in the last 20 years has been in many ways as fascinating as the story of the airship. Small farmers coöperatively manufacture their own fertilizers. They run their own banks, farms and market gardens. The commonest sort of labor paves streets, dredges lands, builds all manner of structures, even to the Reggio-Emilia railroad. It hires engineers, buys material, and pays its own bills from its own coöperative banks. This work now runs yearly into many hundreds of millions of *lire*. The Government and cities are organically committed to a working partnership with these coöperators.

Before the war, coöperators had entered into the world industry and exchange. They were cutting out brokers, jobbers, middlemen, by doing the work with closer economies for themselves and for the consumers. There were five of these wholsales with an annual business of over two hundred millions of dollars. Already, in a new spirit the United States has now begun to take its part in this world change. It is a change toward that democratizing of industry which at least holds the promise of freeing us at last from the proved inefficiencies of autocratic methods, industrial and political, as well as from secrecies which are themselves the mother of privilege.

To return now to its inner discipline. As we were often reminded by believers in "the Great State" that it would have all available resources to preserve order, so the romancers among writers on coöperation in this and other countries have told us why strikes could not occur when business was carried on by consumers. "To make and to distribute things for *use* and not for profit is to harmonize interests so that strikes will be as unnatural as civil war," is one form of this credulity. Even when coöperation developed large manufacturing with a distinct body of "producers," it was urged that their interests were so at one with the consumers that strikes were impossible. Our human pugnacities were not so easily exorcised.

It has seemed to me one of the happiest events that these over-fine expectations have been unfulfilled. Coöperators whose ardor was first roused because industrial peace would be once for all secure, now admit that these quarrels have taught them more about their fellowmen, about business and about the future commonwealth than they could have learned in any other way. "I used to think it absurd," said one, "that a lot of working men owning their own business; all equally concerned in its success and in the wholesale which they had built up, could have the wrangling which goes on among the profit-makers. How could workingmen strike against workingmen? That settled it in my mind.

"Yet we have had rows," he added, "that do not differ a hair from those outside, and they have taught me what we are up against in transforming business."

This is the education which is becoming a power in every branch of organized labor in the world. It is instructing us about ourselves. It is educating men out of sectarian narrowness into some imaginative appreciation of what world-industry will at length require of us. Business is no longer to be done in a corner. It has more and more to be carried on as a part of conditions profoundly different and among races, types, standards varying quite as much.

It is our hope that industry may be so organized that classes within and nations without may learn to produce and to exchange their surplus with some decent regard for each other. It is hoped we may do this without the old blinding appeals to trickery and war. If these rational ways prove possible, we must add to our other cultural devices, severe *economic* training. Neither moral exhortation nor political maneuvering will alone create the habits and ways of thinking upon which a humanely ordered, democratic industry depends.

One saving part of this education is very clearly indicated in these working class groups. They are all learning how human they are; how many weaknesses they have in common with other classes; how easily they develop those weaknesses when power comes to them and when this force is organized for large and urgent duties. These coöperators were very confident that they could cast out strikes and of course "jurisdictional disputes." Even in the United States coöperators have had about all the troubles known to employers. These troubles had to be met very much as other employers try to meet them.

We have had instances inside coöperative stores in this country showing that working-class directors act precisely in the manner of capitalist employers when beset by the same problems. Demands from clerks were met by the same arguments and by the same tactics. Troublesome employees have been quietly dropped by coöperators because they were "agitators." A coöperative manager told me he had discharged seven men in three years. He admitted that he had not given the true reason to the public. "It was safer to say they were unfit for their job."

This "labor problem" is everywhere in the coöperative movement. A large business like the Leeds Coöperative Society had a body of teamsters in its employ. Some years ago, these asked a rise of three shillings in their wages. The demand was finally granted but with restrictions which so angered the men that they struck. This brought on a "sympathetic strike" of teamsters in outside private firms, 4,000 in all. Clerks in the coöperative store refused to touch "tainted goods" and were discharged. A sympathetic strike was least tolerable of all.

The next stage is thus reported. "A meeting of the Leeds branch of the Amalgamated Union of Coöperative Employees thereupon demanded permission from their executive Council to strike in support of the carters, and in order to secure for themselves the minimum wage, which has been the subject of so much discussion in coöperative circles. The members of the Shop Assistants' Union, employed by the Coöperative Society, also decided to take the same course."

At the same time the Gasworkers' Union (city employees) were on strike, so that we have the city council struggling with the same annoyance. A single line in the report shows how near akin we all are. "The city council decided to defer their decision with regard to their employees' demands *until after the November elections.*" Meantime pickets were at work and two labor members of Parliament came hurrying up from London.

For more than a quarter of a century after the English stores had established their great wholesale agency, unionism

INDUSTRIAL DEMOCRACY AT ITS BEST

made little trouble, though the wholesale was hiring men and women by thousands.

Very timidly in 1891, an organization appeared but avoided the name "trade union." It was only an "Employees' Association." Four years later the word "union" was added and in 1911 came openly the gathering of strike funds, an agitation for the trade union label "doing such work for unions in the United States" and even for compulsory trade unions.

We now know that among coöperators a strike may occur which brings into the war zone about every sort of dispute known under capitalism; wage minimum, over-time, discharge of men, trade union arrogance, hours and conditions of work. Capitalism cannot here be made the scapegoat. Labor strikes against labor and under a strictly labor régime. All the taunts, recriminations, responsibilities must be taken by the labor group.

One of the later flour mills built by English coöperators (at Avonmouth) was the scene of such an outbreak in 1913. A section of the mill hands became dissatisfied over wages. The labor section acting as employer hastened to show by figures that the wages were already higher than in outside competitive mills (this quite in the style of private employers). The men who had their own trade union were unconvinced and demanded an increase, together with an eight-hour day, and also a new deal for overtime work. Concessions were granted but the trouble continued until two men had to be discharged. At once the cry of unfair discrimination against these union men was raised. The demand was made that the men be reinstated. A committee from the Coöperative Wholesale decided that the manager was right and the men wrong. After a ballot and twenty-four hours' warning the men struck. Bristol, hard by, is full of coöperators and the society there took the part of the men. Under the constitution, this forced the case before a joint committee of trade unions and coöperators.

The decision was that "neither of the men had been discharged because of trade union activity," and regret was expressed that the case had not been submitted *before* the strike.

The strikers refused to accept the decision until the labor organization which paid strike benefits stopped further aid. This, together with a threat from the Coöperative Wholesale that it would fill the places of the strikers (that is, *itself become a strike breaker*) brought the five weeks' strike to and end.

We may even see that test of jurisdictional feuds among these coöperators, for example, between joiners and cabinet makers as to whether " shop fitting " belonged to one union or the other. These appealed (1903) to the Wholesale acting as employer to decide. The committee, all of workingmen, said like our ordinary employer, that they had no interest in the quarrel. " So settle it among yourselves," and because the men would not listen, a strike broke out. After a ten weeks' loss to the Wholesale (the buying and manufacturing agent of the 1,600 coöperative stores) a Parliamentary committee of the trade unions restored peace through arbitration.

In the autumn of 1919, the author of the " History of the Wholesale " writes me that strikes have not ceased. They have even appeared in the stores among the employees. These have learned the troublesome liturgy about " self-determination " and will have something of it for themselves. He says the strikes have " increased as the militant spirit of the labor movement has increased." He adds further, " The difficulty is that absorbtion in the struggle of labor and capital, and continued thought along anti-capitalist lines, cause many workers and their advocates to overlook the fact that associations of consumers open to everybody, with one member one vote, are radically different from companies of shareholders in which the controlling power is exercised by holders of capital in proportion to the extent of their holdings."

"Personally I think every effort should be made to give the worker as much domestic control as possible consistent with sovereignty (under its rules) of the whole society; but (with human liability to misunderstanding, prejudice and all the rest remaining) I do not think it possible for any form of organization to provide any sort of automatic guarantee against strikes and industrial disputes."

Here are the lessons labor is learning when it takes up and carries the business load upon its own back. Strikes are but one of the lessons.

Not a business trial escapes them, nor can they avoid one of the new troubles fast coming upon us. We are to have long and tedious difficulties in applying the principle of the minimum wage. It is therefore well for all of us that the workers have been compelled to take it up with their own employees. Labor will gather its own chastening experience, so like the trials of private employers that both can weep and smile together over the perplexities involved. As they swap sympathies, both can talk most understandingly with each other over the hopes and despairs in working this standard into general practice. There has been no abler discussion of the "minimum wage" than what went on for years with coöperators before they adopted it in restricted and modest form.

The "shop committee" is now put before us in the American press as something new. Coöperators in several countries as well as unions have for years had this in excellent working order and have already learned some dangers in it which our employers have yet to discover. To no source of instruction could they more wisely turn than to these labor pioneers.

Upon even greater difficulties they can throw light.
A supreme test of democracy in its widening field will be

its capacity to free itself from the demagogue. In every country, the coöperators have come nearer to this goal than any other section. Socialism, syndicalism and the trade union have been about as rank with this pest as our current party politics.

In every function; in its committee work; in the deeper motive of it, the demagogue among coöperators has so little to feed upon that he practically disappears. On the fringe of the movement are demagogues in plenty but they are only trying to use its prestige for other ends.

Again coöperators are almost alone in showing the possibility of ridding democracy of another ever present enemy — the lurking vices of bureaucracy. Mr. Woolf in his recent book [1] admits that this evil shows itself even in the larger retail stores, but much more in the Wholesale. "This," he says, "is because decisions have to be taken instantly in the coöperative movement by the management committee or the officials. To find any broad principle of policy in this mass of details and to follow it is difficult, and it is only by insisting upon such broad principles that the democracy can really interfere in the transaction of business. It follows that the individual coöperator and the community of individual coöperators find themselves separated by an impenetrable barrier of officials and employees from the actual transaction of business, while their ability to influence the actions of their executive officers is limited."

Here is the frankest admission of the evil, but it is safe to

[1] "Coöperation and the Future of Industry." Since Emerson P. Harris' volume in which a successful business man records some ten years' plucky devotion to the cause, another book will richly reward every inquirer: "Coöperation — the Future of Industry" and Albert Sonnichsen's "Consumers' Coöperation" (both by Macmillan, N. Y.). Mr. Sonnichsen, as no writer since Beatrice Webb, clears the whole discussion by his analysis. He shows us what Consumers' Coöperation means as against all the farmers — dairy and profit-sharing schemes so frequently confused with the consumers' movement.

INDUSTRIAL DEMOCRACY AT ITS BEST 281

say — as of strikes and demagogues — that coöperators have so held this mischief in check, that its dangers are few as compared to the evil in any existing state.

Or it may be such a source of incurable vexation to competitive industry as "piece work."

It has been an endless source of wrangling. We still hear it charged up among the trade union stupidities, that they object to piece work. It would be as true to say they object to food. They doubtless object to certain kinds of food, but there are plenty of strong trade unions that would strike at once if piece work were taken away from them. There have been long periods in which far more unionists insisted upon piece work and got it, than those who rejected it.

Why have our international machinists objected to it, while amalgamated engineers permit it? There have been volumes of discussion, reports and investigations in which we see the trade unions differing among themselves as they may differ from employers. Labor's objection has been at those points where it felt that *control over piece work was too exclusively with employers.* At a meeting of the National Civic Association, a president of the employers' organization confessed that piece work had been "too much put to the devil's service" in his own industry.

In those labor democracies here in view, piece work is introduced freely for the same reasons that any enlightened management would suggest. Under its own direction, labor will no more oppose intelligent forms of it than it will exclude inventions. How quickly coöperators learned the meaning of that old conflict in the manufacturing world — the new machine! How quick to see that it makes more wealth from which wages are paid! Labor struck against machinery for a century, chiefly because workmen had no control over its introduction and therefore — *at the time and as long as they could see ahead,*— feared the results for their union or for some part of their membership. But the coöperators have no employers except those freely elected from among themselves. No one can force upon them a new machine against their will.[1] Yet, like certain "labor-copartners," the coöperators have had a most enlightening experience with this difficulty. I saw the Brockton strike of the Lasters' Union against the new machine. If employers had had their way, it would have wiped out their organization. When this same American invention was sent to England, its success in capitalistic shoe factories compelled the great coöperative shoe works at Leicester (1911) to meet the competition. The working men who directed this business saw that their *labor costs* were so much higher than in factories using the machines, that the coöperators must buy them or go to the wall. Here was a situation, the exact counterpart of the problem years earlier in Massachusetts. It was seen that this machine would at once throw out some of the hand lasters, and that their own comrades would suffer. The leaders denied all antagonism to the machine. "We know," they said, "when new inventions come they have got to be put in." "What we shall fight is for some *control* over the machine when it is put in. We want some share in its advantages and not to take all the disadvantages." The head of one factory had gone so far as to have men trained to use the machine in Boston and then sent — man and machine together — to the Brockton shoe shop. This, of course, meant the absolute extinction of the union.

I know no better definition of the struggle between capital and labor than what this precise situation contains. New inventions are the measure of material progress. They must be accepted and put to work. The growing majority of labor men know this as well as the employer knows it. Labor has learned that in the long run the machine in-

[1] The acceptance of new baking machinery in the Belgian Coöperatives is a fine tribute to their intelligence.

creases wealth and even sets more men and women at work on other jobs and at other places. It knows in a word that any new invention may be made a social asset. But labor must be made a party in deciding on conditions under which machinery is to work. The demand is as just as it is intelligent.

Labor has refused and should refuse the old " long-run philosophy " which forced it to bear all the burdens of " short-run," unemployment, insecurity and cut wages. Some of the evils of machine introduction like loss of one's job are inevitable. Labor asks that these evils be fairly distributed, as it asks some share in the advantages. Employers and much of the public have been as slow to learn this elementary justice as labor was slow to admit the value of labor-saving appliances. I have known a strike to be averted in a shoe shop by an employer wise enough to get his men together before the new machine was set at work and talk over the question how the change could be made with the least disturbance and in ways fairest to employer and employed.

That exact question will harass our society to the end — or *until natural resources and applied science (invention) are so far under the people's control as to make any form of private monopoly impossible.*

Leicester coöperators took the new machine and set it at work, finding at once that it raised among themselves the same question as under capitalism. It was found that the jobs of some forty men were threatened — the same issue as in the Brockton shop.

There was not an ugly feature of it from which the democratic hive of industry could escape.

The private employer in Brockton who "talked it all out with his men beforehand," had at least the only true spirit in which society at large must eventually cope with this root problem. It must bring so much of the mechanism of production strictly into the service of the community as to check at its source monopoly privilege in private hands.

What then did the working coöperators in Leicester do toward this end? In that same Leicester shop nearly 20 years earlier, I had talked with one of the managers about their plans for the older workers and the necessary displacements of labor which new machinery compels. He pointed to a man whom I should have guessed to be 60 years of age. "There," he said, "is one of them. We are trying to work it out in connection with a pension plan and giving him lighter work. As a fact," he continued, "inventions have come so gradually that we have been thus far (1890) able to deal fairly with our people." In 1911, this far more disturbing invention brought something like a crisis. When at the quarterly meeting it was known that over 40 men must go as the new machine came in, cries of "Shame" rose from the members.[1]

It was resolved to meet the issue as a whole — on its social as well as on its business side. The men thrown out were not merely promised a job when and if places could be found at some later time. They were not asked to take the whole loss while capital got the advantages. In addition to grants made to the men's insurance or "thrift funds" each one was given 50 dollars to tide them over until work could be secured there or elsewhere.

All this is the more suggestive because at the start, the coöperators set out to do away with the wage system. They were to "work for themselves in a kind of brotherhood." They would at any rate "hire only their own members." Nothing like this has happened. At the present moment, in England alone they must have nearly 150,000 to whom wages are paid as in other business. More radical labor, socialist to syndicalist, calls this the "old slave system." They are more cynical about it than ordinary business competitors are of the coöperators. Even coöperative managers are a

[1] See the excellent History of the "Coöperation Wholesale" by Percy Redfern, 1913, page 285.

little cynical to all breathless inquirers who assume some sentimental value in the movement. "It is plain business with little nonsense about it." They have to "hire and fire." They find the same difficulties in raising wages and improving conditions that private business shows. Here, then, over the new machine and *all* machinery is the spirit and admirable first steps toward that larger organization of distributive justice which industrial society must accept and work out. It is as much an infamy to throw all sacrifices on men displaced by a device which enriches us generally, as it was infamous to throw the burdens of accidents so exclusively on individual victims previous to our compensation laws. The principle of social insurance which must eventually cover these "injustices of the short run" are as a fact being learned and put to initial practice inside our labor democracies. They are being learned there in ways that *may make labor the very best instructor in social conservation.* Nor will any greater or safer measure be taken towards industrial security than by frank admission of this labor contribution and an ungrudging coöperation with it on the part of employers, corporations, the city and the State. Only in this larger coöperation is there hope of meeting a single one of the graver issues now before us.

IV

For general confusion and practical embarrassment, what at the present moment casts a darker shadow than the deepening popular belief about profiteering? Under the wage system with the motive of private profit so all-prevailing: with this profiteering feature now brought under violent condemnation, how can governments discipline large bodies of strikers, either among its own employees or in private undertakings? In more than thirty strikes within six months, we have heard the leaders bewailing their loss of control over their own men. "We can't hold them," says one, "because they believe the profiteers are at the bottom of their trouble and they may be right." This profiteering enters only as one and by no means the most important cause of high prices, but to spread the *belief* stirs revolt while it enables others, who have no convictions at all, to use the advantages offered. To socialists, interest and rent are just as vicious as profits, but except for the flurry over higher house rents, these increments are too obscure to rouse popular emotions. Profiteers are in the pillory. They will stay there until the whole system of private profit making has been "cussed and discussed" as slang has it, to its limits.

I believe a great deal of it will eventually be left in private possession and that this will be done by labor's own choice. Though against every socialist theory, socialists will themselves permit it for sound business reasons. But whether this be true or false, the coöperators are specializing on this subject. To get rid of all profiteering is the very reason for their existence. They can already tell us a great deal about it and within very few years will tell us far more.

On a vast scale, they do now actually eliminate private profit. If plans now on foot succeed, they will carry this elimination out into world commerce and world finance. It was long held even by some leading coöperators, that their movement would be confined chiefly to working class customers, and to the simpler commodities most in use among them. How could they enter the market of luxuries with its infinite caprice of tastes and fashions?

There are two suggestive possibilities (a) that revolutionary strikes with their depletion of output will continue long enough to force people in every class to a far simpler life; (b) that classes next above the coöperators' standard are to be driven from economic necessity into professional sympathy with the whole organized labor contingent so rapidly allying itself with the coöperators.

This would so strengthen the market demand for coöperative products, as to widen the variety of those products and the banking, insurance and other facilities it has to offer. Within three years, consumers' coöperation in America has gained far more working class loyalty than in the entire half century of its existence. It has also won the adherence of " intellectuals," students, and middle class sympathizers as never before.

The educational importance of this is vital because coöperation raises issues about socialism, syndicalism and the new guild that have extreme interest.

Its ideal is that of a world controlled and dictated to by consumers. Nothing is to be manufactured or grown except as it directly serves (is useful to) the buyer and user. Creating wealth " for use and not for profit " is an old socialist principle and a very noble one, but the coöperators have put it in practice with the invincible evidence that it can be carried much farther. They have been canny enough not to try the whole socialist program, and cannier still in not waiting for the downfall of capitalism.

They have bitten from the loaf what they could digest. Their triumphs have given them such confidence that their larger program is now unfolded. They now take up international trade and manage their own finance after their own principles. There are a score of Wholesales in different parts of the world. These have begun already to exchange products. We have this resolution from a recent congress: " Seeing that coöperation alone can provide an economic League of Nations, this congress declares that it is essential that international coöperative trade should be immediately developed; that all coöperators should be looked upon as members of one movement, and mutual exchange and enterprise be undertaken."

We read further that the " English Wholesale is about to embark upon an enterprise unique in the history of coöperation. It is entering the sacred precincts of foreign trade — sacred to competition and capitalism — and is entering them along a road which the angels of capitalism are very fearful of treading. The road leads to Russia, with its 20,000,000 of active coöperators, large factories and banking system of its own." An agreement has already been made under which the English "ship manufactured goods and receive in exchange from the Russian coöperators raw materials and food products such as maize, wheat, oils. The first consignment, consisting of 600 tons of merchandise and including boots and shoes, ironmongery, and textiles, is ready for shipment in Manchester." These Russians already have their organizations in London and New York. They have their own system of credit which entirely ignores the international profit-making banker. The English wholesale "is to be paid for the manufactured goods which it is consigning to Russia, not in rubles but in food and raw materials produced by the Russian coöperators. Such a transaction is only possible because each movement is organized both for production and consumption." Here are coöperative producers and coöperative consumers, each with their own basis of credit which enables them to "swap products" without a penny of private profits.

What fortune awaits this venture, we have yet to see, but in the exact measure of its success, it removes one great cause of revolt — the profiteer. Not one of these fifty millions of working class coöperators can be moved by that argument within the whole field of his activities. Within this field, neither high finance, big business nor the petty usurer can be blamed.

Here, too, great bodies of producers are organized with corresponding bodies of consumers. No deeper question in future reconstruction can be raised. Can their interests be so far harmonized — producers wanting high prices and consumers low prices — as to give world scope to this plan with *no private profits?*

If it should succeed, it is proof positive that society is now ravenously beset by a parasitic class. Bankers and middlemen would suffer until they too were brought into the coöperative alliance. But this temporary suffering would be precisely like the introduction of a new invention which " in the long run benefits us all."

Never could be a fairer challenge, nor one which we can more safely encourage. As with socialism and syndicalism, so many decades will intervene before the coöperative victory is complete, that every chance will be given to judge the merits of respective claims.

The coöperative ideal is spiked with difficulties as it comes in contact with all forms of state socialism, with syndicalism and even with the new guild. These two latter expressly represent labor as producer. Will he yield mastery to the consumer? Not without a struggle so long and of such a character that we have breathing space enough

In its extremer form, this whole consumers' ideal has in it the hints of a dictatorship less sinister than that of syndicalism, but very real. So certain is it, moreover, that we are to have federated groups of labor consciously functioning as producers — proud of this function and its importance — that no purely consumers' association will be granted all it asks. Whatever stable equilibrium, and " balancing of interests " are finally worked out, the old strife for power will have vitality enough. Professor Laski shows insight in his suggestion that real power will remain with the *classifiers*. Some body of officials must deal with callings, and with categories under which all act and work, as well as with necessary services, some of them very unpleasant. It is anarchism in its feeblest form to suppose these choices are to be left helter-skelter to the whim of the individual. Even under any suggested " federalism " the minimum of stability will require a great deal of highly organized authority and direction. Socialism and trade unionism have developed this centralized direction, so far that they conceal it if they can. The coöperators have developed it to an extent that has brought upon them extreme censure from their own ranks. But meantime, more and more of them have learned the necessity of such delegated authority and yield to it. Here are the roots of a sounder representative system in industry. Labor is learning this in the same way that another bit of practical wisdom has been acquired. Many of the noblest of the forerunners were convinced that competition was the devil's own. That "competition is the life of trade" was what one of them called "the great lie." Very strictly they believed it to be the death of trade and of other values more precious still. When Charles Kingsley defined competition as "cannibalism," he was hardly overstating the moral revolt against it in which coöperators were then so conspicuous.

The group to which Kingsley belonged — Maurice, Hughes, Ludlow, Neal — was named "Christian socialists," but only in the loosest possible sense can they be called socialists. They were as one man against competition as it was then viewed. That was the sum of all villainies to the saintly Maurice as well as to the fighting author of Alton Locke. The coöperators know to-day that competition is as necessary as steam in the engine. They know they cannot even select competent leaders without it. To lift the level of competition where the rivalries may be fair is their aim.

It has real interest historically, that one of the intellectual pioneers of English coöperation avoided most of the mistakes about competition into which later writers fell. His own competitive discipline may have saved him. William King won the Wrangler's distinction at Cambridge in 1809. Every superiority had to be challenged in long contests with his fellows. It was a form of competition which seemed to him as fair as it was useful in driving men to their best endeavor. He became physician in chief in a city hospital, but for years gave his best leisure without stint to the co-operative cause. It is in this sense of rivalry in a fair field with no favors, that coöperators accept and encourage competition. They know it has to be "regulated" but not after the manner of trust magnates seeking monopoly. Regulation may admirably serve them in this quest. Coöperators accept competition as a force to be democratized like other forces but no more to be destroyed than life itself.

V

It seems too simple to state, that if labor is to be economically, politically and socially educated, the discipline must come mainly from within. These groups always start with certain proclaimed ideals. It is the ideological stage and has to be passed through. It keeps its hold until the party or trade union acquires influence enough to make its tactics, policies and leadership conspicuous. At this stage, the tussle for power and control begins to be accurately like what is found everywhere else in the rise of parties throughout the world.

No organization — religious, business or labor — ever masters its own inner dissensions without the severest training in those coöperative habits which democracy requires.

As this coöperation gains strength among us, infuriated attacks will be made upon it. We cannot learn too soon what these attacks will mean. So far as they succeed, they will destroy one of the most educationally conservative influences against an uncouth and dangerous radicalism.

There is no peril before society more insidious than those forms of communism led by minorities with an appeal to violence as a means of accomplishing their end.

If this grave mischief is met, it will be chiefly by the working class itself. Especially in this country, property ownership, or the strong hope of it, is so widely spread among this class that, with intelligent sympathy and cooperation, it will furnish the main discipline over every minority bent on methods of destruction.

In the instance following, I am describing a score of other centers carrying the same lesson.

In and about Fitchburg, Mass., are some 5000 Finns — thrifty, hardworking men and women distinctly of the wage-earning class. They have gone into business for themselves. When the men discovered that the manager of a private store, at which they traded, was hand in glove with a local political boss, trying then to control the Finnish vote, they did not like it. This, with high prices and difficulties with the English language, led them to start their own store. They have had extraordinary prosperity. Ten years ago, they did $20,000 worth of business in a year. They now do several thousand dollars more than that each *month*. They have their own clean and up-to-date bakery; a large boarding house of their own, at which I got a much better meal for forty-five cents than I got at my hotel for eighty-five. They have bought the five-story Athletic Club in which is their bank of the credit union type. The extent of their banking business may be judged by loans to other coöperative groups — to the Finnish society in Brooklyn alone, $90,000 for their new bakery now building This is but one of several loans. Europe is tormented by the housing problem upon which nothing adequate has yet been done. We too now feel its pressure. This item is sent me from the office of the Coöperative League in New York: "One interesting example is an attempt by Finnish coöperators of New York City to *cope with the housing problem*. They have bought ground and put up houses in which apartments may be secured by members of the society for from $22 to $27 a month which normally in New York would rent at from $35 to $60. This is probably a socialist group and our sturdy philistines will of course fall upon them as if they were one and the same with the giddiest among the I. W. W. But men so prudent and industrious do not

INDUSTRIAL DEMOCRACY AT ITS BEST 293

stake their all in stores, bakeries and apartment houses without getting opinions of their own on communistic proposals. See further the work of the Fitchburg Finns. They have a publishing company, a daily paper and monthly magazine. A large room is stacked with literature. They mean to have a farm to supply their own milk and vegetables. They want to begin manufacturing. They have nearly forty employees who have their own opinions about wages and hours. These make demands which their workingmen employers have to meet as private employers meet them. They have a labor organization with which they must also cope as best they can. " But if they strike," I was told, " it is a strike in our own family. It is not the old strike of labor against capital. We shall have to settle it as we settle the little differences in our homes, between wife and husband, parent and child." This is like the eloquent pleader for coöperation, Mr. Sonnichsen, who says " when the workers in a consumers' coöperative factory go out on strike, the character of the conflict is quite different from the character of the conflict involved in a strike in an ordinary capitalist factory. In the latter it is a quarrel between the workers and the capitalists over the profits of the industry, over the division of the spoils. In a coöperative strike the quarrel is between the workers in a particular trade and the great mass of the workers in all the other trades over whether they are getting remuneration in fair proportion to that received by the other workers. It is a counterpart of the quarrel between the children of a family disputing over who should wash the dishes and who should wipe them."

But is it so simple as this? Does not one set of workers dispute with other workers over " a division of the spoils?" Coöperators have to set apart the wages of different classes of labor like other business. In one of these stores the employees demand higher wages. The books are opened and together they discuss the possibilities. No one questions that the facts are all before them. In this instance, the demands are withdrawn. I was told of another in which the wages were raised, it being shown that the business could afford it. But the struggle is still over some division of the product. It is a contest not to be eliminated, except in communism with its payment " according to needs " introducing a new order of difficulties greater still. It is yet true that the points of friction and suspicion are so reduced that the strike is of a different order and has an educational reaction which capitalistic strikes do not give. Within the coöperative group, the discontents are directed far less against persons and the " system " under which they feel themselves helpless. Coöperators believe in their system and know they have power to change their managers.

In Fitchburg there are other malcontents. Among the coöperators there are a few I. W. W. who do not like the stores or the bakery because they are " too capitalistic, too slow and too bourgeois." They only " delay the revolution."

So overwhelming is the strength of the membership for the steady hard work which adds economic values and business training, that this disturbing element has little danger to the movement. I heard no wiser word than from one of its managers: " We want them to be free to say what they like and criticize us. The criticism will probably do us good." In what atmosphere, I ask, are extremists safer than in this. What in comparison can the prison or the policeman's club do either to check or to cure the evil? Whether among scholars, diplomatists or fashionable cliques, the criticism that counts and restrains is from those of one's own kind and ways. If the I. W. W. are " class-crazy " instead of " class-conscious," as one of their own officials says, there is little educational value in the censure unless it came from within.

In our own country, labor unions have now so many coöperative stores " to fight the parasites " as to constitute the best possible school to show what the facts and the difficulties are in buying and marketing goods. There is this moment in four large centers an agitation for coöperation because those interested claim " statistical proof that for several food products in constant use the farmer gets only thirty to forty per cent. and the middlemen all the rest." It is argued that sixty to seventy per cent. margin " offers coöperation a perfectly secure basis for large profit — which may be taken from useless middlemen and saved by consumers."

As I deal with this at length in a later volume, I add here only this: if for the ten thousandth time, these coöperators carry out their plan, they will find four or five difficulties where they expect one; they will get a new respect for many of these middlemen; they will finally learn enough of the buying, selling and distributive side of the problem as to make the experiments worth while solely on educational grounds. If by luck or sagacity they secure a manager of unusual skill and rectitude; if further, they command the loyalty of the " two or three hundred families " said to be ready and eager to purchase at the new store, there is no reason why the savings should not be a substantial reward.

There are coöperative stores that return a fifteen per cent. profit on sales and many more which return from eight to ten per cent. Wherever these succeed, they often force a lower price in the neighboring stores that is sometimes more important to the general community than any price reduction in the coöperative store itself.

There are many thousands of coöperative stores in the world that are in a cold business sense successful.

Day by day within this vast democratic organization severe and continuous instruction goes on. *It is an education moreover on the very points raised by revolutionary discontent.* Whether as anarchist, syndicalist, socialist or communist, this critical discontent challenges capitalism for its waste, its exploitations, its corrupting inequalities and its ruthless cunning in fleecing labor.

This attack upon the prevailing financial and industrial system is increasing and will continue to increase. The attack may be met by an appeal to methods that rest on force, or it may be met by enlarging and encouraging democratic organization which has itself become educational — like the entire coöperative movement; like the best of labor organization and a great deal of political socialism.

All these critics of capitalism tell us there is something far superior to the present order. They tell us that any system so dominated by the private profit mongers and resting on the present wage system is a source of increasing injustice and disaster. The voting numbers of those who hold this opinion are, I repeat, a growing force Everywhere the critic wants to get rid of this overpowering management by capital. It wants to substitute its own more democratic management working for other than profit-making motives. It asks to shift the present control of industry and finance from the relatively few who use the system for self-enrichment, to the people as a whole or to their representatives. These are to own and direct our main business activities as directly for the service of the people as Denmark runs her railroads or we manage (or try to manage) our post office.

It is a "large order" but the critics answer, that already in forty countries a most formidable part of every big business is now actually taken from private control and expressly run in the common interest; that the problem is therefore only one of "more or less."

At whatever risks, this issue has to be fought out. Toryism in politics and feudal ways in business will have to make the best of it, adjusting themselves as they may. Is it not therefore all to the good, that we have a political and business schooling on such a scale inside the labor world? In the leading commercial countries, millions of wage-earners are getting this discipline. It has incomparably greater influence because it is *voluntary and self-imposed*. It is a schooling in which every distinctive issue which separates conservatism from radicalism (political and economic) is daily fought out with endless discussion.

There is now great and growing waste in our industrial system because of difficulties in getting rid of those who do bad work or soldier on the job. If they are public employees, politicians will defend them. If in unions, their mates will stand by them. We are told that in ten years, not a teacher among the 20,000 in New York was dropped for poor work. It would be a miracle if, among so many, none were unfit. Boston Common has been filled with navy yard workers and their sympathizers. They were no longer needed because their war work was finished. But they insisted upon staying. They would have work made for them, and two politicians get deafening applause for pleading their case with patriotic fire.

At least so far as private employment is concerned, this protection of incompetence will go on until labor has its own part in business management. When it suffers from the loafer, and sees that it suffers, the labor group will take care of him. In socialist *coöperatives,* as elsewhere, they discover these shiftless or willful ones, but they are not tolerated. They are put upon piece work or they are turned off.

Italy has produced a type of self-governing gang electing its own foreman and doing job-work (in which the labor cost is high) coöperatively. Hundreds of these have proved so successful that Government and cities give them preferential advantages. The societies are registered and work in small gangs. The public inspector sees that the quality of their service is up to standard. If they take a job of city paving for 50,000 lire and can finish it in fewer days than the average for such work, the wage share of each goes up.

One often finds the coöperative store affiliated with this working plan. The profits of each gang go to no outsider, but automatically to themselves when the job is done. They have built city slaughter houses and made whole streets in Parma. The Minister Luzzatti gave them his active sympathy and helped them to the uses of the coöperative banks, of which he was the founder.

The Italian "braccianti" and "muratori" have no boss except of their own electing. If they need a technical engineer, he comes as their fellow counselor and peer, never as a "boss." The gang substitutes its own supervision for that of an employer and also takes the risks. If one can imagine the world's chief business done through such voluntary groups, they would displace the bureaucratic state.

Boston cigar makers have been on strike. As they have not got what they ask, it is announced that a Coöperative Cigar Manufactory has been started. "We can make and market cigars without any big employer and we can undersell him." This has been tried before and the marketing is far from easy. But if they succeed, they will get most valuable instruction and they will not put up with malingering.

CHAPTER XVII

LABOR'S TRAINING FOR THE PRESENT CRISIS

I

THE present hostility of many millions of workers to the wage system in this country is the culmination of a half century of agitation. It is an agitation full of discordant views and discordant methods. The struggle has developed through forms of strife as wasteful to labor as to employer and to the public. No one now knows the ruinous cost of strikes as labor has come to know it. The sense of this loss and the futility of it have given vast numbers of the more intelligent a constructive purpose. To stop this waste is one reason why they ask a closer relation to management. " In the business game, we are no longer to be mere hangers-on like boys clinging to a passing truck. We are going to get inside and we are going to have our share as driver." Among the more radical, it was long the assumption that the present wage system must first be thoroughly upset before labor had any hope of controlling its economic destinies. That so many have learned better is the first awakening to the organic nature of the problem. It is one of these who writes: " To say we workers have no chance until capitalism is destroyed is a return to the intellectual stage of babyhood. There was no such whining among coöperators when they set out in 1844 to beat the middleman. Capitalism is now international and it is only delirium to suppose it can be overcome except by slow replacements made point by point through our own proved capacities." What a challenge is this to the employing class! These may honestly doubt labor's capacity but they must pick up the glove.

We look then to see the instruction which labor has been getting to warrant its confidence. In the trade union in the United States, it is thus far a long, inexorable drill in politics of their own making and in a knowledge of human nature as it " shows up " within their own ranks.

Even in communist colonies, we have seen the education start by self-examination and much plain speaking among the members. After four years in Altruria, one of them says, " We came with the notion that we were very different from other folks, only to find that every one of us brought his own portion of the old Adam with him." This is what the inner group-struggles bring to socialist and trade union organizations. In this discovery, self-criticism and discipline began. In the trade union one form of labor training is very old. It came with the " division of work " incident to applied technical invention. A discovery in the chemistry of dyes was the root of a long angry feud between painters and decorators, one union against another. " We never should have had a row if that d——d machine hadn't come in," was said of an invention that gave new importance to cement. But the " d——d machine " is always coming in.

If twenty different trade unions are at work on a single building; workers in iron, wood, fixtures, paper, plaster, bricks, tiles, decoration, paints, etc., it is clear that opportunity for disputes is there in plenty. Where does painting end and decoration begin; who shall decide? In elaborate piping, at what point is the plumber in order? Steam and Hot Water Fitters have a Union which the plumbers long fought because steam-fitting was said to be plumbers' work. Inventions like those which substitute new and different materials for old (like steel or cement for wood) destroy every classification on which the distribution of work depends. A machine appears which makes it cheaper to cut up timber in the forest rather than in the factory. This alarms the union in the factory. " They are stealing our work." Stone cutting, from the quarry to the finished building, has undergone changes over which many contests have been fought.

If the tile-setters had long put in the metal lathes affixed to the work (as was true until early in 1900) how is this union to get on with the metal-lathers when they form a union of their own. There must be some division of territory.

In putting in electrical conduits, shall the union of electricians cut the brickwork incident to installation? The brick-layers' union says, "That belongs to us." The electricians deny it and the strife continued fifteen years. There is a butchers' union. Should it include those who cut up and sell meat in stores and markets? This has been done, but in any town which has a union of retail clerks it is likely to dispute the claim of the butchers as has often been done. The history of these labor dissensions is at the same time the history of mechanical discovery.

There were years of sharp practice between the unions of the carpenters and the woodworkers. A carpenters' union existed when Thomas Jefferson was President. So few were the technical changes in woodwork and building, that nearly a half century passed before trouble appeared. In the early thirties, the union of the cabinet makers was formed. These were for the most part in furniture factories. Before 1850, a planing machine was so successfully in operation that a part of the carpenters' tasks could be done more rapidly and more cheaply at the factory. The carpenters scattered about town at their work, said they were being robbed by the fellows in the factory, just as later, the union of factory workers said they were robbed by the timber cutters in the forest.

In the building of houses, old fashioned carpenters made sash, frames and doors. Then came the "union of cabinet makers," to dispute "territory" as Jugo-Slavs and Italians now dispute it geographically. As supplementary ingenuities were added to the machine called the "planer," the carpenters in their alarm began a long struggle to form a national organization strong enough to render aid. More than twenty years were required for this; the cabinet makers meantime forming in self-defense their own national body.

Many of these disagreements are met in good temper on the spot; many are arbitrated or settled by conciliation, but thousands of them every year present honest differences of opinion so that the contestants feel it to be a question of " rights," " justice," or of " fundamental principle." As with the old diplomacy, this of course makes it a matter of " honor " and not of compromising or of arbitration. These labor contests have involved a great deal of personal violence and destruction of property. They have often shown contemptuous disregard of the unions' own fundamental law. Nor has any one come to recognize these defects so clearly as labor itself. It is one of many leaders who says: " Most wars have been caused by fights over boundaries. That's what we've been doing, fighting over disputed territory. It's as stupid for us as for capitalists and diplomats. This wrangling among ourselves is exactly like sheep and cattle rangers killing each other over the feeding ground for their animals."

But of still more educational importance is the slow discovery that they have blundered in fixing the blame. From the first, it was obvious that the employer was not the culprit. Labor saw that many employers and contractors were brought to the verge of ruin by trade union wrangling with which the employers had not the least concern. It became as clear that the public often suffered, but clearest of all was it that these family disputes between unions constantly threw out of work other labor bodies that had nothing whatever to do with the squabble; as little indeed as women, children and neutrals in the recent war.

Very slowly labor has been learning to divert its jurisdictional angers *from persons to events*. It was of this that

I heard George McNeil once say: "All the mad has gone out of me. It's too childish to lose temper at the wrong thing. I do not even blame employers any longer. They are victims exactly like the rest of us. All together we have to change a system that injures every one of us and we've all got to take our share of the guilt."

It is nearly a century since St. Simon was dreaming of the time when man would gain the "wisdom to be kind; the wisdom to turn all the exploiting instincts away from his fellowmen and direct them against nature — exploit not the miner but the mine, not the machine tender but the machine."[1] The journey is still long, jurisdictional disputes are not at an end, but a change has come; it sets in the right direction.

The most hopeful of these beginnings are from the long aching experience out of labor's contests with labor.

No definite step yet taken has more suggestive hope in it than what we now read in a new agreement, "entered into between the Building Trades Department of the American Federation of Labor, the American Institute of Architects, the Associated General Contractors of America and the National Association of Builders' Exchanges, to bring this factional warfare under control." It is one in purpose with the "League of Peace" among the nations. For one of the most warlike areas in industry, "there is to be established the National Board for Jurisdictional Awards in the Building Industry, to consist of eight members, three selected by the Building Trades Department of the American Federation of Labor, and one each by the American Institute of Architects, the Engineering Council, the Associated General Contractors of America, the National Association of Builders' Exchanges, and the National Building Trades Employers' Association." This means the building up of

[1] Lord Leverhulm in urging the six hour day revives this language: "I want to put the burden less on to my men and more and more on to my machinery."

a new jurisdictional law to govern the allotment of work. Quite in the manner of the League of Nations we read: " It is a part of the agreement that local unions which do not abide by the decisions of the board shall be suspended and the international union affected shall proceed to man the job. Architects, engineers or employers belonging to any of the organizations involved in the agreement are to be suspended if they fail to observe the rulings of the board." Here as a first step is a sanctioned economic boycott of the sinning party.

I am told that no one was more in earnest or more intelligent in furthering this project than those who represented labor. With every other party it has suffered and out of the long discipline, it joins the new League. No more than the League of Nations will this labor partnership stop all trouble, but with the right purpose, it sets a new standard. It plants it with the approved assistance of all parties who have it in their power to substitute rational action for madness.

We have seen the first alarm of labor coöperators because a trade union was formed among their own employees. We saw the attempt to cope with a strike and even with a sympathetic strike — a much more formidable affair.

It is this experience with all its educational promise that has appeared among our trade unions. They employ large numbers of men and women at wage labor. The recent rapid growth of unionism and its closer relation to Government brings in an ever increasing number of employees. Why should these remain more easily satisfied with a labor boss than with a capitalist boss?

In Italy, what corresponds to our American Federation of Labor, has been savagely attacked for abuse of its own employees and that by the workers themselves. There is indeed no feature of the struggle between master and servant, employer and employed which we cannot study inside the working-men's organizations. It is the oldest story of the sweat shop that the most vicious sweaters are those who pass out of the wage class and become small employers. In spite of the obvious differences, a great deal of this kind of sweating has been found in labor bodies.

The lack of funds and the kind of struggle which these organizations had before them, made it difficult to do otherwise. But this has changed. Labor organization has grown too great for any sentimental definition of its own labor revolt. It has large printing, insurance, clerical service, and a great many stores. An obscure union in Massachusetts carried on business last year of a million and a quarter, which means many employees. These bodies have had painfully to work out all sorts of arbitration and mediation; methods of penalizing incompetence or willfulness, as well as the greater problems that turn on property rights. These have been so far threshed out by labor in its own bailiwick as to offer the indispensable help toward every next step which general industry must take. We see in it, that *the gist of the labor problem is transformed from the capitalistic enemy to the control of labor itself.*

It is transferred where labor must think out and work out the same old problems which have so long baffled capitalism. With vital features of social insurance, with unemployment, with piece work, with the foreman, with minimum wage and hours of labor, these working men have already had long and trying experience of their own and with their own. As these functions grow, we see them face to face with the great test — what to do with their own rebels. They are getting them in increasing numbers. Shall they "hire and fire" in the old way? They have done a great deal of it. They have done it on the same grounds and with the same excuses as those given by the old employers. Shall labor furnish strike breakers (scabs) to bring its own rebels to terms? It has done this often enough and drastically enough to show real working sympathy with bourgeois management of strikes. But labor employers cannot continue these policies any more than capitalist managers can continue them. In this one respect, both have the same task. Together they must devise ways which this common experience makes possible. To show this fellowship in distress, one instance is enough. It was a threatened strike — labor against labor. One of our best investigators most friendly to trade unions was present at the Buffalo meeting. This is what he wrote [1] — " The delegatese, especially those who were officers of international unions, did not feel that they were dealing with a union of coördinate rank "— they were employers who were confronted with a proposition from the union of their own employees. So they acted and talked just as employers do. William Dobson, secretary of the Bricklayers' International Union, remarked, " the employees of the international organizations have no need of a union." He stated that they have short hours, good wages, and that, so far as he was concerned, " I go around every morning and speak to the employees, say good morning, and if any of them are not feeling well, I send them home."

Dobson was very indignant over the attitude of the stenographers' union. He said that because their employers are union men, they think they can hold them up. " I, for one," he told the convention, " refuse to be blackmailed." The convention saw the matter in the same light as did the international officials, and refused a charter to this impertinent organization.

What vexatious feature of capitalistic strikes is left out of this picture? It is true there was no violence or serious intimidation by pickets, yet every essential of the contest is here, even to the humorous details of resemblance to our most popular disorders between capital and labor.

It is of course much that this family quarrel was fought out " on the square " and according to rule without the atrocities of brute force and spying incident to American

[1] John A. Fitch in the *Survey*, December 1, 1917.

enterprise in these misunderstandings. The whole level on which coöperators settle their grievances is so much higher that it requires a different classification. But for *educational value* in dealing with human nature, adjusting conflicting points of view and settling differences of interest among economic groups, these strikes inside the labor world have a disciplining influence more penetrating and more convincing than any to which we may look from all other sources combined.

When we have courage or are forced to take our sins and blunders upon our own backs instead of seeking the scape-goat among outsiders, there is hope for the worst and the weakest of us. On this Buffalo incident a capitalistic sheet became most jocular: " Labor at last gets some of its own medicine." It affects surprise that the national officials should show themselves so astonishingly like other folks with business responsibilities. The hope is expressed that this first lesson may lead to more appreciation of business men's difficulties, etc. Yet this is very far from being a " first lesson." The hiring and managing of wage-workers long since passed inside labor organization with practical consequences that we should not neglect. Let us see the origin of these prudences.

II

Two of the three labor sections — coöperators and the unions — began and long continued exclusively on the economic field. In speech and print they poured out their disapproval of political action. They aimed to free themselves from exploitation under the wage system. The unions strove for higher income and fewer hours with better working conditions: coöperators to eliminate the profits of the middleman. As power over these conditions increased, politics for their own organization had to be created. That it should be " democratic " was a matter of course. As in the United States at large, the word was at first so ill-defined that it became coin for every purpose. No one was more glib in employing it than Southern slave owners or than Northern merchants who stood by the South because " cotton, rice and sugar could not be raised without slave labor."

Neither the trade unions nor the coöperators had this sinister bias, but " democracy " was quite as vague a term to them. It is still vague, but they have made progress. What this progress means in working toward its more intelligent definition, we are forced to consider because labor's part in national politics is now assured. It is passing rapidly from its own private politics into the wider field.

On the world stage, that part of the working class here kept in view, comprises certainly more than fifty millions of wage-earners. To classify them as unionists, socialists and coöperators is a necessary but dangerous convenience. They run into and through each other at many points. Here and there, we cannot distinguish one from the other. They often fight a common battle and are for the most part a unit against the existing wage system, though many of them do not now propose its destruction. They are a unit in demanding far greater control of industry, of its machinery and our natural resources. They are a unit in demanding " government by the people " to a degree that most conservatives would look upon as social disaster.

They are a unit too in asking that democracy shall be applied to the business sphere. The stronger property class has hitherto been amused by this claim. In this country, the first real alarm was at the aggressive rise of " direct legislation." As the meaning of this has grown clear, especially the business men of more thoughtful cast, have " sat up." They see that the logic of direct legislation under popular suffrage, with woman's vote to be added, will certainly disturb many property interests. It is for this reason that these claims offer so good an illustration of labor's political education.

As I look back to the first trade union meeting forming in 1873; as I note the changes since, it seems to me that no conceivable instruction could have done more for the labor concerned, to fit it for the unavoidable exigencies now thrust upon it, than what has gone on within these bodies.

So necessary is it to see this, that I ask the reader to look in at that first meeting in which ordinary working men, with no political preparation, were having their first lesson. They were starting out to do what philosophers had long speculated about — some in fear, a few with hope. Especially after the revolution of 1848, when labor got some real promise of power, publicists became more curious. What would come of it if these vast, inarticulate majorities ever got control of the ship of state? According to temperament, these sages foretold the decay or the saving of civilization. Renan saw only the approach and multiplication of calibans. Long before his death, he said that democracy had so vulgarized French manners that he refused to get into the public omnibus. In Freiburg, near the Swiss border, a man wise in science, Professor Weismann, was watching the growing democracy among the cantons. He thought he saw indications that the higher science was in serious danger and that more democracy would merely vulgarize what remained.

These doubts have not ceased, but speculation to-day shows a new anxiety. For what is it these labor democracies now ask? Not merely for political control in small states, they will have it in great states, while growing numbers include industry and finance in their demands.

The strongest and least sentimental of men in English and American trade unions now set up claims for railway management and actual ownership plus management of vast mining interests. These are to be "democratically administered" and mines and railways are only a beginning.

"The long wars and the *demands of the democracy* had swallowed up the wealth of Athens; the great and splendid works of the Age of Pericles were therefore no longer possible," are the words with which Breasted begins his eighteenth chapter in "Ancient Times." Those alarmed are telling us, this is precisely what will happen over again if demos has its way. This is now what Judge Gary is telling the Senate Committee: even to unionize the steel industry (but a step towards democratizing it) is the beginning of decay.

If the "demands of democracy" swallowed the wealth of Athens: if this resulted on so tiny a patch of the world as Greece, with half the population of one of our states, and with some of the wisest men the world has produced to help them out, what chance have the vast numbers now internationally bound together with problems inconceivably more difficult? Every doubter of democracy cheers up over the prospect, because he believes the very extravagance of labor's claim will prove its unfitness and undoing.

More confident than these open flouters of the demos, are our political realists who make no public display of their doubts. They have learned that the formulas of democracy must be solemnly accepted and publicly confessed. They will swing the censer before the idol, though they gibe at it among friends. They have only to encourage the illusion of the demos that it has the reins in hand. It must be allowed to think it guides, but like a child in its father's lap, the reins in the little fists are manipulated from behind. This veiled management of the people has been the accomplished art of our most seasoned politicians since the secret framing of our Constitution. They get solid comfort out of every weakness that proves the incapacity of the mass to take care of itself. If this view is correct, democracy is indeed "a drunken man in the saddle." Such as these honestly believe all the chesty vaporing about the people's sagacity and self-control to be plain fudge. There is to them no hope for mass-rule except in draped, masterful guidance such as they themselves can give. They look quite literally upon the oratorical and semi-religious tributes to democracy as "the fetish-worship of incompetence."

In their view not only is the people unfit to direct politics, it is far less fit to manage the business of creating and distributing wealth. The masses, in Mallock's favorite figure, are in their opinion, like a horse heady and stupid, that must be ridden or driven with steady hand.

There must be common confession that we do not know how well or ill the masses are to use their power. What we do know is that it is coming to them. It comes so rapidly that labor leaders are themselves stunned by it. The old hands among them are not half able to guide it. By hundreds, they have been roughly cast aside.

Yet a great labor army has long had its severest political schooling — a schooling in which the discipline was real because it came from within. There has been at least a training for *more* democracy; how much we do not know. It is upon this very point that I want to give testimony from labor itself. With the deeper difficulties of mass-rule labor has long had its own tussle. It has learned much and is very frank about it.

It has often seemed strange to me, but from unfriendly critics of labor, I never once heard mention of this schooling for which we should thank our stars. At the present moment, a considerable part of labor is the most truly conservative thing in the world. For safety we depend upon it more than upon the church, the college, the courts or the army.

Three great labor groups have long been creating and paying the costs of many thousands of educational centers in which the rigors are far more strict than in the sheltered aloofness of those private nurseries to which the well-to-do send their offspring.

With each enlargement of the labor structure, the competitive search for capacity becomes more exacting. Those who stand the test are everywhere a very small minority. They are the few against the many.

It has such life-and-death importance that we understand what this labor education *is* and how it has been brought about, that I ask attention to this first gathering of a less skilled body of workers bent upon forming a union.

Unless "old stagers" are there to guide the meeting, we have a crowd certain in time of excitement to demand the "orator." They want his glibness, his epigram and especially his violent opinions. This kind of man was first introduced at that meeting. They had to have him "to get up steam."

These gifts never lose their sway over labor any more than they do elsewhere, but when committee work begins, decisions made and responsibilities taken, another type of man is required. It is these men of executive gift over whom the "tongue-man" soon loses control. They are more likely to jeer at him privately when his sway over the general audience is most impassioned. These cooler "fact-men" learn to take his measure and to use him, very much like adroit managers in the Republican or Democratic campaign.

Year by year, the weeding goes on with much the same result. The conditions of selection become severer with every step in organization. Labor begins with the most "direct" form of self-government. That "no member of the union should be excluded from voting upon every question and for every person nominated" was a sort of axiom in 1803. One century later, we see what the unions have learned in building up restrictions on the voting privilege. We see them refusing the mass-vote and quietly giving power to select committees: we see them build up a caucus and adopt one after another most of the prudences by which political control is kept within the hands of a small minority. The national organization which preceded the American Federation of Labor had in its Constitution direct legislation, proportional representation, imperative mandate, initiative and referendum. To each of these was given the democratic definition. How could the ruling principle " each for all and all for each " be realized unless every man and every woman had equal voice?

All this is the free and easy idealizing of democratic theory. It is an emotional gratification like saying "all men should be in good health and without sin." It has all those mythical conveniences so dear to the master in politics.

This was the atmosphere of the first labor gathering which I was permitted to see by the kindness of George McNeil. At once the question of leadership was the issue. All the men in the special craft were invited. Hardly a fourth of them appeared. It was politely assumed, not only that " one man was as good as another," but that every one was fit to take the chair or hold any other office. McNeil thought the first indication of fitness was "always being present and ready to do anything you were asked." If the humdrum of the meeting interested a man and continued to interest him, it was as good an indication as any, but it was not enough. For months the duties are so simple and ill defined that almost any member may serve, but as the work develops or as the union affiliates with city, district, state or national organization, the selection narrows sharply from the many to the few.

In this instance, one man conceived the idea of a union and first brought the men together. This marked him as one to lead. As he refused office this threw the selection upon the members.

As elsewhere in preliminary organization, some man may come to the front who seems born to it; whose personality, manner, power to conciliate, give him natural leadership and if his influence continues, he is almost certain to have insight into the fitness of other men for the various duties of further organization.

This first instinctive selection by the group is the starting-point. If he survives as leader, this at least indicates a gift on his part for selecting others, and he will be more of a factor in that selection than will the general membership. Here is the beginning of a certain oligarchic tendency to concentrate power in the few; to keep power at the center rather than loosely among the mass. If this first leader has practical sagacity, he will allow the audience to think the selection is entirely its work and not his. Or he may indirectly determine the selection so unconsciously that he would be honest in denying it.

In another craft union of less than ninety members such a leader came to the front. It was said, after ten years, that no official of any importance was ever chosen except by this leader, but that the rank and file never knew this and it was added, "I am not sure the leader knew it himself." When this man voluntarily retired, it was clear that he chose his own successor. When twitted with being a "boss," he replied that somebody had to be a boss because the rank and file could not be induced to take the responsibility for the regular work required by the organization. "Not one in ten of you will come to the regular meetings. Not one quarter will vote unless there is some row on. Of those who do come to the meetings, not one in ten will give the time necessary for the routine, without which the organization can't exist. Of those who are willing to do such work, a great many prove unfit. This leaves a mighty small minority that can do it, or believe in it enough to *stick;* to stick all the time even when nine-tenths of it is drudge work."

"The great majority that stays away," he added, "will probably always call the fellow who carries the responsibility a 'boss' and as the organization gets bigger, the stay-aways will think the executive committee is a hack machine blocking all real democratic rule." I put this opinion before a labor official who has had long experience with the American Federation of Labor and as chairman of large labor assemblies.

He tells me it is pretty exactly the history of labor organization and that it explains why, for example, election of officers by referendum has proved so disappointing in trade union history. " Crowd-selection is the worst possible selection because if the numbers are large, they have no test whatever of a man's fitness for the kind of work demanded by the organization. Only we who make and manage the organization know. It is always a specialized task *with no resemblance to work in the mill or factory.* A committee of experienced members come to know far better what qualities are necessary and what general policies are necessary."

When the American Federation of Labor had hardly more than a million members, the opinion was expressed: " Not one man in a hundred has the qualifications for the more important offices." It was admitted that many of this hundred had the requisite ability but " some kink of character or disposition spoils him for our special purposes. Some of the ablest cannot or will not work with others. We never can tell this at the start. It has to be tried out by pitting men against others, that is, competitively. Others tire of routine. They are first-rate in a crisis, but will not stand the drudgery without which no large organization can hold its own for a month."

In a word, these bodies come to select their own " aristocracy " precisely as do other large organizations, educational, religious or financial.

One may hear among these the same contempt privately expressed for " the crowd." It has to be " managed," " led," flattered and fed on myths as in our national and local politics. This is one reason why labor generates its own share of demagogues. Wherever masses have to be manipulated, whether in the church or secular affairs, the demagogue is a familiar figure. His detection and elimination will prove as good a test of civilization as could be given. Democracy must, however, put up with him as long as the many have to be " led."

That labor should find this out among its own; that it should develop its own safeguards against the evil, is as much a public benefit as it is a benefit to labor. Different forms of workingmen's organizations have been built up into such strength that they are schools of self-criticism in the best sense. It is in these labor discussions that current definitions of democracy and other big words are seen to be inadequate. No one learns better " the bane of the catchword."

There is to-day no gathering in the United States harder to fool with phrases than a trade union convention though men in this body may still be fluent in using them for theatrical effect, after the manner of the congressional record.

In the earlier discussions, one sentence, "*The cure for democracy is more democracy,*" got very wide acceptance. If a plea for the initiative or referendum ended with the proper bathos, this handy effusion never failed to bring a cheer. To-day in any mature union, the men in control would call it buncombe. In great numbers, labor representatives have acquired a critical independence about " the people" probably shrewder than that of the most imposing publicist. Lecky or Sir Henry Maine judges by universal observation. In the labor ranks the judgment, if narrow, may have a higher value because it is closer to the mass; closer to its weaknesses and its apathies.

Many of the unions have learned this lesson of restraint

LABOR'S TRAINING FOR THE PRESENT CRISIS 317

far more quickly and more effectively than the great public. Especially when they have built up a complicated system of finance, taxes, fines and various forms of insurance, they are led, in their own safety, to check innovation and faction and consequently to check these extensions of the democratic ideal. There are always hot-headed men who want to use the funds for strikes. The iron-molders at one period spent nearly three-fourths of their funds on strikes. The hot-heads are often in sufficient numbers to cripple any union if they are not restrained.

This long struggle of experienced men in the union to stop rash strikes with their costs and suffering, has a history which would humiliate many a critic, if he could know the story. The bitterest word I ever heard against these critics came from a leader in this state who had fought his battles with employers but always kept their respect. "The good folks," he said, "are very severe with us, because of strikes. They talk as if we labor men and our families were quite unaware of the sufferings caused, although it is we who do the suffering. Very early, we have cases on our hands where there is neither money nor bread for three days. They have to be cared for and are cared for to the last penny at our disposal. I have looked on mothers weeping like children because the food was gone. But we know all this *beforehand*. We understand that it is a part of all hard contests. The younger men, especially those with no families, are so hard to manage when the excitement comes, that it requires all the resources we possess to keep them back. We have to talk to them as the all-wise folks on the outside talk down to us. We now take it for granted that these critics either can't or won't understand that we *know* the suffering and bear it because we can't get what we think right without it."

It is this less responsible radicalism within the union that has to be encountered over every separate question.

If the impatient ones had free hand, let us say with the "initiative," they could keep the union in perpetual turmoil. They could defeat or hinder every move toward that constructive social policy which includes questions like finance, insurance, charters and strikes, as well as general policies.

This inside record is more rewarding for us, because the workers' first attempts to build their own self-government were by men who not only feared the "representative" but even shied at that more radical agent of democracy, the "delegate." It was first the accepted belief that everybody should take part in deciding "what is one man's business as much as it is another's." For this, the most "instructed" delegate, they thought, might prove a peril. He might change his mind when once out of sight. When the great critic of Amercian democracy (Tocqueville) was converted, it was an "aristocrat submitting to the inevitable." Those early labor men required no conversion. They had a simple and perfect faith that everybody at the meeting should have equal voice and have it all the time.

This "democracy to the limit" had long and stubborn trial by labor, until it was found to be unworkable. There is not a link in the chain stretching from "pure" democracy to the representative principle which has not been forged in these labor schools. For three or four decades, their documents are full of assertions that "trade unions will have nothing to do with politics." This meant the politics of the general public. But meantime they were toiling over their own inner political system. This process is the more to our purpose because it was done without a hint of political or social theory. One by one new rules and restraints were added because necessary business had to be got out of the way. The only theory at the start was one of "equal rights for all." But an airy idealism like this had little real meaning until attempts were made to practice it. As in the instance given, the first steps had a town-meeting simplicity. But as the locals were forced to unite with others until at last they were knotted into a great network of State, National and International organizations, all the practical reasons — numbers, distance, difficulty of communication — which gave rise to the representative system the world over, appeared in labor politics.

III

An excellent example is one of our best drilled and ablest led bodies, the United Mine Workers. It is all the more apt because its proposals now agitate the public. A senator says, "it staggers belief" that any union could make such pretensions. It is as if the single taxer and the syndicalist were speaking with one voice. "Our coal resources," say these miners, "are the birthright of the American people for all time to come, and we hold that it is the immediate duty of the American people to prevent the profligate waste that is taking place under private ownership of these resources." There is even echo of the New Guild, the miners will stand by the Plumb plan of managing railways. Against the old tradition, they will go into politics. They will stand by the coöperators and apparently think well of the Non-Partisan League.

Here is a political program. If even a small part of it is seriously to enlist their efforts, what fitness have they for the political strategy and restraint essential to the undertaking?

This union of miners has no single peculiarity to set it apart from hundreds of others, but its history is well known. It is a story in which we pass from a "local" that may have only a dozen members, to the sub-district, state and national organization. This means a National Convention entrusted with such powers that it can change its fundamental law, the constitution. In 1902 it began to use the referendum to elect officers, but discontent showed itself very early because it did not work as expected. The membership had become so large and the distance so great between one mining center to another that great sections could not be reached so as to get the slightest interest among the men. Except on issues that roused great feeling, or a strike that touched all members, a large part of the membership was as callous about voting as so many "best citizens" who are only nagged into it by their more public spirited neighbors. This lack of response is what every State in the Union with the referendum "direct primaries," and the like, has to learn.

This indifference in the Miners' Union finally led to serious discussion in favor of compelling members (by fines) to vote at the national election. "If the fellows don't take interest enough in the affairs of their own organization to vote, let us soak them by a fine!" How often we have heard this outside the unions! Labor's experience with these compulsions is the most enlightening material we possess on all attempts in politics to substitute force for the slower educational persuasion. In other fields labor has made trial of "absentee voting." It has learned much about the limits of this device.

If lumber camps or Australian sheep shearing leaves multitudes of men beyond the reach of polling booths, the peoples' will is so far unexpressed. To remedy this Victoria has a "postal vote" nearly 4000 persons thus voting in 1908.

Beginning with railway men, Kansas has for several years had such a law and three or four other states modified forms of it. New Zealand has it for "Seamen, sheep shearers and commercial travelers." Norway has it and some of the Swiss cantons for cantonal elections. There have been difficulties both of supervision and expense and nowhere apparently is much enthusiasm over results. One labor opponent says the only thing accomplished is "to stop the cranks hollerin' for it."

To stop the "hollerin'" is not an empty achievement. The miners' trial of the referendum has the same value. Certain uses of the referendum have been found indispensable for special trade union ,purposes, as they have in our general political life. Labor will not renounce these agencies, but long buffeting with the sort of human nature which plagues the politicians of capitalism, leads to the same sharp restrictions of referendum, initiative and recall that we are slowly learning in the world at large. Many of our unions have got this lesson of restraint far more quickly and more effectively than the great public, and they can give the public sound advice as they can on " direct primaries," now rousing such hatred from politicians.

In the political drill of these miners, one by one these vexations have to be met. It is not an extemporized opinion they give. It required nearly forty years to educate the miners' locals in different cities to send delegates to the first national convention. This was to be " the legislative head with power over the separate unions." Their Constitution had to be ratified by the unions in different states. It next required a generation (till 1884) to secure real coöperation among these unions. For many years the locals did not even discuss representative government, but when a single city came to have over 5000 members, " it could not govern it by a general meeting." " Rules of restraint " were found to be absolutely necessary when the meeting was too large. There was often an " outburst of hasty and ill-informed opinion." One by one, these restrictions became incorporated in the Constitution, as amendments have been to the Constitution of the United States. At first every member could vote *on all questions*. Then came a long struggle to preserve the same power for the small union as for the large. From 1884 on, the contests over the referendum and initiative are educationally as illuminating as any feature of our political history. Always the great issues are at the front! Shall there be greater or less centralized authority? What freedom shall local unions have to agitate for amendments in the constitution?

Throughout, the more conservative representative principle gains ground because it steadies the impulsive discontents always present in such bodies. An official says, "To let loose the initiative, without having a brake on, would give us at every session twenty questions where we could deal with only one."

To have given the initiative free play would have discouraged every step in the more rational treatment of burning questions like the introduction of new machinery and the ratio of apprentices allowed. It would have made a chaos of local strikes and in controlling methods of taxation.

It is a long road from this "organized prudence" back to a raw union of mechanics who chose officers eighty years ago in taking names in order, as they appeared on the membership book. There was a democracy in Greece so "pure" that generals, naval captains and high officials were chosen by lot. The Greeks lost a great naval battle by being so democratic as to change the admiral each day.

Early in our own history soldiers were allowed to choose their own officers as in Virginia.[1] We have left these naïve ways as far behind as the wooden plow. Labor organization has learned at least as rapidly and it has learned through experiences so exactly corresponding to outside political experience, that some sense of fellowship and understanding with labor is possible for us all. Labor comes finally to turn to a strong executive (especiallly in all exigencies) just as do corporations, cities and governments. They want the help of a power concentrated enough to be seen, measured and held responsible. This turns the back squarely upon "instructed delegates" and upon every other feature of popular rule which encourages indiscriminate mass voting. More and more it accepts the principle that tried and instructed officials be kept at their posts as long as efficiency requires. Professor Hoxie reports this from a trade union

[1] "Institutional History of Virginia," Bruce, Vol. II, 88.

leader: "The successful officer tends to stay in office indefinitely and grows more competent and more powerful with service. *As a democracy no union would last six minutes.*[1]

Of the referendum in our largest labor body, this author adds, " The use of the referendum in the American Federation of Labor has shown that it frequently results in delay, factionalism and indifference on the part of the rank and file and it is exceedingly expensive."

From one of its most honored officials, at first eager for the referendum, I heard this crisp summary:[2] " I was as hot as any of them for the referendum at the start but it has proved in practice a nuisance." I asked him if he would give it up generally in labor politics. " No," he said, " we can't do that. There are times and conditions when we have to appeal to every voter in order to know what the general opinion is. What we have to do is to find out what sort of political move is helped by the referendum and initiative and what ones are merely bungled by them. So far they have been mostly bungled." He thought the Swiss experience upon the whole was the safest model. But he was chiefly impressed by the hesitation and conservatism of the Swiss democracy in employing these measures.

What more sagacious statement than this could any one give for the entire problem in the United States?

The secretary who says he aided in 1895 " in placing this fad (initiative and referendum) in the union constitution " openly proclaims its mistake. He adds: " In 1906, after 11 years' experience, we kicked the thing out of the union as a useless good-for-nothing scheme and a trouble-maker." He quotes the president of the Boot and Shoe Workers' Union thus: " President John Tobin said at the 1912 convention of the American Federation of Labor: ' I want to be recorded here as one of the original initiative and referendum advocates in the Boot and Shoe Workers' Union. We

[1] "Trade Unionism in the United States," page 180.
[2] The President of the American Boot and Shoe Workers' Union.

had 11 years' experience under that system. The system became so absolutely unsatisfactory and so productive of corruption that we were obliged to abandon it entirely.' From many conversations with Mr. Tobin, I know that this represents his opinion." [1]

I choose the National Boot and Shoe Workers' Union because for thirty years, I saw intimately some of the contests here considered and because, during these years, I had the cordial and friendly assistance of the national president of that union. In deciding upon certain fundamental principles clear enough to admit of intelligent judgment by the mass of shoe workers, Mr. Tobin continued to believe as much as ever. He learned, however, that this instrument could be as mischievous for all administrative details as Switzerland has found it, and that we should use it as rarely and with as much caution as that most democratic people. Listen a moment to the discussion among the 200 delegates at their yearly convention where radical men are always on hand to urge more democracy and the referendum as a means of lessening the autocratic power of the "machine" which "has enslaved the workers at the bench." "The referendum alone will give us freedom." One foe of the machine appealed to history. He says:

"Ever since the twelfth century, since the time of King John and the Magna Charta people have been getting more rights, but here we have an organization that is supposed to be democratic to the limit, that prevents us from voting for our men, and that goes back to the so-called representative form of government."

Another pleads for the referendum because "one hundred men in my factory have lost confidence in the general officers. They tell me and others that you take away our

[1] We read just now "The American Federation of Labor refuses to use this I & R system either for the election of its officials or the enactment of its legislation. In the 1912 convention of this great labor organization all the conservative labor leaders opposed the initiative and referendum."

right to vote for our officers. What have we left? Nothing but to pay our fees. What constitutes slavery? The placing of a man in a position where he must obey the will of others."

Another shouts out that " delegates should be instructed at home how to vote at the convention, so that the will of the people may be carried out."

He is warned by the " machine " that this delegate may get new information at the convention; may see things from a much broader point of view and should therefore keep his mind open. With better information, he may then return to instruct and persuade his mates.

Hours of this discussion (as at the Toronto convention, 1907) brings out every issue on which the superiority of the representative over the instructed delegate depends and upon the restrictions to which all " hurry-up democrats " must submit.

Most vital in this history is the fact that in the earlier periods of labor organization there were no prizes for self-seeking or ambitious men. There were no large funds to administer or honors to award. As these develop, the struggle for office begins and at the same time the needs increase for a higher and more disinterested order of abilities.

To secure men competent to deal with those constitutional and administrative issues which touch the interests of many thousands scattered through hundreds of trades in all parts of the country, is a task impossible except to men — not only of ability but of abilities long and carefully trained.

Here at last is this higher labor leadership behind which is the toil and sacrifice of a century. The story, like that of the printers, has in it far more severe political tuition than any literary institution can give. The slow building up of a constitution, like any of those of the larger unions is a work that no one can study without respectful admiration. That of the shoe makers is a document of fifty pages. There is not one of its 106 sections that has not been toiled over line upon line with as much painstaking thoroughness as was given to any state constitution in the land.

If Hamilton, Madison and Jay helped educate our people to understand and accept our National Constitution in those great letters of the Federalist, this document of the shoe workers did no less for its own membership. Complicated rules of order, finances, charters, elections, sick benefits, labor press, unemployment, relief, strikes, lockouts, methods of auditing down to referendum amendments — these many topics have required the kind and amount of hard continuous labor which trains for citizenship and above all for the " economic citizenship " now before us.

But the framing of a constitution is of little disciplinary value compared to what follows. Beyond the production of such a document is the relentless duty of *interpreting and enforcing its provisions*. There is no vacation in this school. Without a break, working men and women are at the tasks imposed by their fundamental law. Nothing can better illustrate labor's struggle to *carry out* democracy than all the attempts to extend it among the rank and file.

The initiative and recall play their part here too but would add nothing to the point. Italian socialists sized up the referendum as did the English trade unions. They began by taking their democracy very seriously. Again and again they refer decisions back to the whole membership " to learn what every one thinks." Is not democracy " the collective judgment of all?" Nowhere known to me, did the chill in using the referendum come so rapidly as among Italian socialists. As everywhere else, they discover the waste of time, the costs, the misunderstandings and the confusion which Bacon said caused more evil than error itself. Worst of all, they find how little the main part of their body *cares* about the question referred to them. Then the form and mode of the instrument are changed, Dutch socialists trying the "obligatory" referendum, because they could not get any results from the "free appeal." This discovery that the majority "doesn't care" is a great lesson. It is one reason why syndicalism appeared. I quote a syndicalist of great intelligence. Though revolutionary, the Italian — Arturo Labriola — wrote: "The last thing that true democracy means in politics is the influence of all men acting as units of equal influence as though rights were always the sense of the largest assortment of industrial wills. *True democracy, on the contrary, is the concentrating of power in an élite who can best judge of the interaction of social cause and effect."*

This is how labor finally acts, though few of its defenders care so openly to disclose the fact and to give its proper name. A good editor could make up, not one but several volumes on the pros and cons of the referendum from the proceedings of labor conventions.

It is one excellence of this labor discussion that it has not been learned from the printed page. Knowledge and opinion have come from long internal struggles.

There was first among these workers the fervor and simple faith that anything and everything *more* democratic was for that reason desirable. If the "initiative" was more democratic than the referendum, because the people take the first step with the initiative, it was for that reason superior. If a case could be made out that "proportional representation" would bring the voting mass nearer to control, enabling everybody to express his opinion more freely and more directly on all questions of principle or of detail, then proportional representation was to be welcomed. I heard a miscellaneous labor audience, listening to Richard H. Dana on Civil Service Reform, object because they feared the offices would get too permanently into the hands of the few. "Everybody ought to have a show."

In the earlier stages of coöperation, of socialism and the

trade union, this passion for the utmost that democracy can give stirs the imagination as by some mysterious presence akin to a new religion.

In the flush of labor's uprising, these finalities of democratic control have all the unselfish expectations of some great hope for man. It is this which holds our respect, even when the actual attempts to realize the equalities lack every trace of that practical good sense which distinguishes between what is possible and what impossible.

My claim that labor has created its own best schooling is because its organization implies an elaborate constitution, laws and by-laws; it requires provision for the interpretation of these laws; for mediation, conciliation and arbitration, as well as its own severe penalties to enforce discipline. All these have grown up as naturally and with as much justification as our National Constitution and Supreme Court grew up.

It is as if this century of labor legislation were one long preparation for what now so suddenly comes upon us. If we are indeed to do what public authorities, great employers and labor are now actually carrying into effect, namely, to " constitutionalize " industry — to bring it into some harmony with our political traditions, is it not supreme good fortune that labor has been so long at work with these same problems among its own members? They have built up every feature, executive, legislative, administrative and put them to long practical tests under great difficulty. They have discovered most of the weaknesses of visionary forms of democracy.

The century required to produce this whole labor structure has behind it immense sacrifices of time and money. It has cost as much painful drudgery, study, discussion, alternating success and defeat, as any feature of our religious, political or educational life.

If the referendum or direct primary is brought before a labor body still callow with inexperience, it is likely to be received with uncritical enthusiasm. Until experience has come, these are sure to be used with ardent expectation as if all evils would flee before them. But Oregon will not be quicker to learn what the referendum or other devices can do, and what not do, than many a trade union learned long before Oregon heard of it.

It is into this trained labor organism that every radical proposal for further democracy must come for examination.

Is is then seriously to be questioned that capitalism and the public should prudently but fearlessly accept this experience and coöperate with it to the one end of learning together where the new ways lead?

IV

Another discovery made by organized labor in this country and made apparently with no reference to foreign experience, is that the ablest and most trustworthy men will refuse office if their independent action and judgment are continuously threatened by the various devices that grow out of direct legislation. These men do not like openly to abuse anything to which the name "democratic" is attached. They frequently admit the advantage of direct legislation "if held in reserve for extreme or special cases." Their fear is that these limits will be hard to maintain.

After wrathful citizens in two cities on the Pacific coast had secured the requisite petition to "recall" their mayors, it was a labor leader in the East who put the question, "If any bunch of citizens who get mad can run round and get names enough to pull the mayor out of office, what sort of man will think it worth while to run for mayor? Will any one who wants to use his strength to serve the city submit to that? Teetotalers, A. P. A.'s and 'vice experts' are samples of the many 'causes' to be used against any man in office and to be so used that he must be on the watch to defend himself or spend his time in conciliating factions instead of attending to his business duties." "I would not," he added, "put my head into a noose like that even in a small trade union."

Twenty years ago, this man was eloquent as an advocate of the referendum for labor organization. After long watching it in practice he says, "If it was used half as often as a restless minority would like to use it, the best men could not be induced to take office because they would have to be thinking all the time how to defend themselves instead of attending to their job of preserving and building up the organization."

The European labor movement swarms with men, long in power, who are as convinced that the masses should not interfere with the governing function except within carefully defined limits. The answer is often made to this, "Of course those labor men who actually hold power — socialists, trade unionists or coöperators — do not want to be disturbed." The "ins" never want to be shaken up by the "outs." This is not an explanation. Many of the ablest scholars in the labor movement — men who are in the minority — or hold no office, have become as skeptical of direct legislation as the most petted and secure labor officials.[1]

It is a part of labor's political schooling to find how easily its enemies can turn measures like the referendum against its own pet schemes. In Missouri, the unions wanted a "full crew law." It was at least open to the gravest abuses, especially the farming districts so viewed it. When the referendum on which the unions had spent so much time was heavily defeated, a labor paper said:

[1] In Bernstein's "History and Theory of Socialism" we have as penetrating an analysis of the dangers of the referendum and other forms of direct legislation as has been given by any living publicist. It represents the maturer opinion of able men in every country.

"We were gold-bricked by the referendum. In Michigan there was a similar experience under which a constitutional amendment was proposed by the initiative."

It is after trials of this kind, that labor becomes most intelligently critical of these "furtherances of democracy." The line of criticism becomes precisely like that of conservative publicists. One of the commonest arguments of these publicists takes the form of this question, "If the people don't know enough to select competent and trustworthy men to represent them in the legislature, what reason is there to think they can legislate more wisely themselves? Is the mob instinct swayed by the passions of the moment and stirred by demagogues and by ignorant amateurs any more trustworthy?" I have heard the head of a national union, after long experience with the referendum, use this conservative argument with pat illustrations from his own organization. The real reason of this distrust in a "meddlesome democracy" is not seen in the quieter periods, or in the ordinary business. It is always some exigency or crisis in which the executive committee becomes autocratic and acts with as much secrecy as possible. If driven to it by effective attacks from their dissatisfied members, these autocrats have the excuses of a long tradition. "It was a case of great urgency." "Even if we had consulted all the members, there were no safe means of getting before them the most important and decisive information." In church and university administration such exigencies have long shown the same "wisdom," "prudence" or "cowardice" as we choose to name it. Silence is preferred, "but if the lid is removed and the facts come out" we hear some moral justification. Most ethics of institutional and class defense have thus been made up.

For quick action always required in a crisis, labor, like others of old, says with much truth, "We can't wait to consult the whole body. Our opponents will beat us hands down before the returns come in."

Before the Western Federation of Miners joined the A. F. of L. it had these crises in which a close leadership would have no more used their referendum than a general in face of an attacking enemy would send home for electoral approval of his next step. From Lassalle to the Dutch socialist Van Kol, we have had what seems a reckless admission, that for a long period democracy is impossible. There must be, they tell us, a transitional leadership in which the masses are to put implicit confidence.

In a friendly and most appreciative notice of Pease's "History of the Fabian Society," an editorial writer in the London *Nation* refers to the "astute boss-management" of that body. He says:

"This valuable history of Fabianism shows how easily and how completely in a society preserving all the forms and usages of democratic government, a small group of able leaders have been able to impose their will and judgment in all crises on their electorate."

One reason assigned for the great rôle played by Fabians is, that, as they outgrew and cast off the dogmatism of the Marx theories, they also outgrew and cast off other infatuations in the garb of abstract ideas. For all the ceremonial intoning about justice, liberty, equality, reliance is put on close and exact investigation of facts and the ways through which these could be practically embodied. Here lies the distinguished mastery of the Webbs.

So far as assumed power by a narrow and select leadership is concerned, this is no exclusive mark of the Fabians. It is world wide in the labor movement. In the spring of 1918, the chief socialist organ in Berlin, the *Vorwaerts*, showed an angry impatience with comrades who still appealed to the old idealism of the party, "universal justice" and the like. World peace was no longer a question of morals but "of facts and conditions."

As judicious an observer of socialism as Adolph Prins, writes of its dependence on leaders, but they are "chefs très autoritaires." The tendency to faction makes this authority necessary, as does the rivalry for leadership. One of the most astute of living publicists, H. N. Brailsford, watching the concussions at Berlin in 1919, was struck with the sturdy conservatism of the "inner directing wing" of the majority socialists. It is a conservatism born and nurtured by long contests with the less disciplined members of their own party. They have been as strict to curb all factional assertion within the party as the inner circle of bourgeois politicians. The spectre of this dictatorship is never absent from those who revile it most — the anarchists.

The élite among these always look down upon socialists as stodgy and bourgeois, but nowhere do they themselves escape this special danger of the dictator. He gives you, moreover, the same excuse —" the apathy and indifference of the many."

In 1911, there was still existing an anarchist colony within a few hours' journey by boat from Tacoma. My first surprise was to find in a village easily served by one market, two coöperative stores in *active competition* with each other.

An old English coöperator in attendance at one of them said sourly: "They don't know what the word means. They can't coöperate three days in succession."

It was perhaps not strange that anarchists out for field practice, should insist on all the rights of an individualism which is the soul of their faith. If they wanted to sell their goods at cost and thus violate a first principle of coöperation, that was their business. It was less easy to account logically for the "indifference of the majority" on the most vital matters. There were many things to be done together — a large wharf — road making, buildings, water supply and the like. The only bitter words I heard, were over the difficulty of getting the larger part of the members to interest themselves in that minimum of common work without which no group even of three or four hundred people could get on together in town life.

"What it comes to," said one, "is that just a small bunch of us have to do all the planning and all the real work. We shift around and members change, but it's always the few that run things."

If he had thus been describing the entire history of utopian experiments in this country, much of our more highly organized trade unionism and a great deal of our politically developed socialism, his stricture would require little change. Nowhere do we find a sustained interest of the many. They can be stung into occasional activity, but permanent administration cannot be run on spasms of excitement. Out of the total, a small minority is slowly selected that likes the game and develops the aptitudes and patience which lead to professional skill.

These are the "ins" and they are always on their defense against mild or stormy criticism from the "outs." Even in the anarchist colony, there were petulant "outs" who complained that "a baker's dozen of them thought nobody could manage things except themselves." If this necessary "running things by the few" is true of such foes of organization as are the anarchists, what must it be when organization is as compact and nationally efficient as the trade unions in our American Federation of Labor?

A central committee of European socialists often takes so much power into its own hands as to control the selection of new members of Parliament on the ground that the local constituencies are not to be trusted. That is, "the people" are told frankly that they are not the best judges of those who are to represent them. German socialists have many times hotly protested against this, but to no purpose.

Great names like Kautsky and Bernstein have lent their voice to show why the central body in Berlin should be entrusted with so much power. They exhibit much ingenuity. " The party as a whole should select members of Parliament, for sovereignty resides in this whole. An outlying constituency cannot be the final judge of fitness of the man they choose. They may, of course, ' nominate and advise,' but the group in Berlin knows much better what is good for the entire party interest, therefore power must be centered there."

In this spirit is democracy chastened. As European socialists grew great, they again and again refused to refer their conclusions at the congresses back to the party as a whole. No referendum here; it means too much delay, uncertainty and expense. Their radicals always taunt them with destroying democracy and setting up parliamentary government just like the bourgeois. It was said with truth —" The Swiss bourgeois have more confidence in the referendum than socialist executives."

Thus the annals which record the world's labor politics furnish a continuous illustration of small committees trying to get responsibility, interest, initiative out among the masses. Gains have been made well worth all the costs, but no labor group has the slightest monopoly in these achievements. It is bound in with a far wider political constituency. Even in that best of economic democracies, the coöperators, it is the oldest as it is the most recent complaint, and all this in spite of highly organized educational activities to reach and arouse the mass; in spite of the most direct business incentive in their " dividend." Mr. Woolf's recent study [1] is a glowing tribute to and defense of coöperation but he says " the majority of the members are apathetic." He admits that the ordinary view is that " the majority of the members take little or no interest in the working and operations of their society, and still less in those of the whole movement; that the interest of most coöperators does not extend beyond the dividend, and that

[1] " Coöperation, The Future of Industry," pages 51-54.

consequently the real power tends more and more to rest in the hands of the executive; the persons who are immediately responsible for the working of societies, the management committees, directors, and the permanent secretaries." He even adds that "the great stumbling block to democracy lies in the people."

At a meeting of coöperators in San Francisco, after the usual appeal for loyalty and a call upon the delegates to do all their buying at their Wholesale, an impatient listener broke in. "For God's sake, why can't we stop this guff about loyalty and get to the coffee and sandwiches!"

I was told he was one of the best of them, but only the business interested him. It is coffee and sandwiches as part of the real business that attracts the great mass of customers in the movement, yet this growing conservatism in methods and opinions among labor bodies may be stated with as little reproach to labor as it is a reproach to the Christian Church to disclose the facts about its early history. Here was a beginning with all the humilities, the sacrifices, the idealisms of great upward movements. As it grew in numbers and influence, power and property came to it. These attracted for their control and direction a different type of leader. Through these responsibilities the church was forced to affiliate with other worldly powers, economic and political.

As I have said, austerity always has a hard time of it with the rich, so those early ideals and humilities were modified. There is no country where labor has got itself strongly organized politically or economically where the same phenomenon is not seen. Where this labor organization culminates, it affiliates with the old political and economic organizations. This is the atmosphere in which ideals still exist, but the practical men see to it that the day's work is not too much interfered with by the men of visionary temperament and little else.

Thus every phase of labor has the same hard task known

to the oldest societies in efforts of twenty-five centuries to make democracy safe for the world.

I submit that we have in this labor tradition an increasing body of political experience which should make wider understanding possible among all parties. It is a discipline corresponding closely with business experience among all coöperators, all unions and even among those fearsome enemies of capitalism, the socialists.

CHAPTER XVIII

THE EMPLOYERS' CASE AGAINST THE UNION

"Even if the educational values due to labor be admitted, what of the rapacious demands which have also to be admitted?" Among the many European trade unionists visiting this country, I have never seen one that went away unshocked by grave abuses in our American unions. A man as kindly as Keir Hardie told me the problem of ridding some of these unions of their abuses seemed to him as important as any other phase of the contest between capital and labor. To my suggestion that the unions mentioned (just then in the building trades) were up against employers and contractors quite as unscrupulous, and that both were in an atmosphere of corrupt city politics, he still maintained that something was fundamentally wrong with these organizations. While most definite improvement has been made since then on both sides, evils enough remain.

The president of an employers' association says, "Our cause against the unions is God's cause and the country's cause." Union leaders are as prolific in puffery when they pose as the "only champions of democracy." The retort after long argument, "Why can't we both admit that we are human beings, and have done with it," should be kept in mind.

In 1912, I heard from Professor Hoxie his plan of a minute survey of unionism in this country. In its best sense, he was a friend to labor organization. He found a good deal of "predatory unionism" of which four years later he spoke as follows, with unbiased truth. As he had classified the "predatory" bodies, he says, "Prevailingly it is exclusive and monopolistic. Generally it is boss-ridden and corrupt, the membership for the most part being content to follow blindly the instructions of the leaders so long as they deliver the goods." Again, " Now, unionism does violate many of the canons of right, rights, and justice of the business world and the middle class. It opposes freedom of the individual and free contract, upon which our whole legal structure rests. It has little regard for the sacredness of contract or ordinary property rights. It has little respect for our special code of morality; it sneers at and defies our courts; it stands face to face with a great association of employers engaged in a titanic struggle for supremacy." [1]

To the letter, this is exact of that part of unionism in this country of which he writes.

How, then, can one who sees and admits disorders so grave, still maintain that labor organization, in function and structure, is as indispensable a part in social growth as any other section of our political or business organism? Labor in its collective effort has often been shadowed by corruption and self-seeking. It has much of the cheap chicanery of ward politics. It is as jealous of monopoly power as any "trust."

On all hands, it is said, " The unions need antiseptic treatment." " They need house cleaning." Yes, but does capitalism need no house-cleaning? Do the church, our charities, legal procedure, politics as represented in Congress, the States and cities need no house-cleaning? Do they need it less than labor? I have heard two of our foremost men of science say that nothing stood in greater need of reform than the medical profession, while lawyers of eminence have said as much about their own calling.

In this demand for all-round house-cleaning, labor takes its place among its peers. Its right to exist is as easily justi-

[1] " Trade Unionism in the United States," Appleton, 1917, pages 23-50.

fied as are unions of farmers, bankers, lawyers, or churchmen. It is indeed not a question of existing. These labor bodies are to have incomparably greater power than is now theirs. The hastiest glance at their origin and growth in this country alone should convince the most obstinate, that we are not to be rid of them. They can be met by a bludgeon after the manner of too many employers, but that only drives them into policies in which (from the employer's point of view) they are still more dangerous. Labor organization can no more be eliminated than we can eliminate capitalistic organization. Yet always at this point, we hear the reproof: " But because employers are wicked, surely does not excuse wickedness in the trade unions." If it does not " excuse " it does much better; it *explains*. It warns us from the cant of setting up a higher moral standard for labor than for capital. It asks that both of them come before the same impartial judge and submit to the same sentence. A moldy platitude like " two wrongs do not make a right " does not help us here. What we ask is, how may the crookedness and wrong-doing in both parties be brought under influence that shall deflect the evil into channels that can be socially controlled. If, for an indefinite future, these great forces are to exist side by side, they must either fight or coöperate. They will long continue to do both, but neither progress nor order is assured any further than the " all-together-method " is learned and practiced.

But all these educational excellencies; all the changes for the better do not meet the employer's present protest. He notes a great change in the apparent purpose of labor, namely, to get control of the strategic factors of his business. He questions more than ever all the high moralities in the labor ritual. He hears the fine talk about " equality of opportunity "; hears them urge this as one of the workers' fundamental demands. How, then, do they practice it among themselves? Not only are the unions a minority among the wage-earners of this country, they are a very small minority — not one in ten. Organization, however, gives the minority a sense and reality of power precisely as ten well trained firemen are superior to a mob of a hundred in putting out fires.

Against employees as a whole, it is a pretty steady occupation of the unions deliberately to deny " equality of opportunity " to a large part of labor outside the unions. When these come into conflict with outside workers they are fought with as much bitterness as are the most objectionable employers. Strictly inside the unions, we have in rapid succession, " locals defying their own leaders and their own national organization." In the shoe industry, we have a strong body of rebels in active opposition to what they call the " autocratic machine " of their national union. Among the printers we have locals like the pressmen and " feeders " demanding a $32\frac{1}{2}$ to 44-hour week and an increase of $14 per week, with double and triple pay for overtime.

Their own international president " can do nothing with them." He is reported as saying that these secessionists have " introduced industrial chaos into the printing trades." This civil war within the unions — the extent of it and the venom of it — is a queer comment on the beadroll of phrases like the " solidarity of labor."

Not so much about the desired goal, but about what is really important — all the practical ways and means of reaching their goal, there is as much internal wrangling among the entire labor groups and factions as there is between labor and employer.

Between a body as powerful and as ably led as the Amalgamated Textile Workers and all that Mr. Gompers represents, the dissensions are as sharp as between Mr. Gompers and Judge Gary. I take up the organ (*The New Textile Worker,* Sept. 13, 1919) and read this from the pen of the editor: " Does he not know that only a small percentage of American workers are connected with the A. F. of L.? That within the A. F. of L. there are many individuals and organizations whom Mr. Gompers does not really represent, who have in deed if not in name repudiated his leadership? No honest and well informed person would claim that he can possibly represent the whole body of America's workers."

We can have no appreciation of the employer's position, until we see clearly what these inner discords, labor against labor, mean for those responsible for business enterprises. Repeatedly when there is neither complaint nor any proposal for change on the part of employees in a plant, an outside labor official appears with demands which throw everything into confusion. The employer sees himself threatened not by his own men; not by those who represent the least " agreement " in labor as a whole; not even of all organized labor, but by some vague, unknown fragment of it directed by men whom the employer has never seen and bringing demands which he believes to be destructive to business and injurious to his workers.

If such outside labor official entered a Belgian socialist *coöperative* or a factory run by working class coöperators, the labor managers would feel and very likely act like private employers. Only a beginning of genuine labor representation has yet been achieved. Shreds and patches of it only have been organized into anything like unity. It is this disunion both of practice and of aim among labor sections which brings upon the employer real difficulties.

Very acute has become another trouble. In no period of our history have unions, especially locals, so recklessly broken contracts. Trade union officials bemoan this and admit their inability to cope with it. " We don't see what has got into the men." Employers and contractors cannot take too high a tone about " keeping contracts." If the story of what their foremen have been allowed to do in some of our industries in quietly changing the working conditions of the contract and therefore breaking it, were fully known, it would show as little regard for the "sacredness" supposed to inhere in contracts, as are charged against the labor unions.

That the foremen's prestige and value to the employer depends on the amount of work he can get done with the smallest number of men, indicates plainly enough what temptations the foreman is under to "deliver the goods" on which his own advancement depends. It is but another illustration of the superior resources of capitalism to conceal its own sharp practices. Labor has little to learn in these crafty indulgences, but they are more easily exposed. Yet this "parity in frailty" does not change the fact that so many business men are now driven to rough seas with neither compass nor chart. Against a great deal of unionism, they have a very strong case. Everybody, they tell us, is chattering about collective bargaining, but what can such bargain mean without some collective responsibility? The unions refuse to incorporate. Their leaders admit that large numbers of their men and many locals are out of hand. What are we to do?

Can Mr. Gompers give an unembarrassed answer to the employer who now asks so simple a question as this? "As long as hundreds of your own local unions break agreements right and left with their own labor leaders, what warrant have we that any union will keep agreements with us? If they won't play square with each other, how can we count on them?"

There is no honest reply to these employers that can satisfy them or be quite fair to them.

Now comes a new grievance, not lightly to be set aside. The unions ask a kind of monopoly of "recognition." In a plant where there is no trouble between employer and employee — a business that may have its union and collective bargaining — labor claims the right to send its far-off representative to instruct the employees in deciding issues lying wholly outside the business in question. This is the logic of nationalized unionism. Meantime come "shop-committees" organized to settle all local disputes. Here, too, is a logic as invincible as the other. "Self-determination," "home-rule" and decentralization have become very popular and are gaining strength. Many employers who have honestly accepted and recognized the union with its form of bargaining will take this narrower home-rule logic and stand by it. It will be a weapon against the invasions of national interference with local affairs. This means a very long struggle. Employers at present are sure of substantial outside opinion, because all that is worst in unionism has so entangled itself with evils like restricted output, the boycott, picketing, sympathetic strike, intimidation of non-union labor, as to make "recognition," with what that practically *implies,* full of peril. It is the practical logic of these fine words which opposing employers fear. "Peaceful picketing!" a strong case can be made out for it, but so difficult is it to prevent threats, intimidation and actual violence that the employer's resistance is natural. "Recognition" sounds so harmless and so reasonable, but the employer knows well where "recognition" may carry him. I have seen an instance of it; first "closed shop"; then the union acting as the only employment bureau, furnishing all the men — the employer not able to discharge a man unless he got the consent of the union; finally the employer has to collect the membership dues, as at one time an extremely monopolistic trade union in the glass industry forced the employers to do.

Employers in bituminous coal business must deduct from the wages of their men what is owed to the union and pay it over as if they were collecting agents. This practically forces every man to join the union, thus making the employer an abettor of the closed shop.

Next, the union will decide how many apprentices are to be taken on or whether there shall be any. They have often been entirely excluded. Lastly, who is to regulate speed?

Where this is done by the union, it is usually very secret but, if strong enough, it may be set down openly in the by-laws. They explain that it is to prevent " rushing " and to punish the foreman who urges it.

When we add up all these labor exactions, we have the employer reduced to a handy-man of the unions.

That is what many of the unions want and are trying to get. I heard an employer with closed shop say, " They run my business. I expect every day they'll have the key to my office and let me in only when they want me." This brings the employer exactly where the syndicalists, socialists and the new guild are trying to put him. An Italian syndicalist says, " We begin with the foreman and end with the employer."

Boston has just rocked with emotions over its police strike. From what source are the police to take orders? If dissatisfied, are they to look first to Mr. Gompers or to local authorities under which they are sworn in? It is a far less serious issue, but to the employer, the question of the foreman may seem as vital, for where is the " loyalty " of the foreman to be lodged? Whose man is he and who is to give him orders? Unions have many times had him wholly at their disposition. Employers commonly pick him out from those at work in the mine or factory and think of him as under their direction. If they are to lose this, they see in it the first step toward a substitution of trade union management of business for present capitalistic management. While strong bodies among our unions now only ask for " partnership," the employer knows that the more radical forces will not remain content with partnership. These forces have already cluttered the world with a literature claiming that labor needs no capitalistic partner whatever. " Capital," they say, " is already helpless. It has to pick out from our ranks nine-tenths of its ability. Everywhere we see great managers, superintendents, foremen, who, but a few years ago, were common workmen like young Schwab driving stakes at a dollar a day. Now, *we* can pick out 'ability' as well as the capitalists. It is our men who now actually run the railways, mines, and other industries." This radical ultimatum is no longer concealed.

This is what the employer faces and he knows it, but he does not believe labor forces to have at present any such qualifications as they assume. They may some time acquire them, but only to a very limited extent have they thus far proved their case.

Here is the invincible strength of the employer's position. All the swagger about labor-control should be conditional. It must first prove that it *can* control.

The whole batch of new measures like "labor directors" and "shop committees" in which labor is getting about every kind of "representation," is increasingly on trial. At many points, like the Rock Island Arsenal, labor has its opportunity to prove its capacities for business management. The labor representative of these arsenal workers tells a large audience of the Taylor Society in the Harvard Union, what the workers have done and are to do with the new efficiencies for which "scientific management" stands. He even suggested, "we unions will soon beat you at your own game. We know the stupidity of restricted output as well as you. We understand that product must be increased if wages are permanently to go up. We know the necessity of scientific experts and industrial councilors as well as you. We, too, are up to your 'cost accounting' and make rigid use of it. We are doing all this because we see what we can get out of it. We are in for a boom if we see clearly that it booms us."

This is labor's challenge and it has to be accepted. Already many successful employers are taking it like true sports and are giving their employees every chance possible to make good. In the stormy days ahead, this kind of employer is as important as any statesman in the land. In its true sense of getting at the roots, he is more radical than any labor tribune who merely stirs up discontent over which he has no constructive direction. Employers of even more conservative cast are opening new ways for the changes to come and they are doing it with a new purpose. I can hear the ironic laughter of the unions at the very mention of the words, but we are to have a great deal more " management sharing " and general profit-sharing in certain favored industries. All radical labor holds this in derision, but it is going to have trial enough to furnish its own evidence. Employers know what vast silent numbers of wage-earners do not belong to any union — at least twenty-five millions of them. " Let us then see if we can't prove to them that they are better off with us than under union leaders."

Profit-sharing would have no notice here if it had not undergone transformation which makes it an educational venture with the more promise because it professes no finality and it closes no door. An employer who means it says " I am trying it and shall follow it wherever it leads. If it can destroy capitalistic features, let it destroy them. I do not believe it, but I will take my chance."

Let the unions play the sportsman too and meet it in the same spirit.

CHAPTER XIX

THE NEW "PROFIT-SHARING"

An employer now much quoted for successful profit-sharing tells me its older forms are hopeless. He wonders how labor ever tolerated it for a day. We are to have a "new method" with a democratic tang to it. He doubts if business can be carried on except in ways that have an appearance of autocracy. But things have gone so far that there must be a pretense at least of getting the show of democracy into business. He sees most hope in a "new profit-sharing." We must therefore see what the "old" form of it was and what changes have taken place. That a great English engineer should welcome profit-sharing a half century ago, because it would "prevent inroads on the capitalistic structure and protect the manager from all interference from the unions" shows us the reason for labor's caustic and outspoken objections. Many outside the trade unions accept it, a few even welcome it. Only a negligible number within the unions are working profit-sharers.

The National Civic Association investigated the subject in 1916, throughout the United States. This body has had long and intimate touch with representatives of labor organizations. Beginning with the president of the American Federation of Labor and ending with the head of the International Brotherhood of Locomotive Engineers, the opinions on profit-sharing are reported as "unanimous" in opposition both to its theory and practice.

This is thought to be most unreasonable since it is seen at last, that no welfare work can flourish unless labor coöperates with some degree of cordiality. Outside of organized labor, a great deal of this working sympathy is secured because the employees are convinced that the employer's interests are in some real sense at one with labor interests. So far as they believe this they are, for the time at least, content with this modest partnership. But with the unions and their unorganized sympathizers, the doubt of employers' motives and methods is a lion in the way.

The first general explanation of this is in that sense of "labor solidarity" which marks every stage in which power passes over from one class to another. Especially in this country, there is much pure fiction in these shibboleths. But the residue of fact is quite enough to make trouble. With profit-sharing, too, it is a question of labor's allegiance. Is it first to the employer or to the union?

In most countries, strongly organized labor has answered. On all issues that seem vital, labor will stand first by the union if it has the strength for it. A large part of profit-sharing is a bold bid for labor allegiance against the union. Here is the seat of hostility.

If explanation is necessary, it abounds in an old transmitted experience which labor never forgets. From the beginning of labor organization, the union makes up its record. It acquires a documentary accumulation like a campaign book for party warfare. It has an even more important unwritten tradition. Speakers, organizers, trade union journals turn to this for propaganda and defense.

A very innocent example may serve. A "social secretary" concerned for the morals of factory girls under his charge, makes a rule, sanctioned by the employer, that no girl shall visit dance halls. The girls call a meeting in protest. They speak as a group, because it is too risky for individuals to make the protest. They tell their welfare manager that outside the factory their time is their own. Certain girls who "disobey" are discharged, and the fact is scored against the employer and becomes thus a part of the tradition, " The working girl is deprived of her liberty." " Like her employer and other folks, she is not to be allowed to dispose of her own leisure as she chooses."

I have known a strike, because the ways in which the hair was dressed, the waists cut, and shoe heels worn were objected to by the management. More tactful secretaries have persuaded girls quietly to yield, but these cases are poor material for trade union agitation. It is the clumsier interference with " liberty " that gets prominence, and therefore points the moral against beneficent supervision.

The very fact that profit-sharing comes from the top; that it is conceived and applied by the employer, condemns it for all that part of labor which looks toward a society democratized industrially as well as politically.

All labor in which suspicion has become acute is perplexed and offended by the innumerable forms assumed by this advice. One may easily reckon more than thirty varieties of what is named profit-sharing. But more uncertain is the employee about the *motive* of the employer. Is it to increase profits? Is it to enlist labor's good will so that (as a profit-sharing soap manufacturer says) " no walking delegate has any more chance of getting my men away from me than would a vagabond negro preacher." He says his men and women have learned that he has more to give them in wages and in undisturbed regular employment than any union or all the unions.

The chosen ones of trade unionism do not like this, but nothing fairer was ever said to them. If they are to capture the superior millions of the unorganized, they must make a better bid than the profit-sharers. For many years, we are to see a very pretty competition here between those who believe that capitalism is to be reformed, but maintained in its essence, and those who will abolish the wage system and substitute control by labor organization.

There is a still graver difficulty for the employer. In business as now financed and organized, the manager often

THE NEW "PROFIT-SHARING"

sits in the shadow. Unseen by labor, means are in his hands through which every really vital fact about dividing profits can be determined. What is more vital than the method of capitalization, and what can labor know about it? What can labor know about amounts written off for depreciation, or what part has labor in deciding or knowing about official salaries?

Distributing shares on favorable terms to employees is a most frequent form of profit-sharing. But so many and so confusing are the possible forms which these "first and second preferred" stocks may take, that adequate explanations are very difficult. The manager of an English gas company reports that the men never really accepted the plan until they became certain that the entire facts came out in the annual report.

"When they knew exactly what they were getting and *what capital was getting,* the employees coöperated." In a discriminating study, Professor Ashley gives this as a reason why profit-sharing has so far succeeded in some public utilities.

But for business which still conceals information which definitely concerns labor in profit-sharing plans, the workers have learned, or are fast learning their lesson, and it is a tribute to their intelligence that as a rule, they refuse coöperation in which the cards are thus stacked. I have asked employers if they would let their men fully into these secrets. Usually they are frank to say they would not. This raises a hard question.

Can private competitive business generally afford unequivocally to tell the full truth about its inner finance? In making large profits, would they like to have their entire force know what they are? Would they like their own competitors to know all these things? If a few strong ones are willing to do this, will the general run of them do it?

At the Economic Club in New York, I asked George W.

Perkins this question: "Would you let your men know *all?*" He was very emphatic in saying that nothing should be concealed. Now Mr. Perkins appears with a booklet [1] from which I quote, because for thirty years he has really been studying this subject. He has been in the largest business and in many kinds of business as well as in high finance. He too speaks of the "newer" profit-sharing. He is very severe on the popular bonus systems. He writes: "I am convinced that such bonus-giving, erroneously called profit-sharing, has done more harm than good, for in many instances it has caused employees to feel that said bonuses were given because the business was earning fabulous sums of money, a tiny bit of which was thrown to them as a sop to make them feel kindly disposed towards the owners, or in order to ward off a demand for a general increase in wages."

As for publicity, he prints it in large letters, adding: "The annual statement of the concern should be full and explicit, so that every man engaged in the enterprise will know what business was done in the preceding year and on what basis profits were and are to be distributed."

He says it must be a report that wins the confidence of labor — so detailed as to "show the organization in prosperous years how the profits were arrived at and what they amounted to." Like a good trade union objector, he denies the good faith of much of the old profit-sharing.

"Close observation has convinced me," he says, "that practically all the many failures in profit-sharing, both in this country and in Europe, have occurred because at the bottom the plans were not honestly devised nor equitably worked out."

Near the end, he thus expresses his faith: "An industrial democracy of the most ideal sort is found in true profit-sharing; an industrial democracy that makes real partners

[1] "Profit-Sharing," or "The Workers' Fair Share."

of capital and labor, and yet preserves the right of private property; that preserves and promotes the great business asset that comes from individual initiative; that retains the capitalist's incentive to enterprise, while giving the worker a new inspiration for effort that humanizes large organizations of men; that promotes good will and industrial peace."

How far Mr. Perkins takes us from the earlier and most outspoken purpose of profit-sharing! Without turning a hair, the very models among employers in the old days said they introduced it to keep down wages and to hold their workers from unions.

This is what labor knows and does not forget.

Not even in the remotest back pasture of industry today, would any employer dare copy a line from published announcements of great pioneers in this movement. France in many ways led. It was the "land of small industries and great ideas." The classic DeCourcy was actually called radical in his innovation. His profit-sharing required "extra care," "vigilance in the employer's interest," "uncomplaining fidelity," and "each treating the business as if it were his own" and then — the reward! After twenty-five years of this zeal in behalf of the employer, labor was to "share" in profits from the fund. Not a man among them could even guess what he was to get.

Exactly forty years later an English parliamentary report admitted that this uncertainty and all such deferred plans were failures. In 1912, another report which really displays some sense of what goes on in the minds of the worker, tells us that no scheme has promise unless the men know *at the start* precisely what it all means; what they are to get; what the principles and practices are on which the reward is to be based.

Thus we are brought into line with Mr. Perkins. It is now hard to believe that profit-sharing began without shame, by saying to labor, " If you will only work harder, be more attentive to details, and see that nothing is wasted, profits will of course increase. For this extra care and exertion, I will give you part of them. I can't tell you what part, because I don't know. Maybe there won't be any." No employer, either with humor or prudence, would dare say this to-day above a whisper. Yet this was tried until labor " caught on " and forced a change of policy. Schemes were worked out so that participating labor should know beforehand what additional pay it was getting.

From the great banking world, Mr. Mortimer Schiff comes still later with his own plan.[1] He will have as little to do with the popular bonus systems as will the trade unions. He is severe on the old profit-sharing. He wants salaried officers to be a part of his plan. He does not believe in cash payments because this does not consciously identify the men with the business. He wants " non-negotiable, registered, convertible 6 per cent. debentures, convertible into cash at the option of the holder after a certain period, say three years, but even during that period redeemable by the company in case the holder leaves its service." Like Mr. Perkins, he will have " no secrets as to the results of the operations of the business, there must be full disclosure, so that the worker knows he is getting his full share and that it is thus to his interest to secure the maximum results." More boldly still, he tells us what we have to learn about labor's mood. " Above all " we " must realize that it is more than money that the men want; it is a sense of ownership, that can be, in part at least, developed through profit-sharing."

Among the values of profit-sharing, the one of most significance (so far as this volume is concerned) is the test

[1] Reprinted in pamphlet form from the New York *Times*, Oct. 5, 1919.

which the device applies to capitalism. In spite of some intrepid exceptions, profit-sharing assumes a place in the industrial system which socialism in all its forms disputes and what is far more significant — which coöperators dispute.[1]

Wherever the plan succeeds, there is "harmony between capital and labor." We are always told that it brings· out the identities between business and labor interests. We are even told "Wherever the worker becomes a shareholder, he becomes a capitalist and therefore class bitterness disappears."

In connection with the Paris Exposition of 1889 (Centenary of the Great Revolution) profit-sharing was· magnificently "featured." Delegates were either taken or encouraged to visit the best in this kind which France had to show. We went as far north as Guise, where the foundry with its famous Familistère, then offered, perhaps with one exception (Karl Zeiss Stiftung, Jena, Germany) the most arresting of all examples.

In the accompanying oratory, to much of which I listened, nothing was said oftener or more urgently, than that profit-sharing and co-partnership would substitute order for revolution; would preserve us from dangerous innovations, especially from the sinister shadow of socialism and all reckless interference of labor. Never a doubt in that atmosphere, that the employers' prosperity was a sure index of the workman's welfare.

Organized labor in general denies this and capital has to meet the objection. The first step employers have taken is to give guarantees that, in no case, shall profit-sharing be used to lower wages. The start shall be made with a solid minimum not to be questioned.

[1] The best study yet made in this country is "Profit-Sharing, Its Principles and Practice," by Dean Gay of the School of Business Administration of Harvard University and Professor Heilman with three business men,— Messrs. Burritt, Dennison, and Kendall.

This minimum is in no way to be interfered with. It must be a first lien upon the business. Then, upon this minimum and above it, all extra benefits are to be built up. There was much of this constructive practical purpose in this country years before the minimum wage idea had popular discussion. Twenty years ago, not from labor, but from the Chamber of Commerce Committee in Cleveland (1899) we have it plainly:

"The fundamental basis of all welfare work must be found in fair wages, reasonable hours, and sanitary conditions of labor; that these provisions are not a matter of option with the employer, but that every employee has a right to expect them. No amount of special features can rightfully be substituted for fair wages and reasonable hours, clean, light, well-ventilated work-rooms, and adequate provisions for safety and sanitation; and any plans which endeavor to take their place are pretty certain to fail."

With this sure defense against any lowering of labor's standard by profit-sharing employers now have their chance with a vast majority of unorganized workers in this country.

In the long contest now before us capitalism is caught between two fires. Behind it are its own fighting stalwarts who have taken over war methods and a war temper in dealing with labor and would, if it lay in their power, keep things in the good old way. The fire before them is a growing international flame already kindled in this country.

No capitalist management which does not take this into account has the least chance of success. It is far easier to add to this flame than to quench it. We are now throwing fuel into it by methods popularly called "drastic."

One step we have not taken or even seriously tried to take, namely, to *understand* enough of the origin and meaning of the bolder protest, as to face it with that kind of intelligence calculated to divert enough of its incendiary passion into constructive avenues as to make it not only safe, but an actual asset in that reconstruction now inevitable.

I pass to the two final aspects of the challenge which need such understanding.

CHAPTER XX

THE OUTPOSTS OF REBELLION SYNDICALISM

I

Though I cannot find the passage, I once heard a professor of pedagogics quote from Pestalozzi to this effect, " Until we learn to make our educational principles work among the weaker members of society, democracy will remain a dream." I take this as text to my most difficult chapter. Six years ago it could have been written without a protest, but war, which Secretary of State John Hay called " the most ferocious and futile of human follies," has so far put passion in the place of reason, as to make intelligent discussion of syndicalism at present well nigh impossible. Like cave-dwellers, we put it under the hush of the taboo. Yet it cannot be left out of this study. It is as definitely a part of the shifting emphasis about us which we name revolution, as the trade union, employers' association or the new government policies toward labor. In spite of courageous interpreters of industrial unionism in this country, it can have no intelligent or satisfactory explanation if separated from something far larger than its local exhibit.

As this has been denied by some rational writers on this movement, I ask a little patience in considering such proofs as are here presented. French syndicalism is by no means all in the pages of Professor Lagardelle, Griffeuilles or Edward Berth. There is an ignorant hobo-following in other countries too, some of it quite on a par with much of our own. French strikes have had their " apaches " (toughs) who could give points to our most rancorous wobblies.

I went out from Paris to see one of the first syndicalist outbreaks. There was personal violence, there was destruction of property and people were robbed on the roads. On my return, I collected what literature and information I could on the subject — very bewildering to me at that time. I have constantly added to it ever since. When at the Colorado strike in 1903,[1] I was instantly struck by the identity *in idea* of the two strikes and in some of the tactics. Every one of our subsequent uprisings has confirmed my belief that our own vagrant disturbers are in no way separable from a world agitation that is only to be met by some measure of open-mindedness and self-control.

The historic roots of this revolt are English. Even in theoretic detail they were in the Owenite agitation of more than eighty years ago. In this country, one of its main roots springs from the Knights of Labor. Scarcely were the obsequies of that order decently over, when the I. W. W. appear. Less than twenty-five years ago, it developed rapidly out of a crisis in the French trade unions. Some of these had turned into active revolutionary bodies. Chambers of commerce for business men are familiar to us. Locally organized labor in France created its own chambers of labor (Bourses du Travail). They soon won power enough to get substantial subsidies from municipalities. Even among " higher-ups " there was much elation over labor's new power in politics. They were " partners with the city fathers." Waldeck-Rousseau, at the head of affairs, expressed public approval of this partnership because it promised " better understanding between capital and labor." One pulse-beat of the revolution is labor's awakening to the dangers of state socialism, and indeed to every notion of too much government. This reaction against overcentralization has curious illustration in these French labor chambers which induced cities to grant them subsidies. By many of the best labor members, this was soon seen or be-

[1] Described in my "American Syndicalism."

lieved to have corrupting influence. "The politicians are simply using our Bourse to catch the labor vote," which was true. Writers have told us that cities withdrew the subsidies because of abuses in the unions. It has to be added that energetic resistance against subsidies grew up inside the union. "To take subsidies from the city gets us into the toils of demagogues in the pay of the capitalists," became the cry. These labor chambers grew rapidly in different cities to more than a hundred. But as suspicion of capitalistic control through political agents grew acute, we see these labor unions turn into independent revolutionary bodies. They were, of course, called anarchists, and have in fact much in common with the "group anarchism" of Proudhon. Some of their leaders had been of that party, but the National Labor Organization (C. G. T.) openly repudiated all connection with anarchism as commonly defined.[1]

Here in modern form is the origin of syndicalism. One definition is "a protest against a State corrupted by capitalism." It passed into Italy, England and Australia. It has produced a literature in hundreds of books and pamphlets; it has been seriously discussed by very eminent men. When Graham Wallas read his paper on syndicalism, Mr. Balfour was in the chair. Mr. Wallas, twice invited to this country as lecturer on political science at Harvard University, dealt with syndicalism critically, but in the same temper that he would have shown toward our Republican party or the prohibition movement.

This is true of other publicists of the rank of Sidney Webb and J. A. Hobson. It is true of scholars both in France and Italy. In popular series like "The People's Books," we find the volume on syndicalism by a university

[1] This body, though it has been honeycombed with syndicalism, now decides upon the broader policy of a democratic control jointly by producers and consumers, thus approaching the New Guild.

scholar side by side with those on science, philosophy and history. A university professor, Dr. J. A. Estey, with admirable open-mindedness, wrote a book of impartial exposition and criticism.[1] Now Professor Scott, a Scotch philosopher, makes another, more especially on the metaphysical aspects of the movement.

Still another excellent study of 432 pages appeared after this chapter was typewritten. It is under the sanction of the faculty of political science of Columbia University. It is an honest and discriminating account of the I. W. W. in this country. It has plenty of drastic criticism of every half-crazed and lawless feature, but Dr. Brissenden does not lose control of his rational faculties like some disheveled dervishes in politics and in the press. In his preface, he says " There are immense possibilities of a constructive sort in the theoretic basis of the I. W. W., but the press has done its best to prevent the public from knowing it."[2] The press merely reflects the witch stage of discussion.

Even a committee of parliamentarians (Conservatives) took syndicalism into account in their report of 1914, while the elaborate report of 1917, gives much more space and sympathy to syndicalism and its less revolutionary derivative, " the New Guild." These selected agents of the prime minister, even approve one fundamental proposal of the loser and more invertebrate syndicalism in the United States, the I. W. W. After laying it down that labor should be " more closely identified with industry "; that " employees should not be dismissed except with the *consent of their fellow workmen* as well as the employer,"[3] they add: " One industry — one union is, generally speaking, the most satisfactory arrangement. It eliminates all disputes as to de-

[1] " Revolutionary Syndicalism," P. S. King, London, 1913.
[2] " The I. W. W., A Study of American Syndicalism," Dr. Paul F. Brissenden, Columbia University, 1919. Noticed by the writer in the *Survey*, Jan. 10, 1920.
[3] See for example pages 166–169 in our own reprinting of that Report — Bureau of Labor Statistics, No. 237, 1917.

marcation and over-lapping, and reduces the possibility of divided counsel and sectional jealousies on the part of the men." This is as if taken from an I. W. W. pamphlet. Of more consequence than these academic studies and official reports is the fact that syndicalism is in the very structure of that most powerful body known as the International Federation of Trade Unions. It has between seventeen and eighteen million members. Nearly a hundred delegates including French syndicalists have been in session at Amsterdam. There is no intemperate opinion, syndicalist or other, that will not find its correction far more safely within this body than from without. Again, the main drift toward syndicalism has been made inevitable by the organic changes in recent industry. The very magnitude of organization has so weakened the old craft unions as to force them into larger alliances in the direction of industrial unions.

This has become clearly evident in the metal trades, on our own and on Canadian railways and in the packing industry.

But what, it will be asked, has all this to do with " hobo gangs," " blanket-stiffs " and " spittoon philosophers"? It has a great deal and very definitely to do with them. The I. W. W. came among us without metaphysics and without theories. It had no working man of genius like Fernand Pelloutier, in France, " to think it into shape." It came as the hammer's stroke brings fire from flint. It came from one of the bitterest labor contests in this country; a contest in which certain mine owners, or those who managed the mines, were as contemptuous of legal methods as any I. W. W. in the land.

To win in this contest, labor needed in that moment the instant help of every craft union in the mining area, whether they worked in wood, drove teams, tended engines, drilled rock, or smelted ore. All the unions in the industry were a necessity. Wherever this exigency has arisen, the call has been not for *a* trade union, but for industrial unions, and thus in its ideal, " the Industrial Workers of the World."

Yet with defects so common and so vicious, why should an hour's time be given to these " mere marauders "? An employer much harassed by them tells me " they do nothing but live off trouble and sin." He says " they are only a disease." Well, if there were no trouble, disease or sin, what would become of lawyers, doctors and clergymen? If it could be shown that the I. W. W. create all the evils on which they thrive, this employer would be right. It cannot be shown. Wholly beyond the evils of their own making are social and individual disorders arising from unregulated forces like immigration, unemployment, the festering life in cities and many industrial centers with housing, saloons, dance halls and brothels more directly productive of morbidities than I. W. W. pestilence, though it were multiplied by thousands.

These social maladies, as *causes,* can no more be disconnected from phenomena like the I. W. W. than tuberculosis and high infant mortality from rickety and sunless tenements. The late Professor Carleton H. Parker brought not only a saving sympathy, but a cool and penetrating insight into the *social causes* of those sore disillusionments so easily turned to rebellion. It was this insight and sympathy which enabled him to write and speak of this subject without hysterical passion which blurs every fact in the problem.[1]

The commission appointed by the President was really dealing with social causes when it said " Ninety per cent. of those in the camps are ' womanless, voteless and jobless.' " The fact is that about 90 per cent. of them are unmarried. Their work is most intermittent, the annual labor turnover reaching the extraordinary figure of over 600 per cent. There has been a failure to make of these camps communities. It is not to be wondered, then, that in too many of

[1] A volume in which this appears is soon to be published, edited by Mrs. Parker.

these workers the instinct of workmanship is impaired. One conclusion of this commission should be repeated passed forgetting. "Repressive dealing with manifestations of labor unrest is the source of much bitterness, turns radical labor leaders into martyrs, and thus increases their following, and, worst of all, in the minds of workers tends to implicate the Government as a partisan in an economic conflict." For training in collective good sense, we need an anthology of excerpts to make real to us what our general social ignorance and neglect produce in all sorts of rebellious protests. To see what this means, let the reader turn to an article in the *Atlantic Monthly,* May, 1919, the "Diary of a Laborer." It is a brief and uneventful experience of an unskilled worker drifting from job to job. But it shows how I. W. W. may be produced, as clearly as the story of our land-shark companies tells us what armies of fleeced victims go back to the town or to odd-job tasks ready for any I. W. W. or other hallucination that comes their way. Read Mr. Speeks' report in the volume on "Americanization" which deals with these permitted frauds in the selling of land and their mental reactions in terms of social unrest and disenchantment.

After the cry for "more cemeteries" as the proper remedy for our syndicalists it may seem strange authority to quote, but for the proof of social guilt, I turn to Mayor Ole Hanson at the Boston City Club. He said, "I. W. W. swarmed in the lumber camps, and made trouble. Why should this be?" "Because," he said, "of the injustice with which they had been treated in the past. The shacks in which they were housed," he declared, "were unsanitary, and the men were marooned in a wilderness without any amusement whatsoever, even a chance to read. When they were paid off and visited Seattle, nobody greeted them but the I. W. W. agents, and the only places where they got any welcome were the saloons, where they dumped their dunnage and even deposited their pay checks."[1]

With the logic of this sobriety we should be perfectly safe, as we should be altogether unsafe with reported utterances like this. "We closed up every 'wobbly' hall in town," said the mayor. "We didn't have any law to do it with, so we used nails. When there was serious opposition, we trotted out the Department of Health and had the buildings condemned. We didn't need any more law than we did to stop the red flag. We just stopped it." Or, that reported from his chief of police after a raid on a coöperative market run by union labor. It was said I. W. W. literature was printed in a coöperative shop. "I had no warrant ordering the place closed. I was tired of reading the revolutionary circulars that were printed there, and decided that I had already let them go too far, so I just locked them up." In this exact spirit, I have heard "best citizens" North as well as South, defend the lynching of negroes though every necessary law was at hand.

We need nothing recondite or far afield to answer the practical demands of the I. W. W. and of a very much larger body of labor now asking to take on their own shoulders the main direction of business and politics.

On the I. W. W. "philosophy" and their claim to take control of industries because "labor" created them and, therefore, the mills, mines, etc., are already their legitimate possession, I wrote in my note book from a forgotten source, this half-remembered line — "trying to explain things that ain't so, to a world that knows better." It is mere hallucination that the I. W. W. are in agreement on principles or their practice. The difference in opinions among socialists and trade unionists is bewildering enough, but among American syndicalists these differences are both more violent and contradictory. I have tried to classify them along

[1] *Boston Herald,* May 14, 1919.

lines indicated by the "One Big Union," "General Strike," "Direct Action," "Sabotage" relation to government, politics and especially over that minimum of organization which the most anarchist group admits to be necessary for making and exchanging products. If everything claimed by their complete program were put at their disposal to-morrow, they would be more fiercely at odds with each other in their first meeting, because the prizes of place and power would be immediately at their disposal. From the first hour, there would be a conservative, middle of the road and a radical section. The most clear-headed syndicalist I have met in this country, held a most interesting view of "Direct Action." It was to be "the gesture of the folded arms." Never was there to be an exercise of force. "Direct action" was to be the great mediator between the fanatics of violence and those trusting in political agencies. If labor was refused "industrial self-determination" it was quietly to drop tools and wait; seeing to it meantime, that no one of their members used force or even threats. There was to be only the "terror of a great silence." If we are to judge by every documented account of their many conventions, this I. W. W. intellectual would not hold his influence for two hours in any time of excitement.

Of their more popular propaganda and its assumption of fitness to carry out the plans proposed, another comment may be added.

I saw years ago a passage quoted from Xenophon's Memorabilia. It is charged with the kind of penetrating good sense which makes it ring as true for our day as when Socrates uttered it. He is talking to a youth ambitious to play the statesman. As compared to our day, the economic and political education of the Statesman was then of the utmost simplicity. Fiscal resources and trade, at that time, compared to the present world market, finance and industry were as a dugout against the last ocean liner. But Socrates wants to know what this lad knows about the dugout,[1] which I give at length, not only for its raciness and application to the over-hasty proposals of the I. W. W. but as descriptively exact for a great many of us outside the ranks of the "blanket-stiffs."

Glaucon, the son of Ariston, desiring to be a leader in the city, began to speak in public before he was twenty years old, and amongst his friends and relatives none was able to restrain him from making a laughing-stock of himself except Socrates. He, meeting him, began in such a way as to induce him to listen, saying — "Well, Glaucon, I hear you intend to be a great man in our city?" "Yes, I do, Socrates." "That's right," he said, "it's one of the best things a man can do; for if you succeed you will not only be able to do whatever you like yourself, but you will be in a position to help your friends, and to raise your family, and to increase the greatness of your country."

Hearing this, Glaucon was much flattered, and willingly stayed to listen, so Socrates went on —

"I suppose since you are going to be so famous you mean to be very useful to the city?"

"Of course."

"Come then, don't make a mystery about it; tell us where you will begin your reforms."

Glaucon hesitated, as if just beginning to consider what he would do first, and Socrates continued —

"I suppose if you wanted to exalt a friend's household, you would try to make him richer; shall you try to make the city richer?"

"Certainly."

"It will be richer if the sources of revenue are increased?"

"I should think so."

"Tell us then from what sources the revenues of the city are *now* derived, and how great they are; for you must have considered this, so as to be able to increase what are

[1] The full text may be found in the third book of the Memorabilia.

deficient and to replace any which may have dropped out."

"Why, no," said Glaucon, "I have not considered this."

"Well, if you have omitted this, tell us the *expenses* of the city; for you will want to cut off those which are superfluous."

"Indeed," he said, "I have not yet had time to look into this either."

"Ah, well," said Socrates, "we'll put off making the city richer; for how is it possible to look after her expenses and revenues unless you know what they are?"

"But, Socrates," said Glaucon, "it is possible to make the city richer at the expense of her enemies."

"Why, certainly, if we happen to be the stronger, but if we are weaker, we should lose even what we have."

"No doubt."

"Then if you want to advise war you must know the strength of the city, and that of the hostile powers; and then if the city is stronger you may advise her to declare war, but if the enemy is stronger you may persuade her to let it be."

"Quite right."

"Come, then, tell us first what is the strength of the city by land and sea; and then the same of the other powers."

"Indeed," said Glaucon, "I am not in a position to tell you that out of my head."

"Never mind; if you have got it written down, go and fetch it, for we should like to hear."

"But I've not even got it written down yet."

"Then we must refrain also from giving counsel about war," said Socrates; "perhaps the magnitude of these matters put you off undertaking them so early in your career. But I am sure you have been thinking about the defenses of the country, and know if the forts are well placed or not, and how many are sufficiently garrisoned, and that you will advise us how to strengthen those which are well placed, and do away with those which are superfluous."

"I shall do away with all of them," said Glaucon, "for they are so badly garrisoned that the countryside is actually plundered."

"And if you take away the forts any one who likes will be able to plunder! But did you go and look into it yourself? or how did you know that they are all badly garrisoned?"

"I imagine it to be the case."

"Might it not be better here again," said Socrates, "to put off giving advice until we no longer imagine, but know?"

"Well, perhaps," said Glaucon.

"I suppose you have not been to the silver-mines," resumed Socrates, "so as to be able to say why they are yielding less than they used to?"

"No, I have not been there."

"Why, no, indeed; the place is said to be unhealthy and that will be quite sufficient excuse when you are called upon to speak about it."

"You are laughing at me," said Glaucon.

"One thing, at any rate, I am sure you have not neglected, and that is, how long the corn in the country suffices to feed the city, and how much it falls short in the year; so that the city may not run short without your being aware, but that you may know exactly what is necessary, and by your advice to the city may help and save it."

"You are making it out to be a tremendous affair," said Glaucon, "if I am to have to look after such things as these."

"Why," said Socrates, "no one would ever be able to manage his own household properly, if he did not understand just what was needed, and if he were not careful to supply it. But since the city consists of more than ten thousand households, and it is a difficult matter to manage so many all together, why not try first to improve *one,* that of your uncle?— it needs it."

"I would certainly put my uncle's house in order," said Glaucon, "if he were willing to obey me."

"Do you really think, then, that though you are unable to make your uncle obey you, you will be able to make all the Athenians, including your uncle, obey you?"

Very early in the I. W. W. career, it was seriously proposed to show the world what could be done in the way of business. Leaders like Moyer, " Big Bill " and Vincent St. John were in it. It was announced that a mine should be bought with union money. They said assessments would bring it in. They would then show the world how to do business without exploiting labor. They could run the mine and secure the entire profits for union purposes. We should then have seen these revolutionary spirits making a test of industrial democracy as they defined it. The foremost figure among I. W. W. said capital got three-fourths of the product. If labor bought the mine, running it in its own interest, this tidy sum could be added to the workers' income.

To see how sore was the need of business training among these pioneers of the I. W. W. we have only to watch them at work in their conventions from 1905 on. They could frame large plans of a New Jerusalem; draw charts of a re-ordered world-industry that resemble nothing so much as a Greek map of the unexplored world in Glaucon's time. They could predict the fall of Mr. Gompers' hated craft unions and a general merging of skilled and unskilled labor into class-conscious unities, all far more naïve than Bastiat's classic " Economic Harmonies," between capital and labor. The first immediate and simple task was too much for them. They could not put their own preliminary organization on a business basis. They could arrange for the world's financing, but not for their own. They even seemed afraid of any serious effort in this direction for fear of factional opposition. Four of these leaders had pressed for the purchase of a mine to show what " the real pro-

SYNDICALISM 371

ducers" could do. All the risk and responsibilities would then have been theirs. No capitalist could be made the scapegoat.

The mine would have failed, but one of those elementary lessons which "go-it-alone-labor" has got to learn would have gone on record. These extreme spirits who tell us that wage-earners are to make their first fight without any compromise or coöperation with employers or with the State, have no alternative except in business experiments of their own or in revolutionary attacks from without. Side by side on the world map, we are now watching both methods. We observe the ways of the violent "taking over" of all sorts of properties, factories and mines with no penny of compensation. But even here, labor has painfully to learn its entire lesson. It will be harder and longer to learn because of habits deliberately cultivated by the revolutionary membership. Openly to teach insubordination, sabotage and the breaking of contracts, becomes a peril within the household of syndicalists. To instruct men in the devices of sabotage is to put weapons in their hands which will not be used alone against the bourgeois parasites. Nowhere was the threatening logic of this feature of I. W. W. education more clearly seen or more warningly expressed than by a few men active in the movement, notably by that sinister intellectual of the Socialist Labor Party, Daniel De Lion. But the educational process *begins* even among the I. W. W.

It begins at the earthy foothold on which the labor ladder is planted. For dare-devil ignorance, we literally touch bottom in the extremer factions of the I. W. W. It is "anarchism" upon which the philosophical type — Tolstoi, Reclus, Thoreau, Tucker, Auberon Herbert — would look, not with the popular ferocity of some of our investigating committees, but rather with pity, as for men suffering from disease. No country furnishes such a record of this "ignorance plus insanity" as the United States since 1904. In every Convention since 1905, we may see a struggle as if the stone age were pitted against our twentieth century. Yet in this lowest stratum education *starts*. It starts in that immemorial strife between individual willfulness and some degree of discipline in the group. It starts as educational opportunity; an opportunity to be met more than anywhere else in other labor unions which have learned something of the restraint demanded by all constructive organizations. In its most lawless stage, the Western Federation of Miners linked arms with the I. W. W. These miners found the fellowship impossible, as did two other unions. Many I. W. W.'s made the same discovery and passed into the older bodies. If two score I. W. W. delegates met in a Chicago Hall, it instantly became a question whether individual caprice was to prevail, leaving a mere noisy rabble, or should an officer be appointed with at least authority enough to get through the most elementary business.

If ever anybody devoted to social renovation thought itself secure against bosses and machines it was our I. W. W. Nothing was more fundamental with them than their " mass rights." They would " endure no dictation or secret cabal." In the spirit of their chant, " Hallelujah, I'm a bum," they would preserve intact the free initiative of minorities however humble. There should be neither " Organized Snobbery " nor " Organized Scabbery." At the first informal meeting in 1904, from which the I. W. W sprang, were six well known men in the trade union world, two editors, a president and secretary of two Railway Unions, Secretary of the American Labor Union and a representative from a great union of engineers in England.

W. E. Trautman, as editor of the *Brewers' Journal,* was already trained in an industrial union as distinct from a craft union. He was very prominent even as late as the Lawrence Strike, yet in 1913 he thus summed up his case against the would-be oligarchy: [1]

[1] *Weekly People,* July 5, 1918.

"A convention of the I. W. W. is the last place where a change of things could be expected. Only when the rank and file get wise to the facts, will they, possibly by a referendum vote, eliminate all these features, and break the monstrous machine of officialdom that is plunging its fangs into the organization.

"Such a convention nominates the candidates for office. That means that in the last convention two individuals had it in their power to dictate who would go on the ballot or not. Progressive legislation was spurned, and the election of officers by referendum was to be established if the ring could have had its way."

At the very outset (1905) we are told in these words what the crusaders are to bring about.

"Asserting our confidence in the ability of the working class, if correctly organized on both political and industrial lines, to take possession of and operate successfully the industries of the Country." As *ideal*, this is what many millions in the labor movement also proclaim. But with experience, they learn that many other classes must be included. They slowly broaden their definition of labor so that everybody using his mind productively is also of the working class.

At an I. W. W. meeting reported to me, a callow member said "the boss (a foreman in the mill) did no work." He was at once set upon. "There isn't a man of us that works harder or more hours than he does. When we take things over, we shall have to employ him. What you mean is, he don't work for *us.*" This is the kindergarten stage of discussion, and I. W. W. documents are rich in illustrations showing how the first steps on the ladder are taken. We can help them up or we can kick them down making more of them in the process.

It is my belief that a wiser way can be found than by shunting them further into the criminal classes.

The first step is to encourage every form of labor organization in which discipline has really developed. Even the I. W. W. began with those rudimentary organs on which civilization is built. They worked out a Constitution with officials and agencies to interpret and carry it into effect. This " fundamental law " forced them at once to face that oldest and hardest of problems, *how shall the assumed powers be distributed?*

They explain their object. It is " to take possession of and operate successfully the industries of the country." Here, at the threshold of so formidable a task, that ancient mystery of *" sovereignty "* appears. Where is power to reside? How is it to be assigned and to whom? Fearing all " authority," it had been expressly laid down —" powers should rest in the collective membership." They were afraid of all leaders. " Leaders," it was said, " are too easily bought up. If we delegate authority to officials at this convention, it must be exercised all the time until the next convention." Charters could be issued or refused, funds disposed of, assessments laid and their press controlled. " Can we trust any man or set of men with authority like this? " They decide on this issue, yet if anything like national organization were formed, then these local I. W. W. bodies, scattered throughout the country, must be " connected up." How is this possible unless the locals parted with some of their powers? Wrangling over this question went on year after year, with the same heat that we now observe among the nations clamoring for international order, but clamoring still more to preserve their own local sovereignty. When the organizer of an I. W. W. local calls the officials at Chicago " a bunch of Czars," it is a language as old as documentary history. When a member of the Executive Board says the hot-heads among the locals must be under some control or " irresponsible strikes " will wreck the cause and moneys cannot be collected or any national business be transacted, he too talks a dialect familiar to every age. Yet extremists would have no President, or even Executive Boards. "Let us do all through the members." With infinite turmoil and blundering, this is what the race has had to go through. In no other way has it ever learned its lessons of social restraint and cohesion. It is not even an unkindness to compare our American syndicalists to the son of Ariston. Of the magnitude and complexity of their enterprise, they have as little comprehension as Glaucon. In their own words, they are to "take possession of the earth and the machinery of production and abolish the wage system."

For the organic work of production as related to market processes, they have only Glaucon's equipment. Not only does the old uncle refuse obedience, they cannot get obedience for any conservative task, from their own membership from one week to another.

But for another reason, one wishes they had bought the mine. Had a few hundreds of them put their money into it with that "practical knowledge of mining" which they said they possessed far more than directors and owners, some sense of proprietorship would have developed among these I. W. W. investors. They would have had real pride in showing the capitalists what the "actual workers" could do. They were careful to say that "two or three years" might be required to get the mine into flourishing shape. Let us imagine the I. W. W. mine at this prosperous point and put a very simple question. In a neighboring town or state, other I. W. W.s hear of this prosperity. Some of them are very radical but have no prosperity whatever. In good communistic terms, they ask to share the acquired affluence of their brothers. This is what our syndicalists have done in three western states with flourishing capitalistic properties. They said "labor" had created these properties and labor should own them. The legal owners said they themselves had taken all the risks, put their own and other people's savings into the business and with very hard work, built it into a paying concern. When this was seriously threatened by I. W. W.s who said this ownership was a theft which no honest man could respect, they were "deported." It was very high-handed and destitute of legal sanctions. It is not here recommended. But when Haywood, St. John, Moyer & Co. had made their own mine a success, what would they have said and done to outside communists proposing, on such easy terms, to divide a melon in the growing of which they had not lifted a hand? If they threatened force, they would have been lucky to get off as well as their hardly used brothers in Bisbee, Arizona. In a group of successful socialist coöperators, I have within a fortnight listened to a definite communistic appeal from such an outsider. It had as little chance of acceptance as if it had been made at the office of one of Mr. Wood's Woolen Mills in the neighborhood.

It is this extension of "economic self-determination" among all the stronger labor groups that is to be our main safeguard.

It is from the pen of one of the mainstays of international socialism that one reads in the *Daily Chronicle,* this incisive word: "The grand program of syndicalism is a mere delusion, its immediate action is mischievous. Sabotage, destruction of industrial capital, perpetual strikes, injure the workers far more than any other class, and rouse in society reactionary passions and prejudices which defeat the work of every agency making for the emancipation of labor. They put labor in the wrong. The Syndicalist might be an *agent provocateur* of the capitalist, he certainly is his tool. In so far as he succeeds it is only by the old and most primitive methods of trade unionism, and to get his small successes he spends extravagantly the money, suffering, energy and loyalty of his followers. In all crusades of reformation a defiant enthusiasm and a hope that will accept no denial are necessary, but when these are substituted for reflection, good sense and persuasive wisdom, they are the furies of destruction rather than the energies of progress. That fatal substitution is made by Syndicalism."

Is there then nothing in their protest that will remain over after the excesses of thought and action have spent themselves? Have we in a word nothing to learn from syndicalism?

II

Before the war, I was asked by the *Survey* to summarize the objections to the I. W. W. movement. These paragraphs (no syllable of which I would now change) hold the gist of them: " What I shall call its immaturity applies even more to its methods, especially in the United States. Its glorification of impulse and ' direct action '; its almost flaunting ignorance (or ignoring) of the whole *organic* character of modern industrial and political life, are too obvious for serious criticism. Its strident talk about a ' fighting minority '; its raw conception of the ' general strike '; its excessive and credulous emphasis on the ' class conscious ' idea,— all convict it of an immaturity so naïve that capitalism will lose no sleep except in taking the necessary trouble of making the whole body of wage-earners and the larger body of consumers understand clearly what kind of substitute the I. W. W. offers."

As a "philosophy" the rational condemnation of the I. W. W. is set down in the first line of its Preamble —" The working class and the employing class have nothing in common."

This is an assumed first principle on which practical policies are forthwith to be based. There is as much wild exaggeration in that first line as there is lack of good sense in its proposed remedy. There is a vast network of up-and-down ties between employers and workers in which economic interests of the most vital sort are strictly in common.

This common interest moreover will hold *until labor learns its own independent superiorities in producing and distributing wealth.* It may some time accomplish this, but its success at every step will depend on a long coöperation with industry in the hands of employers. Labor is not through with this schooling. It must learn to direct the work better than employers now do it. It is a task of many decades. In vast numbers, the coöperators are now engaged in this difficult undertaking. But their methods are not those of delirious persons who cannot wait for things to happen. As coöperators, they work together at a thousand and one points with employers and with a system which they propose to transform by slowly putting something better in its place.

"We have never taken out a brick," says one of them, "from the capitalist edifice, that we haven't put a solider one in its place."

Though there are still people who become hysterical over the term " trade-union," we can be rational in discussing it. Yet a little less than one hundred years ago, men trying to get collective bargaining were hung. There was a popular fury against them closely akin to the New England mania over witches. All dangers to society could be put upon these new conspirators just as our I. W. W. are now made a scape-goat for every sin, real or imagined. Though many of our older trade unions have outdone the I. W. W. in sabotage and in violence a hundred to one, we do not become suddenly insane by saying or writing "trade-union" as is so commonly the case in saying above a whisper, "I. W. W.!" We are now publicly assured that a careful investigation has been made in eleven western states with the result "that union men as a rule first pass resolutions demanding the return of beer and light wine and then turn to radical organizations." We knew that prohibition was filling our asylums, multiplying drug addicts and corrupting politics — as the report says —" by a new source of graft." But the opinion that prohibition would swell the ranks of the I. W. W. and fasten the pest upon us to our undoing has original merit. It is among the most alarming findings of these investigators that all I. W. W. leaders are earnest advocates of prohibition. In this last statement there is at least a gleam of sanity. I met an engineer who told me he joined the I. W. W. after being four times blacklisted for trying to unionize the men in the plant. What interested him most when I saw him was organizing teetotalers among the I. W. W. He had stumped a western state for prohibition.

Yet these Industrial Workers of the World have come among us. With their internal changes, they are a force with which wise statesmen will reckon as they have already learned to reckon with the trade union and a great deal of the socialist plan. The essence of syndicalism can no more be ignored than can the general labor situation. We cannot ignore it because it is passing too widely into the practices of that larger labor body feared by politicians because of votes, as they are feared by the community because of their power. Lacking the artist's touch, our American Unions are cultivating the most winning ways of the French syndicalists. In the present year, many unions conscious of their strength and bent on using it, are turning to French models.

Paris postmen have twice struck. They did not bother to leave their work and reduce their pay. For about half the morning, they sat, arms folded with leisure to tell the public why they were thus posed. Every train on a Southern line was stopped for one minute; the theatres turned dark for a quarter of an hour, while audiences were instructed about the cause of the protest.

In two of these cases the leaders were jailed, but they could not be kept there. Those they represented were too many and the unions (like Boston carmen) were doing a work which the community cannot and will not see held up too long.

Labor discovers this and takes advantage of it. The very heart of the first syndicalist protests in France was entire loss of faith in the political machinery for setting things right. " Direct Action " is the result. This is why a former Prime Minister, Mr. Balfour, told English militant suffragists that if they wanted proper attention they should make a row. Because of these indirections and delays, Chicago school teachers unionized and joined the A. F. of L.

In spite of much gross popular abuse and misunderstanding, I have no temptation to idealize our I. W. W. The assumption that the least skilled of the labor-mass " if it once have a chance," can take over the management of industry is among the most fantastic of utopian freaks. Nor do I suggest any coddling or sentimental treatment. The I. W. W. cannot be allowed to have their own way. They ask too much and they ask it in ways which no organized community can grant. I raise no question that fairly proved law breaking should be punished. These I. W. W. have no class privileges in this respect. Nor have I a doubt that what is called " free speech " must have restrictions. I have seen two strikes in which, at the most critical moment, a fiery appeal would have turned the crowd to a destruction of property more ruinous to their cause than to employers or to the public. This twice happened in the most disastrous uprising of labor we have yet had in this country — the railway strike of 1877.[1]

[1] There is real instruction about labor turmoils in looking back upon them from a distance. The worst strike in our history was that upon the Railways in 1877. In a short chapter, Rhodes gives a masterly account of this outbreak in his eighth volume (" History of the United States "). We see there how railway managers broke agreements with each other by the score. Because of their own reckless mismanagement, they twice reduced the wages of the employees — did in a word about everything in their power to drive the men to resistance. That on three occasions soldiers were

It is certain that a good deal of individual law breaking has gone on among them in this country. Nor do I for a moment accept that flabby theory, that "*society*" is to be held alone accountable for I. W. W. iniquities. Whatever the weight of social accountability, we all have a margin left over of our own. Even modern " determinists " (deniers of free will) insist on this personal responsibility for wrong. "Within the range of our character," they tell us, are choices — good and evil — where praise or blame is ours alone. Every sound social code will recognize this, even if we improve so far as finally to expunge the word "punishment" altogether and put discipline or education in its place. Our real danger now is in a stark conservatism trying desperately to revive the old "herd penalties" indiscriminately applied to groups and, worse of all, to the expression of opinion and ideas. We have old criminal law in abundance to punish such expression if it can be made plain that overt acts are due to such expression.[1]

There should not be the least difficulty in so understanding the larger movement of which the I. W. W. are a part, as to guard against lawless and unjust ways in dealing with it.

It is a wise sentence from the Webbs, " If the anarchist creed did not exist, it would almost be necessary for the socialists to invent it, as the drainpipe to carry out of their organizations those nuisance-elements of revolt, envy, mortified vanity and the impulse to bear false witness against one's neighbor." No existing society is safe without this drain-pipe. Each society has its swampy miasma to be made wholesome by social engineers who know their bus-

found untrustworthy, because of active sympathy with the strikers was commented upon at the time as "the most ominous sign of social insecurity that had appeared in our annals."

[1] No one has stated this more convincingly than Professor Chafee of the Harvard Law School.

iness too well to revive again the ways of the medicine man.

A traveler, quoted by Fraser, tells of a tribe stricken by miasma. The mists they said were full of devils only to be driven off by howlings and throwing of spears. It was not a question of drainage or destroying mosquitoes, but of drums, shouting and hurling of darts.

This was the local patriotism of the time. We are not yet rid of these medicine men. Some sit in Congress and other high places. They still put faith in noisy activities having as little relation to the *causes* of our trouble, as the contortions of their ancient brothers. In method they are strictly on a par with the I. W. W.

It would be a good thesis: "The Two I. W. W.s." In Oregon, an official asks for a "blanket annihilation" of all I. W. W.s. He thinks it a waste of time to make distinctions. Another says: "The only thing needed is plenty of rope." If these, and such as these, could have their way, they would soon prove an incomparably greater danger to social order than the I. W. W. even if as bad as its worst enemy depicts it.

This "blanket annihilation" with "plenty of rope" would have to apply to what is now as distinctly a world movement as socialism or the trade union. When shall we get statesmen with sagacity and forehandedness enough to recognize that heavy-handed ways as crude as this, *merely close the factional strife and apathy within radical labor ranks* thus arming them with the very weapons they most need? There is at this hour, no danger so great as this playing into the hands of the least responsible in the labor class.

The remedy of the heavy-hand has had long and thorough trial. As the sense of power spreads among the people, reliance upon force, as a primary or even secondary principle, is the most treacherous of allies. There is one reason for this which the whole "stamp-'em-out" brigade should learn, and until they learn it, they are a greater peril to "law and order" than any syndicalist. From the judge upon the bench, who says they must be "crushed like a snake in the grass," to Mayor Ole Hanson with his demand for more cemeteries, we have humiliating numbers to whom the policeman's club symbolizes the final appeal in saving civilization. Between Mr. Gompers and the unions loyal to him, there is a kind of conjurer's chain of links — now fast, now loose, reaching down to obscure, temporary groups criminally bent on mischief. Inside the Federation which Mr. Gompers has led are hundreds of these linked unions bitterly opposed to him and eager to break away. Just outside of them are definitely socialist groups hating the I. W. W. on one side, but as hostile to the A. F. of L. on the other. The main strength of organized socialism in this country is squarely pitted against every most distinctive tenet of the I. W. W.

But what happens when judges, attorneys, citizens' alliances, editors, politicians, police and vigilance committees composed of "the best people in town" fall to, in this frontier cry for physical force, as chief agency in dealing with rebeldom? If the job is roughly and indiscriminately done, as has been the case in at least thirty instances in the last five years, the general sense of justice is affronted in the larger outside community. The moral protest appears in official reports and very freely in our more independent press and among large numbers of the clergy. It appears more quietly but effectively in the student world. English officials shut up a philosopher and man of sciences. They are afraid of his *ideas,* but instead of checking the ideas, they call attention to them. A group of students, but two of whom had read a line of Bertrand Russell, not only begins to read and reread, but resolves to spread his literature. After a circulated report that Mr. Russell had been denied a hearing in one of our Universities, a class forms on the outside for a special course of lectures on his most radical book. Men with academic honors, not yet suspect, including two college teachers are among the instructors of this class. If this philosopher's ideas are really dangerous to social order, what do we think of an official clumsiness that tumbles upon the one unmistakable way, both of scattering those ideas and of preparing the soil for their rapid growth? So far as real influence is concerned, nothing within Mr. Russell's own resources compares for a moment with what was done for him by public authorities. Through these ineptitudes his ideas have gained at least fivefold range and influence in our country.

I do not forget most important differences in the cases, but so far as practical results are concerned, in what least spiritual item do these modern panics about *opinions* and attempts to punish them differ from the treatment of Socrates? That "son of a stone-cutter" gathered followers upon every street corner in Athens. His questions seemed to reflect upon "law and order" as then conceived. The wittiest playright, Aristophanes, poked fun at him on the stage. Especially the religious people took alarm. They said he was corrupting the youth. He was, moreover supremely concerned with politics and the State. This especially was an offense. He omitted altogether appeals to religion as if it had no bearing on moral behavior. They effectually shut him up with consequences which school boys can recite. But this was not the end. Among his listeners was a youth named Plato on whom the ideas had done their work. He began to set them down on those immortal pages making these same impious opinions an open classic for the entire world.

Never had the saying fitter application:—" The murderer is for the moment; the victim is for eternity." Just before conviction, John Brown wrote: " I am now fully persuaded that I am worth inconceivably more to hang than for any other purpose."

With pretentious backing, an expensively printed document is now scattered through our country, urging us all to unite in a campaign of destruction against "Socialism, Anarchism, I. W. W.s, Bolshevism, and the *Non-Partisan League.*" Another boggles these together and adds "*and all radicals.*" Here again is the witch mania in perfection. What a comment on "The Great Bad," this mixing things that don't belong together. When, as at the present, passion is added to a fuddled judgment like this, voluntary and legislative acts will follow. These will hit blindly at guilty and innocent alike. Much social as well as labor sympathy, so revolts at this as to defeat every end aimed at. Let me illustrate:

In many strikes, the public is puzzled to know why so small a per cent. of the men (as the employers say have quit work) exercises so great an influence. I. W. W.s would tell us it was "the power of the militant minority." This does not explain it. Those who refuse to join the strike and are proudly pointed out by the employer as "perfectly satisfied" easily find ways, if their sympathy is aroused, to assist the strikers.

Every conspicuous unfairness against the strike will draw from the non-participating workers not only money but powerful indirect support. The Federal Report on the Lawrence Strike of 1912, after careful investigation, gave the victory to the strikers. I wrote of this ("American Syndicalism," p. 27): "To cut such a wage scale as Commissioner Neil's Report has now made clear; to cut it because fifty-four hours took the place of fifty-six; to cut it with so little regard for those affected, that no sort of adequate warning or explanation was given, shows how sure of itself the mill-ownership felt.

"It could (it believed) hold organized labor effectively at bay. It could have for itself all that organization gives, but refuse it to labor. It could have generations of paternal, tariff coddling from Government to protect its own product, at the same time that unprotected and competing labor was at its disposal. These were advantages which beget confidence that easily breeds arbitrary habits of mind."

Thousands of non-strikers in Lawrence and elsewhere did not like this. They knew it to be unfair and even where leaders of Mr. Gompers' organization appeared to be traitors, " scabs " and " fakirs " to the I. W. W. cause, there *came from the American Federation membership large sums of money to assist the very men whom Mr. Gompers so bitterly repudiated.* From outside sympathizers — socialist, trade union and people amply supplied with this world's goods, came in a daily average throughout the long strike of a thousand dollars a day, as estimated by Federal investigators. Yet the members organized in that strike were less than one in twenty of Lawrence employees. They were indeed a " militant minority," but they represented an issue and a struggle which brought in the sympathy and support without which they would not have had the slightest hope. A good part of this outside sympathy springs from a dawning sense that hordes of our unskilled home and alien workers have suffered from neglect. None of the advantages of organization have been theirs. Packed away in congested centers of industry or city life, they have become in many ways a social peril. An explosion of " Americanization " schemes throughout the country is now one illustration of this new anxiety.

Meantime, the troublesome sympathy of which I write will increase in importunity. It brings in the hated " outsiders," or it brings in State and Federal authorities upon the scene of conflict. As at Lawrence in 1912, so in its recent strike, the most feared and hated of all enemies to local property interests was this " outsider." Wholly human and natural as this local irritation is, it will every month prove more difficult to ward off the obnoxious interference of this larger public.

A university President and diplomatist as well known as Andrew D. White, gave a long and special study to crime and lawlessness in the United States. It was among his milder strictures that " law and order " in Western Canada had much firmer foundations than on our side of the line. Yet we have seen at Winnipeg 35,000 men for six weeks in " general " or " sympathetic " strike. An old friend — a veteran correspondent for Canadian papers, George Iles, sent me from the first the capitalistic and labor sheets. The city police were so favorable toward the strike that they voted for it. Many war veterans refused to take the places of these police. Firemen also struck. They were not I. W. W. outbreaks but it is among the greater events that strikes having a great deal of I. W. W. impulse in them are now in order — as at Seattle and Winnipeg. They move as by instinct toward the " one big union." They rebel against their own traditional leadership. Though internationally allied with our American Federation, the strikers in Canada say they are tired of it. " We will manage our own affairs and leave Yankee labor to its own business." They are very impertinent toward their own national officials in Canada. They will have " more control and more definite control " in their respective industries. Here too the outsider is annoying.

Editors, aldermen, Methodist clergymen and returned soldiers are on trial. A former President of the Methodist Conference tells 8000 people that the sympathetic strike " is just as religious a movement as a church revival. It is just as ethical as the fight at Flanders. Those who oppose this strike do so because they are individualists; the workers support it because they put the interests of others ahead of their own interests. The individualist has no program, hence he attacks the man or the body that tries to work out a program." Methodists are a very powerful body and they are eminently " of the people." They have drawn up and sanctioned one of the most advanced programs of social reconstruction. It is an unequivocal challenge to the capitalistic order. Many of our super-patriots could easily convict it of "seditious conspiracy" but in the effort, they must attack very similar programs in four other most influential sections of the Christian Church. There are few men in the United States better fitted to report on the general strike in Winnipeg than Edward T. Devine. When it was so far over that men on all sides could talk with some calmness, he made his investigation. It is a model of thoroughness and impartiality. (Survey Act 4, 1919.) He closes his report as follows: "Believing in freedom of discussion and in freedom of the press, I find no trace of danger in the Calgary Labor Conference or in the strikers' bulletins or in the Labor Church; but I find some danger of Bolshevism *as a result* of the repression of speech, the deportation of aliens without public hearing on specific charges, the imprisonment of labor leaders without bail, and the arrest of men like Woodsworth and Dixon on such flimsy evidence as has been made public." It is this kind of strike that now comes on apace. On its more radical side, it touches syndicalism, but in its saner following, it is full of constructive hints which ally it to a movement so alive in industry that we may see in it some real promise of the next step in more democratic reorganization.

CHAPTER XXI

THE NEW GUILD

I

THE spirit of the syndicalist protest is very much abroad. It appears politically in Sein Fein [1] and in Sir Edward Carson's rude defiance of the English Government; in Mr. Gompers' threat that he and his followers will disobey any law which makes the strike illegal. It is everywhere among the trade unions, laughing at their own leaders or telling them bluffly to step one side. Boston carmen recently stopped the entire service in and about Boston in the same spirit.

One of the greatest of our railroad builders was long abused for saying that if the public didn't like his management, "it could walk." This is what the Boston union said to a large community. It cared neither for its own agreement nor for the advice of some of its own councilors. Boston Police have given us further illustration. Now the miners send out their challenge to Government and public alike, as outlying locals force the leaders to declare a risky strike in the steel works.

In suggestion and in idea this syndicalist protest now appears in a new and greatly improved form.

No one willing to learn can weigh the claims of the New Guild without admitting that our thought has been quickened and enlarged by its criticism and analysis. It is far less destitute of some sense of the economic and political solidarities than is syndicalism. This latter so cut itself off from the State, from politics and from the facts and necessities of large trading communities as to leave it fragmentary and unrelated. The New Guilder avoids this eco-

[1] With syndicalist emphasis in the meaning of the words "ourselves alone."

nomic provincialism. Against all capitalism, it is more disdainful than the railway magnate of long ago, or the Boston carmen, police and miners of the present day. Its most dashing leader tells us, with no mincing, what is proposed. "Step by step the Unions must push their control higher up the industrial scale by bringing into their ranks foremen, supervisors, experts, professionals — all those grades of management which are now regarded as preëminently in the employers' service." Here is a "functional," rather than a representative, democracy. Geographical areas are at a discount.

In its loathing for the big State, its politics and commercialism, the syndicalist reaction was too extreme to hold the loyalty of those who thought "socially." It could hold anarchists to whom the State is anathema,— it could not hold men with enough political sense to recognize that the State is not to be willed out of existence in this or the next generation; neither is it to be politically ignored. It is to be dealt with organically. This means political accommodation. The Guilder recognizes the State, as employers are learning to recognize labor organization, because it is for the time an unalterable fact and certain long to remain so.

Thus with wholesome English compromise, the New Guild takes the field. It abhors state socialism. It is acutely critical of the present trade union because ill-organized and too much on the defensive. It will turn it into a constructive economic organ including all the craft unions of an entire industry. Syndicalism gave far too much power to the union. It would even have ownership vested in these unions "working at the point of production." This is the opposite of state socialism which gives ownership to the community. Guild socialists aim to reconcile this conflict. Mr. Cole speaks of the "fear and mistrust, the overwhelming claims advanced on behalf of even a capitalist State in every sphere of life; and many are looking eagerly for some form of social organization capable of holding the State in check." Differing from the syndicalist, the New Guild does not flout the State. It sees that consumers also have their rights. These are to be represented by the State. The new movement has accomplished leadership, even an academic dialect ready to hold its own against all disputants. Convinced that parliaments, deputies and congresses are no more to be trusted, they demand that hand and brain workers create their own industrial legislature. Representation based on territorial areas alone has lost all touch with those occupational interests that should now take control.

There has been much idle criticism of these Guildmen, as if they sought again the petty economic monopolies of the " dark ages." There is hardly one working analogy between the two. We are not dealing here with the medieval Guild. That wrought its service until invention, transportation, with a widening market, destroyed it. In its time, it gave the thing most needed, stability. Catholic scholars in economics long pleaded for the Guild, but in its more ancient sense of preserving the employer and " social authorities." It is no belated ghost like this that the heralds of The New Guild call up. Benevolent employers shall play at most a minor part. Labor, including every one who contributes to production, is to be supreme. Organized into groups, corresponding to different industries, the perfected trade union is given new powers. It is to have social reorganization through the "producers." Organized labor is to represent these; but the wage system as we know it is neatly disposed of, as stated in their Constitution, " the abolition of the wage system, and the establishment by the workers of self-government in industry through a democratic system of national guilds working in conjunction with a democratic State."

No one is less fooled by popular shibboleths about democracy. That we now have *political* democracy is not only denied; it is denied that in any sense we *can* have it until industry is democratized. To secure this, they turn like the syndicalist to the trade union but they put it under restraints. They not only ally themselves to the State and to political action, but — more important still — they do not claim *ownership* for the Union. Their claim is for administrative control. Here, as with Sein Feiners, it is "ourselves alone." They give a far broader definition to "labor." Not a thinker, writer, dreamer, teacher, inventor, manager or "intellectual" of any sort who contributes "creative energy in production" is to be excluded. Every man and woman who "renders service" is the real producer. Salary earners, organizers, foremen are laborers in this sense, and all alike necessary to production.

It is here the revolutionary character of the Guild appears. As in Consumers' Coöperation, private profit is at an end. They are to give us a new kind of " General Strike " against the whole wage system. It is here the reformed union is to do its work. Not the present distracted unionism, full of intensive conflicts of its own, but " amalgamated " unions of entire industries. Under the wage system, the employer says his manager and foremen belong to him. They are first to obey him or he loses all control of his own establishment. This loss of employers' control as now exercised, is precisely what Guildsmen want and mean to bring about. They propose to shake him off by doing his work better. The unions are to have the manager and the foremen and, that there may be no uncertainty, the unions are to *pay* them. All these former agents of capital are to pass over into the direct service of the unions. How else can the wage system be destroyed? It is admitted that this requires first of all an entire overhauling of unions as they now exist. Not only are they to be more compactly organized in all the important industries, they are to begin at once a higher technical education to insure fitness for the new duties.

Both for reorganization and for training, the first instruments are already put into the hands of the Guildsmen in our much adopted " Shop-Committees." " Beginning in the workshop, they must more and more take control out of the hands of the employers and transfer it to their own organizations. This involves, not joint control with the employers, but actual transference of control from the employers to the Trade Unions." Here already is a tentative partnership with the employer, but it is to be carried *through*. One by one, the henchmen of the employers — technical experts, bosses, supervisors are to be won over to the unions, until the partnership is perfected between the Guild of unions and the State.

Thus the New Guild is to become the administrator in wealth-production. Each is to manage its own politics and working conditions. Workers are not to receive " wages " as determined by competition. They are to get " pay " as an officer in the army. If we take fright at the monopoly and " closed shop " which this control of industries by unions implies, we are told that every door is to be left open for free admission. There are to be no heavy fees to pay, as in so many of our present craft unions. We are also to remember that the " State " is to be a people's possession with the direct aim of destroying all class distinctions. Its ownership of land and the machinery of production will then become complete as its bureaucratic dominion is checked.

Government may have the say as to *what* is to be produced. They must figure out the quantities or product needed by the consumers, but the hours, conditions, and methods under which production goes on, rest with the Guilds. These are not to set what prices they like on the goods turned out. Nor are they to buy their raw material at figures of their own determining. The State representing the public is to have a voice in these decisions. Nothing more than this acknowledged partnership with the public, differentiates the Guild from syndicalism. Far beyond the syndicalists, the guides of Guild socialism have some adequate sense of the organic and social character of these problems.[1]

They do not for instance, like syndicalists, go wild over the General Strike. They know too well what resources of self-defense the communal whole will show if its safety is really jeopardized. They see the necessity of a strong centralized authority. How else could a stubborn capitalism be properly taxed? It will indeed be one task of the Guilds to see that the State has stability. The State must help with the great problem of unemployment, with the minimum wage and with finance. Between it and the Guilds are commissions and committees on which labor has full representation. As brainworkers are included, there are to be guilds of architects, artists, schoolmen, doctors, lawyers and men of science. There is thus full provision for a functional organization of producers where brain and hand workers are in theory at least to exercise real sovereignty.

II

Until 1908, I had heard no word of this movement. My first serious look at it was suggested by an employer who

[1] The super-Guilder, A. D. H. Cole, has given as succinct a definition as I have seen, "a community in which production will be organized through democratic associations of all the workers in each industry, linked up in a body representing all workers in all industries. On the other hand, we look forward to a democratization of the State and of local government, and to a sharing of industrial control between producers and consumers. The State should own the means of production: the Guild should control the work of production." "Where we have now a single Parliament, elected by geographical constituencies and claiming universal authority, Guildsmen want two 'Parliaments,' one geographical to represent all 'users,' the other industrial to represent the 'producers.' Matters affecting producer and user alike they want settled by joint agreement made by the two bodies."

had read Arthur Penty's book, among the first, if not the first, to introduce the subject. This employer had come to believe that in some way the unions were to get far greater control of industry in spite of all opposition, but to do that with any safety to the Commonwealth, *they must have entire reorganization with responsibilities thrown upon them in such way as to educate them into constructive agents in industry.*

The impression I first derived from Mr. Penty's study was that of a visionary person of artistic temperament with an idea so utopian as to be outside all practical discussion.

A careful reading of the literature from that date and above all, the actual changes taking place under our own eyes, even in this country, have brought the conviction that this Guild idea deserves (as it is getting) the most serious attention. To call it merely " interesting " and " perhaps fruitful," as one now hears and reads, is not enough.

Already most important features of it are plainly observable about the world as they are in our own industry and in politics.

It outlines a partnership between labor and the State. Though with far different aim and definition, employers here and there are moving definitely in the same direction. Shop-Committees, labor representation in all its forms so far concede the Guild idea. But with still more significant hint, it appears in those half-conscious " felt necessities " expressing themselves inside specific industries like those of the garment workers, the railway men, and in the Union of the Photo-Engravers.[1] Here it is the union men who show anxiety — about the " cost of production " and of " unscientific methods of selling," as well as other " ruinous practices carried on by many employers which capitalist organization seems utterly unable to rectify." Here labor twits the employer with gross inefficiencies. Here, says Mr. Fitch, is " a union that does not make requests concerning

[1] See John Fitch's account of this in the *Survey,* Nov. 16, 1918.

working conditions; it issues directions with respect to the very nerve-center of business arrangements; the price at which goods are to be sold; and the employers do not make any retorts about running their own affairs — they comply with the directions!"

There are employers who are not even frightened at this tendency. I hear from a Boston employer, as successful as he is widely known, that he sees the time ahead when his employees will have the training fitting them for entire control of his business. In helping them toward this control, he believes he is serving the only form of democracy that will secure either liberty or economic safety.

Other employers, who feel the ground shake under their feet, are thrown into a panic. A New York dispatch of October 31 tells of a trade union in one branch of the meat industry demanding so much control that the employer describes it, "as the first step in a Bolshevist movement to take over his plant. He was informed by an insider that the unionists planned, after accomplishing their purpose by a series of strikes, to allow him six per cent. on his investment and divide all profits over that among themselves."

At the heart of labor's struggle, this is now a tendency as certain as the rush for "shop committees."

In that portentious center of biggest industry, Pittsburgh, the syndicalist impulse toward the "One Big Union" now comes to the surface. Twenty-four labor bodies instead of fighting alone, resolve on common action. More than a million are represented:— sailors from the great lakes and men in the mines send delegates. The most aristocratic unions which ask entrance fees higher than a social club are to step down. The less skilled are welcomed. This requires low fees. The Guildsmen have given careful theoretic justification for union control of mines and railways. Government ownership is assumed. There were remarkable prophecies that labor would rapidly increase its political demand for nationalization. We have seen this prove true. They foresaw that labor would grow more antagonistic to the existing State. The present State, they tell us, must take these properties in order that a start be made. Step by step, it must give up all *management* to the Guild and thus be shorn of its most dangerous possession.

And so we are offered a definite and practical policy for starting and developing the New Order. They do not wait for a new heaven. Like socialists grown wise, the Guild asks to take over "what can be conveniently managed." Railways and mines are so ripe on the capitalistic tree as to be ready for plucking. Others as they grow mellow are to be gathered in.

They point to the labor manifesto in France where "State Ownership" is also demanded, but only as a strategic step toward the elimination of the old bureaucracy. The first step taken in England was a cautious one. At their Conference, the resolution closed with the words, " we believe that national welfare demands the railway should be acquired by the State, to be jointly controlled and managed by the State and representatives of the National Union of Railwaymen." Parliamentary control it is said, " would mean in practice, not control by the people for the people, but control by the cold-blooded bureaucrats of Whitehall." " In place of the profiteers who control the railways to-day, we must set up not a bureaucracy of state officials, but a self-governing community of railwaymen." Here in this business of transportation is their ideal of "industrial self-Government." They point to the capitalist system of promotions which continually picks the abler men from the unions to place them in the employers' group, thus weakening the labor class as they strengthen capitalism. "Only the one big union can stop this practice." In organizing "joint control," already begun, this process is to be reversed. Not only shall capital quit picking away from the union its best men, these shall be plucked from the other side.

From the very pets of capitalism, the union shall select every expert capacity for its own collective management. Of what use, they ask, is the present average type of railway director? There is much amusement in describing many of them. Even of the better minority, we hear it asked: "Are not the railway men, with leaders of their own, more capable of running the service in the public interest than Lord Claud Hamilton or Sir Guy Granet?"

What meantime is to become of the present shareholders and of their pretty coupons? State socialism would merely shift interest on shares to interest on state bonds, thus preserving the old evils of private profit. Here is a real difficulty. The Guild will have no private profit. It ends by passing ownership to the public. But the Guild is after *all* private profits, not merely those of the railway. Railways and mines are chosen as the best practical illustrations of what can be done. They frankly tell us what this means. The private profit system " will be ended only when all the workers in all industries, organized in blackleg-proof Industrial Unions, pull down capitalism and the capitalist State from their place, and set up National Guilds and the democratic State instead."

And the other little matter of buying out the present owners? Are they to have no compensation? Yes, but one over which, it is admitted, there is to be a fight to the finish. Here the Guilders are not to compromise. Their ultimatum is " that the bonds issued to railway shareholders shall be state bonds chargeable, *not on the railways, but upon the whole revenue of the State,* and further that they shall be issued in the form of annuities, strictly terminable at the end of a given period, so that at the end of, say, fifty years, the whole burden of interest will be automatically extinguished, and the railways will be, in fact as well as in name, the property of the public." When this minimum is reached and the true people's State arrives, what as owner, is the State to get? It is there to represent the whole community — the consumers. It must raise taxes for national expenditures. It is admitted that these will be very great and increasingly great. The Guilds therefore are to pay rent to the State. They are vocational bodies and will exist in great numbers. Some of them, it is suggested may be untaxed, perhaps the Guild of the actors, the " Guild of Applied Sciences," the Clerical Guild. It is already hinted that the Railway Guild may be let off because travel should be free. There has been much said about a free theatre.

These open questions about taxation — the amount of it, the uses to which it is put and method of raising it, will present difficulties enough for State officials in the Guild World. But it seems to be assumed that the very multiplicity of interests will somehow fall into happy equilibrium to make possible the industrial brotherhood to which they look.

The latest news is from the other side of the world. It is a plan for the " Democratic Control of Mining "[1] in New Zealand. Its five graphic diagrams are as much superior to those published by our I. W. W. as the New Guild is superior to syndicalism in general.

It pits democracy against bureaucracy. It will have nothing to do with " State Ownership of Mines," as hitherto proposed. This would only " officialize the industry." What is now asked is " democratic, local, and departmental autonomy," so that every miner may have a conscious and defined interest in the mines *to stimulate greater output*. This will give him " an inducement to produce his maximum." It will also give him an inducement to economize waste and save the enormous losses due to methods of exploitation under competitive private ownership.

[1] To be ordered from D. A. Davis, 38 Cemetery Road, Porth, Rhondda Valley, South Wales.

The State is to be the owner of the mines; appointing its Minister of Control, who will order such supplies as the nation needs. The Miners' Union is to meet this demand. The author says, the Federation of Miners already "contains the necessary skeleton structure on which such an organization could be constructed. It is co-extensive with the industry; it has the forms and machinery — albeit imperfect — for democratic control, and with the alterations and improvements we suggest, could well become the steward to administer the nation's coal resources."

Each pit is to have its technical staff to be then and there democratically elected. "Theoretical knowledge and administrative capacity will be essential." No man shall become a candidate for the technical staff who does not bring his certificate of competence. Who, it is asked, is so much interested in the trained ability of the staff as the miners? Do we not risk our lives under them? Does not everything we want — safety, more output, saving of waste, depend on their abilities? Every mine is to have its main "Pit Committee." There is also to be a "deliberative assembly which supervises the activities of the Pit Committees, composed of all the workmen of whatever grade necessary for the working of the colliery. It is the only authority competent to judge any proposal for more facile or productive working of the colliery. Here its "industrial politics" are to develop.

There is to be (a) a Legislature, (b) Executive to carry out the demands, (c) Initiative for discussing proposals and for dealings with other industries. There are to be "tuitional classes" free to all students and to encourage all workmen to become technically equipped, especially for "all young lads coming into the industry." No boy is to pass from school at fourteen years of age direct to the mine. If, after examination, he is pronounced fit for the work, he is to have two years special training, "supplemented by visits to, and working short periods in, different mines during that period. This would turn them out at the age of sixteen with a good theoretical knowledge of the industry."

I omit the elaborate detail over the organized relation between the State Controller and the various mine committees. It is not questioned that present owners should have some measure of compensation when the State takes over the mines. But the miners, we are assured, " would jealously investigate the prices paid for these properties."

The pamphlet closes with a paragraph which voices a growing sentiment among miners in many countries: " To the miner the choice lies between Industrial Democracy and some form of Industrial Serfdom; to the nation, between efficiency and harmony and a series of disruptive struggles leading to chaos and anarchy."

If a plan like this were a lonely inspiration of some eccentric and fanciful person, it would deserve but slight attention. If it were suggested by a book like Bacon's " Atlantis " or Camapanella's " City of the Sun," it might pass as an exercise in poesy to be reverenced as Plato would have men reverence the poets, but be sure to keep him (as a practical nuisance) well out of the Republic. These miners are not concerned with any such fairyland. Their scheme grew slowly from instincts bred in hard experience. They have lost faith in all distant, financial management. They have come to believe they can do it better themselves. Both the doubts about private ownership and faith in their own abilities are international in their range. We ask therefore, how is capitalism to succeed against an awakened hostility of this character and extent? Will it not be forced to concessions along these lines that shall at least give labor experimental opportunities to prove or disprove its case? Sulky and disgruntled with the old order, can labor be induced or forced to methods in which its faith is gone? A body of such numbers and strength as our United Mine Workers join the Railway brotherhoods and the Plumb

Plan. I hear this plan scoffed at as an imbecility. Even by Mr. Plumb, the plan is admitted to be faulty and very imperfect. But no critic should forget that this plan is not a local and accidental explosion. It draws its strength and such authority as it has from many peoples about the globe and from many industries. As we have seen, so much of it is already embodied in practical business operations that we have to take it at least with some seriousness.

I recognize the risk of stating Guild opinion as if it were a unit of consent. Views differ here as in every other party, sect or faction. It has its "right," its "center" and its "left." Some are in great haste, others cautious. Some are wise enough to see that the most advanced employers may prove their best aids in the transformation and will for the time make common cause with them. These are, of course, abused by the more revolutionary, as "sold out to the capitalists." These latter appear however to have but very slight influence in the propaganda. Thus far this has been in charge of a select intellectual leadership. It is from these that the idea has spread so rapidly to at least a dozen important American periodicals, economic reviews, and even government publications.

III

Without asking, one knows what most practical American citizens will say, as they first look upon a scheme like this. It will seem more fantastic than socialism and more intolerable, because of the privileged powers granted to the unions. The very definiteness of its proposals will make it seem to these objectors the more repellant. Socialism is at least elastic with infinite interpretations. It has its poetic and nebulous charm. But a society run by trade unions with a medieval spelling — No! No!

After some experimenting in this line, I found, with some most interesting exceptions, that American business men refuse to be reconciled to the guild idea in spite of limitations imposed upon the unions by the State.

The Guilder asks: Is not the State to *own* the industries and therefore have a saving control over them? The answer (I fear with some truth) is that the proposed ownership is far too shadowy; so shadowy as to threaten constant feuds between officialdom and these guilds with all their super-powers of collective bargaining and possible political influence.

Yet these same business objectors admit the practical certainty of radical economic and political changes now impending. This of itself should insure the readiest hospitality at least to the idea so quick to catch the loyalty of thousands among the younger and best equipped of those seeking their way toward such new order as lies before us. I step into a single small bookstore catering especially to the student class. I am told that the demand for syndicalist and New Guild literature constantly grows; that " Coles' books are eagerly read by thousands of students in the United States." As guild leader, he writes the leading article in the *American Economic Review*. This Oxford scholar is the most skilled interpreter of the movement. He is not raided in England, but given very responsible positions in the new plans of social reconstruction But, to the American business man I have in mind, serious treatment of a faddish eccentricity like guild socialism, will seem labored and ridiculous. I should like if possible to make him listen.

I submit, therefore, a bit of evidence. It comes wholly from the long and secure experience of a business man who did two things. He was successful in large mercantile affairs. He won the highest distinction as a cautious investigator of social questions. Joseph Chamberlain, master in great business as in politics, spoke of him as the highest authority in his field in England. As early as 1885, Charles Booth began those investigations with " The Life and Labor of the People" which resulted in the monumental work under that title. He won distinction as a statistician which made him president of the society. Not even the hardest headed among "practical men" can call him "a theorist." For more than twenty years he worked as hard at these labor and social questions as other men work in successful private business. I saw him last when he was turning to more general issues, troubled about trade unionism and its relation to the industrial future. He said his investigations had shown a more dangerous social condition than he had believed. Syndicalism had just caught his attention and two years later he sent me a pamphlet from which I quote ("Industrial Unrest and Trade Union Policy," Macmillan, 1913). He had no superstitions about the unions. He subjects them to trenchant criticism. He says they are "responsible for many of the evils that have caused industrial unrest" but unlike the vocal members of our manufacturers' association, he is not gleeful in writing it. Two years before the war he was asked for a public statement on industrial unrest.

Before answering, he carefully examined the origins and claims of syndicalism and especially of its sectarian offshoot — the New Guild. He admits that he was helped to his conclusions by syndicalism and even more by guild socialism. He says "The views of the syndicalists, guild socialists, and socialists generally on the whole subject are very interesting and particularly useful to its discussion, from their extreme and logical character." The guild socialists, "approach nearest in their aim to the proposals set forth in my paper." That is, *he was willing and eager to learn from them.* But here, again, he does not lose his head. Bag and baggage, he does not go over to socialism, syndicalism, or the rejuvenated guild. All three condemn the wage system. Mr. Booth says he believes in the wage system. He trusts, moreover, "largely to competition." Like a syndicalist, he distrusts political reform. He sees that radical economic readjustments have to be made and that these should have first emphasis. He says expressly that syndicalists are right in urging the precedence of economic to political reform. He insists upon more attention to what he calls the "neglected values" in this dark problem, adding that employer and employee must learn to "work consciously together with a common aim," both looking upon capital as a tool to "be obtained at the lowest possible price."

One promise of the guild organization is very real. It gives the amplest field for practical experiment in our most perplexing special problems.

No practical difficulty of the uniform eight-hour issue has been more obvious than the varying abilities of many men and women to work easily within the limits of fatigue far longer than others. The great argument for the shorter days rests on studies of nervous fatigue. To pass this line is pure waste and often the beginning of disease. Some are at the end of the day's energy at six — others at seven, others at eight or nine. To set the limit for *all* at seven might prove a waste as real as under the old system. Now the guild has absolute control of this question. Its responsibilities are localized. It has the elasticities which admit of experiment and classification. It may have its four, five or nine-hour workers as it will. It may avoid the tyrannies of uniformity or huge organization spread over areas within which are innumerable variations for which allowance should be made.

Criticism at this stage is so far futile that I leave it with a little questioning. That there is a good dose of utopia in the proposals is clear, especially in the imagined facility with which "the whole burden of interest will be automatically extinguished": in the cheerful elimination of the wage-system and of all "class-conflict."

It is claimed, too, that politics will be wholly eliminated from industry but not a stray atom of proof is given us to show why or how this is possible.

What, again, is to keep these guilds at peace among themselves? They will assume enormous proportions. Bakers, garment makers, textile workers, railway men, miners, timber and woodworkers with scores of others must have their guild. They are all organized producers leagued to the State representing the public and its many interests. In theory these guilds will watch each other, that no one makes a sharper bargain or secures preferential rates from the State over the others. Councils that stand for "inclusive social interests" are to supervise. Science, the professions, the arts, the educators all are to have their chosen ones to interpret and to defend.

Though the State is to be owner, it has apparently no real power over the manner in which its properties are to be conducted. If this is "ownership" it requires a new definition.

It has a very different meaning from ownership in our present habits of thought. It is communal ownership with no such personal responsibilities and solicitudes as now go with that word.

Decisions about the social wealth are to be made by elected officials. These are to act and to decide under pressure of producer's opinion and consumer's opinion. They must decide upon rentals and site values. They have to make an infinitude of bargains over pay and prices with the many guilds. There are delicate questions like piece work, foremen, technical men and general management, the right to strike, from which the consumers represented by the State will hardly allow themselves to be excluded. What are the guilds to pay for raw materials? These guilds are to be industrial and therefore in many cases to cover at least the entire national area. This means some gigantic bodies with corresponding political influence such as we should have in our mining and transportation guilds. The railway guild would include every worker from the candy boy and colored porter to the highest official.

Again the relation in which these guilds are to stand to each other, and also to the State is not a static, but an ever-changing relation. Unless invention and applied science are to be " slowed up," both structure and function are always in flux. No one lays more stress upon technical invention and entire freedom of choice of movement than these guild pioneers. These changes of themselves would require powerful equipment both among the guilds and between them and the State.

These objections are of the simplest and most obvious. They may prove groundless, but they are not to be ignored. Diderot, when guest of Russian Queen Catharine, had read her some fine passages on desired social renovations. They impressed her, but she thought it easy to note these down in manuscript. Her task was to write them, not in a book, but " on the sensitive human skin "— a matter safer with a practical statesman like herself than with one possessing only a dazzling imagination and a pen. Yet the spirit of Charles Booth should be our spirit. This " merchant student " was not afraid of the New Guild or of any other new idea. So far as our employers and other guides rise to that level, the industrial future is as safe as available human wisdom can make it. We may differ as we will from Mr. Booth's approach, but not to study in his spirit; merely to turn sniffingly away from the challenging idea is a blindness never more dangerous than now. Certainly a very long period will be required for its high accomplishments — so long indeed, that we shall have plenty of time for practical and searching tests of the project.

CHAPTER XXII

THE GREATER TASK

I

PESTALOZZI was right, democracy halts until our fine principles are applied to the weak. In a lawyer's minute study under the Carnegie Foundation, we have an informing word about justice and the law as applied to the poorer and weaker citizen. How often we have heard it magisterially delivered that "justice is impartial"; that "rich and poor alike are equals before the law." An approved and selected member of the Boston bar elaborately reports upon this through 270 pages. For three years he has been about the country observing the law as it is practically administered. Already ex-President Taft, himself a judge, had said his word about our administered justice: that "under present conditions, ashamed as we really are of it, this is not a fact." It is from a high legal organ that we hear of "the harsh fact that, with all our prating about justice, we deliberately withhold it from the thousands who are too poor to pay for it."[1] It is in a report of a government commission that we find this "denial of justice" set down as one cause of industrial unrest. It is from a chief justice of one of our greatest States that we hear what this denial of justice means: it "incites citizens to take the law into their own hands. It causes crimes of violence. It saps patriotism and destroys civic pride. It arouses class jealousies and breeds contempt for law and government," with a great deal more from unimpeachable authorities, thus plainly printed in this study of "Justice and the Poor." Of the moral havoc this legal denial causes, the author writes, "it actively encourages

---

[1] Judicature Society *Bulletin VIII* (1915), page 24.

THE GREATER TASK

fraud and dishonesty. Unscrupulous employers, seeing the inability of wage-earners to enforce payments, have deliberately hired men without the slightest intention of paying them. It enables the poor to rob one another; it permits the shrewd immigrant of a few years' residence to defraud his more recently arrived countrymen. Everywhere it abets the unscrupulous, the crafty, and the vicious in their ceaseless plans for exploiting their less intelligent and less fortunate fellows. The system not only robs the poor of their only protection, but it places in the hands of their oppressors the most powerful and ruthless weapon ever invented." The foreword to this report is by Elihu Root, who says it " should be useful to the members of the American bar, who during the past few years have been gradually awakening to a sense of their responsibility." He explains the conditions " which to so great an extent have put justice beyond the reach of the poor," concluding that it is *" time to set our own house in order."* [1] Strongly approving the report, Mr. Root says it is a " systematic treatise and practical handbook on the administration of justice in the United States in the direction which is at this time of the most critical importance." " It is full of trustworthy information and suggestions." In part first, we read " The administration of American justice is not impartial, the rich and the poor do not stand on an equality before the law; the traditional method of providing justice has operated to close the doors of the courts to the poor, and has caused a gross denial of justice in all parts of the country to millions of persons." There is not a page of this report that does not apply to something more than " the poor." Another volume should be forthcoming to tell us of the organized cruelty under the name of justice against so many of these embittered ones who have spoken or written opinions which brought upon them these same harsh discriminations. It is here, too, that " we must set our house in order."

[1] My italics.

"Denial of justice — to millions of persons!" What more substantial reason could be given to show why this most important part of the social order should be challenged. Times quite innumerable, I have heard these same opinions by Judge Taft and Mr. Root expressed by labor and socialist agitators or read them in their papers. But lawyers and good folk generally were angered by such low-down fault-finding. Before other lawyers in my own house, one of their most honored leaders treated this labor criticism of the bar with an air of pity, as a thing so ignorant that one despaired of reaching it. He said there had not been an abuse even of the injunction against labor. But now "we must set our own house in order." It is most worthily spoken.

This, too, is a challenge to our time. These complaining classes have now to be convinced that slow and ordered reconstruction will promote their welfare more surely than any revolutionary promise. For two reasons, it will be a thorny and up-hill road. First, because of the long "sacrificial transition" before world prosperity returns. Second, because the necessary legal and social remedies are so slow in maturing. These delays will give the iconoclast his chance and his excuse. It is for this reason that (as we work openly and unafraid with the collectivist, and the trade union) we have also the harder task of learning so far to understand the revolutionary groups as to see why they are there; to see that social causes are behind them as behind other phenomena. If Athenian society required a gad-fly in Socrates, every "social order" needs and will have its critics with whip and sting. We may hang them and thus "make the gallows sacred as the cross." We may imprison them and redouble their influence. We may banish them, only to make them work the harder and more dangerously where they are sent. No old line or fence checks in the least the final influence of these victims.

Look at Bismarck again, trying this child's game with

the Catholic Church as he tried it against socialists. With the stupendous prestige of his three victories and the most powerful military and bureaucratic force at his disposal, this imperial master was stung by ideas that he did not like. During some half dozen years after 1872, he attacked these ideas with heavy battalions, as our committees attacked the socialist Rand School in New York with toy pistols. He put banishment and the prison to wholesale use. The English ambassador, Odo Russell, noted down the increasing temper and nervous irritability of the "Master of All Europe," as he saw himself beaten by the ideas he would crush. With every clumsy hammer-stroke, he saw the thing he hated grow in numbers and in strength. He saw finally that he had closed up every serious factional squabble inside the Catholic Church. His heavy weapons failed him as completely as they did in his attempt to crush socialism. When he saw he was beaten and meanly laid the blame upon his creature, Falk, we recall an incident. One of Bismarck's biographers [1] quotes Thiers' story of Napoleon. Some wag or sycophant said, "Sire, the enemy has lost thousands of men." "Yes," said Napoleon, "but I have lost the battle." He tells another of the fascinating gossip Pepys, who had been watching a fight against ideas that even in those days fortified the dissenters far more than it weakened them. Flunky as he was, Pepys, watching them on their way to prison, sighed, "I would to God they would reform or *not be so well catched.*" In the days of his greatness and in humorous mood, Bismarck sent a message to Gladstone. "Tell him, while he is felling trees, I am planting them." We now know the kind of tree he was nurturing. We shall find neither good timber nor shelter from such planting. It is already among the platitudes that Germany's tragedy was in her worship of force as the "great ultimate." It is no truer of Germany than of ourselves, so far as we copy it.

[1] Grant Robertson.

German naval officers with the same obliquity heard of mutinous ideas among their sailors. They must be "stamped out." For punishment, the suspected were packed off to trenches, where they at once began their work of creating still more dangerous opinions among the soldiers. Strikers and their leaders from three parts of the empire were also sent to the front "for punishment." They carried there the same message of revolt that the sailors carried, only to be later spread more widely still by wounded, furloughed soldiers in their home towns and hospitals. On an even keel with this were the various botched raids like that upon the Rand School in New York. There is not a follower of that school whose fidelities will not be strengthened by that raid. But this does not measure the aid which the raiders render to the cause represented by that school. Thousands over whom this institution had no slightest influence have had their attention called to it and sympathy excited for it. I heard one such say, "Well, an idea as stupidly persecuted as that, must have something in it." Against blind muddling like this, we have here and there hints of sanity and statesmanship.

In Morley's "Reminiscences" we read how long and patiently he argued with the English authorities in India to change their entire attitude toward the rebellious element there. As Secretary of State, he too had responsibilities. We must, he says, keep order, but "excess of severity is not the path to order — it is the path to the bomb."[1] Again he urges, "Triumphs of violence are for the most part little better than temporary makeshifts, which leave all the work of government to be encountered afterward by men of essentially greater capacity than the hero of force without scruple." And nowhere are the ways of the violent so inciting to evil, as when sanctioned or winked at by those most strident in their talk about "law and order."[2]

[1] Vol. II, page 269.
[2] S. K. Ratcliff, long an editor in India, tells me that if Morley's

We have heard of that "self-searching humility which alone makes men wise and merciful to those who err." No people ever needed this compunction in dealing with the victims of our political and economic disorders more than we need it. Until we get far more of that spirit we shall not only fail to cure I. W. W.s, but we shall increase their influence. We shall do it precisely as we do in every lawless act against another weaker member — the negro — and with the same result. Negro sentiment in this country has its radical party and its conservative party. Negro radicals always spoke of Booker Washington as "a white man's nigger." They spoke of him exactly as radical labor men and I. W. W.s speak of the American Federation of Labor as "bought up by the capitalists."

White folk generally saw more hope in Booker Washington's methods because of his more peaceful and conciliatory spirit. I sat beside him when he made one of his last public addresses. He said the *real* prosperity of the white race was one with the real prosperity of the black. He said they must rise or fall together. But what happens with every lynching or other coward's act against this race? This happens: Every sanctity in this message of a common welfare which Washington left is weakened. It is weakened to the delight of every extremist in the colored race. The white lyncher becomes the chief partner of these extremists. He directly helps them prove their case.

If, in the desperate struggle over the realities of collective bargaining, the extremists among employers get their way, they will as directly become partners of the syndicalist impulse now seething in the world and have their full share of the blame. Between a syndicalist tribune like J. J. Ettor and the employer, there is no inch of common footing. Every bridge is destroyed. When Ettor writes in his "In-

conciliatory spirit had not prevailed, England would have lost India in the war.

dustrial Unionism "—" Certainly there can be no common interests between those who own the tools, the machines, factories, mines, mills and land, with the workers who do all the producing, who can be so stupid or knavish as to talk of peace between these two classes?" We have here nothing left even for a truce. Rawness like this plays into the employers' hands because it brings the full weight of public opinion to his side, as well as that of the most intelligent labor. But the ways to help Mr. Ettor and all his kind, are as easy as " the slopes to hell." We have only to stop up those " drainpipes of discontent "; we have only to fall back on a legal technique which the great ones of the law now tell us is in immediate need of reformation. Imperfect as it is, to refuse coöperation *with the best that labor has to offer* is deliberately to encourage and revive hope in every radical and " direct action " section of labor in the land.

Do we want labor more disaffected than it now is? It is easy to make it so. Do we want more revolutionary leaders? They can be had for the asking. So far as capital succeeds in defeating collective bargaining, it will close the safety valve. To bargain with the full strength of the union is the one avenue through which labor is to enter the new partnership. It is the avenue through which business responsibilities are, one by one, to be taken on by labor. So deep is the unrest that the one problem is to fix these responsibilities on labor groups *at the safest points.* This will force labor to select the kind of leader required for these duties, as we have long seen among coöperators and in the old and steadier unions. I heard an enraged criticism against Wallace Short, mayor of Sioux City, because he went to an I. W. W. hall and spoke to the members. He wished to be sure that he understood them. On request for the facts he sent me a stenographic report in full. He read their constitution and preamble, noting the principles, one by one, and saying plainly what he thought of them.

With the more rebellious I. W. W. utterances which he held in his hand, he said, " I am not wholly blind. I want you men to cut out the idea that you can get anywhere with that sort of thing. I do not expect you all to agree with me; but that won't go; and so far as I am concerned, it cannot go in Sioux City." After warning them that he would not tolerate the least show of violence, he appealed to them " to do everything in your power to rid yourselves of the idea of violence, and so far as possible to rid the public of the idea that you are here trying to take the world by violence. For you can never do it. It is just a matter of plain common sense to cut that out, because it won't go." Of further details here, I know nothing, but the spirit of that man is the only spirit to which we can look either for security or for hope.

As against the acceptance of socialism, I hear much of a " new liberalism." It comes from those who know well that the older political liberalism with its negations is a thing of the past.

If the spirit of it, as I hope, may be revived and made a power in the social remaking, its first, hardest and most essential task will be in creating positive agencies to replace the crude reactions of deportations and jail sentences. If well removed upon some sea-girt space, the really dangerous could be set down to fight it out among themselves and point the better way to a benighted world, the spectacle would be worth its costs. But no such welcoming spot is known to us.

In a panic, Canadian politicians pass a law in forty-five minutes to deport a group of English-speaking agitators of whom a great many estimable people had a good opinion. Would they have been less dangerous in England or Australia? Would their departing have quieted a single wave of unrest in the home country?[1]

[1] Has the "Dublin agitator," Jim Larkin, been less injurious *to England* by carrying on his agitation here rather than at home?

Here are rare chances for a "liberalism" which, if not new, may, in saner spirit, "first set its own house in order." There is one sorely neglected reason for this. Only as we learn to meet our problems where they *are* shall we find out the persons competent to the high tasks which a true liberalism must set before it. A further word must be said about this.

II

To look back for forty years through chronicles so imperfect; to compare remedies, conflicts, hopes, opinions, legislative enactments on subjects here considered, is to get one clear conviction. It is that anything which humanizes the prevailing mental temper of men is the one fundamental achievement. If the spirit in which a man argues is more important than his argument, it is as true socially. If "as a man thinketh, so is he" is true, it is no less so of the community.

If, in 1630, the thought was general that devils do actually get into old women, then torture will follow. It was long the custom to roast live cats over a fire, not from ill will to the cat, but to get the best of the devil. The real reform there, as it is to-day, was to change the community thinking on this subject.

We have Tyler's authority for it that the Mbayas of South America believed that their God bade them live by war: by watching and preparing to catch other people unawares, take their property, children and kill their men. There is no cure for such hallucination except through change of ideas. They must learn to think differently about their god, or to get a new one.

After ages of casting girls into the Yellow River in China, a magistrate appears with a new thought. He was said to be impious and worthy of death, but he took his chances. Against the whole bevy of witches, whose office it was to select the victims, this agitator turned. He bade them leave the girl and throw the whole bunch of witches into the river, saying with the edged humor that great leaders often possess, " Let the old god have his choice among the witch-hags for a wife." These demonic ideas come down into our own time, oozing up from muddy depths to leave their stain on everything they touch.

For those among us who look to force (whether by police club or jail) as a saving agency against troublesome views, I want to recur to August Bebel in prison. I knew the man imprisoned with him, who taught him French and English — French so well, that Bebel translated a very radical book by the French economist, Yves Guyot,— writing out an appendix on the future of woman. This latter was the beginning of a still more radical book (" Die Frau ") which several years before the war had passed its fiftieth edition, read by millions of people. It appeared in more than twenty foreign languages. As he was condemned at this time for thirty-one months, he made the most of it. The Government was putting him to school, paying all the bills, giving him ample leisure, making a hero of him and enormously adding to his influence.[1]

In " My Life " he tells us what occupied him behind the bars. " I read Marx's ' Capital ' for the second time; Engel's ' Condition of the Working Classes in England '; Lassalle's ' System of Acquired Rights '; Mill's ' Political Economy '; Lavelaye's ' Primitive Property '; Stein's ' History of Socialism and Communism in France '; Plato's ' Republic '; Aristotle's ' Politics '; Machiavelli's ' Prince '; Sir Thomas More's ' Utopia.' Of the historical works which I then read, I was most captivated by Buckle's ' History of Civilization ' and Wilhelm Zimmermann's ' History of the German Peas-

[1] It was in an earlier imprisonment that he was elected to Parliament by a large majority although the general party vote had fallen to a low figure because of the patriotic election following the Franco-Prussian War.

ants' War.' I read Darwin's 'Origin of Species'; Haeckel's 'Story of Creation'; Büchner's 'Force and Matter' and 'Man's Position in Nature'; Liebig's 'Letters on Chemistry.' I was seized by a veritable passion for reading and learning."

When the story is told of our own jailed masses since the war, we shall add scores of lesser experiences, but in their essence like that of Bebel.

With utter certainty we have to learn an appeal to what lies neither in new legal severities nor in any shaky precedent. Already upon one side, we have the fact that every organized group,— employers, unions, socialists, coöperators are experimentally working together to enlarge the basis of common interests. The bravest step in this learning together is this:— resolutely to leave open every door where new ideas and new attempts express themselves. It must be our one reply to radical protesters of every sort, "You shall have the fairest chance to speak out what is in you and the largest opportunity which social cohesion permits to state your case and to try out your scheme before all men." In spite of inherent defects of socialist theory and practice, it is criminal to shut the door upon further tentative trial of it. These "socializers of the three rents" may be nearer right than their individualist opponents. They have proved already that parts of their program are strictly in line with a progressive society. Because of our ignorance, we should take the moral risks of further trial. We shriek at communism and I think rightly, if there were the least danger of its general adoption. A child of a neighbor, hearing that she must share her new bicycle with the brothers and sisters, exclaims, "I am tired of living in a family where everybody uses everybody's things." Even in the most utopian of our communist colonies, with a membership largely composed of those who believed in common property, this child's protest is never for a moment silent. The protest becomes contagious among the stronger characters. What then must this protesting instinct be in the world at large? Yet we have deliberately organized enormous properties communistically. There are no more beneficent possessions than what we now hold in common. As society strengthens, these will be enlarged. I saw a school garden in which a wise teacher was experimenting. Each child had its own plot of ground. There was private ownership over every head of lettuce and hill of beans. These could be marketed and the money put down in a bank book. It was said, " You ought to see their delight when they draw from the bank the first interest." Here was most effective teaching of the property instinct. I was told that most of them worked more willingly and more intelligently under this stimulus, as one would expect. But this was not all. There was also a large plot set apart where they could work *" for the school ";* where none could say " this is mine to do with as I like," but " when it is sold the profits go to all of us alike." What impressed this teacher was that some of the " very dearest children " worked as faithfully and heartily " for the school " as any of the others digging for themselves alone. I tried to induce a rich man who had started an open air school, with a large number of children doing garden work, to extend this experiment. If carefully tried, what would it disclose after adequate tests? If it were shown that goodly numbers would sweat as gaily for the common benefit, what values would be put in jeopardy? That large numbers — probably the majority — of children require a strengthening of the more personal property instinct, I believe to be true. But is it not also desirable that those who work with less self-seeking motive should have every encouragement to increase this type and motive, which adds to our social riches and strengthens social texture?

If we cannot train a great deal more of this disinterested aptitude, to what leadership for the future do we look for some of our highest and hardest tasks? Without these aptitudes, we can have neither a Mazzini in political agitation nor a Pasteur in science.

For most of the new changes on which social growth depends, some of the greatest adventurers are of this type. At every further advance, we shall need more of them.

Even in the more commonplace betterments which we see about us, this cleaner passion can nowhere be so clearly traced as to some man or woman ill at ease with mere private possessions. During many years of journeying about this country (with one exception) into every State, I tried to find the origin of any conspicuous local improvement. So invariably does one find it inspired and started by a *person,* that its later institutionalized or organic form seems secondary and derivative. One may safely submit the test to any reader. Seek in almost any community for the best thing that has been done: the most fruitful idea with its embodiment outside or within some institution; seek for the inspiration awakened in small groups of men and women who have carried things on and up in the politics, education and health of the town. In finding the source of that uplift, we pretty certainly come upon some individual moved by an innovating impulse he could not himself explain.

The coöperators from the first were experimenters. From the store to the Wholesale; from the Wholesale to great factory industries; to banking, farming, mining and shipping, it is all a history of a new way with a new motive. At every step, they have discovered and trained the emerging talent " to work for use and not for profit." It is a most sobering process. One hears little of those quackeries which promise over-hasty changes in human nature that only ages can bring about. " We have learned to laugh at the man with a panacea," is a phrase I was glad to hear in a gathering of coöperators who, by the hardest work, had come to their own.

For the intricacies of social change here in mind, we must learn to laugh at the man with a " remedy " and perhaps more at the man with a " solution." One as great in practical business achievement as Godin, published in 1888 a fat volume, " The Social Solution." Our libraries have long lists of pamphlets in which " solution " is the conspicuous word, although tests of primary-school simplicity would show how inappropriate the word is. It not only starts the mind on the wrong track, but *keeps it there.*

I have read an address from a summer school, " How Society may be Reformed," in which " Society " is treated as if it were an ailing baby with something wrong in the gums or bowels. But " Society " is some millions of times more complex than this. It is not one thing, but a thousand and an ever-changing thousand. At one point, the growths are far advanced, at others they lag as far behind as the spinning-wheel (which my farm neighbor still uses) lags behind the latest textile mill. This world-tangle of habits, customs, institutions, is full of taints, survivals, atrophies, and all manner of sticky imperfections. Behind us is a vast, dateless body of traditions, all created by those long and safely dead. Upon this jagged and uneven mass, the present generation lives. With much uneasiness it quivers on this last outer edge, during what we call a " generation," and then, with its little deposit, drops back into that overpowering majority which rules and subdues us far more than the rule of those who live. All this unfathomed depth of human usage is such a part of the present society we seek to change that we cannot stir hand or foot without measuring our little strength against it.

Much of this past is integrally a part of the " social question " and of the narrower " labor question." We may select any tiny, recent fragment of this total — let us say, the trade union. We cannot touch it with hostile or friendly hand without touching, even in America, a full century of tragic human experience. The problems of those early

American printers, ship-calkers and carpenters are as passionately alive as ever; overtime, apprentices, fines, hours, wages, conditions, and, most fateful of all, the seat of power. What part of it shall be held collectively by labor and what part by the employer? Not a strike of yesterday or to-day in which these older memories are not still alive. Yet in the Senate a grave man warns us that "trade-unionism will never be '*solved*' until we compel them by law to be 'incorporated.'" What this gentleman means is probably this, that if labor organizations were made legally accountable, they would behave better. Such better behavior is extremely doubtful, but I do not here press that point. If " incorporation " did improve behavior, that increment of better conduct is precisely what we should get, and in no sense should we get a " solution."

If I am asked " what is the solution of a growing child," I cannot answer, because " solution " is a misnomer. I can see that a child may be trained, guided and improved, but not " solved." This is not so grotesque as to ask, " What is the panacea for a growing child? " but as applied to our economic disturbances and proposals for their removal, " solution " is scarcely less confusing.

Our politics are as confused and imperfect as are our industrial relations, but we do not ask, " What is the solution of politics? " In depths of perplexity beyond anything which " capital and labor " presents to our time is the question of race adjustment, yet ever and again we hear it, " the solution of the race question." So far as the inhabitants of the globe in the coming centuries can learn to live together with decency and self-respect, so far as they come to practice with each other the most elemental virtues in our religious and moral codes, so far, especially, as the strong learn to respect property and persons among weaker peoples, to that extent only can " solution " have intelligible meaning.

Is there a " solution " of religion?

Where on the scale of intelligence should we place a man or woman who set claim to a "solution" of the sex problem? Yet we have had an utterly inane thesis on that very topic.

To ask for a "solution of human nature" is a fairly exact equivalent of these other "solutions," even as applied to the lesser term, "labor question."

There is a contest of opinion over the distribution of what is produced; what shall go to capital, what to the employing manager, what to those who take wages. Economists the world over are still theorizing about this division, and the disagreements among the best of them are many and abrupt. But in the roar of the mill, in the machine shops, in mines, and in railways, where labor is thrown together and organizes itself, this dispute over the respective shares has become so charged with hostilities that the legal and police system in most countries is put to the greatest strain.

This strain is increasing, if we mean by that, a growing determination on the part of labor to break down the kind of authority which ownership and management have assumed to be theirs. The strain means more than this, because that part of our wage-earners, bent either upon the destruction of the wage system or upon very radical changes, is a growing and more determined proportion of our population.

Now it is this strain; this struggle over the division of the product, that we ask to "solve." We will have a "remedy" for it. I say again, it is like asking for a solution of human nature. We cannot stop this strain, and even more, we do not want to stop it. We hope to guide it. It is a part of economic and political readjustment, as essential to growth as it is unavoidable.

Our cry for solutions has, however, one intelligible meaning. We wish to make the struggle over the respective shares as fair and rational as we can. We wish to check the waste and savagery of the conflict. Terms like "relieving the friction," "civilizing the struggle," "raising the plane of competition," are all terms accurately describing such possibilities as are before us.

A very simple word like *improvement* sets us right before our problem. It does not excite absurd and premature expectations certain of disappointment. Education, politics, the child, race contact, sex relations are open to improvements. Both within and without ourselves certain changes of temper and external regulation are possible. These may lessen antagonisms, undermine economic privileges, and widen opportunity. It is with these rather humble betterments that we must learn to grow content.

But to get even these, we need an intellectual tolerance that is still rare. We must learn to bear with the critic and listen to him. Mill said no man understood his own side until he understood the other side.

That "bundle of race habits" which in any time and place constitutes existing society, has never taken on new and better ways except under criticism that hurts; hurts man's vanity and threatens his interests. Criticism arouses consciousness of imperfection and unfitness of the thing that is. When Rev. Mather wrote down his half timid strictures against the torture of witches, he was severely blamed and, what seems stranger still, blamed by those who suffered from the superstition.

Thus a few fiercely abused critics in New England compelled men to doubt the sanctity of this witch feature of their folk-ways. This has always been the service of both critic and agitator as it is to-day.

The difference between the wise and foolish agitator is in the sagacity to know what constitutes the evil, and what better thing may be substituted, and — hardest of all — how practically the substitution may be made. This constructive step defines the statesman as distinguished from the politician. There was never a more fatal superstition than that we of our day have none. We are still, for instance, much more than knee-deep in superstition about "laws." It is from a brilliant light in the legal profession that we read "At the last legislative session in California 2,877 bills were introduced. Of these the Governor vetoed 227 and 771, an appalling number, became laws. The Session Laws of Arkansas for 1915 comprise a book of 1,046 pages and of Massachusetts 1,100 pages."

From another lawyer we learn that "our 48 state legislatures enact a yearly average of about 25,000 laws." Yet Blackstone thought that as we became more democratic, the people would show great caution in making laws.

What has been called "the stage of scape-goat development" is accurately described by this dense belief that our safety is in this heaping of law upon law. A mother tells her daughter, "Why, since you went to college, have you brought home a new ideal about something, at least once a month?" "Well, mamma, I *have* to have a new one, because I can't do anything with the old ones." Here was one reason of Nietzsche's contempt for socialists. He spoke of them as whimperers and half degenerate because always railing at and making a scape-goat of the social or industrial order. "Don't cover society with pitch, until you get the pitch well off yourself." In other words, "first set your own house in order." We are already in possession of more laws than we can use or show the slightest desire to enforce. Our need is for a new *temper in applying those we have*. This touches that blacker phase of our superstitions. Until the recent rage for more drastic laws against ideas and criticism of the present order, I never before realized why the very greatest of the race came to think so lightly of the mass-total of laws. If we could revive the very noblest of our dead; those who did most to break the tyrannies of their time, many bills now before state legislatures and one bill before Congress would put every heroic one of them in jail. Jefferson, John Adams, Sam Adams, James Otis and Patrick Henry would go there, as would Thoreau and Emerson. What troops of others would go, from Montaigne to Tolstoi! Montaigne said "the State was built on man's inertia. He said many laws held over not because they were just, but solely because they were laws. He said they were often made by dullards (elles sont souvent faites par des sots) and oftener still by those who hate equality and will have nothing of it."[1]

The philosopher of "all's well in the world," Leibnitz, would be as vulgarly jugged as any pitiful I. W. W., for the great moralizer said "the mightiest among the living have little respect for tribunals." Carlyle is among our noblest ethical advisers. In putting Cromwell before us as one of the sublime figures in history, nothing more delights the Scotsman than his hero's capacity and readiness to break laws. Cromwell not only said "There is but one general grievance and that is the law," but he acted vigorously on that opinion. It is a socialist (Albert Thomas) who turns to the German jurist, Professor Köhler, quoting from him words like these: "No law is so sacred that it must not yield to necessity; and this act performed under the pressure of necessity — does not constitute a violation of law." It is only "weak and timid people" who hesitate in such moments to override the law.

Midway in the 19th century, we had in this country no more intellectual or highly moralized men and women than those who defied the law. To a mind as serene and penetrating as that of Emerson, the Fugitive Slave Law was an infamy, and obedience to it moral turpitude. In his Phi Beta Kappa oration last summer, Bliss Perry called this man "who lived in the spirit" "Harvard's most distinguished graduate." Not only did he say "Republics abound in young civilians who believe that the laws make the city . . . that any measure, though it were absurd, may be imposed

[1] See further the Essay *De l'Expérience*.

on a people if only you can get sufficient voices to make it a law. But the wise know . . . that the form of government which prevails is the expression of what cultivation exists in the population which permits it. The law is only a memorandum. We are superstitious and esteem the statute somewhat; so much life as it has in the character of living men is its force," but he added, " a good man will not obey the law too strictly." It was one of the subtlest of agitators and ablest scholars who quoted the words of Gladstone in 1869 —" If the people of this country had obeyed the precept to preserve order and eschew violence, the liberties of this country would never have been obtained."

These " concessions of the august " are now the commonplace in labor literature.

These are other words of Elihu Root in 1915, before the New York Constitutional Convention: " We found that the legislature of the State had declined in public esteem and that the majority of the legislators were occupying themselves chiefly in the promotion of private and local bills, of special interests, . . . upon which apparently their reëlections to their positions depended, and which made them cowards and demoralized the whole body." If Mr. Root had been an obscure and " foot-loose " person with trousers chewed off at the heels, and had thus spoken upon a soapbox what would have become of him last year or this year?

We can neither hush up these opinions nor play the ostrich. We may raid every haunt of the I. W. W. and jail every mother's son of them, we shall still have to cope with these unsettling views in a long, uncertain future before us. We cannot in this discussion ignore the opinions of a long list of intellectual and moral leaders of the race. We can range them wholly on the side of greater freedom. The spirit of them all may be summed up at its best in Benedict Spinoza. At his bicentenary at the Hague, another philosopher, Renan, quoted from Spinoza with express and warm approval, a passage as noble as that of Milton and clear as that of Mill.

"The final end of the State," he says, "consists not in dominating over men, restraining them by fears, subjecting them to the will of others. The State has not for its end the transformation of men from reasonable beings into animals or automata; it has for end, so to act that its citizens should in security develop soul and body, and make free use of their reason. Hence the true end of the State is liberty. . . .

"Even if we admit the possibility of so stifling men's liberty, and laying such a yoke upon them that they dare not even whisper without the approbation of the sovereign, never can they be prevented from thinking as they will. What then must ensue? That men will think one way and speak another; that consequently good faith — a virtue most necessary to the State — will become corrupted; that adulation — a detestable thing — and perfidy will be had in repute, entailing the decadence of all good and healthy morality. What can be more disastrous to a State than to punish honest citizens as evil-doers, because they do not share the opinions of the crowd, and are ignorant of the art of feigning? What more fatal than to treat as enemies men whose only crime is that of thinking independently?"

Throughout the war, what racy irrelevancies and even rubbish we heard about Nietzsche! Yet he speaks to the fact about everything in modern Germany and in every other country which shouts for more and more virulent measures against expressed opinions. As for the Germans, he says they think "that force must reveal itself in hardness and in cruelty and then they subject themselves gladly and admiringly,— that there is force in mildness and quietness they do not readily believe." In the best book ever written about this strange genius, Mr. Salter admits that Nietzsche saw, as our masses became mixed, averaged and democratized that they would need a strong man as they need daily bread. But what kind of a strong man? Least of all the swashbuckler; least of all one to "keep the masses down" and hold them in order, but one with power high enough and wise enough to bring them "relief and benefit" It is made clearer to us by examples, even that of a Cæsar, who after Pompey was at his feet, said, "I will conquer after a new fashion and fortify myself in the possession of the power I acquire by generosity and mercy." [1] Nietzsche makes his pet hero say, "thoughts that come with the feet of doves rule the world."

As a youth, almost sixty years ago, I recall the song in the streets, "We'll hang Jeff Davis to a sour apple tree," and they meant it. I remember (especially from the stay-at-homes) the angry cry for the hanging of "all the leaders," and of one man who would add luster to any period of known history, Robert E. Lee. We recovered from those sombre insanities, and who to-day does not rejoice that we so recovered? I heard Lincoln brutally named because of generosities and forbearances which now endear and make him sacred to the people. The "quality of mercy" is as true as when the poet wrote the words.

But mercy is perhaps even less our present need, than the intelligence of a sympathetic imagination before the nature of our problem. This, I say, we shall get mainly through actual practice in trying new ways and tolerating new thought.

The daily cry (no, let us name it from its proper origins), the daily *howl* for more drastic net-work of force is worse than a futility, because it incites and adds to every evil it would abate. Passion and hate against persons has this devilish ingenuity; *it turns every thought and energy away from the real sources of our trouble.* Though it is upon a

[1] "Nietzsche, The Thinker," page 370.

single page, no nobler essay was ever written than that of Bacon on " Revenge." He says it is " a delicacy that should be eaten cold."

It is a " wild justice which the more man's nature runs to, the more ought law to weed it out." It " putteth the law out of office."

But a few weeks since, the author of " The American Commonwealth," James Bryce, as true a friend as this country ever had, wrote, in a letter to a friend, these words:

" In my judgment there has never been a time at which the systematic and impartial study of social and economic questions has been so urgent as at the present day. We stand on the threshold of a new age. The problems which confront us and the other leading democratic States of the world are of the most complex and the most vital character, and can only be solved by patient examination conducted in a spirit of scientific detachment, accompanied by a wide diffusion of adult civic education. To avert grave conflicts between classes and interests we must in good time enquire into and determine so far as possible their causes and conditions. We need, therefore, to-day and at once, a much more adequate provision for social research and for giving publicity to the results of such research. But to be most fruitful our work must be conceived in a large and liberal spirit."

" Patient examination of causes and conditions "— conducted with " *scientific detachment* " and all " in a large and liberal spirit."

If there is a gleam of hope for democratic fellowship among men, it is in the braver faith of these great teachers. If in any sense, there is to be a Commonwealth of America and of the world, it is in their spirit that we must learn to think and then to act.

War has left the dwelling places of men foul with vindictive passions, but it has also left there such hungers, as were never felt, for the ways of peace and good will among men. Here is the choice that is open to us. It is the choice in industry. It is the choice among the nations.

INDEX

Act of Freedom, in France, 46.
Acton, Lord, on freedom of supreme achievements from state control, 236.
Actors, trade unions among, 2; strike of, in New York, 3.
Advertising, one aim of coöperation, to abolish wastes of, 264-265; effect of coöperation as foreseen on, 267-268.
Agents provocateurs, use of, 92.
Agents, secret, used in industrial warfare, 54-66.
Amana Community, the, 155-156.
American Federation of Labor, trial of initiative and referendum by, 323-324; leadership by the few in, 334.
American Woolen Company, pension plans of, 105.
Anarchist colony, attempts at coöperation in, 333.
Apprentices, question of, decided by labor unions, 344.
Arbitration courts in Australia, 29.
Ashley, R. L., study of profit-sharing by, 351.
Atchison, Topeka & Santa Fe R. R., pension plan of, 105.
Australia, new industrial conditions in, 2; struggles of labor with political democracy in, 28-29; utopian colony from, in Paraguay, 165-166; questions concerning government ownership in, 198.

Bacon, Francis, on "Revenge," 430.
Balfour, A. J., advice of, to militant suffragists, 380.
Bank clerks, trade unions among, 2.
Barth, Theodore, views of, regarding public ownership, 189.
Bebel, August, 8; "Die Frau" by, quoted, 208; advantages to, of imprisonment, 417-418.
Belgium, coöperators in politics in, 255.
Bellamy, Edward, 147; "Looking Backward" by, 148-149; consumers' coöperation as depicted by, 265-266.
Benson, A. L., former socialist leader, 180.
Bernstein, E., "History and Theory of Socialism" by, 330 n.
Bismarck, political tactics of, 37; "reptile fund" of, 57; policy of, concerning public ownership, 189-190; warfare waged by, on Catholic Church, 410-411.
Blanqui, Louis, as a revolutionist, 8.
Bon Marché, Paris department store, 95; welfare work at, 104; strike at, 104 n.
Bonus systems, argument against, 352.
Booth, Charles, testimony of, concerning New Guild, 403-405; admirable spirit actuating, 407.
Boston, feeding of school children in, 226-227; proposed coöperative factory of cigar makers in, 298; police strike in, 345.
Brace, Charles Loring, view of, of coöperative movement in England, 259.
Brailsford, H. N., on conservatism among majority socialists in Berlin, 333.
Brissenden, Paul F., study of syndicalism by, 361.

British Commission on Industrial Unrest, report of, 19.
Brook Farm experiment, 158 n.
Bryce, James, on present-day need of study of social and economic questions, 430.
Buffalo meeting of trades unions (1917), 306–307.
Bummery element in I. W. W., 372.
Bureaucracy, vices of, among coöperators, 280–281.
Burial system, public regulation of, 216–217.

Cadillac Lumber Company, pension plan of, 105.
Canada, war-time profiteering in, 76–77; coöperative wheat-growing in, 260.
Capitalism, increasing friction between wage labor and, 21; the changed position of, 22–25; fighting powers of, 25–26; predictions as to evolution of system of, 33–34; welfare schemes, pension plans, etc., introduced by, and results, 94–117; value of profit-sharing as a test of, 354–356.
Carnegie, Andrew, criticism by, of modern business methods, 22.
Catholic Church, results of Bismarck's attacks on, 410–411.
Cherington, Paul T., "Advertising as a Business Force" by, quoted, 267–268.
Chicago, unionizing of school teachers in, 380.
Children at school, care of, by public agencies, 220–233.
Christensen, A., "Politics and Crowd Morality" by, cited, 182 n.
Christian socialists, group of, 253, 290.
Clapp, Professor, article by, cited, 72.
Clemenceau, and Louis Blanqui, 8; capitalist leadership attacked by, 22.

Closed shop, the, 134.
Cohen, J. H., "An American Labor policy," cited, 3; on labor struggles as war, 60 n.
Cole, A. D. H., leader in New Guild movement, 390–391; definition of New Guild by, 394 n.; popularity of writings of, 403.
Colorado, communistic colony in, 165.
Commons, Frank R., quoted, 72.
Communism, wars followed by, 144.
Communistic settlements, account of, 145–167.
Competition, conflicting views of, 290–291.
Consumers' coöperation. *See* Coöperators.
Contracts, breaking of, by labor unions, 342–343.
Coöperation, in anarchist colony near Tacoma, 333.
Coöperators, troubles of, with labor, 30; achievements and experiences of, 252–298.
Crane, Charles R., on progress of coöperation in Russia, 268–269.

Davies, Emile, quoted on U. S. government printing office, 191–192; "Collectivist State in the Making" by, quoted, 192–193.
Debs, Eugene, 7.
De Courcy, French profit-sharer, 353.
De Leon, Daniel, dangers of I. W. W. perceived by, 371.
Democracy, definitions of word, 26–27; has to do with uses to which power is put, 33.
Denmark, coöperative societies in, 263–264; rapidity of growth of coöperation in, 273.
Destitute Children's Dinner Society, in England, 227–228.
Devine, Edward T., report by, on Winnipeg strike, 388.
Direct action, a tool acquired by

INDEX

labor, 4; syndicalist view of, 366; tracing of causes of, 379–380.
Division of work, labor troubles over, 300–302.

Education, of labor for present crisis, 299–337; of the I. W. W., 370–377.
Egan, Maurice, quoted, 264.
Eight-hour day, discussion of, 237–251.
Employers, warlike temper of, toward trade unions, 132–135.
Endicott, Henry B., as an arbitrator of strikes, 197.
Endicott-Johnson Shoe Co., eight-hour day in factory of, 247.
Engis Chemical Works, trial of eight-hour day at, 247.
England, new acquisitions to union labor's ranks in, 13; National Union of Teachers in, 46 n.; public care of school children in, 221–222, 224–225; coöperators in politics in, 255; achievements of coöperatives in, 260–261; extent of coöperation in, 267; roots of syndicalism found in, 359.
Estey, J. A., "Revolutionary Syndicalism" by, 361.
Ettor, J. J., syndicalist tribune, quoted, 413–414.

Fabianism, "astute boss-management" of, 332.
Fall River Textile Mills, experiment with sliding scale at, 70.
Farmers' Alliance, the, 68.
Farming, coöperative experiments in, 260.
Filene's, Boston, "not a store but a university," 102.
Finland, coöperative societies in, 263.
Finns, coöperative work of, at Fitchburg, 292–293.
Firemen, progress of unionism among, 125–129; involved in great Winnipeg strike, 387.

Fisher, Irving, quoted concerning inheritance system, 205–206.
Fitch, John A., quoted on Buffalo convention of 1917, 306; article by, cited, 395.
Fitchburg, Mass., Finnish coöperative at, 292–293.
Foley, Margaret, woman suffrage advocate, 13.
Forbes, John M., cited on public control of railroads, 187.
Foreigners, industrial unrest not to be laid to, 51.
Foremen, question of loyalty of, to employer or to union, 345.
France, socialistic character of labor organization in, 43–44; school teachers and public employees as trade-union members in, 44–49; public care of school children in, 220, 228–229, 231; experiments with shorter working day at glass works in, 246; profit-sharing systems in, 353; appearance of syndicalism in, 359.
France, Anatole, "Sur la Pierre Blanche," quoted, 191.
Free speech, necessity of restrictions upon so-called, 380.
Froude, J. A., "History of England," quoted, 34.
Funerals, over-stimulated extravagance in, 216–217.

Gay and Heilman, study of profit-sharing by, 355 n.
General strike, results of, economically and politically, 49.
George, Henry, doctrines of, improved on by socialists, 172.
Gerard, J. W., "My Four Years in Germany," quoted, 90–91.
Germany, strikes in, during the war, caused by profiteering, 78–79; state ownership under Bismarck in, 189–190; concealed deficits in, 201; dangers of glory of "The Great State" shown by, 235–236; coöperative societies in, 262–263, 273;

INDEX

conservatism of leaders of majority socialists in, 333.
Glasgow, coöperative bakeries in, 267.
God, utopian leaders and, 155–156; from the German point of view, 156.
Godin's Iron Works, 150.
Gompers, Samuel, 6, 16, 81 n., 341–342, 343.
Government ownership, 184–204; inefficiency of, from capitalistic standpoint, 194–196.
Grey, Albert, pioneer coöperator, 254.
Gronlund, Laurence, quoted on inheritance, 210–211.
Gruber, E. L., pious saint and boss, 155–156.
Guise, Familistère at, 145–146.

Hall, B. R., "The New Purchase" by, quoted, 164.
Hanson, Ole, quoted on the I. W. W., 364–365.
Hardie, Keir, on evils in trade unions, 338.
Harris, Emerson P., book on coöperation by, 280 n.
Harrison, Frederic, quoted on political capacities of labor, 34–35.
Haywood, W. D., 7; quoted on strikes in the East, 60; as an I. W. W. leader, 370.
Hazzard, Frederick, report by, on length of working day, 245.
Helper, H. R., "Impending Crisis," quoted, 96.
Hillebrand, Karl, quoted on danger of "The Great State," 236.
Hillquit, Morris, socialism defined by, 174; "Socialism in Theory and Practice" by, quoted, 175.
Hinds, W. D., "American Communities," quoted, 158.
Hours of work, length of, 50, 237–251.
Hovey, C. F., anecdote by, 261.
Howard, Stanley E., article by, cited, 70.
Hoxie, R. F., "Trade Unionism in the United States," quoted, 322–323; quoted on "feudatory unionism," 338–339.
Hunter, Robert, "Violence in the Labor Movement" by, cited, 58.
Hyndman, W. H., "Future of Democracy" by, quoted, 233.

Icarian utopian colony, 165.
Idea, grave views of a new, 67.
Ignorance, element of, among I. W. W., 371–372.
Iles, George, Canadian journalist, 387.
Individuality, effect of communistic life on, 159–164.
Industrial warfare, characteristics of, 54–66.
Inheritance system, 205–207; proposed changes in, 207–210; views of leading socialists on, 210–212.
Initiative and referendum among labor unions, 319–326.
Insurance, state control of, 199–200.
International Coöperative Alliance, growth of, 271, 272.
Inventions, a source of labor disturbances, 281–284.
Italy, feeding of school children in, 232; coöperative societies in, 263; extent of coöperation in, 273; self-governing coöperative gangs in, 297–298.
I. W. W., the, 7, 41; attempts of, at trouble-making among Fitchburg Finns, 294; advent of, after demise of Knights of Labor, 359; discussion of, 359–388.

James, William, quoted on difference between men, 94.
Jamestown Colony, communistic features of, 167.
Japan, coöperative societies in, 263.
Justice, charge of denial of, to the poor, 408–410.

Kahn, Otto, warning by, against

state socialism, 186; ill-grounded optimism of, 187.
Kansas, postal vote for railway men and others in, 320.
King, Mackenzie, on analogy between strikes and wars, 60–61.
Kingsley, Charles, a Christian Socialist, 290.
Knights of Labor, one root of syndicalism found in, 359.
Kropotkin, Prince, effects of coöperation as foreseen by, 268.

Labor, new conditions resulting from power recently acquired by, 1–11; position of, in changed social conditions following the war, 12; greater political power secured by, 12–14; investigation of uses made by, of political opportunities, 27–32; means of accomplishment of overthrow of capitalism by, 33–34; results traced of new ideas among ranks of, 67–93; effect on, of excesses in war-time profiteering, 75–78; effect on, of lessons of violence learned from rulers, 92–93; attitude of, toward welfare schemes, 95–96; pension plans distrusted by, 105–106; consideration of aims and purposes of, 118–143; object of, in demanding government ownership, 196–197; past education of, for present crisis, 299–337.
Labor party, planks in platform of (November, 1919), 203.
Labor turnover, annual cost of, 106.
Labor unions. See Trade unions.
Lassalle, Ferdinand, theory of, 159.
Lawrence, Mass., strike of 1912, a victory for strikers, 385.
Leadership in trades unions, qualifying for, 311–316; by the few, 329–336.
League of labor, a new, 303–304.
Lee, F. G., article by, cited, 246.

Leeds Coöperative Society, strike in, 276.
Leverhulme, Lord, experiments of, with hours of labor, 248–249; quoted on six-hour day, 303 n.
Library workers, unionizing of, 2, 13.
Lunn, George R., socialist mayor and congressman, quoted, 179.

Macaulay, disbelief of, in mass-capacity for stable government, 52.
Machines, labor troubles caused by, 281–284.
McElwain, W. H., trial of eight-hour day by, 247.
McNeil, George E., discussion of eight-hour day by, 242–243; on fixing of blame for wrong industrial system, 303.
Manitoba, politics and government ownership in, 198.
Massachusetts, report on hours of labor in, 244; experiments in shortening working day in, 245.
Mavor, Professor, on public ownership in Manitoba, 198.
Methodists, program of social reconstruction drawn up by, 387–388.
Milk supply, socializing the, 213–216.
Mill, John Stuart, disturbance of, over social problems, 154–155.
Mining, plan for democratic control of, in New Zealand, 399–402.
Moltke, General von, quoted on war as instituted by God, 156.
More, Sir Thomas, 147; the Utopia of, 149.
Morley, John, F. Harrison quoted by, 34–35; quoted, 236; conciliatory policy of, toward India, 412.
Mormons, autocracy of Brigham Young among, 151–152.
Morris, William, negative atti-

tude of, toward "dividing up," 208–209.

National Civic Association, investigation of profit-sharing by, 348.
National Industrial Conference Board, investigations by, of hours of labor, 250.
National Labor Organization, anarchism repudiated by, 360.
New Guild, the, discussion of, 389–407.
New Harmony, Owenite Colony at, 160.
New Jersey Bureau of Statistics, investigation by, of hours of labor, 250.
New South Wales, government control of business in, 202.
Newspaper men, trade unions among, 2.
New Zealand, politics and government ownership in, 198; plan for democratic control of mining in, 399–402.
Nietzsche, truth in sayings of, 428–429.
Non-Partisan League, the, 40 n.

Ogden, Robert G., on relations of capital and labor, 95.
One Big Union, present tendency toward, 396–397.
Orchestra, loss of individuality by members of, 234–235.
Owen, Robert, the "new employer" of his day, 256; attainments and achievements of, 256–258.

Paraguay, Utopian colony in, 165–166.
Parker, Carlton H., writings of, 363.
Pension plans for workmen, 105–106.
Penty, Arthur, subject of New Guild first treated by, 394–395.
Perkins, George W., quoted on profit-sharing, 351–353.
Perry, Bliss, quoted on Emerson, 426–427.

Philadelphia, municipalizing of gas in, 195.
Piece work, a source of wrangling among coöperators and union laborers, 281.
Plumb, Glenn, proposals of, concerning railroads, 265.
Plumb Plan, socialist note in, 172.
Plunkett, Horace, quoted, 253.
Plymouth Colony, communistic features of, 167.
Policemen, as members of trade unions, 2, 45; strike of, in Boston, 345.
Political experience gained by labor, 299–337.
Postal clerks, trade unions among, 2.
Postal voting plans, 320.
Poverty as treated by socialism, 173.
Prins, Adolph, observations of, on socialism, 333.
Production and wages, relation between, 238.
Profiteering, effect on labor of excesses of, in war time, 75–78; examples of, and strikes caused by, 78–85, 285–286; treatment of, by coöperators, 286–288.
Profiteers, enemies of society in peace time as in war, 15.
Profit-sharing partnership in England, 239–240.
Profit-sharing plans, 101; discussion of, 348–357.
Prohibition, favored by I. W. W. leaders, 378–379.
Property, principle of sacrifice to, 88–90; attitude of socialism toward, 168–173.
Pryor, Judge Roger, opinion by, on violent tactics in industrial warfare, 58–59.
Public employees, labor organizations and status of, 44–48.

Quakers, spiritual impetus of, 157.

Races, clashes between, 39.

Rand School, effects of attacks on, 411, 412.
Ratcliff, S. K., cited on Morley's policy in India, 412 n.
Rathenau, Walter, results of the war foreseen by, 76.
Rea, Russell, impressions of, concerning American labor situation, 32.
Read, H. E., "The Abolition of Inheritance," cited, 207.
Recognition, unions' demand for, 343-344.
Redfern, Percy, "The Coöperation Wholesale" by, cited, 284.
Referendum, use of the, by workers' unions, 320-326; criticism of, by labor unionists, 330-331.
Revenge, avoidance of ideas of, 427-430.
Rhodes, James Ford, account by, of railway strike of 1877, 380 n.
Rockefeller, John D., Jr., quoted on a new brotherhood in business, 22-23; opposing views of, by socialists and capitalists, 23.
Root, Elihu, on denial of justice to the poor, 409; quoted concerning selfish interests of New York Assemblymen, 427.
Rousier, Paul de, cited, 38.
Russell, Bertrand, results of attempted suppression of, 383-384.
Russia, coöperation in, 268-270.

Sage Foundation, investigation by, of European coöperative movement, 259.
St. John, Vincent, an I. W. W. leader, 370.
Salter, W. M., "Nietzsche, the Thinker" by, quoted, 428-429.
Salt monopolies, 191.
San Remo, Italy, free feeding of school children in, 232.
Schaffner, Mr., quoted, 72.
Schiff, Mortimer, new profit-sharing plan of, 354.
School children, public supervision of, care of, 220-233.

School garden, lessons from a, 419.
Schwab, C. M., at Atlantic City convention, 22.
Scotland, extent of coöperation in, 267.
Self-governing workshops, 153.
Separatists, the simple life among, 154.
Shakers, religious devoutness a mainstay of, 159 n.
Shop committee, the, 279, 344, 346.
Short, Wallace, and the I. W. W. in Sioux City, 414-415.
Simons, A. M., quoted on socialist political organizations, 180-181.
Sliding scales, experiments with, 69-70.
Socialism, use made by, of political opportunity, 31; progress of, in France, 43-44; question of results of, to labor, 110-111; communism to be distinguished from, 144; necessary intermingling of communism and 144-145; discussion of, as a world fact to be reckoned with, 168-183; definition of, 174; political weaknesses of, 179-182; pros and cons of government ownership, 184-204.
Socialists, leadership by the few among, 334-335.
Social remedies for disturbed conditions, 18-20.
Socrates, a dialogue of, 366-370.
Solvay Process Company, welfare work at, 102-103.
Sonnichsen, Albert, "Consumers' Coöperation" by, 280 n.
Spargo, John, quoted on political aspect of socialism, 180; on necessity of increasing productivity of labor, 200-201; on inheritance systems, 207-208.
Speed, regulation of, by labor unions, 344-345.
Spinoza, on liberty as the true end of the State, 428.
Spy system in industrial warfare, 54-66.

Standard of living, value placed upon, by all classes, 12.
State socialism, 14; discussion of, 184–204.
Stevens, R. B., quoted on losses in shipyards from labor disturbances, 77.
Strikes, new conditions surrounding, after the war, 15–18; viewed as warfare, 57–64; caused by profiteering during the war, 78–79; among coöperatives, 274–279; among labor unions themselves, 306; results of, in solidifying labor forces, 385–388.
Sweden, government ownership in, 195.
Switzerland, state and city ownership in, 195; public regulation of burial system in, 217; coöperatives in, 262.
Syndicalism, purpose of the "One Big Union" of, 38; discussion of, 358–388; point in which New Guild differs from, 394.

Taft, William H., on withholding of justice from the poor, 408.
Tarbell, Ida, "New Ideals in Business" by, 101–102.
Teachers, unionizing of, 2, 13, 45.
Townley, Mr., and the Farmers' Alliance, 68.
Trade unions, new sections of workers included in, 2; change for the better in character of, 9; public employees as members of, 44–48; among firemen, 125–129; antipathy of many employers toward, 132–135; admitted improprieties of, 139–140; among coöperative workers, 276–278; faults of, 338–347.
Training of labor for present crisis, 299–337.
Trautman, W. E., quoted on the I. W. W., 372–373.

Union Pacific pension plan, 105.

United Mine Workers, **example** of well-drilled labor body, 319–320.
United States, coöperative movement in, 259–260.
Utopian colonies, accounts of, and lessons to be learned from, 145–167.

Vanderlip, Frank, attention paid by, to labor disturbances, 73–74.
Venezuela, government monopoly of salt in, 191.
Vercelli, Italy, questions raised by feeding of school children in, 232.
Victoria, N. S. W., government ownership in, 195; postal vote in, 320.
Victor plant, New Jersey, shortening of hours of labor at, 248.
Vienna, coöperative bakeries in, 267.
Violence, use of, in labor struggles, 54–66; lessons of, learned by labor from the great, 92–93.
Voting, question of compulsory, 320–321.

Wallace, Henry, quoted on communists, 161–162.
Wallas, Graham, treatment of syndicalism by, 360.
Walling and Laidler, "State Socialism Pro and Con" by, cited, 184.
War, analogy between industrial struggles and, 57–64.
Warren, Josiah, communistic experience of, 160.
Washington, Booker T., methods and spirit of, 413.
Webb, Beatrice, 280 n.
Webb, Beatrice and Sidney, on value of the anarchist creed, 381.
Welfare schemes, beginnings of, 95–96; account of, and labor's attitude toward, 96–111, 349–350, 356.

INDEX

Wells, H. G., views of on inheritance, 208, 211.
Western Federation of Miners, leadership of, 332.
White, Andrew D., on law and order in Western Canada, 387.
Whitely Plan, the, 75; adoption of, by British government, 42.
Whitlock, Brand, quoted, 59.
Williams, J. E. labor arbitrator, quoted, 60.
Wilson, Henry, 243.
Winnipeg, strike in, in 1919, 387-388.
Woolf, L. D., book by, 256; on bureaucracy among coöperatives, 280, quoted, 335-336.
Working day, question of length of, 50, 237-251.
Wright, Carroll D., view of, on violence in labor struggles, 59.

Young, Brigham, personal power of, among Mormons, 151-152.

Zeiss Optical Works, 150; experiments with shorter working day at, 246.
Zelenko, Mr., Russian coöperative director, 270.